Northern Development
The Canadian Dilemma

Northern Development
The Canadian Dilemma

ROBERT PAGE

Canada in Transition Series
McCLELLAND AND STEWART

McClelland and Stewart Limited
The Canadian Publishers
25 Hollinger Road
Toronto, Ontario
M4B 3G2

Canadian Cataloguing in Publication Data

Page, Robert, 1940–
    Northern development: the Canadian dilemma

(Canada in transition series)
Includes bibliographical references and index.
ISBN 0-7710-6928-6 (bound).   ISBN 0-7710-6927-8 (pbk.)

1. Canada, Northern – Economic conditions.
2. Canada, Northern – Economic policy.
3. Natural resources – Canada, Northern.
I. Title. II. Series.

HC117.N5P33 1986   330.9719   C85-099974-X

Figures 6, 7, 11, 18, 19, 20, 26: James Loates *Illustrating.*

This book has been published with the help of a grant from the Social Science
Federation of Canada, using funds provided by the Social Sciences and
Humanities Research Council of Canada.

Printed and bound in Canada by John Deyell Company

Contents

Figures and Tables

Abbreviations

AAG	Alaskan Arctic Gas
AERCB	Alberta Energy Resources Conservation Board
Alyeska	The Trans-Alaskan Oil Pipeline
AMOP	Arctic Marine Oilspills Program
APP	Arctic Pilot Project (LNG tankers)
CAG	Canadian Arctic Gas
CARC	Canadian Arctic Resources Committee
CASNP	Canadian Association in Support of Native People
CDC	Canada Development Corporation
CIC	Committee for an Independent Canada
CIDS	Concrete Island Drilling System
CJL	Committee for Justice and Liberty
CNF	Canadian Nature Federation
COPE	Committee for Original Peoples Entitlement
CRI	Caisson Retained Island
CYI	Council of Yukon Indians
DIAND or DINA	Department of Indian Affairs and Northern Development
DOE	Department of the Environment
EARP	Environmental Assessment and Review Process (federal)
EIS	Environmental Impact Statement
EMR	Department of Energy, Mines, and Resources
EPB	Environmental Protection Board (Winnipeg)
FERC	Federal Energy Regulatory Commission (U.S.)
FH (ML)	Foothills (Maple Leaf) Pipeline
FH (Y)	Foothills (Yukon) Pipeline
FPC	Federal Power Commission (U.S.)
ITC	Inuit Tapirisat of Canada
LNG	Liquid Natural Gas
NAG	Northern Assessment Group
NEB	National Energy Board
NEPA	National Environmental Policy Act (U.S.)
OEB	Ontario Energy Board
PIP	Petroleum Incentive Program
Probe	Pollution Probe (now Energy Probe), Toronto
YCS	Yukon Conservation Society

Editors' Foreword

The volumes in this series, *Canada in Transition: Crisis in Political Development*, attempt to place our current national situation in historical perspective. As a country embedded from the outset in the political and economic fortunes of powerful neighbours, Canada has encountered unique social, economic, and political obstacles to unity and cohesion. Indeed, the term "crisis" denotes for us the central features of the Canadian experience: a fascinating mix of dangers and opportunities in a rapidly changing environment.

The North has long held a special place in the Canadian imagination, providing a continuing source of dreams, escapism, and myths. It has presented competing visions of immense national treasure and bankrupt desolation, alternating bouts of boom and bust, of hope and despair in the native communities. With the opening of the Trudeau era the isolation and the environmental purity of the Arctic rapidly disappeared. It was as if the many earlier isolated events – the famous voyages in search of the Northwest Passage, the whalers, the Hudson's Bay Company, missionaries, the Yukon gold rush, Norman Wells oil, the Alaska Highway, the construction of the DEW line, Diefenbaker's Roads-to-Resources, and many others – had finally yielded fundamental changes in context and future directions. The S.S. *Manhattan's* first dramatic sail through the Northwest Passage, coupled with the discovery of oil on the Alaskan North Slope a year earlier in 1968, represented the end of an era. Would the new developments destroy or serve the North and the country as a whole?

For Canadians, for the northerners, and above all for the Inuit and Dene, the decade of the 1970's was one of unprecedented turmoil. The U.S. challenge to Canadian sovereignty over Arctic waters was itself a harbinger of the new stakes: not just the Canadian Arctic, but the circumpolar region as a whole faced growing absorption into global resource and military rivalries. The preservation of the Arctic environment became a call to battle. The intense national debate concerning the future of the North galvanized environmental and public interest groups, the churches, government, regulatory agencies, and the public sector in general. More importantly, it signalled the political revival of native northerners in Canada. For a time the debate broadened into a national discussion of Canadian-American relations and helped to feed a nationalist groundswell. Never before in Canadian history had such a powerful consortium of resource corporations confronted such a highly mobilized opposition.

By the mid-1970's, the national media were covering the North in unparallelled detail and depth. Public attention was riveted by a proposed natural gas pipeline from Alaska up the Mackenzie River Valley to U.S. markets to the south – an outsized engineering project that sharply juxtaposed the clashing visions of the future and the coalitions marshalled in their support. Then the pipeline proposal failed and public interest shrank as rapidly as it had mushroomed.

What lessons would the 1970's hold for northern development in the following decades? This vibrant, turbulent period clearly produced irreversible changes in every aspect of northern life and relations with southern Canada. To date, however, we have lacked a major reflective study of the nature and significance of this change.

Professor Robert Page's *Northern Development: The Canadian Dilemma* provides the first comprehensive evaluation of the post-1968 debate regarding the future of the Canadian North. As a scholar who was also a participant at the height of the controversy in the mid-1970's, Professor Page writes with uncommon authority. For readers, both specialists and the general public interested in the future and curious about the past, the book is essential reading. It has implications for the country that range well beyond northern development and touch on some of the vital issues affecting our future survival as a nation.

David V.J. Bell
Edgar J. Dosman

Preface

The controversies over northern development provided the sharpest focus for the political issues of the 1970's. The list of components in this debate is long and curiously disparate, and includes environmental protection, native rights, economic nationalism, energy conservation, the limitations of high technology, political sovereignty, public participation, and government regulation. The pipeline proposals mobilized powerful economic interests from the multinational oil companies, banks, steel companies, and North American gas utilities. The projects aroused the widest and most powerful coalition of public interest groups in Canadian history.

For many, Arctic pipelines became a symbol of what was wrong with our growth-oriented, energy-intensive society. In spite of the massive public relations campaign by the applicants, the liberal conscience of middle-class Canada became disturbed by the environmental and native issues. The Mackenzie Valley Pipeline was subject to the most thorough public hearings of any Canadian project. Yet when all the rhetoric of testimony and cross-examination was completed and the government decisions were announced with great fanfare, surprisingly little had actually been decided. While the Mackenzie Valley Pipeline was indefinitely postponed, the successful applicant, Foothills, was little better off.

Nine years later, in 1986, the project was still not off the ground because of financing problems. As a result, a sense of frustration remained from the experience for governments, the corporate sector, and public interest groups. The first two absorbed the lessons of the 1970's, regrouped, and devised new strategies for the 1980's. The public interest groups, having mounted a massive effort in the 1974-77 period, seem less powerful in the 1980's. Financial viability and the need to retain experienced personnel are ongoing and continuous problems. The public interest group phenomenon, so much a feature of the 1970's, has not evolved into a permanent and self-sustaining "third force." The early hopes of many exponents have been only partially realized; for many of those involved it remained an unsatisfactory and incomplete experience.

This book reflects a mixture of motives and concerns. It is the reflections of an active participant, but one who deliberately chose to wait several years before putting pen to paper. Here, my own academic instincts were surfacing through an attempt to allow some of the fires of controversy to cool. My determination to proceed was increased by the first two books to appear, *People, Peregrines, and Arctic Pipelines* (1977) and *Super Pipe* (1979). The first of these was published through the financial support of one applicant and the second written by the former head of public affairs of the other. Both of these works cast serious doubt on the validity of the Berger Inquiry process. In the first the inquiry and the report were dismissed as "romantically utopian" and a product of Berger's own "socialist background." In the second Mr. Justice Berger was accused of promoting a vision of a separatist "Northern Marxist Nation."[1] It is not the purpose of this book to defend Berger, for his report rests on the evidence cited. But these two books, in their search for a scapegoat, have ignored many of the policy issues involved in the hearings. As one who participated in both the Berger and the National Energy Board (NEB) hearings I found it curious that Berger aroused this reaction, given that his conclusions were similar to those contained in the NEB report.

This volume is not assumed to be a definitive work on northern pipelines and northern development; but it is designed to put the topic into a wider perspective and hopefully a more balanced view. It seeks to look into the process employed by a public inquiry and by an energy regulatory board. As Canada moves through the closing years of the twentieth century a further series of northern projects are under consideration or on the horizon. Given these future needs it is useful to probe the strengths and weaknesses of the process applied to decision-making on northern pipelines in the 1970's. Also, we approach public policy issues like northern development with a series of attitudes and assumptions. But these are conditioned by our perception of what has happened in the past. Through the hearings I continually saw at work this historic legacy, which some call the myth of the North. In the first chapter I try to probe the roots of this mythology for an understanding of the southern response to northern development. In the second chapter I try to probe the intellectual ideas that brought the different public interest groups into a uniquely Canadian coalition. The existing literature in both these areas is very thin and my comments of necessity constitute a very personal and subjective view in a highly controversial area.

After assessing the Berger and NEB formats for decision-making, the study goes on to consider the issues within the four main areas of concern: geotechnical, biological, social, and economic. I am not a specialist in all these areas; no one person is. However, I have taken great pains to present the scientific evidence as it has been debated in public. I have gone into some detail because without it the reader would not get a proper perspective on the substance of the debate and the uncertainties facing the experts in all four fields. In each area northern development was straining our existing knowledge and systems in ways often not evident even to the participants. Also, it shows the confusion of motives and priorities involved at every step for government and, to a lesser extent, for the corporate applicants. These venues did not present a normal business environment governed by the principles of the Harvard Business School. Victory went to the smaller consortium, which interpreted more astutely the political parameters in which the project had to be judged. There are a number of lessons here for the aspiring corporate executive. Corporate social responsibility is a newly emerging concept that has expanded in the last decade. It is important for all corporations, but it is imperative in the special circumstances of the North. The new social and environmental standards were not fully appreciated in many boardrooms, as the following pages show. These matters are now not just a question of public relations but of regulatory requirements essential for project approval. The northern pipeline debate helped to trigger these changes and in the process increased the levels of government intervention.

When these issues of northern pipelines were first raised late in the 1960's, I was an academic historian teaching in southern Canada. I had always been particularly interested in the problems of resource development in modern Canada and it appeared to me that Canada was headed to repeat some of her historic mistakes in exploiting and exporting raw resources. In the years between 1972 and 1977 I chaired the northern pipeline efforts of the Committee for an Independent Canada to research the issues and intervene before regulatory boards. In addition, I prepared evidence and appeared as a witness for the Native Brotherhood of the Northwest Territories before the Berger Inquiry. These experiences have undoubtedly coloured my perspective. In fact, it was the most profound educational experience of my life. The subtleties and complexities of economic development and regionalism took on new meaning. When it was all over I felt strangely unsatisfied with the whole experience. By then I had come to appreciate that some of my original ideas and arguments were a bit simplistic. My original environmental and native rights concerns had widened to encompass engineering and economic aspects of northern energy policy. This book attempts to sort out some of these wider issues from the jumble of events that involved northern development.

One of the basic themes of this work is public participation. While there has been a great deal of talk about public input in the last decade, there has not been much serious analysis of its extent or of its influence on public policy. The Mackenzie Valley Pipeline debate is useful because it demonstrates public input through both the inquiry and regulatory board routes. Berger attempted a number of innovations to try to increase public participation; these were a continual annoyance to some of the participants, who wanted a speedy resolution of the issues. I hope that this study will show the degree of success some of these initiatives achieved and their influence on the final outcome.

I have tried to avoid the temptation to turn this book into a narrow academic treatise. The issues involved I hope will be of wider interest, given that this is such an important area of public policy. I have also deliberately avoided the type of ideological rhetoric that creeps into some works on contemporary affairs. This volume is neither a justification for free enterprise nor an explanation of the North using the Marxist paradigm. As a result, I expect to be attacked from both wings. However, I do feel strongly that the North has suffered from the colonial nature of the government and from economic dependency to southern financial interests. I am not concerned with finding heroes and villains *per se* and I leave it to the reader to make his or her moral judgements from the evidence presented.

The sources used to write this book are many and varied. I have my own notes and correspondence relating to many of the events I observed. I have talked at one time or another to most of the major participants, including government and corporate figures. Canadian Arctic Gas and Foothills Pipelines provided me with copies of their filed testimony and were generous with their time in answering questions. Both companies allowed me to visit their northern installations and question their own personnel. I consulted the small collection of Berger Inquiry Papers (RG 126) at the Public Archives of Canada; Terry Cook and Marc Hopkins also supplied leads in other directions. The Bata Library at Trent University and especially Bruce Cossar, the former Government Documents Librarian, were tremendously helpful throughout. Many other libraries and archives were consulted, including Imperial Oil; the National Energy Board; Energy, Mines, and Resources; Canadian Arctic Resources Committee; and the Arctic Institute of North America. I am grateful to all of these people and organizations for their courtesy and their support for wandering scholars like myself.

The research for this book was made possible by financial help from the Social Sciences and Humanities Research Council, Trent University Research Committee, and a research grant from the Nova Corporation. I am also extremely grateful to many of my friends and co-workers in the public interest group coalition who shared their insights with me at one time or another. Canada has been well served by people like François Bregha, Nydia McCool, Bruce Willson, John Olthuis,

Ian McDougall, and many more. For two summers Mr. Peter Paul worked as my research assistant and did some excellent background work for several of the chapters. Mrs. Mavis Prior, Maggie McTavish, and Taru Freeman did yeomen efforts in translating rough notes into typed manuscript. I am also grateful to the series editor, Ed Dosman, for his advice and encouragement, as well as to Dick Tallman, whose careful editorial work on the manuscript improved it considerably.

Finally I owe a great debt to the patience and wisdom of my wife Jocelyne, who made sure that this manuscript did not suffer the same fate as the Mackenzie Valley Pipeline. Among her many contributions was compiling the index. For this and for much more, I want to thank her.

Bob Page
Fraserville, Ontario
October, 1985

Were we the harbingers of a brighter dawn, or only messengers of ill-omen, portending disaster?

Diamond Jenness, *People of the Twilight* (1928)

CHAPTER 1
The Vision and the Need:
The Myth of the North

The year 1968 revolutionized the development planning for Alaska and Canada north of 60°. In that year, on the frigid wind-swept wastes of Prudhoe Bay, Atlantic Richfield discovered the largest reservoirs of oil and natural gas to be found anywhere on American territory. Once the news was out, a stampede followed to get leases and then to drill in the Canadian and American North. The hope quickly spread through the boardrooms of the major oil producers that the future solution to energy supply problems for North America could lie within Canadian and American territory. In Canada the new exploration focused on two areas – the Mackenzie Delta and the High Arctic islands from Melville to Ellesmere. In both areas, significant discoveries of natural gas were made, but no oil in commercial quantities was found. While this exploration was proceeding there was a vigorous debate on a delivery system for the Prudhoe Bay reserves. In spite of an offer from Canada, the Americans quickly approved an oil pipeline across Alaska to Valdez and tankers down the West Coast. The logistics and costs of liquefying natural gas for tankers made a land route across Canada much more attractive for gas than oil.

With the backing of such giants as Exxon, a powerful consortium of twenty-seven companies proposed to build a 48″ high-pressure pipeline from Prudhoe Bay in Alaska across the Mackenzie Delta, and then south to near Calgary where one branch would service California and the other the American Midwest. It was expected to be the largest project privately financed in the history of free enterprise capitalism. In Canada, Prime Minister Trudeau compared it in importance to the building of the CPR, then being celebrated on television by the CBC series "The National Dream." Yet hardly had the project been announced before opposition began to coalesce from disparate sources. Part of the reason for this response involved the historic role of the North in the Canadian imagination and identity. For the sponsors of the project, this was something they could neither understand nor

1

control. This project was putting in doubt aspects of the northern mythology of Canada that went deep into the consciousness of many Canadians. To understand some of the subliminal aspects of the battle over the Mackenzie Valley Pipeline, one must first try to unravel some of the historic mythology of the North that has conditioned Canadian assumptions.

Southern attitudes to the North have traditionally been based on a powerful mixture of romanticism and greed. The mysterious nature of the polar North with exotic wildlife and heroic native peoples has always provided an outlet for the Canadian imagination. These factors helped to foster the image of Canada as a vigorous northern nation, "the true North strong and free" to quote the national anthem. This did not mean they took a deep interest in caribou or native peoples. Successive governments dealt with the North with an absent-minded paternalism and benign neglect that quietly ignored the poverty and related problems. The romantic feelings about natives a long distance away only produced the Canadian version of the "white man's burden" and some curious descriptions of Dene and Inuit that were linked to the idea of "the noble savage."

The other extreme of southern attitudes to the North has always involved greed and economic exploitation. The early explorers sought the riches of China and the contemporary ones, the profits of oil. In following through the northern pipeline hearings, I was fascinated to watch the public response to a distant area of the country where only a tiny percentage of Canadians would reside or ever visit. I came to realize that a romantic vision of the North was deeply implanted in the national consciousness and this vision was a potent political factor surrounding the Berger Inquiry. It was impossible to define because it had been slowly emerging for a century. It was also impossible to appreciate the nature of the southern response to Berger without first trying to understand the myth of the North lurking within the Canadian identity.

As W.L. Morton has ably demonstrated, the northern character of Canada springs not only from geographical location but from "ancient origins in the northern and maritime frontier of Europe."[1] The North Atlantic was a cultural as well as a commercial highway. Ironically, the first explorers into the Arctic sought not Canada but only a route around her to the riches of the Far East. This frontier of exploration had two great phases: the Elizabethan and post-Elizabethan eras of the sixteenth and seventeenth centuries and the modern era of the nineteenth and twentieth centuries. The recent *Manhattan* and *Polar Sea* voyages are merely the latest chapter in this long saga of the Northwest Passage. Until the twentieth century, most of the assaults on the Arctic were mounted from the United Kingdom and Northwest Europe. However, by the mid-nineteenth century they became part of the adopted folk mythology of Canada. From my own schooling I can still remember the vivid lesson on the sad end of Henry Hudson, set adrift with his young son in 1611 in a small boat on Hudson Bay when his crew mutinied rather than continue on with their arduous exploration. These views were captured in school texts such as those produced by Ryerson Press.[2] Canada, which lacked the heroic martyrs of a revolutionary war of independence, had to create a national mythology in other directions. The early and later phases of Arctic exploration helped to fill this gap. Through their school system and popular literature, Canadians gradually acquired what Farley Mowat has termed the Polar Passion and Richard Rohmer, the Arctic Imperative. A search through any second-hand book store will show many examples of this phenomenon from the mid-nineteenth century to the present.

It is interesting to speculate on the reasons for the enduring interest in Arctic exploration. In the history of exploration on this planet, the search for the Northwest Passage includes some of the most incredible feats of human endurance. Although Hollywood has chosen to ignore it, the search for Sir John Franklin in the Canadian North was every bit as dramatic as the search for Livingstone in Africa. Both ended with fitting memorials in Westminster Abbey. In the Arctic without modern technology, the explorers pitted their fragile wooden ships and stubborn willpower against the iron grip of Arctic ice and weather. It appeared to be *the* classic example of man versus nature. Canadians

As Canadians have drifted into an urban and sedentary existence in the twentieth century the attractions of the northern mythology have in no way diminished. Stephen Leacock, that rare combination of humorist and economist, caught the sense of escapism that attracted so many. He wrote: "Arctic exploration, in so far as it can be carried out from an armchair before a winter fire, has long been for me a pursuit that verges on a passion." In pursuing this hobby, he had "spared neither hours nor effort." He felt a personal sense of involvement with the tribulations of Franklin on his famous journey to the Coppermine. "Let the hour be as late as it likes, let the snow beat at the window as it will, let the trees outside groan and creak with the frost. I can stand it. With the help perhaps of an odd glass of hot toddy kept warm on the hearth, I can face any arctic winter that ever was. No igloo was ever snugger than my study-library on the Côte des Neiges road, with a volume of arctic adventure to centre its warmth and comfort."[3] In this as in other things, Leacock caught the spirit of Canadians in his age.

Figure 1.
Areas of the High Arctic Named after Early Explorers or Well-Known
Nineteenth-Century Figures. From EARP Report on Arctic Pilot Project
(1980), p. 2.

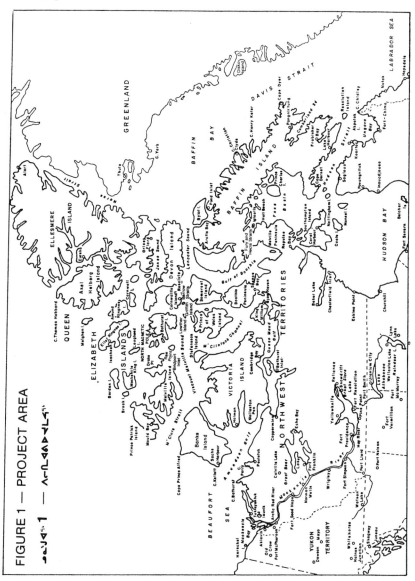

proud of their tradition of being a northern people avidly followed the drama and the mystery of the explorers.

In the years following Waterloo, the Royal Navy was looking for new worlds to conquer and when the whaler William Scoresby reported open sea lanes in the Arctic to the Admiralty in 1816 and 1817, the latter offered a prize of £20,000 to the discoverer of the Northwest Passage. In 1819-20 Sir William Parry nearly pulled it off, for he penetrated to within 250 miles of the Beaufort Sea. The extent of British interest in the Arctic increased significantly in 1845 when the Admiralty outfitted its most ambitious expedition, with *HMS Terror* and *Erebus* under the experienced guidance of Sir John Franklin. When this expedition was lost without trace, thirty-eight official and unofficial expeditions were sent from Britain and North America in the following decades. The full story of the loss of the ships and the slow and agonizing death of the men profoundly shocked Victorian Britain and created great interest across the English-speaking world. Even in the 1970's, books were still appearing to explain the mysterious circumstances of the ill-fated Franklin expedition.[4]

In 1854 Dr. John Rae of the Hudson's Bay Company published some of the first hard evidence on their final fate. He had heard from Eskimos that a party of Englishmen had starved trying to flee southward from the Arctic straits south of Victoria Island. Dr. Rae reported that their final days had been as "melancholy and dreadful as it is possible to imagine." The natives had reported from "the mutilated state of many of the bodies and the contents of the kettles, it is evident that our wretched countrymen had been driven to the last dread alternative, as a means of sustaining life."[5]

That English gentlemen had been driven by weather and starvation to cannibalism seemed profoundly disturbing to the Victorian conscience. In the ensuing controversy, Charles Dickens rushed into print in his weekly *Household Words* to challenge the validity of Rae and his native witnesses. No doubt the vision of officers and men of Her Majesty's Royal Navy abandoning discipline and the values on which the Empire rested seemed impossible to many Victorians. If Englishmen were capable of resorting to the eating of human flesh, then the civilization that set them apart from the people they had conquered was only a surface veneer. The Arctic obviously held strange powers to bring men down, and as such it was the ultimate test not only of courage and technology but of civilization as well. The stories of cannibalism in the Canadian Arctic have continued right through to the present day as the recent Gateways aircraft crash showed once again. Dickens went on to write a play with Wilkie Collins called *The Frozen Deep*, probably based on Sir John Richardson's memoir of the first

Franklin expedition. He wrote to John Forster, "I think Richardson's manly friendship, and love of Franklin, one of the noblest things I ever knew in my life. It makes one's heart beat high, with a sort of sacred joy."[6] In this decade of the Crimean War and the Indian Mutiny, the drama of Arctic exploration attracted the romantic imagination in both Britain and North America. Even the good Queen felt obliged to attend one of the performances of *The Frozen Deep*. As a result of the search for Franklin, Mother Britain drew Canadian attention north to focus on her own Arctic as never before. If it was important to Britain then it was deserving of Canadian attention.

In the early twentieth century, when Franklin's exploits were presented in Canadian school texts, the message was clearly designed to promote Canadian patriotism. The exploration of the Canadian Arctic was an example of those stern Victorian qualities and values on which the Empire had been built. As one school text put it: "It is as though one listens to the muffled heart-beats of a nation and an empire. And it is fitting that here the name of Franklin should be preserved, for of the qualities of body, heart, and mind which made Britain great among nations there is no nobler embodiment."[7] Franklin was part of that heroic naval tradition from Drake to Nelson as it applied, through the North, to Canada. In addition, these traditions had migrated with the British immigrants to North America and became truly Canadian with the purchase of Rupert's Land from the Hudson's Bay Company in 1870 and the transfer of the Arctic archipelago from Britain in 1880.

Tied into the early concept of the North was the idea that racial characteristics were a product of climate. As the *Toronto Globe* emphasized in 1869, "bracing northern winters" will preserve us from "the effeminacy which naturally steals over the most vigorous races when long under the relaxing influence of tropical or even generally mild and genial skies."[8] In the year following Confederation, the Canada First movement attempted to awaken in Canadians a sense of identity based on race and climate. As the "Northmen of the New World," Canadians possessed all the vigour, endurance, and stamina of the Norsemen of old. R.G. Haliburton, one of the leading Canada Firsters, put it this way: "If climate has not had the effect of moulding races, how is it that southern nations have almost always been inferior to and subjected by the men of the north." Canada drew most of its immigrants from the vigorous peoples of northern Europe where the germ of political liberty had been developed. In the bracing climate of Canada the racial stock and the political institutions were destined for further refinement. Cold weather determinism provided a convenient rationalization for Canadian assumptions of superiority over southern cousins in the United States. In practical terms, the Canada Firsters advocated the speedy absorption of the Northwest into the new Dominion.[9] In the era of British imperial expansion these new territories provided Canada with its own imperial vision.

The links between climate and race resurfaced many times in the following decades. Late in the nineteenth century they were given a particular impetus by the application of Darwin's ideas to the study of history and political science. This "racial Darwinism" appeared to give a pseudo-scientific basis for elements in the Canadian northern myth. Canadians read with interest the works of some of the leading British writers of this school. Benjamin Kidd, for instance, wrote about the struggle for survival between nations and races in a way that buttressed the ideas of imperialism then current. Kidd wrote: "Throughout history the centre of power has moved gradually but surely to the north into those stern regions where men have been trained for the rivalry of life in the strenuous conflict with nature in which they have acquired energy, courage, integrity, and those characteristic qualities . . . of social efficiency."[10] If Britain was the successor to Rome as the great imperial power, then in time Canada would succeed Britain because of her more northerly location.

Kidd's ideas were reflected in the debates on northern topics in the Canadian House of Commons. In 1903 S.E. Gourley, a Conservative MP from Nova Scotia, argued that a Canadian explorer should be the first person to reach the North Pole. He denounced those who worried that the image of Canada's northern climate would interfere with the flow of prospective immigrants, for Canada's climate was "her glory." A cold climate was one of the profound forces involved in the shaping of history. Countries like Germany and Russia dominated the world and had achieved such high civilization while southern states like France, Italy, India, and China "are the dying nations of the world." Canadians must be prepared to sacrifice themselves and their children if need be on the altar of their new country. If there was any doubt about Canada "owning every foot of territory from here to the North Pole" they must physically take possession of it. Canada ought to buy Greenland and secure Alaska from the Americans. In the race for the North Pole, Canadians must show that they possess the seafaring qualities of the old Vikings and demonstrate that they are a "bold and intrepid race."[11]

Some of these ideas of geopolitics, race, and the North continued in the post-World War One era in the writings and speeches of the explorer and scientist Vilhjalmur Stefansson. He was a great publicist of the potential of the North and a policy adviser in both Ottawa and Washington. In his widely read *The Northward Course of Empire* he

7

wrote that man's "fight upward in civilization has coincided in part at least with his march northward over the earth into a cooler, clearer, more bracing air."[12] In a chart opposite the title page he showed how the great centres of political power and culture had followed a gradual path northward from Greece to Rome, Paris, Washington, London, and Berlin. This pattern would continue, he claimed, with future developments in the Soviet Union and Canada. But Stefansson was far more than merely a theorist; he had personally travelled 20,000 miles across the Arctic by sled and dog team. He had shown a remarkable ability to live off the land and to survive the most gruelling of journeys. He had argued that the Arctic was not a frozen wasteland but a land of great potential awaiting development for those who knew how. "There is no northern boundary beyond which productive enterprise cannot go till North meets North on the opposite shores of the Arctic Ocean."[13] One recent scholarly analysis concluded that "Stefansson created more interest in the arctic among Canadians than any other individual of his time."[14] As late as the Second World War he still played a role as policy adviser in Washington on projects such as the Alaska Highway and the Canol Pipeline, which cut through the Canadian North to supply Alaska.

As Canada approached the Second World War some of the wording became more subtle but the message was essentially the same; the challenge of a northern climate would provoke the evolution of a vigorous and great nationality. Stephen Leacock, writing in 1938, saw physical, economic, and intellectual benefits flowing from the northern experience. "The vision of a vast northern empire, rigorous and stern to its children but kindly in its very rigour, rich in resources, not such as to fall into the idle hand and nourish the languor of inertia but such as come as the reward of effort and courage; this and the prospect of the intellectural culture that arises on such a foundation, is the view."[15] As late as 1958 one of the official handbooks of the federal government reiterated this climatic determinism: "It is a curious fact that civilization has been expanding northward ever since the dawn of history . . . converging from both sides of the world toward a common centre. That centre is the arctic."[16]

The boundary extensions and consolidations of Confederation were a further stimulus to the northern myth. The acquisition of Rupert's Land from the Hudson's Bay Company has already been mentioned as being central to Canadian aspirations in the post-Confederation years. The question of the High Arctic islands was brought to the attention of the Mackenzie government in Ottawa in 1874 by London. Both British and American groups had applied for land grants on Baffin Island and the British were faced with the ticklish question of

Figure 2.
Stefannson's Chart on the Northward Migration of the Centres of Civilization. From V. Stefannson, *The Northward Course of Empire* (New York, 1923).

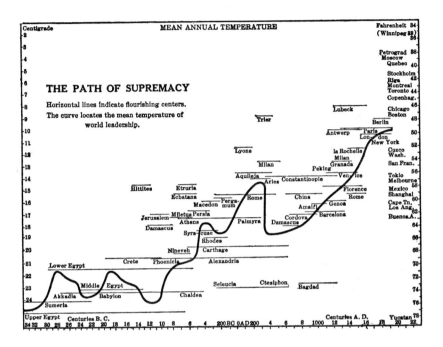

sovereignty. They were reluctant to exercise their own jurisdiction in the area for they had enough territorial concerns in Africa and Asia at the time. But if they renounced the area it would likely be claimed by the United States, which had purchased Alaska from the Czar seven years earlier, and would be lost for future Canadian expansion northward. The Mackenzie government was reluctant to act and, consequently, let the matter rest.

In 1877, with American interests commencing to ship out graphite and mica, London pressed Canada to act. When resolutions for extending the northern boundaries were presented to the House of Commons they were strongly supported by the Conservative opposition. Macdonald emphasized that they were laying the foundations for the country's future. This new territory was "rich in mines of iron, copper, gold, silver, and large deposits of mica." They would be "unworthy" as founders of Confederation if they failed in this charge.[17] When the Conservatives returned to power they completed the trans-

9

fer of the islands to Canada in 1880. However, once the new property was acquired they did nothing to establish their sovereignty by any effective presence in the area. The transfer was effected quietly to avoid arousing an American response; it was 1897 before the Laurier government passed an Order-in-Council that described even in general terms the islands acquired. There is no evidence of international recognition at this time, nor did Ottawa provide any services for the native people in the islands.

In the 1880's serious interest in the economic potential of the Canadian North began to surface. The Senate appointed a select committee to investigate the resources of the Mackenzie Basin. This committee reported in the session of 1888, with an optimism that seems incredible today: there were, they announced, 656,000 square miles of northland suitable for potatoes, 407,000 for barley, and 316,000 for wheat. The potential for agriculture was said to stretch all the way to the Arctic Ocean along the Mackenzie Valley, and this myth of the green North was continued in the twentieth century by such writers as Stefansson and by many less-than-candid government pamphlets. The area was also alleged to possess a huge mining potential, in the mountains west of the Mackenzie River for silver, gold, and iron and along the Coppermine River for copper. One of the northern industries, whaling, was in severe danger of extinction from American vessels armed with explosive harpoons and swivel guns. The committee urged Ottawa to regulate the trade by licences, which would conserve declining numbers and bring revenue from the trade. Thus, both conservation and sovereignty were concerns of the committee.

The committee reserved its greatest enthusiasm, however, for the petroleum potential of the region. In the Athabaska and Mackenzie valleys existed "the most extensive petroleum field in America, if not in the world." In words with a contemporary ring, they emphasized that with increasing world demand for petroleum these reserves would assume "an enormous value in the near future" and would become one of "the chief assets" of Canada. Because of its value and significance, it was recommended that 40,000 square miles of the key property be excluded from public sale as a Crown reserve. What form development would take in this area was not explained by the report although the author did talk of petroleum exports to Britain through Churchill or some other Hudson Bay port. The committee's aspirations for economic development seem to have been the basic thrust. With the CPR barely completed and the Prairies still largely silent and deserted, the report opened the prospect of even further development by tapping the greater riches of the North.[18] For years this volume continued as a basic reference book on the potential of the North, and its work was continued by the Geological Survey of Canada.

While the vision of black gold slumbered on in the Canadian mind, a much more pressing reality surged to the foreground of public attention in the 1890's. The discovery of gold along the creeks near Dawson in the Yukon triggered the wildest stampede of population in Canadian history and made the Yukon a household word around the globe. Since Confederation, Canada had suffered through long years of recession and the internal feuds over Riel and separate schools. Considerable doubt about the viability of the nation was reflected in heavy immigration to the U.S. Then two events in the late 1890's burst that bubble of gloom and self-doubt: the beginning of a great wave of European immigration to settle the West and the gold rush to the Klondike. Together they had a profound impact on the national psychology, pushing back the inferiority complex of the earlier years. The National Policy was finally bringing prosperity to the country and unexpected riches were tapped in creeks like Bonanza.

It is difficult to isolate events that excite the national imagination, but the Yukon gold rush was certainly one for Canada. Possibly Robert Service's poetry caught the mood of the moment better than any historian. In his *The Spell of the Yukon:*

You come to get rich (damned good reason),
    You feel like an exile at first;
You hate it like hell for a season,
    And then you are worse than the worst.

It grips you like some kind of sinning;
    It twists you from foe to a friend;
It seems it's been since the beginning;
    It seems it will be to the end.[19]

The Canadians were very determined to protect their northern goldfield and, following the British imperial tradition, they sent in a para-military police force and a bureaucracy, very different from the American frontier. Troops were also dispatched because the bulk of the miners were Americans and there were rumours of conspiracies by alien groups with such exotic titles as "The Secret Order of the Midnight Sun." There were fears that these Americans hoped to pull off another Texas during the winter months when the Yukon was isolated from communications with Canada. With so many Americans and others flooding through the passes into the Yukon, there were worries about maintaining Canadian sovereignty. This helps to explain why Canadians were so defensive about the Alaska Boundary Dispute.

In terms of the impact of the Klondike on the public, it is ironic that only a few thousand Canadians went to the Yukon and few of them made their fortune. As with other extractive staples, the gold boom did little to spawn permanent economic activity in the North; after five or six years the population and activity largely evaporated. Only a little dredging remained. But the incredible tales of hardship and instant fortunes gave the North a greater attraction to those in the south. The drama and romance of the Klondike Days are still celebrated in Edmonton each year; and the tales of gold gave a new stimulus to the drive for northern development, which fed on visions of profit.

The concerns about Yukon sovereignty that surfaced during the gold rush migrations and the Alaska Boundary Dispute reappeared in connection with whaling in the Beaufort Sea and the Arctic islands. When Canada acquired the Arctic archipelago from Great Britain in 1880, Ottawa made no attempt to establish an effective presence in the region. Throughout the nineteenth century, whaling vessels from the U.S. and U.K. had been active in areas such as Davis Strait and Hudson Bay. With the application of steam power to ocean navigation after 1850 the potential for Arctic penetration increased considerably and the Americans were most prominent in the post-Confederation years. With no internationally recognized jurisdiction in the area, Ottawa was apprehensive that her claims could be effectively challenged. These worries increased in the last years of the century when American whalers from the Pacific pursued the declining whale population into the Beaufort Sea, north of the Mackenzie Delta. Wintering in the protected harbour on Herschel Island, the whalers not only depleted the numbers of beluga and bowhead whales but the caribou, muskox, and other wildlife on the mainland. Severe social impacts resulted as the police reports warned: "This liquor is sold or traded to the natives for furs, walrus, ivory bone and their young girls who are purchased by the officers of the ships for their own foul purposes." In addition, the whaling crews brought such diseases as measles, which killed off most of the original Inuit population of the Mackenzie district. For Ottawa, these reports were an embarrassment because they graphically illustrated the absence of any government presence in the area. These events also left a permanent memory with the local native people as to the dangers of white "development" for Dene or Inuit.[20]

During the years 1898-1902, while Canadian attention was focused primarily on the Yukon and the troops in the South African War, foreign explorers were busy in the Arctic archipelago. The Norwegian expedition of Otto Sverdrup ranged over Ellesmere, Devon, and the islands to the west. On his return he tried unsuccessfully to get the Swedish and then the Norwegian governments to claim the territory. With the Laurier government hesitant to act, some individual Canadians tried to seize the initiative to protect their territory. The veteran Captain J.E. Bernier worked furiously to raise funds for Arctic exploration from private and government sources. He used the nationalist appeal that a Canadian must be the first to reach the North Pole and found support for his arguments on both sides of the House of Commons. John Charlton set the tone: "We have recently awakened to the possibility of having an active and aggressive national life in Canada. We no longer feel like apologizing for being Canadians. We no longer have the sense of provincialism . . . inferiority. We have found in South Africa . . . that we have gained an enviable position in the world." Canada would not only be solving a serious geographical problem but would be laying claim to the "enormous mineral wealth" in the islands between Greenland and the 141st parallel of longitude.[21] As no one was sure exactly how many islands existed it was easiest for Canada to claim "the sector" from her mainland north to the pole, although there is no indication that they wished to claim the sea as well as the land.[22]

As the parliamentary debates of 1901-03 show, some Canadians feared Teddy Roosevelt would buy Greenland from Denmark and then seize the High Arctic islands to link them to Alaska, in the same way that Washington had seized territory on her southern flank in the Spanish-American War. In response, some newspapers called for a Canadian "Monroe" Doctrine that would prevent disposal of Greenland or St. Pierre et Miquelon to anyone except Canada. The papers were particularly militant in defending Canada's right to expand in the Arctic. The Quebec *Chronicle* boldly announced that any "purchaser of Greenland must be prepared to defend his purchase by force of arms" and Canada should be prepared to separate from the Empire if the Foreign Office in London refused to support its claims against American "filibusters."[23] Laurier, on the other hand, feared that bold Canadian moves might provoke "official" American concerns where little existed. The lesson he had learned from the Alaska Boundary Dispute was that Canada could not mobilize the imperial alliance with Britain in any dispute with the United States. In the end, Laurier supported Captain Bernier with rhetoric but little money. "If a son of Canada were to plant a flag of this country at the north pole, if he were to achieve what so many brave men have struggled in vain to achieve, there is not a Canadian heart that would not beat with pride."[24] Not all members of the House were carried away with the topic. A.W. Puttee, the Labour MP for Winnipeg, commented sarcastically: "I very much fear that the country will question the sanity of this House . . . when we have nothing better to talk about than discovering the North Pole."[25]

When Bernier sailed north, he went really as a government Fisheries officer and part-time explorer, with far more mundane duties than discovering the North Pole. He posted various government plaques and collected licence fees for fishing and whaling. In 1909, after several attempts, the American Robert Peary planted the Stars and Stripes at what he believed to be the North Pole and claimed the entire area for the United States. Although some Canadians were upset, Laurier refused to be provoked into denouncing the American claims. Between 1909 and 1918 various Canadian explorations and police patrols were sent into the High Arctic to show the flag. In a temporary aberration in the early 1920's Canada laid claim to Wrangel Island off Siberia. This confusing international incident with the Soviet Union involved territory clearly outside the Canadian sector theory of Arctic sovereignty. Under the sector theory Canada claimed all the islands in a wedge-shaped area from Greenland west to a line extending north from the Alaska border (141° west longitude) to the pole. This concept was never recognized in international law. Fortunately, the Mackenzie King administration abandoned the claim within two years because it would have been impossible for Ottawa to have occupied the island without provoking the wrath of Moscow. After the Allied interventions in Russia in 1918-19 in support of the anti-Bolshevik elements the Kremlin already had reason to suspect the Western democracies. By the late 1920's the United States was applying for permits in Ottawa for scientific exploration in the Arctic islands. It was not until 1930, however, that the Norwegian government recognized Canadian sovereignty over the Sverdrup Islands after Ottawa had paid $67,000 to Sverdrup for his maps, notes, etc.[26] In the interwar years the books and articles of Stefansson and others kept the image of Arctic exploration before the Canadian public. But as the nature of the work changed from physical discovery to scientific analysis, the extent of the press and public interest declined and the romantic rhetoric cooled.

The North has always provided another attraction for those seeking to get away from it all. Anti-establishment rebels from the days of the Hudson's Bay Company in the eighteenth and nineteenth centuries to the Company of Young Canadians in the 1960's and early 1970's have sought escape in the northern wilds. One such figure was John

Hornby, who came out from England in 1904 and for nearly a quarter of a century created a reputation for his ability to live off the barren lands. He was seeking release from the degenerate materialism of the modern world as he saw it. World War I "confirmed, rather than initiated, his conviction that civilization was evil and social man diseased."[27] Yet the lonely experience of hunting and trapping produced a brooding introspection rather than a release from the evils of this world. Hornby's protest, however, took on a greater glory with his martyrdom. In the spring of 1927 he guessed wrong about the caribou migration in the Thelon area and along with two young companions starved to death. It seemed to emphasize the harsh reality of the North where Hornby's superb talents were not enough if luck ran out. The struggle with nature was an unrelenting one where man even in the twentieth century required all his cunning to survive. For whites the Arctic was the ultimate Darwinian challenge.

In the long history of the North, the role of the RCMP in maintaining law and order has always attracted wide public interest. Its image made the Mounties an international symbol of Canada and hero figures in literature and movies about the North. Probably their most exotic case occurred in the early weeks of 1932 when they attempted to bring the "Mad Trapper of Rat River" to justice. With incredible ingenuity and endurance, Albert Johnson defied a posse of white trappers, Dene, and RCMP in a forty-eight-day running gun battle across 150 miles of mountainous terrain southwest of the Mackenzie Delta. In midwinter with the temperature averaging forty below, he engaged in a series of shoot-outs with his pursuers, leaving one dead and two wounded, and then he disappeared when he seemed to be cornered. For the first time in Canadian history an aircraft was used to help locate a fugitive; the pilot was the famous "Wop May," who had duelled with von Richthofen in World War I. The pursuit of the Mad Trapper of Rat River was a leading news item on the radio and in newspapers across the English-speaking world during January and February of 1932. By the time Johnson was finally gunned down on February 17, 1932, along the Eagle River his exploits were known far and wide; for the Mounties it further substantiated the slogan that they got their man.

In the nearly fifty years since then, the legend of the Mad Trapper of Rat River has shown no signs of losing its public appeal. There is still no rational explanation for the animosity that had built up in his mind to all other human beings. Some have argued that the loneliness of the Arctic trap lines warped his sanity. Yet his skill, his cunning, and his amazing endurance aroused deep admiration. His exploits have become part of the folklore of the North. But mention of his name can still start an argument between those who pity and those who damn him. Papers such as the *Toronto Globe* gave the hunt vivid front-page treatment and in the period since, thanks to the efforts of Pierre Berton and others, the story has never been allowed to drop from sight.[28] Public controversy erupted in April, 1980, when a Hollywood crew began filming a version of the story in Alberta. The American company was attacked in the local media for distorting Canadian history to fit its commercial purposes. Clearly the story had now become part of the legacy of the Canadian North and Albertans resented any efforts to tamper with it.

Only infrequently did the North capture attention during the interwar years. Southern images were dominated by the noble trinity of the missionaries, the Mounties, and the Bay. Each was viewed as a means of civilizing the North. With the church saving souls, the Bay buying furs, and the kindly Mounties preserving law and order, there seemed to be little reason for alarm. While these activities did not capture frequent headlines, they still received media attention. The exploits of the northern bush pilots for fire-fighting and rescue made them into folk heroes. In popular and juvenile novels they became a symbolic equivalent of the American cowboy. The photo-journalism of *National Geographic* magazine often featured the Arctic and its peoples. The establishment of the National Film Board and the film documentary allowed for frequent portrayal of northern themes even if some of them, like *Nanook of the North*, added to southern stereotypes. In artistic circles in the 1920's and 1930's there was growing acclaim for the Group of Seven and their portrayal of the rugged northern shield country as the aesthetic heartland of Canada.

During these years some economic development was taking place to strengthen the concept of a northern treasure chest of natural resources. Imperial Oil discovered a small oilfield at Norman Wells on the Mackenzie in 1920 and later built a small refinery to supply local needs in the western Arctic. Although some exploration work followed this discovery there was no oil boom such as those triggered by the news of the Turner Valley and Leduc discoveries in the south. The absence of a viable means of transportation to southern markets acted as a discouragement to those who were convinced that huge pools of oil existed under the Arctic wastes. After all, by 1940 the average production of the Norman Wells field was still only 100 barrels per day, which was hardly in keeping with the fabulous predictions of the Senate report of 1888. The reason for even this limited production at Norman Wells was the local demand from mining operations started up in the 1930's on Great Bear and Great Slave lakes.

Gilbert Labine discovered a major silver-pitchblende (uranium) deposit on the east shore of Great Bear Lake and by 1933 Eldorado

Gold Mines had a concentrating mill operating at the site, which they named Port Radium. Further south at Yellowknife Bay, gold had been discovered by miners on their way to the Klondike in 1896, but it was the relative increase in the value of the gold during the depression that made the mine profitable. The only reason both these operations developed was because the final product was valuable enough to cover the heavy costs of pioneer air travel. Other mineral bodies were known but required land transportation systems. Resource development and transportation facilities would have to move north in the provinces before development could spill over into the territories.

The stillness of the Canadian North was shattered by Pearl Harbor and the Japanese attack on the Aleutian Islands of Alaska. This northwest corner of the continent now became a strategic line of defence for the continent, and with Japanese submarines sinking supply ships on the Pacific an overland transportation corridor became essential. First the Americans established the Northwest Staging Route, which consisted of a series of landing strips north of Edmonton to ferry aircraft to Alaska. Next came the building of the Alaska Highway by the U.S. Army, permanently destroying the isolation of northern British Columbia and the southern Yukon. Finally, the Canol oil pipeline was built from Norman Wells on the Mackenzie over the mountains to the Alaska Highway in the Yukon, to allow expanded Norman Wells oil production to supply the war zone in Alaska. About $150 million was spent by the United States on the project, which was completed in 1944 and operated for about one year, with an upward capacity of 3,000 barrels per day.

In order to supply this quantity and allow for future American military needs, extensive drilling privileges covering large areas of the Yukon and the western Northwest Territories were granted to Washington for the duration of the war. Only slowly did Canadian officials realize the extent of the resource commitment involved; their embarrassment was great, for Canada possessed only very limited oil production to supply the domestic market. Warnings also came from the British government with regard to American attempts to get control of petroleum reserves in the Middle East.[29] Norman Robertson, the Undersecretary of State for External Affairs, warned the Canadian cabinet that the Canol arrangement might be part of a wider U.S. policy to line up post-war petroleum reserves at the expense of others and that access to oil could become a serious international issue. Even Mackenzie King was profoundly disturbed. He confided to his diary:

I attended War Committee at 11. Almost two hours were spent on discussion the Canol Project. I held strongly with one or two others to the view that we ought to get the Americans out of further development there, and keep complete control in our own hands. As discussion went on and it became apparent that that part of Canada may possess oil areas as vast as those countries like Rumania and California areas, etc., the thought came to my mind that Canada might well become the occasion of another great war unless matters are handled with the greatest possible care. . . . With the tiny population that we have, relative to what we possess in the way of resources, this country will become a scene of battle and pass into other hands. I know of nothing which has grown out of the war which seems to me to require more careful consideration.[30]

The scenario King outlined in his diary seems more appropriate for a Richard Rohmer novel than for two allies working in close co-operation to win a war.

During the Cold War of the 1950's the United States became acutely interested in the Canadian North. With the Korean War and other examples of confrontation, the Pentagon in Washington was determined to eliminate the chance of a sneak attack on the industrial heartland of the United States by enemy forces flying over the pole and across poorly defended Canadian territory. As a result three great radar lines were built across the country, including the Distant Early Warning (DEW) line on the shores of the Arctic Ocean. In addition, northern bases like Goose Bay, Labrador, became key components in the Strategic Air Command nuclear strike force poised for retaliation against the Soviet Union.

While Lester Pearson tried to carve a name for Canada as an "honest broker" and peacekeeper to the Third World, events in the North, the establishment of the joint North American Air Defence Command, and the involvement in NATO showed the real nature of the Canadian position in the world. Many Canadians had the uncomfortable feeling that the Americans would intercept any northern air attack over Canada anyway; but co-operation would allow the zone of interception to be hundreds of miles north of the main Canadian population centres. But even this argument seemed a little hollow in terms of the extent of the sacrifice of sovereignty. The year before the Diefenbaker election of 1957 Ralph Allen of *Maclean's* filed a devastating article after visiting the DEW line stations. In order to avoid costs to Canada, he argued that the St. Laurent administration had surrendered our "independence" to the American military. "In law we still own this northern frontier. . . . In fact we do not."[31] Press reports flourished of American censorship of Canadian news reporting from the DEW line, of American flags flying at the radar bases in

Canada, and of the Canadian Minister of Northern Affairs having to secure clearance from Washington before he could visit the DEW line area.[32] These events were annoying to Canadians who resented this curbing of their sovereignty for the needs of American defence.

With these northern events as background, the St. Laurent government, led by a determined C.D. Howe, decided to push ahead in 1956 with the Trans-Canada Natural Gas Pipeline scheme to supply new markets in Ontario and Quebec with the rapidly expanding gas reserves of Alberta. The scheme had great attractions for Canadian energy supply but it required massive government support to get it off the ground and, at the eleventh hour, extensive American involvement in financing. When it appeared that this strategic energy facility could fall under the control of American interests, John Diefenbaker and a number of others exploded in righteous indignation. Incredible scenes followed in the House of Commons, with the opposition parties abandoning all the normal etiquette of Parliament and the government ramming the bill through using the technique of closure. C.D. Howe got his pipeline bill but it was a Pyrrhic victory for the Liberals. With the public already sensitive about American influence in the North, the electorate responded to the Conservative campaign. Diefenbaker's nationalist appeal would never have been persuasive had not the fears about northern sovereignty already been present in the minds of the people.

After gaining a slender minority in the 1957 election, Diefenbaker went back to the people for an increased mandate early in the following year. Part of the reason for the tremendous response of the electorate was that his "Northern Vision" caught the nationalist undercurrent of the late 1950's. His appeal was not to some vague romanticism but to a clear development concept. "We will open that northland for development by improving transportation and communications and by the development of power." His Roads to Resources program and railway subsidies were designed to provide the infrastructure so that private enterprise would be encouraged to invest in new projects. He wanted to give Canadians "a transcending sense of national purpose" in developing the North; this would "safeguard our independence" and restore "unity." Like the experience of the pioneers in settling the prairie West, Diefenbaker believed this would give Canadians a new imagination, a new hope, even a new soul![33] Canadians bored with the dull materialism of successive Liberal governments responded to this idealism of the frontier spirit and of developing the North for Canada's future greatness. In appealing to the myth of the North, Diefenbaker brilliantly caught the mood of the day and secured the largest electoral majority in the history of the country.

Although John Diefenbaker came into office expressing great concern for northern and nationalist issues, his administration was largely incapable of translating those aspirations into effective policies. In 1959 he attempted to assert Canada's control over the DEW line stations, but they were declining in importance as the intercontinental ballistic missiles became the strategic weapons in the Soviet and American arsenals. In the same year the National Energy Board was established to regulate the oil and gas industry; in its early years, however, it remained dependent on the multinationals for information, thus allowing the status quo to prevail. In 1961 the Diefenbaker government established its new Oil and Gas Land Regulations but these contained many loopholes for the expansion of the majors. Finally, in the last months of his administration, he had a furious row with the Americans over his refusal to accept nuclear weapons. It was sadly ironic that a man of such immense oratorical talents proved to have such limited administrative capability. By the end of his term the Northern Vision had become a basis for sarcastic jokes.

The concept of northern development, however, continued strongly irrespective of the fall of the Diefenbaker government. By the late 1960's a new, grandiose concept, the Mid-Canada Corridor, emerged. This idea, promoted vigorously by a foundation led by Richard Rohmer, the lawyer and novelist, called for a new brand of development from Churchill Falls, Labrador, to Kitimat in B.C. In the West there would be two wide northern extensions along the Mackenzie Valley to the Arctic Ocean and along the Alaska Highway to the Canadian border. Its purpose was to exploit the green belt south of the tree line in a planned and orderly fashion. A number of very prominent Canadians were attracted to support the foundation, including the Governor General, Lester Pearson, the former Prime Minister, and Leslie Frost, the former Premier of Ontario. Rohmer wished to strengthen the independence of Canada through a new national policy of widening the narrow band of development along our southern border. In the large conference on Mid-Canada two years after the centennial of Confederation, Rohmer summed up his own view of the implications of the scheme: "Canadians need a new nation-wide purpose – a national goal – like they need new blood. It should be a purpose which relates internally, patriotically, to our own people and their material and spiritual growth."[34]

Rohmer and his colleagues failed in their efforts to mobilize the country in such a huge co-ordinated effort; there were too many competing and conflicting jurisdictions involved for a very clear consensus to emerge. Also, some of the business leaders were sceptical of Rohmer's ability to keep fact and fiction separate. At the same time, in one part of the Mid-Canada Corridor, rapid events were unfolding as a result of the largest oil strike in North American history across the border at Prudhoe Bay, Alaska.

During the 1960's, northern policy received a lower priority after the exit of Diefenbaker; the Pearson years were dominated by the flag debate, bilingualism, medicare, and Expo '67. When news of the Prudhoe Bay oil discovery first reached Ottawa in early 1968, few realized the future implications for Canadian northern policy. It was believed that the news would spark new drilling in the Canadian North while the sovereignty issue was discussed solely in terms of Russian penetration of Canadian waters. There was no apparent awareness of the revolution in the development of supertankers and the new potential they possessed for Arctic waters. When Humble Oil and its partners decided in October, 1968, to refit the *S.S. Manhattan* to demonstrate the practicability of tankers navigating the Northwest Passage, Canada was informed and data on ice conditions were requested. The assumption implicit in these communications was that the passages from Lancaster through McClure Strait were international waters, which directly violated the policy of successive Canadian governments.

Worries in Ottawa gradually increased when it was learned that a U.S. Coast Guard icebreaker would accompany the *Manhattan* through Canadian waters. As Coast Guard ships were considered military vessels, they had a responsibility (not merely custom, as with commercial vessels) to request permission to enter Canadian territorial waters. When Washington refused to apply for permission in spite of the Canadian request, it was clear that the Americans intended to challenge Canada's definition of her territorial waters. Fearing that Washington might cut off oil imports from Canada, the Trudeau government followed a conciliatory approach, trying to make the best of an embarrassing situation. They offered the support of a Canadian icebreaker as an indication that the two countries were co-operating in the project. In spite of strong criticism from the opposition parties, the Trudeau government refused to admit that Canadian sovereignty was being challenged. The official position of the American government was clear: the Northwest Passage was an international strait through which they had the right to innocent passage. As a maritime power they clung firmly to the traditional principles of the freedom of the seas enshrined in international law.[35] Public opinion in Canada, however, was not convinced that the Canadian response was adequate in terms of protecting sovereignty or the northern environment from oil spills. Besides, important oil or mineral resources might lie under the Arctic continental shelf. Toronto lawyer Michael Galway warned that unless Canada established the baseline for her territorial waters around the whole archipelago "we may end up being handed another Alaskan panhandle," and Richard Rohmer stated that Canadians were "prepared to do battle, if necessary, against any American intruder."[36] Yet the official government position appeared weak and vacillating, until in 1970 the Arctic Waters Pollution Prevention Bill was passed by Parliament as a response to the threat of marine pollution. Detailed analysis of these events will be presented later in this volume.

The *Manhattan* incident rekindled Canadian fears about sovereignty in the North and forced the government's hand. It brought historic feelings and deeply felt passions to the surface as Canada entered the decade of the 1970's. Edgar Dosman caught that point when he wrote that "one of the few shared and deeply felt beliefs in Ottawa is that Canadian sovereignty in the North is non-negotiable. The political cost of retreating publicly . . . is perceived by both senior officials and the leaders of all political parties as intolerable and a certain defeat for any government in office."[37] Canadians had always assumed that the Arctic climate and ice would protect their northern waters from commercial traffic around the northern flank of the continent. The voyages of the *Manhattan* and, later, the *Polar Sea* shattered that illusion and reminded Canadians that their empty North was attracting visitors.

Mr. Justice Berger, in his famous report, saw the North as a zone of confrontation, between southern-based white development pressures and the defenders of a traditional native homeland. The concepts of a development frontier and of a homeland are both ingredients in the historic myth of the North as presented in this chapter. From the time of the Yukon gold rush the northern development ethic has appealed to the southern sense of greed. With current dreams of an oil bonanza in the Beaufort, there is a combination of the desire for profits and of the need for energy. This contemporary drive is giving concrete substance to the rhetoric of John Diefenbaker's Northern Vision, which the Canadian electorate endorsed so enthusiastically. But equally relevant are the romantic or spiritual ingredients in the mythology.

Traditionally, the churches and the RCMP had provided the "civilizing" mission to the "primitive" North. In the 1970's the pipeline brought out into the open the dichotomy between the two ingredients. Some Canadians opted for the pipeline as the symbol of "progress" while others saw it as a threat to the "native people," the virgin wilderness, and the exotic wildlife. Some southern middle-class Canadians with their neon advertising, their urban high-rise apartments, and their post-Christian agnosticism found new attractions in the historic values of Dene and Inuit society. As pollution mounted in the cities, the cause of protecting the pristine northern wilderness became a symbolic means of avoiding the full implications of the overwhelming materialism of Canadian life. In this sense the North provided a spiritual escape and a new idealism for middle-class southern Canadians. These two conflicting ingredients in the myth of the North, the greed on one side and the romantic idealism on the other, made the pipeline debate and later events so fundamental for northern history. As well, the greed and the idealism in the debate were a reflection of the conflict of values inherent in Canadian society of the 1970's and 1980's.

The myth of the North that has emerged in the years since Confederation is a complex and potent mixture of hopes, fears, and ideas. At no point could it be defined with precision, as this chapter clearly demonstrates. Yet the North has played a substantial and continuous role in Canadians' image of themselves and their country. In the twentieth century northern events have continually fuelled Canadian nationalism. As we approach the present the importance of the North increases as a result of technology, resource scarcity, and the strategic defence needs of the continent. The old concept of isolation and distance is breaking down with television news transmission via satellite, air travel, and even our highway system now penetrating the Arctic Circle. Yet, with all the wonders of modern technology, Canada retains much of the traditional mythology, including its basic split between materialist development goals and idealism. This historic struggle is the Canadian dilemma over northern development.

CHAPTER 2

The Politics of Ecology

One of the distinctive features of the political scene in the 1970's was the rise of the environmental movement to challenge the existing practices of government and business. The movement was part of a wider revolt of public interest groups against existing political structure and attitudes; but it developed out of its own ideological base, which had been slowly evolving in the twentieth century. While the roots of the movement emerged from a variety of sources, they are worth examining because they demonstrate the reasons for the appeal to middle-class Canadians.

Traditional concerns for parks and conservation were joined in the 1960's and 1970's by a number of new intellectual ingredients, giving the movement intensity and ideological coherence. In the 1970's it probed a whole series of philosophical questions about growth economics, the conserver society, and the ecological viability of the planet. As it challenged many of the assumptions of Western industrialized society, environmentalism was viewed with deep suspicion by many within government and business ranks. Yet it defied the usual categories of ideological analysis because it was separate from the free enterprise or the traditional Marxist schools. In Canada the movement drew support from various camps, including "progressive" conservatives, left-wing liberals, social democrats, and some Marxists. The politics of ecology brought together advocates of wildlife protection, pollution control, limits to growth, and economic sovereignty and had links to aboriginal rights. It was an impressive coalition of interests, ideas, and people. Above all, the issue of the northern pipeline was a marvellous catalyst in bringing all these ingredients together and giving them a clearer and more direct public policy focus. The purpose of this chapter is to show the historic evolution of the extra-parliamentary public interest groups, the emergence of an environmental ideology in Canada, and it links to similar movements, which gave it such depth and political strength. This analysis is essential background to understanding the progression of events and ideas of the 1970's and demonstrating their significance.

Democracy, by its very nature, assumes a participatory role for its citizens; yet in most countries it remains an elusive goal never fully attained, despite the rhetoric of constitutions and politicians. From the early days of the Greek city-states, through the rise of Parliament and parties in England and the evolution of the Town Hall meeting in New England, people have sought political structures capable of combining mass input with efficiency of action. In the last few decades the problem has intensified with ever-growing government structures, huge multinational corporations, and the depersonalization of computer-based administrative systems. Government ministries seemed to be divorced from the people and the needs they were designed to serve. They even developed their own language, which seemed to obscure the obvious or even directly mislead the average citizen. The Canadian civil service, which possessed a remarkably high public reputation in the 1950's, was confronted by public cynicism by the 1970's. It seemed that some of the basic principles of liberal democracy had become eroded. As our society and government became more complex, the individual lost any sense of involvement and alienation set in. The major political parties, faced with a huge variety of complex issues, were ill-equipped to handle them with any degree of precision. Often this led to frustration for interested individuals, who retreated from political parties to public interest groups. Following the arguments of John Kenneth Galbraith and others, they attempted to organize "countervailing" forces to prod the system into action.

The massive increase in the number of these groups in the 1970's was a reflection of the failure of party politics to confront directly the new issues. Parties were caught up in the homogenizing search for consensus. The arrival of these groups added a new dynamic and non-elective force to the political scene. In the age of Watergate, they reflected some of the public cynicism toward a political process that sought party unity through ambiguity; serious policy was reduced to generalities that would avoid offending conflicting interests. These groups were also a reflection of the rise of regulatory agencies, which operated very largely independent of the checks and balances of the parliamentary system. The issues considered by these tribunals were often technical in nature and the decisions unintelligible to interested members of the public. As a result, they suspected the lobbying power of big business or the sinister motives of "faceless" bureaucrats. While many of their claims might be exaggerated, these protests represented deep democratic stirrings even though the ideology of liberalism seemed to be in decline. In an age of big business and big government, the public had to organize pressure groups to protect consumer, environmental, and other public concerns.

Although there were no public interest groups in our contemporary sense of the word prior to World War II, there have always been protest groups challenging the power of the two-party system. The roots of the modern public interest group go back to the huge coalitions of groups that formed to press the temperance cause in late Victorian years. Working outside the party system they attempted to impose a radical solution for a series of social and economic problems. Like many public interest groups today, there was a clear moral tone to their political message. They attempted to combat the indifference of the parties by mobilizing especially the women of Canada for public demonstrations and protests. Early reform owes a tremendous debt to the extra-parliamentary activism of Canadian women, who were excluded from the vote and took their protests into the streets. In the 1890's and the years following World War I the farmers were another group who felt alienated from any meaningful influence in the political process. While beginning as protest movements they eventually elected governments in Alberta and Ontario.

A third type of early revolt against the party system was that of the Social Gospel. Important elements in Canadian Protestantism believed that the social and political responsibilities of the Christian forced him to speak out against the economic disparities of laissez-faire capitalism and the political system that buttressed it. The Social Gospel emerged in Canada in the years before World War I and reached the peak of its influence in the years just following. After a decline in the mid- and late 1920's its message had a resurgence in the depression, with links to the early development of the CCF, more radical social reform, and Christian socialism. These Christians attempted to apply Christianity as a working political philosophy, not just a spiritual message, and this emerged in some of the pronouncements of groups such as the League for Social Reconstruction. Needless to say, they created intense divisions within the church, especially among upper-middle-class elements who were distinctly uncomfortable with such a message. These social critics were raising fundamental ethical questions about social justice within a free enterprise economic system. It is interesting to note that exactly the same kind of debate took place in Catholic and Protestant circles over the stand on the northern pipeline by such church leaders as Primate Ted Scott of the Anglican Church. Through organizations like Project North, the churches took an active part in the political debate on the North, in terms of both the ethics of the pipeline and the justice in settling native land claims. Theirs was a legacy of the Social Gospel.

In the post-war years, the development of the Consumers Association of Canada was the real beginning of the modern "public interest" group movement in Canada. The CAC traces its origins back to 1941 when the Minister of Finance and the Wartime Prices and Trade Board sent out a plea for the help of Canadian women in the task of monitoring wartime price ceilings. Women's organizations from across the country swung into action to support their efforts, forming regional advisory committees to provide the board with local eyes and ears.[1] When the consumer branch of the Wartime Prices and Trade Board was disbanded in 1945, the women's groups decided to carry on and a permanent consumer organization was created in 1947, long before anyone had heard of Ralph Nader. Since that time, the size and the scope of the organization have gradually increased.

The CAC concerned itself with the quality of food, the safety and durability of appliances, fair pricing to protect consumers, and a wide variety of related questions. With the rising tide of corporate concentration and its lobbying powers in Ottawa and the provinces, the CAC tried to make the public aware of shoddy goods and price gouging in the hope that this would embarrass the government into action. By the late 1960's, the organization had developed a research component and experienced legal staff capable of intervening to protect the public interest before regulatory boards, such as Bell Canada rate increase applications before the Canadian Transport Board. It has also received government grants from the Ministry of Consumer and Corporate Affairs for its consumer advocacy program. This funding has led to some criticism that the group can become dependent on public funds and too sensitive to the point of view of the donor. Generally, the CAC has done an outstanding job as the leading pioneer in the development of the concept of a public interest group in Canada and as the champion of consumer concerns.

These four examples – temperance, farmers, the Social Gospel, and consumers – illustrate how frustrated individuals have attempted to combat our party system. In the 1960's this "public interest" movement picked up steam with news events from the U.S. of black power and anti-war demonstrations. In addition, the rising international movement against nuclear power and nuclear weapons spilled over into Canada with Pearson's decision to acquire nuclear weapons and the development of the CANDU heavy water reactors by Atomic Energy of Canada and Ontario Hydro. On a variety of issues, the parties and Parliament seemed unresponsive to the new policy ideas. Pierre Elliott

Trudeau, when he came into office, seemed determined to reverse this closed approach and campaigned in 1968 on a plank of "participatory democracy" that attracted many young voters in a wave of "Trudeaumania." But the expectations of 1968 were doomed to failure, for one man, even if he wanted to, could not change the complex system of government decision-making. As a result, public interest groups proliferated and expanded in the early 1970's to reflect the inability of the major parties to articulate the many specific policy concerns of individuals.

Pressure group politics has always been part of the twilight zone of democracy. Lobbying on Parliament Hill has been viewed as an essential function for the corporate sector in pursuing its goals. In Ottawa, lobbying is not licensed and regulated in a formal way, as in the U.S.; Canadians try to avoid recognizing the lobbyist for fear of casting doubt on the integrity of the system. With modern communications and Nader's Raiders in Washington, it was inevitable that militant and outspoken public interest groups would emerge in Canada in an attempt to counter corporate pressure groups.

The rise of public interest groups has changed some aspects of the political process. Some groups have enjoyed a public profile in exposing bureaucratic errors and denouncing corporate exploitation. Ironically, the more success they have achieved in public, the more government bureaucrats have distrusted and excluded them from influencing policy. Often, politicians have resisted change until public opinion could no longer be ignored. The groups have increased the air of confrontation before government regulatory boards and, unlike other special interest representatives, they have lobbied out in the open. In fact, their only strength was in arousing media attention and, through it, influencing public opinion. To get that media attention, wrong-doing was presented in the most dramatic way. They changed the tone of regulatory hearings by raising the issue of business ethics, and by insisting on the need for natural justice. Their crusading zeal and air of righteous indignation infuriated many of the old hands in the business world, who had no interest in discussing their "social responsibilities." Dress added a further feature to the air of confrontation when the beards and jeans filled hearing rooms previously inhabited only by three-piece suits.

In addition, the young representatives of the public interest groups used the new jargon of the social sciences, which corporate lawyers and executives believed to be at least mildly subversive and tainted by Marxist assumptions. As the procedures of so many of the boards were drawn up by lawyers for lawyers, it was hardly surprising that these new intervenors felt frustrated by the definitions of evidence or the rules for cross-examination. It was a conflict of values and generations with many tensions for all involved in the early seventies. With time and experience these tensions eased some. Boards learned it was better to give public interest groups their day in court than to face the adverse publicity from excluding them. Public interest groups, in turn, learned to marshall their arguments in more effective and convincing ways. By the time of the appointment of Mr. Justice Berger in 1974, both sides had come to a *modus vivendi.*

In the evolution of public interest groups to challenge the Mackenzie Valley Pipeline, there were a number of separate but inter-related constituencies. The consumer rights efforts of the Consumers Association of Canada were background to the pipeline issue as the costs to consumers of frontier energy supplies were frequently raised. In addition were a whole series of ecological issues that led to the formation of the Canadian Arctic Resources Committee. As has been suggested in Chapter 1, nationalism was also a very potent ingredient in the "public interest" response, especially to the Canadian Arctic Gas proposal. There was very considerable overlap and interchange between the groups,[2] but the distinctive approaches are of importance in recognizing the origin and nature of dissent against the applicants.

In the early evolution of environmental concerns in Canada prior to 1945, there were four main outlets: the development of national and provincial parks; the struggle for wildlife preservation; the emerging concept of wilderness; and the conservation movement. Each in its turn contributed to the early environmental movement and to the evolving intellectual pattern of ideas from which our current assumptions spring.

One of the first ingredients was the movement for public parks, which began when the U.S. created the first national park in the world at Yellowstone in 1872. Behind the movement was the idea that the public had the right of access to places of great beauty as opposed to commercial exploitation and private ownership for the rich alone. In 1885, with the CPR nearing completion, the Canadian government declared a ten-square-mile Crown preserve around the Banff railway station where the hot mineral springs were located. Their prime concern, however, appeared to be "sanitation," not aesthetics. The hot springs were to be kept free of private owners so that bathing would be available for railway workers and holiday makers.[3] In 1893 the Mowat government of Ontario established Algonquin Park at least partially as a response to those concerned about Ontario's declining natural resources. It had the added benefit as a timber preserve, for the lumber interests were determined to keep homesteaders out. With these events, our parks system began in Canada with modest results from mixed motives. They were not a means of preserving wilderness but they were a means of limiting development for the commercial benefit of lumbermen or tourist operators.

By the 1890's, there was already a vigorous wildlife preservation movement in the United States. In Canada, in spite of the disappearance of the buffalo in the 1870's and 1880's, wildlife was not considered an important natural resource and hunting was a national pastime. There were a few token efforts for endangered species, such as in 1894 for the wood buffalo in the Northwest Territories, but there was no general perception of the need for wildlife preserves, except for very practical reasons, as Arthur Meighen argued as Minister of the Interior in 1919: birds helped to control insects, significantly increasing farm production; furs and meat held great commercial potential for the northern barren lands; and wildlife was an essential social condition and source of food for the continued existence of the Indian and Eskimo population, who otherwise would be forced back on government aid.[4]

Government itself knew little about wildlife habitat, breeding, diseases, and so on. Initially, the federal authorities hired interested amateurs, not professionally trained biologists. Yet, the movement began from this group of officials in the period around World War I. As Janet Foster has argued convincingly, "it was at the level of senior civil servant that the awarness was born and that new concepts emerged and took shape."[5] Many local naturalist clubs from one end of the country to the other were dedicated to observing rather than preserving nature. One of them, in London, Ontario, was founded in 1863. Most did not view their role as an activist one to seek changes in official policy. In this sense, they were significantly different from some of their American counterparts.

The conservation movement of the first decades of the twentieth century in the U.S. and Canada may appear to be an antecedent of the present-day environmental movement; but the semantics here can be misleading. There were two streams of thought involved in the movement: one was genuinely concerned with preserving natural resources and wildlife and the other in the efficient harvesting of these resources. In Canada the latter view, held by professional foresters and lumber executives, clearly had the upper hand. They wished to see large-scale capital apply scientific approaches to forest harvesting and they wanted to control unrestrained competition. This creed has been termed "the Gospel of Efficiency."[6] When Laurier established the Federal Commission of Conservation in 1909, he appointed businessman and former cabinet minister Clifford Sifton as chairman. During the next decade, the Commission spawned a good deal of research, primarily into forestry, fishing, water power, minerals, civic planning, and wildlife. The basic approach was summed up in their 1911 report: "The principles of conservation . . . do not stand in the way of development, but make possible the best and most highly economic development and exploitation in the interests of the people for all time."[7] In the evolution of the conservation movement in the twentieth century – including the current debate on energy conservation – there has always been this ambivalence between those whose primary aim is efficient use and those who actually wish to conserve natural resources or wildlife.

One of the key factors in the development of the politics of ecology in the last decade has been the growing acceptance of the value of wilderness. This idea, which appeared to be innocuous on the surface, challenged some of the basic tenets of the development ethic. Growing out of our nineteenth-century experience in settlement, there was a strong belief in the expansion of the agriculture frontier to its greatest extent across North America. Where agriculture was not possible, then lumbering, ranching, and mining should be developed. Man was ordained to harvest the mammals, vegetation, and minerals for his own use. With this kind of frontier development ethic, there was a built-in hubris that stubbornly refused to recognize the environmental forces conditioning man's existence.

There was also an element of patriotism in the myth of clearing the land for both English- and French-speaking Canadians – the back-breaking toil of the pioneer who had converted the potential of the forest into the economic reality of farms. Those who called into question the usefulness of draining swamps or clearing forests were questioning fundamental assumptions that had created the country and allowed it to prosper. The settler was one of the great forces of "progress" in the march of Western civilization, especially in North America. In the United States, this idea had found its greatest champion in Frederick Jackson Turner, who had argued that the successive frontiers of settlement across America had shaped the American character and institutions. In both countries, wilderness was viewed as wasted or unused potential for national development.

In 1968, Roderick Nash, a leading American writer on the conservation movement, claimed that Canada was at least two generations behind the United States in its "posture regarding wilderness."[8] In spite of the fact that Canadians by nature may have been more reticent in expounding the wilderness doctrine, there is more than a little truth in Nash's contention. The Sierra Club of the United States was founded in 1891 and by 1913 was mounting large public campaigns, but similar efforts in Canada really only began in the 1960's. Wilderness appeared to be available to Canadians without great effort in a way in which it had been long since lost to Americans. Most provinces had an open-ended northern frontier. When the parks system was developed, it was designed to provide recreational opportunities or to be a stimulus to the tourist trade. Wilderness tripping brought little economic return to the country.

For over a century the praise of the wilderness has been an important theme in American literature. The works of New England writers Henry David Thoreau and Ralph Waldo Emerson are merely two examples. Ironically, Thoreau, who was inspired by his trips to Canada, had only a limited impact on Canadians, who intellectually were not ready for his message. In New England in the 1860's, many ideas central to our contemporary environmental movement were already in vogue.

In 1864, George Perkins Marsh declared in *Man and Nature* that man was abusing his relationship with nature and disrupting the natural harmonies. From his vantage point in Vermont, close to the Canadian border, he warned that "man has too long forgotten that the earth was given to him for usufruct alone, not for consumption, still less for profligate waste." Man had used his power to alter nature by clear-cutting forests in the Mediterranean area. History showed that the resulting erosion, flooding, and drought had humbled great empires. Wilderness had flood control and wildlife refuge advantages for modern society.[9] As well as his efforts as a writer, Marsh had an illustrious career in Congress and then as an ambassador in Turkey and Italy. His ideas resurfaced in books by Stewart Udall, David Lowenthal, Roderick Nash, and Arthur Ekirch in the 1960's and 1970's.[10] The Canadian wilderness movement, which was attacked as being anti-American by some oil companies, had a profound intellectual link to a number of the New England writers and thinkers of the nineteenth and twentieth centuries.

In the 1960's attitudes were changing quickly and the size of the minority concerned with wilderness steadily increased. In 1963, the National and Provincial Parks Association was founded and well-established organizations, such as the Federation of Ontario Naturalists, became more activist in pushing for wilderness areas. For many Canadians there was a psychological barrier to open political agitation for even the most laudable of causes; it was just not the Canadian way. By the late 1960's the establishment of the Algonquin Wildlands League attempted to do battle with the provincial policy of logging in Algonquin and Quetico Parks. Flowing north from the U.S. through the media and the activist press came a steady stream of environmental commentary that struck home on Canadian university campuses. In the highly politicized atmosphere of the late sixties and early seventies, wilderness became one of the political catch phrases for the rhetoric of dissent. If development represented the corruption and pollution of industrial capitalism, then wilderness represented the opposite pole. If the cities had become sterile dehumanizing "concrete jungles," then wilderness was the means of salvation. For many who had no immediate intention of experiencing it, wilderness was the symbolic escape from their feeling of entrapment.

Wilderness to Canadians of 1970 was something more than the absence of development; it was a creative process of positive renewal. As an undisturbed natural ecosystem, it provided refuge to preserve species elsewhere in danger. It was a standard from which we could judge the degradation of other areas. There was a profound intellectual and scientific value in studying systems in their natural state of equilibrium as opposed to a man-altered environment. Man has a moral responsibility not to eliminate species or habitat, for the whole of nature, including man, is interdependent; future generations have a right to enjoy a natural heritage similar to our own. Wayland Drew argued there was a revolution in progress with the emergence of a "new Biology and its affirmation of an ancient understanding. We have never doubted our animal nature . . . and . . . we have begun to take the first steps toward a non-anthropocentric social science of what must be recognized. . . . We are one animal among many."[11]

Only when man came to see that his destiny was linked to the natural forces around him could he appreciate the value of his natural inheritance. Canadians have always assumed that they possessed this natural heritage in abundance; now, for the first time in their history, this was called into doubt, and with it their own survival. Unless they moved quickly and militantly their biological heritage would slip through their fingers and be gone. Unless wilderness was preserved, one of Canada's greatest attractions would be slowly but remorselessly eroded, and nowhere in Canada were there greater wildlife and wilderness resources than in the 40 per cent of the country north of the 60th parallel.

But wilderness by 1970 was more than a biological concept to Canadians; it had now become part of their cultural and intellectual heritage. In the literature of the early 1970's, with novels such as Margaret Atwood's *Surfacing* and Wayland Drew's *The Wabeno Feast*, a cult of the wilderness began. It was a literature of protest against the development ethic implicit in the evolution of Canada. As Drew wrote, "our history itself becomes the beast from which we must escape or perish."[12] At the same time, many Canadian historians were attempting to give substance to the importance of wilderness and wilderness values for the evolving identity of Canada. W.L. Morton, the general editor of the Canadian Centenary Series and one of Canada's most distinguished historians, wrote: "Canadian life to this day is marked by a northern quality, the strong seasonal rhythm which still governs even academic sessions; the wilderness venture now sublimated for most of us to the summer holiday or the autumn shoot; the greatest joys, the return from the lonely savagery of the wilderness to the peace of the home; the puritanical restraint which marks the psychological tensions set up by the contrast of wilderness roughness and home discipline. The line which marks off the frontier from the homestead, the wilderness from the baseline, the hinterland from the metropolis, runs through every Canadian psyche."[13] Morton wrote *The Canadian Identity* because he believed that identity was in doubt.

During these years, the art of the Group of Seven with their aesthetic portrayal of the shield country's wilderness seemed to have caught the mood of the people irrespective of the fact that Canada is not a country noted for its concern for painting. Native sculpture and prints also enjoyed a great popularity, and they, too, reflected wilderness values as well as being, like the Group of Seven, a very distinctively Canadian contribution to the world of art. Bruce Littlejohn, a teacher at Upper Canada College, put it succinctly in an article for the Conservation Council of Ontario: "Our history, our arts and our letters, proclaim such direct experience of wild nature as part of our rightful heritage. Furthermore, wilderness is important to us as a people even if we never set foot in it. It is important too as an idea or abstraction, or inspiration – as an integral element in our cultural geography."[14] Wilderness was tied into our concept of the nation and our concern for the North. One biologist entitled his exposé of northern environmental policy *The Violated Vision*, which showed how biological concerns about wilderness had become wrapped up in the national mythology.[15]

Even some of the political leaders of the day reflected in their words and their actions this concern for the wilderness ingredient in Canadians. Prime Minister Trudeau lamented that "Canadians seldom attempt to explain even to themselves their spiritual attachment to the wilderness." He then went on to quote from his canoeing companion, the journalist Blair Fraser: "What held such people together was not love for each other, it was love for the land itself, the vast empty land in which for more than three centuries a certain type of man has found himself uniquely at home." Trudeau then went on to draw out the lesson of all this for Canada: "If part of our heritage is our wilderness, and if the measure of Canada is the quality of life available to Canadians, then we must act should there be any threat to either." By moving resolutely, such as on northern pollution, Canadians were protecting the freshness of the air, the purity of the water, and the living resources. "If necessary, we must offer leadership to the world."[16] The only difficulty with all these idealistic words was that there seemed to be a wide credibility gap between the speeches and the reality of Canadian environmental policy. As a result, they added to the growing cynicism toward politicians and the political process within the environmental movement.

In the evolution of the rhetoric of ecology, wilderness and pollution were the two key pillars, the two sides of the coin, the two extremes like virginity and rape. Having looked at wilderness, we now must turn to pollution, for the absence of pollution in the North made it so attractive to those concerned with the growing environmental degradation in the south. The battle in southern Canada was attempting to reverse a process already well advanced. In the North, it was a chance to define environmental standards prior to development so that impacts would be minimized. Thus the southern movement to curb pollution was a potent force behind the environmental concerns about the North.

In the development of the politics of ecology and pollution, a number of environmental pressure groups emerged in Canada in the late sixties and early seventies. Unlike the United States, they were mainly local rather than nationally based, concentrating on specific projects or problems. One of the most successful of these, which is still flourishing after more than a decade, is Pollution Probe at the University of Toronto. It began in February, 1969, as the spontaneous response of a group of faculty and students at the university concerned that the CRTC might try to censor CBC television for a good piece of probing journalism on air pollution. Partly because of its university connections, Pollution Probe always emphasized thorough research, and with such faculty members as Don Chant, chairman of zoology, involved the group got expert advice. This helped to give scientific authority to the movement even when the corridors of power at city hall or the legislature were closed to them. As Don Chant emphasized: "There is scarcely an aspect of pollution . . . on which one or more members are not acknowledged experts." This meant that Probe could speak confidently on virtually any pollution problem, "sure of its facts and without the vagueness that so often characterizes anti-pollution groups."[17]

A stream of students spent a year or two or even longer working full-time for Probe on a wide variety of issues. They built a formidable collection of data and expertise. They recruited some high-profile corporate figures to raise money for them and the university allowed them the use of one of the stately old mansions opposite the provincial legislature. Their strategy had two basic goals: confront the minister with the relevant factual data and keep the media well informed. They developed important allies; for instance, the *Toronto Telegram* not only gave full news coverage of their activities but printed their educational and promotional material free of charge. They attempted to combine the roles of a research institute, a forum for public education, a lobby for environmental legislation, and, as a last resort, a legal challenger through the courts. Their efforts were strengthened by the development of the Canadian Environmental Law Association in Toronto and close links to the faculty at other Ontario universities. Probe was merely an example of what was happening across Canada with the rising tide of concern for the environment.

One of the problems for Probe was the politicians' obsession for job-creation projects. Both Liberals and Conservatives accepted the necessity of the Growth Ethic. Unless there was a grassroots revolt by people, the politicians would never act. Organizations like Probe tried to act as catalysts to speed up public concern by showing through dramatic examples how serious the issues were. The campaign was an attack on the individualism and materialism of the free enterprise consumer economy, and, consequently, there were spiritual and ethical overtones. Laws of nature were more basic than free enterprise, and since Western social, economic, and political structures had ignored these principles, the day of reckoning was fast approaching. The sooner changes were made, the easier the transition would be. Like "old-time" religion, there was a vision of hell-fire and damnation, but this time it would be experienced in this world, not the next.

Yet, in the early flush of a few victories, the environmentalists overestimated their political strength and success. In 1970, Don Chant wrote that "the present Ontario and federal governments are becoming sophisticated and knowledgeable about pollution and moving in the direction of effective environmental control. Members of these governments, with few exceptions, have received Probe freely, listened to its cases and in most instances, been convinced."[18] Only with time did it become clear that the inertia to change was greater than expected and bold words did not always lead to bold actions in the political arena. As economic times worsened the impetus for environmental action seemed to weaken, and some politicians now talked of environmental standards as a luxury one could no longer afford.

Some of the first meetings of concern about the Mackenzie Valley Pipeline took place in Pollution Probe's offices at the University of Toronto in 1972, the year Canadian Arctic Gas was formed. Sandford Osler and Brian Kelly organized these meetings and a wide spectrum of individuals – private citizens and people from Ontario universities – attended. One of the great problems at the time was information; the meetings were an opportunity to share scouting reports on the applicant and discuss hard information on the ecology of the Mackenzie Valley. At this early stage, Probe played an essential role as a clearing house for ideas and analysis. The group also made approaches to Donald Macdonald, Minister of Energy, about funding for the public interest groups intervening on the Mackenzie Valley Pipeline; although Macdonald appeared to be sympathetic, nothing concrete emerged from the cabinet discussions.

While Pollution Probe is an example of the broad-ranging environmental movement, a number of individuals wished to focus specifically on the problems of northern ecology. Their fears came to a head in 1971 with the ministerial statements about the desirability of a Mackenzie Valley Oil Pipeline; the rest was "spontaneous combustion," in the words of Doug Pimlott, the first chairman of the Canadian Arctic Resources Committee (CARC). In order to avoid oil tanker traffic down the West Coast and to provide stimulus to the Canadian economy, Ottawa was prepared to offer a land corridor across Canada for the new pipeline.[19] With northern environmental problems still such an unknown factor and native land claims unresolved, Pimlott, Kit Vincent, and Dick Passmore went to work to forge CARC into an organization of concerned citizens. Their plan was not to form a national public interest group with membership and local chapters but to mobilize a few professionals to do research and then spread the results of their work to as wide an audience as possible. As a result, CARC has been challenged on occasion (such as at the National Energy Board in July, 1979) that it represents no one but a few intellectuals and therefore does not qualify for intervenor status. They have also left themselves open to attacks as an "elitist" organization with this type of structure. They possessed a clear idea of their goals and they proceeded to achieve them in the most efficient way possible without having to waste time and money servicing an extensive membership. They hoped to be viewed as an "honest broker" providing objective information on northern development issues to the Canadian public. They had a small steering committee of prominent Canadians from the universities and business and appealed successfully for funds to a number of large corporations, including Labatt's,

Molson, and Simpsons-Sears. They also received financial support from American environmental organizations, including the Audubon Society, the Sierra Club, and the Wilderness Society.

In appealing for funds, Doug Pimlott tried to define CARC's role in such a way that it would defuse some of the potential corporate opposition. In discussions with industry: "We have reiterated that our approach is a very positive one, that CARC will not be assuming adversary positions on matters of policies that relate to development."[20] This turned out to be a difficult and controversial approach, suspected by some activists as a constraint on CARC's ability to operate publicly and deal with issues directly. Later it became a matter of some bitterness in the corporate community when CARC appeared to be taking sides and assuming an adversarial role. But the latter reaction was inevitable if CARC was to play any serious role in the public debates and the regulatory proceedings. In its fund-raising, CARC encountered some scepticism about there even being a role for a small third voice in the process. Pimlott wrote: "On one of our trips, an executive . . . told us bluntly that in his opinion where two elephants were involved, there was no role for a mouse."[21] But CARC very rightly stuck to its guns, for the organizers were worried about the quality of environmental input into corporate and government decision-making and about the need for an "honest broker" in the process. The government's own processes for environmental impact assessment were as yet very limited; the Department of the Environment was barely established and the responsibilities for the northern environment were still retained by the pro-development Department of Indian Affairs and Northern Development.

CARC was strengthened in its early months by all the public discussion of the *Manhattan* voyages and northern pipelines. As Doug Pimlott had written, "The idea of transporting oil through the Arctic ice packs in 250,000 ton tankers causes ecologists to go green around the gills because sooner or later one will sink." Here the sovereignty concerns of the nationalists combined with the pollution scare to form a potent compound. As John Livingston wrote in the *Ontario Naturalist*: "I propose for Canada a thoroughly respectable form of neo-nationalism which might be described as ecologic independence."[22] But the government seemed apathetic in meeting this challenge. There was no assurance that the U.S. would abide by the Canadian Arctic Waters Pollution Prevention Act or that Canada had the will or the capability to enforce it. The Northern Land Use Regulations were still in draft form and, until promulgated, their provisions were uncertain. The Yukon Minerals Bill (C-187) was under attack from mining interests and its fate was in doubt. The Arctic Land Use Research Program was just nicely under way but it would be years before the baseline data would be adequate for planning such northern development as a pipeline. Yet, at the time, it appeared that a pipeline might be under construction by 1973: the country was woefully unprepared. In granting exploration and drilling rights to millions of acres in the North, the government had given only very limited consideration to the environmental implications or the native land claims in the area. Yet the impacts of exploration on wildlife and the native way of life were increasingly clear. The Canadian North seemed headed in the direction of a Greek tragedy where events overwhelm the ability of the characters to cope.

The individuals who formed CARC experienced a number of mixed feelings. They felt "awed" by the strength of the forces pressing for immediate development; they felt "frightened" by the pro-development bias within government; and they felt "frustrated" by the public's inability to know or influence decisions.[23] The social implications were clearly evident from the work of Peter Usher and others.[24] But were there any means of stopping the juggernaut? From informed discussions with Jean Chrétien, Minister of Indian and Northern Affairs, it appeared that there would be no formal means of public input and even the Standing Committee of Indian Affairs and Northern Development would not have any significant role. The only route remaining appeared to be to go public and raise a storm of popular protest. To this end, CARC held the first of its large public conferences in Ottawa in May, 1972. In mounting this effort the organizers worked in conjunction with the Arctic Institute of North America, and representatives of business, government, the universities, native people, and public interest groups attended. By the time Berger was appointed in 1974, CARC was already well established to participate from an environmental point of view.

The specific concerns of some of the preceding groups inevitably were part of the larger international matrix of ideas that constituted environmentalism. Here one encounters the depth of philosophic and ideological dissent. Because of the particular conditions and ideas within Canada at this time, these international influences had a greater impact than would have been the case earlier in our history. Environmentalists were not just confronting a few items of public policy; they were challenging a way of life that had been evolving since the early days of the Industrial Revolution, a way of life held together by a steel chain of ideas that formed a formidable barrier to ecological reform.

The late 1960's and the early 1970's were a time of tremendous intellectual ferment in Canada. The 1960's had witnessed a vast expansion of the university system, upsurge in interest in Canadian novels and poetry, and a flood of new small magazines and publishing ventures. In most social science disciplines, especially history, politics, sociology, and political economy, many new figures were emerging from the graduate schools to challenge the existing orthodoxy in their fields. The environmental movement was thus part of a wider wave of dissent and intellectual debate – Canadians were entering a period of changing values and concerns.

The most fundamental challenge to the intellectual status quo came with the rising interest and acceptance of the Marxist paradigm in politics, political economy, and history. The role of Mel Watkins and Jim Laxer brought many of the ideas to centre stage through the public battles of the Waffle, a left-wing movement within the New Democratic Party. The concept of nationalizing the resource sector was their special concern. With foreign ownership expanding, Canada's dependent industrial status made her a colony and resource hinterland of the United States. With the Waffle, class analysis overlapped with clear nationalist priorities in a way that was uncommon for Marxism, given its usual international perspective. The dependency of Canada on American multinational corporations had to be broken as a precondition for the class struggle in Canada. In the late 1960's and early 1970's serious ideological debate came back into the universities and the major urban centres as at no time since the depression. At the University of Toronto Press a new socialist scholarship series was established under the title of Studies in the Political Economy of Canada. Tom Naylor, Leo Johnson, and Stanley Ryerson were three of the leading exponents in history. As background to the Mackenzie Valley Pipeline, Black Rose Books in Montreal published the first full-length "exposé" of capitalist exploitation and colonialism in the North.[25]

The Marxist intellectual group was never more than a minority among the pipeline critics, but it did present a coherent world view and a number of clear answers to the seemingly confusing and illogical pattern of events involved in the energy crisis. For the environmental movement, the Marxist attack on multinational corporations fitted in well, but class politics seemed less appropriate for building the united sense of community for ecological action. In addition, many of the leading environmentalists reflected their own middle-class backgrounds.

Curiously, the intellectual origin for that sense of community came from a very different ideological source. In the thought of eighteenth-century conservatives like Edmund Burke was the aristocratic sense of trusteeship or stewardship for society as a whole. With their organic view of the state based on balance, harmony, and interdependence, they were the antithesis of both Marxism and aggressive entrepreneurial individualism. Burke's concept of aristocratic privilege was no longer valid but his concept of an organic union of classes came down to the present through such later figures as Disraeli. In the environmental movement today, there is distrust of unchecked liberty and democracy as being the basis for corporate power and its abuses. There had to be restrictions on the self-interest of the individual in order to preserve the common good. Thus the politics of ecology is based on both radical and conservative principles, which is why the Red Tories in Canada felt comfortable with its ideology. The state was the embodiment of principles that transcended the individual. Preserving the natural legacy of the environment was similar to preserving the historic legacy of the nation. In both cases, a fundamental continuity had to be understood and protected. While the traditional liberal suspected the state, the traditional conservative welcomed it as a means of preserving this sense of continuity.

A few environmentalists were prepared to take the Burkean concept of authority much further. William Ophuls, one of the leading American environmental thinkers, questioned whether the public on its own would ever go far enough.

> Accordingly, the individualistic basis of society, the concept of inalienable rights, the purely self-defined pursuit of happiness, liberty as maximum freedom of action, and laissez faire itself all become problematic, requiring major modification or perhaps even abandonment if we wish to avert inexorable environmental degradation and eventual extinction as a civilization. Certainly democracy as we know it cannot conceivably survive.[26]

Such dramatic words left authoritarian overtones in the minds of readers who had no idea how these new philosopher-rulers would be chosen or to whom they would be answerable. Yet for some of the ecological activists, the existing political structures were so subservient to vested corporate interests that it was ridiculous to talk about them as democratic. They firmly believed that without some type of revolution, environmental goals could never be achieved.

Another of the areas of intellectual dissent involved the field of history. Among some of the younger practitioners was a strong belief that the focus of the discipline had been too restrictive, largely ignoring the social, economic, and environmental factors. They sought to demonstrate that the social costs of industrialization and urbanization had been heavy. The "National Dream" of a transcontinental railway had been built on the backs of the Chinese and other immigrant navvies, some of whom had paid with their lives. Likewise the expansion of the agricultural frontier across the country had meant that the native people and their way of life had been shunted to the margin. These historians challenged the liberal belief that economic development produced "progress" for society, which seemed to be the central principle of resource policy historically in Canada. Development was not leading to a reduction of poverty and social tensions; economic disparity between classes and regions seemed alarmingly permanent in spite of transfer payments and welfare programs. The proposed Mackenzie Valley Pipeline seemed to be a continuation of some of the worst aspects of the historic pattern of Canada as a resource hinterland for the United States.

A smaller group of historians were directly stimulated by the environmental lessons of history. Influenced by Fernand Braudel and the "Annales School" in France, they sought a history that reflected not only the social sciences but the biological factors as well. Many of them saw Darwin, not Marx, as the greatest thinker of the nineteenth century. The environmental historian was concerned that the techniques involved in resource development were often in defiance of nature.[27] The land policies of the Laurier government and the farming practices of the early settlers had intensified the prairie dust-bowl conditions of the 1930's. And the clear-cutting techniques of some Canadian forestry companies were a serious threat to the long-term viability of the industry. But behind this type of specific analysis was a fundamental interpretation of the weakness of Western industrial society.

It was common sense that infinite material and population growth was impossible upon a finite planet. The Western nations had lived through the most rapid period of economic growth in the history of the world (1945-73). This prosperity had been achieved on the basis of great technological advancement, abundant natural resources, and cheap energy supplies. Suddenly, it was seen, man was beginning to enter an era of resource scarcity and rapidly escalating energy costs. As a result, levels of economic activity in the 1980's were reverting toward the historical norm after an unprecedented period of growth.

The faltering drive for economic growth and industrial expansion encountered the further dilemma of rising pollution levels. Profound changes were now under way in the biosphere on which all life depended, and these changes were on an upward escalating curve reflecting the historic pattern of industrialization and the proliferation of non-biodegradable wastes. The equilibrium of natural forces was being distorted by man-made technology. This scenario presented an enormous problem for man because of the long lead time involved for changes in values, policy, and structures. Historically, man is resistant to change and there is real danger that the long-term biochemical impacts of pollution on the human body would be irreversible before the danger would be fully perceived. This attack on the biosphere is a rejection of the organic origins of man, who is subject to the laws of nature, not independent of them.

In the last two centuries man's hubris had been demonstrated in his overriding drive for material wealth. In harnessing energy from coal and other sources, he had learned to mass-produce goods and enjoy greater leisure. But the new chemicals, including pesticides, could not be recycled by nature, and their accumulation took a savage toll with habitat and biological food chains. Man failed to appreciate that the decline and extinction of other species were eroding his own basis for existence, even though over three-quarters of human cancers are environmentally related. The net result of all this meant that we had now entered an important watershed in Western history: the costs of continuing the present pattern of the industrial revolution were greater than the benefits. Historians and biologists had to combine to convey the message that the eroding ecological balance was the most important event of twentieth-century history. The crucial issue was anticipating what lay ahead and commencing the changes required.

Now, we are entering an era of transition between growth economics sustained by fossil fuels and the steady state of the conserver society. Historically, such periods of transition have been filled with political upheavals and social tensions. But it does not necessarily mean apocalypse now, or the start of a new dark age, provided that man can see the lessons of history. He must commence the process of change before he is forced into it by the collapse of the present economic/ industrial society, such as portrayed in *The Limits to Growth* of The Club of Rome. The historians' role has been to show that the environmental revolution was not a passing fad, or merely a calling for changes in a few aspects of public policy. It went right to the heart of our economic and political system. An ecological interpretation of history was essential to recognizing the depths of the dilemma.

The new environmentalism had a number of spiritual ingredients in it that gave it overtones of becoming a type of post-Christian religion for some adherents. If God did exist, he existed in the natural forces of the environment, which were all pervasive. As a result, there was strong criticism in some quarters that traditional Judeo-Christian beliefs were at the heart of the environmental crisis. Historians such as Arnold Toynbee in Britain and Lynn White in the United States went back to Genesis 1:28 when God instructed Adam:

Be fruitful, and multiply, and replenish the earth, and subdue it: and have dominion over the fish of the sea, and over the fowl of the air, and over every living thing that moveth upon the earth.

Later, after the Flood, similar directions were given to Noah. These passages appear to put man outside of nature and superior to it. Some environmentalists claimed that this helped to explain the historic drive in Western capitalism to exploit resources irrespective of the consequences. Such contentions triggered a great debate among Christian scholars and agnostics about the intellectual role of Christian theology in the overall environmental crisis. For many Christians there were serious ethical as well as spiritual issues involved in this controversy.[28] This in turn became part of the wider debate about Christian ethics and corporate capitalism, which will be discussed in connection with the formal pipeline hearings.

While there was a great deal of this type of general intellectual analysis entering Canada from the U.S. and Britain, the points were really driven home by revelations on northern policy from within Canada. In 1975 Ed Dosman of York University published a provocative book on the politics of northern development covering mainly the period from 1968 through 1972.[29] Dosman, who had had access to a wide range of government documents, presented a sorry tale of Ottawa's attempt to protect the public interest in public, while pushing furiously for the pipeline in private. In environmental circles, it created a sensation overnight, for it appeared to document the critics' worst suspicions of the pipeline and "development at any cost." On the eve of the opening of the Berger and National Energy Board hearings, it seemed to show the government had already made up its mind, that native land claims would be ignored, and that all the crucial decisions were taken in camera between government and business leaders free of parliamentary scrutiny. The book was even referred to in the opening day of the NEB hearings as part of the case against Marshall Crowe, to be discussed in Chapter 6.

In the United States, one of the great achievements of the environmental movement was the National Environmental Policy Act (NEPA) of 1969, which ushered in the age of the Environmental Impact Statement (EIS). One of the first major projects to confront this new legislation was the Trans-Alaska Oil Pipeline (Alyeska). The Department of the Interior, under strong White House pressure, produced a report favourable to the project. However, when environmental groups challenged through the courts, the project application was ruled to be deficient under NEPA regulations. In 1972 a proper EIS was issued by the Department of the Interior allowing the injunction to be lifted.

A further challenge by environmental groups was successful in the U.S. Court of Appeals, which issued a new injunction, this time under the Minerals Leasing Act (1920). This statute limited a pipeline right-of-way to a maximum of fifty feet while Alyeska required a 300-foot corridor. The environmental groups also argued that the Canadian alternative had not been sufficiently investigated, as was required under NEPA. Rather than wait for the outcome of all these legal battles, the Nixon administration passed special legislation through Congress that declared the project to be in the national interest; ordered the Department of the Interior to issue the necessary construction permits; and established unexpectedly heavy spill liability penalties of $50 million on land and $100 million on the sea irrespective of negligence. The bill overriding the NEPA regulations only passed the Senate by one vote, when Vice-President Spiro Agnew cast the tie-breaking vote. Thus, after three and a half years of legal struggles, the project was legislated into existence. For many environmentalists and members of Congress, this action was a damaging precedent and serious erosion of NEPA. In Canada, the case had been watched closely because of the proposed tanker traffic down the West Coast and was viewed also as the first test case of major northern development and environmental protection.

In the intellectual debate of the 1960's and 1970's, environmentalists experienced a growing sense of frustration with the discipline of economics and the process of cost/benefit analysis. Economics had now become the tool to provide all the answers for government and corporate decision-makers. In its rigorous determination to confine itself to questions of market forces, allocation, and efficiency, economics kept itself aloof from many of the wider questions of political economy that concerned such founding fathers as Adam Smith, David Ricardo, and John Stuart Mill. In constructing a "science" free of moral and political judgements, "conventional economics has ensured its technical virtuosity and its internal consistency, but at the cost of its social relevance."[30]

Part of the revolt against Keynesian economics came from within the discipline and partly from without. In the U.S., John Kenneth Galbraith, Kenneth Boulding, Robert Heilbroner, and other economists called for radical changes to create a "New Economics" or a "Post-Keynesian Economics." With the contradictory combination of high inflation *and* high unemployment, the credibility of the discipline eroded in the 1970's. But there were much more specific criticisms from some of the environmental critics. They rejected the relevance and the efficacy of market forces for weighing relative values of the commodities in our society. Clean air and water are as much a component in our standard of living as purchased goods and services. Also, the viability of market forces as a self-regulating mechanism appeared to be in steady decline with producers' cartels like OPEC, government incentives, and growing corporate concentration in the hands of the multinationals. From 1944, when Karl Polanyi published *The Great Transformation*, there had been a growing literature criticizing the social costs of the market economy. The environmental movement picked up these arguments, utilizing them for its own purposes.

In corporate allocation of investment capital, the main criteria were productivity and profits. Investment in environmental equipment was a non-productive use of capital; therefore it should be avoided except insofar as required by the state. In making these decisions, traditional cost/benefit analysis of economics was applied where social and environmental costs were usually downgraded as "externalities" or the social costs of production not accounted for by the price mechanism. In my own work at the National Energy Board, it was clear to me that cost/benefit analysis contained a built-in bias in favour of the developer. The price mechanism allowed him to quantify the benefits of his project while the social costs, which were much more difficult to quantify, were largely discounted. Government regulatory boards welcome hard dollar statistics, for this type of cost/benefit analysis can free them from having to make value judgements about ecological damage or rights of native people. This approach seemed to be further evidence of how the system was loaded against a just consideration of environmental evidence. There was also a hidden ideological barrier in the economists' commitment to free market forces that conflicted directly with the interventionist role for government required for environmental protection. Economics widened the gulf between private enterprise and the environmental movement by providing a pseudo-scientific rationale for laissez-faire policies.

Economics was also attacked because of its heavy emphasis on individual property rights, while environmentalists were concerned about the "Commons" – the air, land, and water – that mankind had to share for his continued existence. Corporate development had come to depend on a legal system where private ownership rights were sacrosanct, so that any individual legal challenge to a company had to be on the basis of direct personal financial loss and not on the basis of general "class action" suits of damage from pollution to the population in general. This meant that there were far fewer challenges through the courts in Canada than in the U.S. It also provided an indication of the primacy of economic thinking in official circles, which allows business to ignore its social responsibilities.

In March, 1972, The Club of Rome research report *The Limits to*

Growth was released for general circulation. This study of the inter-relationship among population, agriculture, natural resources, industrial production, and pollution created an immediate storm of controversy because of the apocalyptic scenario of the imminent decline and collapse of Western society. While some of their numbers and equations were successfully challenged, many of the impressions and arguments became firmly entrenched in the environmental movement. Out of the ashes of *The Limits to Growth* came the concept of the Conserver Society, the new environmental blueprint for the future. While the battle of the Mackenzie Valley Pipeline was underway, ecologists all over the world were seeking to put the pieces in place for the new post-industrial society. Canadians played an important part in that debate[31] and felt that their country was on the firing line in the battle for environmental priorities.

As is already evident, the challenge to the northern land had to provoke a nationalist response; but the details of the *Manhattan* voyage and the U.S. multinational oil companies behind the pipeline project ensured a deep and emotional reaction. As the previous chapter attempted to show, nationalism and the North have enjoyed a type of symbiotic relationship both in terms of economic development and national symbolism. Diefenbaker caught that theme and tried to exploit it for political purposes; but he could not convert the rhetoric of his speeches into effective policies for his government. In the late 1960's Richard Rohmer and the supporters of the Mid-Canada Development Foundation had attempted to do the same thing, but they were eclipsed by the news from Prudhoe Bay.

However, there was a different stream of nationalism emerging in the late 1960's, best exemplified by the intellectual writings of Abe Rotstein, editor of *Canadian Forum* and one of the founders of the Committee for an Independent Canada. The movement was a combination of cultural, economic, and political concerns, and it worried as much about the question of values as it did about ownership. For some, Rohmer was as great a threat as Imperial Oil. Excessive levels of foreign ownership were merely symptomatic of a deeper malaise in Canadian society. With the expanding foreign control of the publishing industry, the Canadian identity came to be viewed as an endangered species. American television, *Time*, and *Reader's Digest* demonstrated the stifling mediocrity of the media blanket conditioning Canadian thought and action. Although Walter Gordon's efforts to counter the continentalism of the Pearson years were unsuccessful, they did help to rally the troops and bring individuals together with a growing sense of commitment.

The roots of intellectual nationalism go back to a number of figures of the sixties, with George Grant as the brooding philosophical conscience. In two slim volumes, *Lament for a Nation* (1963) and *Technology and Empire* (1969), he laid out the dilemma of a distinctive Canadian society whose values were being eroded by the all-powerful expansion of the American industrial empire. His writing was not bitter, but rather reflected the sadness of a doctor commenting on a terminally ill patient. "In this era when the homogenising power of technology is almost unlimited, I do regret the disappearance of indigenous traditions, including my own. It is true that no particularism can properly incarnate the good. But is it not also true that only through some particular roots, however partial, can human beings first grasp what is good." To Grant it was clear who the villains were. "Canada was allowed to slip into the slough of despond in which its national hope was frittered away to the U.S. by Mackenzie King and the Liberal Party." Earlier in the century, the national vitality had been drained away in curbing German aggression in Europe, and those who returned had retreated into commercial activities with a weakened concern for public affairs. "Canada's survival has always required the victory of political courage over immediate and individual economic advantage."[32]

Nationalism was concerned with the twin themes of spiritual identity and physical independence. For Grant and many others, the loss of the former left the latter as an empty shell. Environmentalists, who saw industrialism and growth economics as the great threat, responded to Grant's arguments about the link between industrialism and values. Preserving the nation-state from the American multinationals was essential for environmental as well as intellectual preservation. From Grant's writings, environmentalism and nationalism came to have a strong interrelationship. For most of his readers, Grant's despair was a stimulus to positive action, for historically Canadians have always been stimulated by the immediate prospect of the demise of their nation. Only at this point in time, the stimulus was from Quebec separatism as well as the American impact.

Historian Donald Creighton was another Tory nationalist, but there was nothing philosophic or detached about some of his pronouncements in the 1970's. Earlier he had written the majestic two-volume biography of John A. Macdonald and the profoundly influential *The Commercial Empire of the St. Lawrence*, which contributed in the Innis tradition to the development of the staples thesis. In works like *Canada's First Century* (1970) he denounced the abandonment of the principles of Macdonald by the Liberal Party in the twentieth century, both in connection with the constitution and the relations with the U.S. Although his influence was weakened on occasion by verbal overkill, Creighton correctly saw the central role of natural resources and the Canadian willingness to use public ownership when it fitted their purposes. In 1970, he wrote: "Canadians instinctively regard their natural resources in a very special light. . . . These natural resources are not looked upon as ordinary assets – things the Canadians have built or acquired themselves. They are regarded as part of the original endowment of nature, as the birthright of Canada. Many of them are not owned absolutely, as they would be in the United States, by private enterprise. They are properties in which the Crown retains a right which it has sometimes converted into public ownership, for the beneficial interest of the people in Canada."[33]

In the coming battle on northern projects, this concept of natural resources belonging to *the people*, not to corporations, was to resurface again and again. This was a Tory attitude, not a liberal one, and especially not an American liberal one. The failure of the oil industry to appreciate the concept of public ownership and the people's resources was a major mistake, which allowed them to dismiss as "socialism" Petro-Canada and other state initiatives basic to a nationalist ideology. They ignored the historic origins of the public enterprise tradition in Canada, which goes back to the Conservative creation of Ontario Hydro in 1905, and in so doing they seriously underestimated the strength of the opposition to their project until it was too late.

In the rise of intellectual nationalism, the greatest figure of all was Harold Innis, the father of Canadian political economy. When he died in 1952, his critical analysis of Canadian-American relations was not overly popular in the days of Korea and the Cold War. By 1969, however, the revival of interest in H.A. Innis was abundantly clear for political and intellectual reasons.[34] His staples thesis gave a coherence to Canadian economic history and his discussion of dependency opened the way for both liberal and Marxist schools of thought. When traditional economics seemed to have so little to say about the distinctive economic problems of Canada, his analysis of the development of the various export staples – cod, furs, wheat, timber, minerals – showed how vulnerable Canadian prosperity was. The staples required capital-intensive transportation systems (like the CPR) and access to external markets, where the processing often took place.

Each new staple brought in its wake social and economic adjustments for the Canadian people and influenced the evolution of the political structure. Even Confederation was a product of the Commercial Empire of the St. Lawrence (to use Creighton's phrase). Staples ensured that Canada remained dependent on more highly developed economies for capital, technology, and markets. These dependency relationships helped to explain both regional disparity within Canada and the overall weakness of her branch-plant industrial base. In 1930, Innis wrote, "No country has swung backwards and forwards in response to such factors as improvements in the technique of transport, exhaustion of raw materials, and the advance of industrialism with such violence as Canada." Innis, who had travelled widely in the North by canoe, saw clearly the instability that had accompanied resource development there. "No one can travel down the Mackenzie River without realizing the importance of the economic cyclone on the Klondike to that area."[35] To those who saw the pipeline project as another boom/bust economic cycle this was all grist for the mill.

One of the central contributions of Innis to Canadian nationalism was to call into question some of the techniques of economics and their relevance in any study of the Canadian scene. Economics as a discipline was a fundamental tool for the liberal democratic state and the international financial community. It preached that nationalism, and especially economic nationalism, interfered with the optimum allocation of resources and free flow of trade. Innis warned as early as 1929 that there were problems in applying economic theory to a country like Canada. He wrote: "A new country presents certain definite problems which appear to be more or less insoluble from the standpoint of the application of economic theory as worked out in the older highly industrialized countries." Economic theory has to be amended by the specific features of local economic history. For example, English and American textbooks pay little attention to "the problem of conservation and public ownership which are of foremost importance" in a new country such as Canada. The handicaps of this process led to distortions with "dangerous consequences," including a "new form of exploitation." The only escape from this theoretical strait jacket was an intensive study of Canadian economic problems; hopefully from that empirical work would develop economic theory or a philosophy of economic history appropriate to understanding the actual problems of Canada.[36] To the young nationalist who was upset with the apparent political and cultural sterility of economics, these words of Innis acted as a type of rallying cry.

At the University of Toronto and elsewhere, there was a new emphasis on "political economy" and out of it came both Marxist and non-Marxist schools. They were challenging the "market" concept of free enterprise economics, which assumed automatic and self-regulating networks of supply and demand factors determined by price. The theory assumed a supply-demand relationship between two relatively equal parties operating voluntarily and at arm's length. Yet to the nationalist, the development of trade between components in a multinational corporation was anything but arm's length, was governed by no market forces, and was unresponsive to local concerns. As Abe Rotstein put it: "Left to itself, a market system threatened to erode the very fabric of social existence by subordinating the twin pillars of society, i.e., man and his environment, to the autonomous forces of the economy."[37] With the growing phenomenon of corporate concentration, there was too much of the natural wealth or economic rents being diverted to foreign multinationals. This was a long-term hemorrhaging of wealth from the country, and a transfer to those foreign boardrooms of basic investment decisions on the Canadian economy. For the liberal wing of the Innis school, it meant that the ownership pattern must be returned to Canadian hands, to finance further Canadian development from the profits and to promote a Canadian entrepreneurial class. Walter Gordon was one of the key figures in that campaign, which was attempting to counter the traditional laissez-faire economics of the Economic Council of Canada and private research foundations such as the C.D. Howe Research Institute, financed and controlled by the multinationals.

A group of Canadians, however, was not prepared to accept the "liberal" interpretation of Innis and pressed on to develop a nationalist Marxist paradigm. Led by Danny Drache, Mel Watkins, and Tom Naylor, they used the staples thesis to show the stagnation and deindustrialization of the Canadian economy. In the era of the Vietnam War, America was the new imperium reflecting the international interests of her corporate citizens. Canada had become a state dependent on multinationals who could now manipulate the federal government by influencing Canadian affairs from within. In the Marxist view, there was no point in replacing American capitalists with Canadian ones when the fundamental problem was capitalism, including the dependency relationships and economic disparity it spawned. While drawing much of their analysis from Innis, they criticized him for not taking his analysis to its logical conclusion, "the blunt reality of American Imperialism."[38] They pointed to Innis's analysis of Canadian dependency on American capitalism: "Canada moved from colony to nation to colony."[39] In a way that was particularly relevant for northern development questions, Innis had stressed the interrelationship between social, cultural, political, and economic factors that was also of central importance to the Marxist point of view. Concentration on export staples to Europe and then the U.S. had profound implications for the evolution of "the Canadian economic, political, and social structure. Each staple in its turn left its stamp, and the shift to a new staple invariably produced periods of crisis in which adjustments in the old structure were painfully made and a new pattern created in relation to a new staple."[40] Out on the northern frontier, the oil and gas exploration was already under way and the potential for distortions was even greater with this new staple, given the ownership pattern and American demand. With Exxon behind the Mackenzie Valley Pipeline, it appeared to be a classic case study for Marxist economic analysis, and for demonstrating the need for radical changes in the Canadian political structure.

Both the Marxist and the liberal nationalist wings were united in their belief in the interventionist role for the state; without preserving and expanding the nation-state, there could be no initiatives for social welfare, economic equality, or cultural development. Technology and computers had made the role of the individual steadily less satisfying and added new social strains. Nationalism was not a movement but a reaction to these points of stress. In 1965, Abe Rotstein had tried to put this feeling into words in describing Canadian nationalism.

Its implicit premise is that existence is not individualist but collective. The weakness of present-day liberalism is that it views our present situation as simply an attempt to graft the twentieth century welfare state onto nineteenth century individualism. But the interdependence of persons in a complex industrial society has made such a position obsolete. The spontaneous countermovement to protect the centres of power in such a society is a consequence of their crucial importance for our lives, particularly for the fulfilment of the varied objectives we have assigned to the nation-state.[41]

Nationalism, with its commitment to communal values, was seen by at least some as a means of countering the depersonalizing process of technology and an attempt indirectly to restore dignity to the individual. This dignity was partly a product of this sense of continuity with the past, including its traditions and its prejudices. With the state itself under attack from the multinational corporations and computer technology, these historic communal values had to be preserved by the only tool available, the state.

During these years, however, the nationalist intellectuals were not without their critics. Many of these were academics or writers who viewed with horror the ravages of nationalism in Europe. Some liberals, like historian Ramsay Cook, saw nationalism as a force of intolerance trying to create a monolithic uniformity that was unhealthy for the country. Biographer and literary critic George Woodcock expressed a type of philosophical anarchism. In his "A Plea for the Anti-Nation" he bitterly attacked what he terms "the cold-minded centralizers" who would draw Canada into "centralized competition of the existing nations for space and resources." But Woodcock was prepared to give his blessing to some true form of decentralist federalism espoused by those who "value the independent, pluralistic, and unpredictable way of existence which Canada offers." He saw nothing wrong with trying to free oneself from political and cultural subservience to the U.S. The novelist Wayland Drew had similar reservations about nationalism, based on his wilderness concerns. In the *Canadian Forum* in February, 1973, he wrote: "The only context in which Canadian nationalism can be acceptable is in the service of the ecological conscience, as a decentralist and anti-statist movement. If it can be conceived as a responsibility to the land, then the term nationalism would transcend its connotations and acquire significance as a means rather than an end."[42] What is interesting about the comments of both Woodcock and Drew is the similarity of motives between some of the nationalists and their critics.

While the intellectual debate about nationalism raged in the country, a number of political events fomented the nationalist response, especially in relations between the Trudeau and Nixon administrations. The *Manhattan* diplomacy has already been mentioned. One of the most curious events took place in Washington in December, 1971, when Trudeau emerged from a summit meeting with the American President. The Canadian Prime Minister announced jubilantly to the press that Canada would be treated henceforth as an independent country, as if this marked a major change in U.S. foreign policy. In the House of Commons the next day, he explained that Nixon had assured him it was in the American interest "to have a Canadian neighbour not only independent both politically and economically, but also one which was confident that the decisions and policies in each of these sectors would be taken by Canadians in their own interests in defence of their own values, and in pursuit of their goals."[43] It was an interesting comment on the politics of the day that Trudeau felt it necessary to get such assurances and to make such a point of making them public. Bruce Hodgins, a Trent University historian, showed some of the feelings of desperation that many Canadians felt on the independence issue: "Our choice is between some form of Canadian nationalism, dangerous as that might be, and continued drift towards absorption in American nationalism, seductive and easy as that would be. American nationalism is already too dangerous to Americans, to us, and to mankind."[44]

The political response to the growing debate on Innis and the Canadian economy was brought to a head by three federal government reports, all of which found that Canada had unacceptably high levels of foreign ownership. In 1968, the Task Force on the Structure of Canadian Industry headed by economist Mel Watkins (but including a cross-section of economic views, including those of A.E. Safarian) came to the unanimous view that the American multinational "erodes Canadian sovereignty and diminishes Canadian independence." This presence, in other words, creates political costs that seriously undermine the economic benefits of foreign ownership. "No other country, however, seems prepared to tolerate so high a degree of foreign ownership as exists in Canada." Two years later the litany of the evils of foreign ownership continued with the Wahn Report of the Special Parliamentary Committee. In 1972 the Report of the Hon. Herb Gray on Foreign Direct Investment in Canada was finally released formally by the government after the report was released informally as a special issue of *Canadian Forum* in December, 1971. The government was forced into publication of the report, which clearly catalogued a great number of the deficiencies of Canadian policy in dealing with foreign ownership. These events are important as background for understanding the rise of economic nationalism and its particular focus on the oil and gas industry where not a single integrated oil company remained in Canadian hands. When Arctic Gas was put together by Imperial, Gulf, and Shell, it immediately attracted the attention of the economic nationalists.

At the end of the 1960's the nationalist movement burst forth with two political action groups reflecting the two widely divergent nationalist ideological positions. The Waffle Movement led by Mel Watkins and Jim Laxer tried to push the NDP leftward toward a truly socialist position, creating tremendous strife within the party, especially from the large trade union component with its American links. When it failed to gain the upper hand, it was gradually purged by the party leadership, who were determined that the NDP could not advance with a party within a party.

The more moderate wing of the nationalist movement planned in 1970 for the launching of a large non-partisan nationalist organization called the Committee for an Independent Canada. Originally the brainchild of Abe Rotstein, Walter Gordon, and Peter Newman, it was launched with great fanfare in 1971 with Flora MacDonald as executive-director. The leadership of the CIC attempted to found local chapters of the organization from Halifax to Vancouver Island, from southern Ontario to Inuvik inside the Arctic Circle. With close links to the *Toronto Star* through Walter Gordon and Beland Honderich, the support of media people like Pierre Berton, and links into universities across the country, the CIC started off with great expectations.

After collecting nearly 200,000 signatures on its founding petition, the CIC presented it personally to Prime Minister Trudeau. The latter expressed his sympathy with the aims of the organization and thanked the CIC for helping to prepare public opinion for the kind of program his government intended to enact.[45]

The Committee for an Independent Canada initially tried to cover a wide spectrum of policy issues: foreign ownership of industry, land, and cultural forms; its first collection of readings included some writers, such as Jim Laxer, who were more radical than the organization. At the founding conference at the Lakehead, where publisher Jack McClelland presided, there was a groping for concrete policy answers to give the group focus and some substance and meaning and to help it to get away from motherhood platitudes about identity and autonomy. As a result, a large policy conference was held in Edmonton in September, 1972, during the federal election campaign to try to prod the parties into stronger stands on CIC issues. With the dynamic publisher Mel Hurtig running for the Liberals in Edmonton, there was real hope that the CIC might penetrate the Ottawa establishment. Prior to the opening of the conference, Rotstein led a group of CIC researchers north to view at first hand the locale for the building of a Mackenzie Valley Pipeline and to allow a CBC film crew to tape some shows with Adrienne Clarkson.

When the discussions took place at the Edmonton conference, the northern topics created the greatest interest. The resolutions passed included calling for a moratorium on all major northern development projects until there had been a native land claims settlement and adequate northern environment research. There were also worries that Canadians did not need frontier gas and that financing the project would distort the Canadian capital markets and increase inflation. The CIC established a task force to pursue further research on the project, to publicize the results, and to intervene if and when public hearings took place.[46] From that point in 1972 through to the end of the NEB hearings in the summer of 1977, the CIC played a major role in the evolving debate on the pipeline. It is of some significance that a broadly based nationalist organization like the CIC, concerned with the foreign ownership of land, culture, energy, industrial strategy, science and technology, books and periodicals, would put so much of its efforts into the northern pipeline issue.

Both the Liberal and Conservative parties were split by the issue of nationalism. When the public returned the Liberals to power in 1963, Walter Gordon was in a central position as Minister of Finance to influence the economic policy of the new administration. But Gordon's beliefs ran counter to those of Prime Minister Pearson and the majority of his colleagues; as a result, Gordon was never as effective as he had expected. Both Pearson and then Trudeau were traditional liberals who were suspicious of nationalism and sympathetic to North American economic integration. In Pearson's case, his years at External Affairs made him uncomfortable with anything that might disrupt quiet diplomacy or interfere with the "special" relationship between Ottawa and Washington. For Trudeau, it was a philosophic problem. As a result of watching Quebec under Duplessis, he viewed nationalism as a reactionary force used by unscrupulous politicians to preserve the status quo and resist change. He also possessed the classical liberal contempt for European nationalism, which he feared was spreading to English Canada. With the Foreign Investment Review Agency, the Canadian Development Corporation, and Petro-Canada he only went as far as he felt he had to in order to appease Liberal nationalists or, from 1972 to 1974, the NDP caucus in a minority house. Five or six members of his cabinet were clearly in the nationalist camp, including membership in the CIC.

On the Conservative side, Robert Stanfield had a mental block about nationalism that he carried in his quiet way through all his years as Tory leader. From my own discussions with him, I can only believe it went back to his Nova Scotia roots and their links to the great families of New England. He feared English-Canadian nationalism because he believed there lurked in the movement sinister anti-American motives that he distrusted. He never seemed to realize that the Nixon administration or the corporate planning of Exxon might be based on very different sentiments than those demonstrated by his cultured friends in New England. His own staunch integrity sometimes interfered with his ability to appreciate realistically the motives and methods of others. Yet within his party and his caucus were people such as Flora MacDonald who had contributed greatly to the development of the CIC and the nationalist movement in Canada.

Even the NDP had its own internal agony over the nationalist issue. The rifts were not healed quickly because the trade unionists wanted to rout out every last remnant of the Waffle. Dennis McDermott of the UAW took particular interest in stopping any return of Laxer or Watkins to the fold. Unions like the Steel Workers and the Auto Workers saw nationalism within the trade union movement as an attack on the big American unions in Canada. In addition, foreign ownership, far from being an evil, was part of the rationale for international unions; the power of the multinational corporation could only be countered by the power of the multinational union. On the other hand, after the collapse of the Waffle, the members of the NDP caucus had very cordial relations with the CIC. For instance, Tommy

Douglas, the energy critic, had close liaison through the years of the debate on the Mackenzie Valley Pipeline.

Nationalism in Canada is a curious amalgam of hopes and fears reflecting the Canadian experience, including the overriding influence of the United States. It is concerned with territory and the territorial imperative to preserve and protect. This includes the state of nature in that territory and the aesthetic values that flow from the natural environment. The specific issues include: ownership of land, especially in the provinces of P.E.I., Ontario, and the West; the independence and the vitality of the various components in the media; the book publishing trade; and the course content at universities. The focus was on how we saw ourselves and whether Canadians were in control of the images and analysis being transmitted by everything from news magazines to university lectures. But above all nationalism in Canada was concerned with the intangibles that help to give shape and substance to the symbols employed by any nation. They include those things taken for granted and seldom expressed but which provide the intellectual sinews that give a community the will to survive. This is why images and mythology have always played such a central role in the evolution of any nationalism.

Two very potent yet interrelated movements were coming to the fore at this time when the Arctic pipeline was being planned in the corporate headquarters of Arctic Gas just off Bay Street in Toronto. The nationalist movement in Canada was a moderate one by international standards and focused on the economic, cultural, and political dependency of Canada to the United States. The dependency had been growing in a hundred subtle ways that were hardly apparent to the average Canadian. In the terminology of the political scientists, the phenomenon was really a form of patriotism, not nationalism in the classic European meaning of the word.[47] Nationalism demands a paramount position within men's thoughts and actions while patriotism allows for a variety of links and commitments of a social, religious, occupational, or political character. Patriotism often tends to be a more defensive mechanism, stressing loyalty to the defence of a nation and its institutions, including culture. In the Canadian case it was very hard to define the nationality or culture in any very strict ethnic sense. The main unifying links were residence within the geographic boundaries, participation in the recent historical experience of Canada, and allegiance to our political institutions. The Canadian "nationalists" sought to preserve what they liked to call the Canadian identity not because it was the highest level of civilization in the world, but because it was distinctively Canadian. It also had a heavy emphasis on the land as Canada's greatest asset and this allowed for the building of such close links to the environmental movement. There was no point in protecting the physical independence of Canada if it was turned into a wasteland by commercial operations.

In some ways, the environmental movement was even more intense than the nationalist. Environmentalists believed that neither government nor industry reflected any serious commitment to environmental values and that the speeches—such as those by Trudeau—were sheer hypocrisy. Because there were no national environmental organizations such as the Sierra Club or the Wilderness Society in the U.S., CARC had to be formed if there was to be an effective campaign on the pipeline issue. CARC not only succeeded in this, but did it with a high degree of professionalism that was a direct product of the elitist or non-elective structure of the organization. Like nationalism, environmentalism had an ideological content and a common attack on laissez-faire liberalism and the growth ethic of international free enterprise. While the nationalists were concerned with the future of Canada, the environmentalists saw that as only part of the wider struggle for the future of man. Each also was concerned about the future of Canada's native people, who were even more directly concerned with the outcome of the pipeline debate.

CHAPTER 3

The Northern Sense of Grievance

The renaissance of Canada's native peoples is one of the most positive and exciting aspects of late twentieth-century Canada, but it has aroused widely differing reactions within the white community. After two centuries of social and cultural erosion, a powerful internal movement in the native communities aims to turn this all around and to start anew. Like environmentalism and nationalism, the movement for native rights was steadily mounting in the turbulent early years of the seventies. With the confrontation tactics of the American Indian Movement and the cultural rebirth of native people across North America, these wider currents of opinion inevitably influenced native attitudes in the Northwest Territories and the Yukon. Part of it was the result of the growing number of young people attending southern schools and returning with a pride and determination to reverse the trends of social and cultural decay. I was amazed at the number of northern native leaders who were in the 18-26 age group in a society where much stock is put in the advice of the elders of the tribe. They were determined to change how their people had been treated in the school books, in the economic world, and historically in connection with their land. They had to rebuild a sense of pride, a sense of identity, a sense of purpose in their people.

Long before oil was discovered at Prudhoe Bay in 1968 the native communities in the Yukon and the Northwest had begun to experience profound and destabilizing psychological, cultural, and economic impacts from increasing white presence. Learning from the southern native experience, the Inuit and Dene were profoundly worried that the pipeline would be the beginning of the end for their traditional social structures based on the experience of hunting and trapping; for without this relationship to the land, the values could not be perpetuated by each new generation and their culture would die off. It is absolutely essential to understand the central significance that the land, the land claims, and the historic perceptions of the treaties

59

played in their attitude to the pipeline and their scepticism of all relations with the federal government. Their history and that of their southern native brothers showed that their fears were well founded. Northern native people demonstrated a real sense of history and the legacy of the treaty negotiations had bred a real sense of grievance. To understand the intensity of feeling on the "aboriginal rights" issue, it is necessary to consider briefly native perceptions of their history.

The northern native people constitute three main ethnic groups – the Inuit (Eskimo), the Dene (Indians), and the Métis (mixed blood) – with each group possessing a distinctive and complex culture. The tree line that arcs down from the Mackenzie Delta to Churchill on Hudson Bay roughly divides the Inuit (on the barren tundra lands) from the Dene (in the bush country). Each has developed a complex social and cultural structure over thousands of years that enables them to utilize on a sustaining basis the limited wildlife available in their harsh environment. All native people in the Americas are a product of a series of migrations beginning about 30,000 years ago from Asia across the temporary land bridge to Alaska. The ancestors of the Dene crossed to North America probably about 10,000 to 14,000 years ago, and the third wave of migration, about 5,000 years ago, brought the Inuit to the northern margin of the continent. Scholars today are attempting to map these migrations and understand their significance. Because parts of the Yukon were never glaciated, it is a key area for archaeologists attempting to reconstruct the pre-Columbian history of the Americas. Some artifacts found in the Yukon are believed to be over 30,000 years old, some of the oldest ever found on this continent. Because of geography, the pipeline through the southern Yukon will tend to follow the same natural routeways as these early migrations. Hence, such a project, with its huge super-ditcher, raised the serious possibility of the destruction of important archaeological sites, which would not be known until construction cut through the area. This is a matter of some concern to the National Museum of Man in Ottawa and to academics.

The third ethnic group was the Métis, the offspring from the sexual relations between French or Scottish fur traders and Indian women. The Métis played an indispensable middle role for commercial operations like the Hudson's Bay Company, and by the late nineteenth century they had emerged as a distinct people with a separate identity, especially in areas such as the western Prairies. With the coming of white settlement, their frustrations peaked in the efforts of Louis Riel and Gabriel Dumont. The demise of the buffalo ended their staple source of food and their great social institution of "the hunt." The arrival of the CPR ended their usefulness in transporting goods across the Prairies and symbolized a new technology they neither understood nor controlled. When the Métis land claims along the North Saskatchewan were not recognized by the Macdonald government, they rose in revolt in 1885. They had no hope of permanent military success but did aspire to repeat the negotiated settlement of 1870 whereby Riel had brought Manitoba into Confederation with guarantees for the future of his people. However, with the railway nearing completion Macdonald was in a very different position to put down the insurgents than had been the case in 1870. Militia regiments were rushed west with all possible speed.

The collapse of resistance not only signalled the political failure of the provisional government, but brought on the destruction of what had been a functioning and stable society. Some individuals, like Gabriel Dumont, fled at least temporarily to the United States; many more drifted to the social quicksands of the new settlements. But many proud and defiant Métis trekked north to the Mackenzie Valley, where in seclusion from white settlers they could re-establish their way of life. The Mackenzie was the last refuge from the onslaught of white civilization for these political refugees of 1885. They brought with them a political consciousness and sense of grievance that became a permanent part of the Dene and Métis folk culture. To their descendants, the Mackenzie Valley Pipeline appeared to be the same kind of basic threat to shatter their isolation and way of life as had been the CPR and the settlers ninety years earlier. All the glossy public relations pamphlets had no chance of overcoming this historic perception of how the native people had lost their lands and their dignity on the Prairies to the south.

The Dene of the Mackenzie Valley and the western Arctic are part of the Athabascan language and cultural group. This group is one of the most widely dispersed in North America with bands all the way from Alaska to the Navaho and Apache of the southwestern United States. Within the Mackenzie Valley there are five subgroups: the Kutchin (or Loucheux), Hare, Slavey, Dogrib, and Chipewyan, each speaking a different dialect; yet all refer to themselves as the Dene (the people). There are similar divisions within the Inuit of northern Canada; the Inuvialuit of the Mackenzie Delta consider themselves separate from the Copper Eskimos and other groups further east. Elaborate cultural and social systems have been developed via the hunting and trapping technology through thousands of years of experience in surviving. Although the differences among the Dene and between the Dene and Inuit made absolute unity impossible for the public hearings, one could not help but be impressed with their common concern to preserve the land from which all life flowed. There seemed to be a curious degree of arrogance in the white assumption that their "book" learning was more dependable than those thousands of years of cumulated experience passed down by the elders of the band.

At the centre of the current debate on native affairs is the complex concept of "aboriginal rights" to land. The basis of the claim rests on the fact that the native people have traditionally occupied and habitually used areas of North America predating the arrival of the Europeans. For half the area of Canada, these rights have been extinguished (at least from the government's point of view) by treaties signed between the Crown and specific bands. Today many of these treaties are being challenged by Indian protests as being unjust or never fulfilled by Ottawa. In addition, up until the 1980's there were no treaties with the Inuit of the Northwest Territories and almost no land cession treaties with the Indians of British Columbia, Quebec, the Maritimes, and some parts of the North. Those Indians and Inuit who are outside of treaty are dependent on acceptance of the theory of aboriginal rights by Parliament and the courts in order to pursue their land claims. Yet this theory has never been defined in legislation nor ruled upon clearly by the courts. In 1969 the Prime Minister appeared to repudiate their existence when he emphasized that they are "so general and undefined that it is not realistic to think of them as specific claims capable of remedy."[1] Because land claims are of such central importance to native people, this legal vacuum creates intense frustration for them. Yet, many in government are exceedingly fearful of opening up the issue because it could turn out to cost billions from the public exchequer and create chaos for their development plans all over the country.

The legal foundation for native land claims goes back to the first efforts at white colonization in the Americas by Spain. Some early officials based their approach on Aristotle's arguments that some peoples are inferior and therefore born to subjection and slavery. Some observers, especially within the church, contested that philosophy and argued that the Indians were the true owners of the land; that they were no less intelligent than Spanish peasants who held legal rights; and that their non-Catholic beliefs were irrelevant because heretics in Europe had not been stripped of property rights. Spain had no pre-emptive rights from discovery for this concept only applied to unoccupied lands. These views were confirmed by Pope Paul III in 1537 in a papal bull that was to have an influence on all future Catholic thought. He wrote: "Indians are truly men . . . they may and should, freely and legitimately, enjoy their liberty and the possession of their property . . . should the contrary happen it shall be null and of no effect."[2] These two conflicting philosophies continue right down to the present day; during the NEB hearings I heard many private comments based on the concept of native racial inferiority and the need to abrogate their land rights in the name of "progress."

When the British colonists came to settle the eastern seaboard of North America in the seventeenth century, the land was purchased from the Indians. In 1832, Chief Justice John Marshall of the U.S. Supreme Court summed up the colonial and American experience: "The occupancy of their (Indian) lands was never assumed except on the basis of contract, and on the payment of a valuable consideration."[3] For Marshall, Indians could only tender their land to the state, not to private individuals, which afforded them some protection. Native rights to their traditional homelands could only be extinguished through purchase or conquest in war. Given the provocative nature of relations between the expansive white frontier and the Indians, this weakened greatly the legal protection for Indian lands. Native rights did not extend to unoccupied land, which reverted with Manifest Destiny to the white sovereign state. Marshall's analysis and interpretation helped to shape American legal opinion and have been cited in Canadian court cases as well.

Turning to the Canadian experience, a similar pattern emerges. During the French regime, native lands were not an issue because the small colony along the banks of the St. Lawrence did not force the removal of any Indian villages for white settlement. Also, the French were closely allied to neighbouring tribes (except the Iroquois) for military and commercial purposes. The legal origins of aboriginal rights in Canada go back to the Proclamation of 1763 that followed the British conquest. Determined to preserve peace with her Indian allies, Great Britain chose to exclude white settlement from the Indian territory to the west of the Appalachian Mountains, including the Ohio Valley. If further land was required, it would be purchased by Crown agents through formal negotiations with the tribes concerned. Individual settlers were forbidden to enter Indian territory. In this proclamation, meant to cover most of present-day Canada, it is clearly evident that land rights reside with the native people until extinguished by the Crown. This position was not a product of any great principle of international law, but resulted from the pragmatic needs of the British treasury to avoid war with the Indians after war with the French. Ironically, with this land policy, in preserving peace with the Indians, they helped to provoke war with the colonists in 1776.

The Inuit were clearly not covered by the Proclamation of 1763 and their case must be dealt with under a general theory of aboriginal rights or some of the vague provisions of English common law for the acquisition of new territories.[4] It is difficult to believe that their position or that of the B.C. Indians (also not covered by the Proclamation) will be handled in any significantly different way from those outside treaty elsewhere in Canada. This approach leaves many legal questions unanswered; they will only be answered when negotiations have been completed and the results are enshrined in parliamentary legislation. The negotiations will be difficult, for they will challenge the federal control of northern development. For instance, the Inuit claim that their rights extend to all renewable and non-renewable resources, which the federal government has quietly ignored in issuing oil, gas, and mineral leases in the North.

It is frequently forgotten that in the early years of the British regime Indian policy was extremely important and that the Loyalist migrations to Canada included the Six Nations Confederacy (the Iroquois), who had lost their lands because of their commitment to His Majesty. Under the able leadership of Joseph Brant, they were settled along the Grand River on land purchased by the colonial government from the Mississaugas. During the first fifty years of the British administration in Upper Canada, Lord Simcoe and his successors were busy purchasing Indian land to clear the way for white settlement. Joseph Brant and other Indians did not try to stop this process but did attempt to force up the price from the basic level of three pence per acre. Governor Bond Head attempted in the 1830's to remove a large number of Ottawas and Chippewas from their traditional lands to Manitoulin Island. They surrendered over one and a half million acres for which they received virtually no compensation.[5] Their new lands proved unattractive and unsuitable in comparison to their old area; as a result, in 1862 the island was surrendered back to the Crown except for the eastern portion, which remained a reserve. Although all of these transactions were legal, they hardly reflected the principles of natural justice.

By the 1850's, some improvement was evident in the negotiations further north in Ontario. Here the proceedings were open and formal and the lands allocated for reserves could not be resold or leased to individuals but only back to the Crown. Annuities were paid to all members of the band, with greater amounts to the chiefs and leaders. Hunting and fishing rights were to be allowed in the unsettled portions of the surrendered territory. Later this same approach to treaties was followed in the 1870's in clearing the way for the CPR and white settlement of the West. From this historic pattern, certain general conclusions colour the native attitude to treaty questions today. There is no clear consistency between the treaty provisions in one area of the country and another. Some feel cheated as a result. Even in the

West, where some of the terms were the most generous, the Indians were in no real position to negotiate and bargain. Social impacts had been so great they were suffering in a state of shock and despair. The disappearance of the buffalo on the Plains had signalled the end of a way of life. With the white man, too, had come alcohol and disease to ravage the ranks of a once strong and independent people. With their spirit killed, many chiefs saw the treaties as the lesser of two evils; they would allow them to avoid starvation and control disease with government rations and medical help. As a last resort, they provided a means to preserve what remained.

Today the Indian people of Canada believe they were robbed of their lands and their heritage, herded onto inadequate reserves, and left to die off through malnutrition and disease. This is the basis for their charge of "genocide," which surfaced frequently during the Berger hearings. Whites who were used to the term as applied to Hitler's extermination of the Jews were shocked and annoyed by the charge. From a white point of view, the land allocations for reserves (160 to 640 acres per family) were not ungenerous and roughly similar to the land allowed for white settlers. However, this assumed that the Indian would voluntarily accept agricultural cash crop society and that the reserve lands were well suited to it. But the social transition to farming was a difficult one and was completed successfully in only a small minority of cases. For the young northern native leaders of the 1970's, where there was no chance of an agricultural society, the southern pattern of treaties and reserves had to be avoided at all costs or they would merely repeat in a worse way the tragic failures of the south.

The constitutional position of the Indian people was established at the time of Confederation when they were given special status under federal jurisdiction by Section 91:24 of the British North America Act. With this and the Indian Act that followed, the federal government was given extensive powers over land and development questions within Indian areas. This has created some tensions with the provinces, especially when native people are adversely affected by provincial development schemes such as the James Bay Project. In such cases, the federal authorities have had great difficulty enforcing their position as trustee of native rights, and for the Indian, the degree of federal paternalism and intervention in Indian affairs has been increasingly resented by those on the reserves who wish to run their own show. This is background to the Indian demand that they had to be party to the federal-provincial negotiations for constitutional reform.

The treaty negotiations of the 1870's ended at the northern fringe of the arable Prairies, for Ottawa had little interest in areas unsuitable for white settlement. This complacency evaporated with the gold rush to the Yukon in the late 1890's, which raised the fears and hostility of the native people along the route who faced this sudden influx. In June, 1898, the press reported that 500 Indians encamped at Fort St. John were blocking the route north for the miners and police until a treaty had been signed. They had had horses and goods stolen and were fearful of losing everything with the white stampede into their country.[6] As a result, treaty commissioners were sent north in 1899 and 1900 to sign up the native people of (present-day) northern Saskatchewan, Alberta, and British Columbia and the southern fringe of the N.W.T. and the Yukon. At each settlement the treaty was usually presented in one afternoon and the Indians expected to sign the draft wording prepared in Ottawa by officials largely ignorant of local conditions. Missionaries such as Father Lacombe were there to reassure the Indians of Ottawa's good intentions. Each individual was to receive $12 the first year and $5 each year thereafter, as well as ammunition and school and medical services. When white settlers would arrive they would be offered 640 acres (one square mile). The Métis were given the option of coming under treaty or accepting script, which entitled them to $240 or 240 acres of land.[7]

Father Fumoleau of Yellowknife, who researched the circumstances of the signing of Treaties 8 and 11, concluded that "The Indians and the treaty commissioners did not understand each other. The Indians considered the treaty to be only a treaty of friendship."[8] The explanations were given in very simple terms, which the commissioners believed the Indians could understand. There was no immediate intention to place these people on reserves and therefore the details of a land settlement could be delayed to a later date. The commissioners had orders to get speedy agreement so the last thing they wanted was to raise the issue of extinguishing aboriginal rights to the land, which was the chief purpose of the treaties. Instead, the native people were given oral assurances they would be "just as free to hunt and fish all over as they now are."[9] Within twenty years these hunting promises were contradicted by the game protection laws and the International Migratory Bird Convention with the United States. As the Indians possessed no concept of individual land ownership but only the collective occupation of an area by the band, there was little likelihood of their understanding the legal implications of the land transfer implied in the treaty but not orally explained.

The oil discovery at Norman Wells in 1921 prodded the federal authorities into further treaties to cover the Dene north of Great Slave Lake. Once again, the wording of the formal document was clear and precise: "the said Indians do hereby cede, release, surrender and yield up to the Government of the Dominion of Canada . . . all their rights, titles, and privileges whatsoever to the lands included within the following limits. . . ."[10] As the treaty wording was incomprehensible to the native people, the contents were explained in their own language by missionaries or others. It was emphasized that they would be allowed to continue their hunting and trapping on their traditional lands. From the surviving records of the native people and the surviving witnesses of the 1921 ceremonies interviewed by Mr. Justice Morrow in the Caveat case (1973), it is evident that the native people had no clear idea that they were relinquishing rights to their land. As in 1899, they believed them to be treaties of friendship and co-operation with promises of aid and support from Ottawa. The oral assurances and explanations were never part of the written treaty texts. Bishop Breynat later complained to the minister responsible, T.A. Crerar: "I have given them [the Indians] my word that the Government would be true to their promises and this is the reason why I feel I must insist that the promises made at the time of treaty be not overlooked any longer."[11] The treaty commissioners had used the credibility of the missionaries to reassure the Indians and get the needed signatures. When the promises were not kept the missionaries felt they had been used and that they had failed to protect their flocks. The government, for its part, viewed the treaties as a legal hurdle they had to get over before the great oil boom they expected to materialize along the Mackenzie. When the great hopes for massive development quickly collapsed, so did their interest in and concern for the North and its people.

The interwar years were hard ones for the Dene, with white trappers increasing the competition and fur prices falling. White diseases took a heavy toll: in 1928 alone, an influenza epidemic killed 600 Dene or about one-sixth of their people in the Northwest Territories. In the midst of the depression one medical report concluded: "I can see no hope for them [the Dene]. They seemed doomed to extinction." But the government did have the time and the money for a few things in the North. In 1922 it established Wood Buffalo National Park and enlarged it in 1926 to 17,300 square miles. Ottawa appointed more rangers, game wardens, and veterinarians to Wood Buffalo Park than there were Indian agents and doctors in the entire Northwest Territories. The park was carved out of traditional hunting and trapping areas and some Dene were convicted for attempting to continue to use it. At the same time, there were hopes of government revenue by attracting rich American hunters who would pay a heavy price to bag a buffalo.[12] The northern natives believed they should have the first priority as the treaty commissioners had promised. They did not understand why, when the Hudson's Bay Company gave up its trading monopoly it received extensive lands, the native people who predated the Bay should be less generously treated. To them it did not seem that matters had progressed very far from 1626 when the Dutch bought Manhattan Island for goods worth $26. Also, in both 1899 and 1921, Ottawa extended treaty coverage north not out of concern for native welfare but for reasons of resource exploitation.

In the struggle for their aboriginal rights, Canadian Indians have suffered a number of severe handicaps. The courts and the political system were alien and expensive vehicles for redress where the deck seemed to be stacked against them. For instance, in June, 1926, the B.C. Allied Tribes petitioned Parliament for recognition of aboriginal title and to be allowed to participate in discussions between Ottawa and Victoria on their own future. A joint Senate-House committee considered the petition, and the politicians' strategy was to reduce the document to a list of grievances, which, avoiding the principle, could be handled by existing practices. The final report unanimously found that "the petitioners have not established any claims to the lands of British Columbia based on aboriginal or any other title." In addition, at the same time the Indian Act was changed to make it an offence to raise funds for the purpose of pressing any Indian claim. For some Indians it was "the darkest hour" in the history of the Canadian Parliament, and this restriction remained on the books until 1951.[13] Clearly, the native peoples had reason to believe that the system was tilted against any fair consideration of their concerns.

After the signing of Treaty 11 in 1921, the issue of northern native land claims remained largely in abeyance until Diefenbaker's "Northern Vision" raised new development pressures. In 1959, the Nelson Commission was sent north to investigate the unfilled provisions of Treaties 8 and 11 and to canvass native opinion. Five alternatives were offered to the Dene: (1) take land as offered in the treaties; (2) take a portion of the land plus cash; (3) in lieu of land, take mineral rights plus cash; (4) take cash plus hunting and trapping rights; (5) any other reasonable alternative.

No clear consensus emerged from the hearings with the Dene, who were generally suspicious of government motives. The Commission expressed a sense of frustration in its failure to get the local people to understand the legal complexities of the options open to them. Many of the Dene believed that because they held hunting and trapping rights the land belonged to them. The Commissioners concluded that the reserve system was an anachronism and should not be reconstituted in the N.W.T. The treaties should be renegotiated to give the Indians title to the land where their homes are located, a lump sum payment of $20 per acre to cover the loss of their land entitlement under Treaties 8 and 11, and an annual payment of one-half of one per cent of any revenues derived by the Crown from mineral, oil, and natural gas resources in the areas covered by the two treaties. They also reiterated the Indians right to hunt, trap, and fish and suggested a uniform rate of welfare assistance to residents of the Mackenzie District.[14] Although the Indians were promised in 1959 that the land claims would be settled as soon as possible, now close to thirty years later, these commitments of the government of Canada remain unfulfilled. As development requires the use of more and more of their land, the Dene believe strongly the old adage that "justice delayed *is* justice denied."

Native fears about the land claims issue were brought to a fever pitch by the first major statement on native affairs produced by the Trudeau administration. The Prime Minister put it bluntly: "We can go on treating the Indians as having a special status. We can go on adding bricks of discrimination around the ghetto." The treaties, in other words, should not go on forever because one section of our society should not have treaties with another. "We must all be equal under the law." To the question that native people have aboriginal rights because they were here first – "our answer is 'No.' If we restore the aboriginal rights to the native people, what about the French who were defeated on the Plains of Abraham?"[15] The government would respect specific treaty obligations at least for the present; but the more general, the more nebulous concept of aboriginal rights was not a viable principle the government could accept as a basis for negotiations. This policy statement appeared to dash the hopes for a land settlement for that half of the country not under treaty and for those additional areas where treaty provisions had never been fulfilled. It appeared as a provocative challenge to the native position and was curtly and emphatically rejected. To the Prime Minister, however, it was merely a long overdue application of liberal principles of equality and individual advancement in a competitive society.[16]

In the early 1970's a series of events forced the government to begin to reconsider its position. In December, 1971, the United States government legislated a land claims settlement for Alaska's 70,000 native people through which they received ownership to 40 million acres or 11 per cent of the area of the state (about 570 acres per person). In addition, they were granted $962.5 million over twelve years as compensation for their giving up of claims to the remaining lands, including rights to the oil, natural gas, and minerals (or about $13,750 per person). Twelve regional native organizations were established to invest the cash payments with a thirteenth to handle the capital for those no longer resident in the state.

Some critics have argued that the settlement involved too little land and the corporate structures assumed the assimilation of Alaska's native people when the whole purpose of the settlement should have been to protect their way of life. Certainly the end result after over a decade of operation is that the settlement has not met the expectations of either the native groups or the government. The social, economic, and cultural erosion of the various native societies in Alaska has continued. From the Canadian point of view, there were two very important conclusions from the Alaskan settlement relevant to the Canadian scene. The Americans, having accepted the legitimacy of the aboriginal claims, had paid a heavy economic price to settle. More land was involved than held in trust for all other American Indians, while the cash value was four times that awarded by the U.S. Indian Claims Commission in the previous twenty-five years.[17] It only got through Congress with the heavy backing of an oil lobby anxious to get production started. Also, the Americans had settled prior to the commencement of construction, which is something Ottawa refused to commit itself to. The Alaskan settlement provoked wide discussion in Canada, where some benefits were received because of migration and family ties. And, equally close to our story, in 1983 Thomas Berger was hired by the Alaskan native groups to do an in-depth study of the success of the settlement.

When the White Paper of 1969 appeared to eliminate the chance of redress through the political arena, the native groups had to fall back on their only alternative means – the courts. There were three main court cases, the most important involving the Nishgas of northwestern British Columbia. Being non-treaty, they sought a declaration that their native title to a large area of the Nass River Valley had never been extinguished. They lost at both the trial court level and the B.C. Court of Appeal. The latter ruled that the Royal Proclamation of 1763 did not apply to British Columbia. Thomas Berger, counsel for the Nishgas, was determined to press on by carrying the case to the Supreme Court in Ottawa. Although it was the first instance in which Canada's highest court had been asked to consider the merits of aboriginal rights, only seven of the nine justices heard the case and in January, 1973, in a narrow four-to-three verdict, they found in favour of the province and against the Nishgas. On the central point of aboriginal rights, Justices Hall, Laskin, and Spence ruled in favour of the Indians while Judson, Martland, and Ritchie found in favour of the province. The verdict was decided by Mr. Justice Pigeon, who came down in favour of the province on a technicality unrelated to the issue of aboriginal rights.

As a result, the case did not resolve the point of law at issue and sparked tremendous controversy in government and native circles. Although they did not win, it did appear to give greater credibility to the native case for aboriginal rights. However, as Professor Peter Cumming has emphasized, "the court is the least appropriate forum for dealing with native title." Even if the Nishgas had been successful it would have required more costly and time-consuming litigation, for in this case they sought only a declaration that native title existed.[18]

In 1973, two additional cases involving native land rights were working their way through the courts. The treaty Indians of the N.W.T. followed a different route by attempting to file a caveat with the registrar of land titles in respect to land they had traditionally occupied and used. (A caveat is a legal device to declare an interest in a property that does not imply ownership of the property but does preclude others from having clear title to it.)

Clearly, the caveat would bring development to a stop. The basis of the native claim was that the literal wording of the treaties was different from the oral explanation so that the native people were unaware of any surrender of land title. In September, 1973, Mr. Justice Morrow of the Supreme Court of the N.W.T. found in favour of the Dene. "That notwithstanding the language of the two Treaties, there is sufficient doubt on the facts that aboriginal title was extinguished that such claim for title should be permitted to be put forward by the caveators."[19] Judd Buchanan, the Minister of Indian and Northern Affairs, and his officials saw this decision as a basic challenge to their northern development policy, for a land freeze would disrupt such future projects as the Mackenzie Valley Pipeline. As a result, they successfully appealed the decision. The Indian Brotherhood viewed Ottawa's determined stand in the case as a further indication of the federal policy to fight aboriginal rights at every turn.

The third case involved the James Bay Project in Quebec. Here the Liberal Bourassa government had decided to proceed with the massive hydroelectric project without negotiating a native land claims settlement, and this decision created great hostility among the Indians and Inuit of northern Quebec. The flooding of huge areas directly eliminated hunting and trapping grounds the native people had traditionally used and they challenged through the courts to protect their rights. Mr. Justice Maleuf, on November 15, 1973, granted the native petitioners an interlocutory order of injunction stopping the James Bay

Development Corporation. With incredible speed, the Quebec Court of Appeal suspended the injunction until the determination of an appeal, which later ruled in favour of the Quebec government.

Following the legal battles, the Bourassa government improved its offer to the Cree and the Inuit and eventually a settlement was reached, in November, 1975. In return for the loss of their aboriginal title, the 10,000 native people received ownership rights to 1.3 per cent of their traditional lands, hunting and trapping rights to a larger area, and $225 million to be paid over a number of years. On a per-capita basis it was slightly more generous in cash but less in terms of land than the Alaskan settlement. The James Bay Agreement was publicly criticized by native leaders elsewhere in the country because of the very limited land base they retained. However, with the bulldozers already at work and with a very unsympathetic Quebec legislature, Billy Diamond and the other native negotiators were determined to get what they could in the light of very unfavourable circumstances. The federal government, the trustee for native people, was not prepared to exert public pressure on their Liberal counterparts in Quebec for fear of giving ammunition to the Parti Québécois charge of federal intervention into provincial affairs. Once again, fear of separatism hurt the native cause. In addition, even if they had successfully appealed the issue to the Supreme Court of Canada, under a parliamentary system there was nothing stopping the Quebec authorities from legislating a settlement to cover their actions. For the natives outside Quebec it was viewed as a serious blow for it constituted a precedent for future settlements largely on the basis of cash rather than land.

Although the native people had failed to win any of the cases, they had forced a new respect for their arguments. In each case, some member or members of the bench had sided with them and thus enhanced their credibility. In the days following the Nishga case, the Prime Minister told them that he was impressed with the minority judgement that had upheld their case: "perhaps you have more legal rights than we thought you had."[20] Members of the opposition called on the government to negotiate a settlement that would do justice to aboriginal claims, and with the government lacking a majority the opposition arguments carried a little greater weight. On February 14, 1973, the Yukon Native Brotherhood presented its land claims to the federal government[21] and native leaders from across the country waited to see the response. Trudeau warmly received the proposal and agreed to set up the requested negotiating committee. This response was *de facto* recognition that aboriginal rights had some substance, which constituted a fundamental change from the 1969 government position. The native people, however, were not certain it was anything more than a change of tactics rather than a change of policy. For the sake of public relations it was better to be appearing to negotiate in good faith (even if conceding nothing) than to be rejecting in principle the whole concept of aboriginal rights.

The failure to get the courts or the political process to define the legal status of aboriginal rights made it a very weak bulwark to defend Indian land rights from white encroachment. Governments never intended the term to be a basis for Indian rights but a means whereby whites could acquire Indian lands in a peaceful and orderly fashion for settlement and resource development. The assumption was that the Indian wished to give up his land entitlement. After all, the Indians had far more land than they knew what to do with and white agriculture was so much more profitable that the country could not afford to allow large areas to remain underdeveloped.

Now the current generation of native leaders is attempting to use the term "aboriginal rights" as a means of entrenching land claims, not extinguishing them. In the North it is claimed that the treaties involved no relinquishing of land rights but were only treaties of friendship. Those like the Inuit who have never signed treaties are in an even clearer legal position for they have signed away nothing. Even the word "treaty" seems curiously out of place in this context because it implies an international agreement, freely negotiated, between two independent parties that cannot be altered unilaterally. Some evidence supports the contention that this is how the treaties were originally viewed.[22] Now the bureaucratic practice is to view the treaties as a type of contract given by the federal government to a specific group and these contracts are subject to change any time through statute. The lands in question are subject to all the normal regulations, including expropriation when in the public interest. The curious irony is that if the treaty commissioners had been emphatic in explaining the legal implications of land alienation in Treaties 8 and 11, there is no reason to believe that the Dene would ever have signed. However, their legal position would be no better today and they would have lost the treaty benefits received during the intervening years.

Native land claims remain one of the great unresolved questions for Canadian public policy. The Trudeau government took a hard line in its 1969 White Paper. Liberalism could not endorse such special rights for one ethnic group without compromising its ideals of equality and a fully integrated classless society. In addition, there were strong bureaucratic arguments against recognition of "aboriginal rights." No government could afford to have its development policies, including oil and mineral leases, put into mothballs for decades while the land claims and related issues were resolved. The legal status of the land was far too fundamental a question to be thrown into doubt in order to satisfy the idealistic minority who wished to "give the country back to the Indians." Yet, in spite of ideology and administrative convenience, the Trudeau cabinet did move to negotiate land claims and to fund the research behind them, all the while having no idea where they were going or what constituted aboriginal rights. With the failure of the courts to resolve the issue and with the political uncertainties of a minority Parliament, it was hardly surprising that the Trudeau government resorted to the age-old Canadian device of appointing a commission of inquiry when the application for a Mackenzie Valley Pipeline was received. It was clear that aboriginal rights could not be separated from energy policy.

CHAPTER 4

The Pipeline Applicants: David and Goliath

In countries like Canada with long distances, cold climates, and high
energy consumption, pipelines are the arteries sustaining the economic life of the nation. In the 1950's the building of the great interprovincial pipelines had contributed a major component for
consolidating the post-war industrial growth as well as creating new
industries, such as petrochemicals. The oil pipelines were built first,
largely as a corporate extension of the major oil companies, led by
Imperial. The natural gas pipelines followed, but at arm's length from
the oil majors, reflecting American anti-trust policy. These facilities
were important in their own right but also provided economic spinoffs for the municipalities located along the right-of-way.

Construction of the Trans-Canada Pipeline in the 1950's provoked
intense controversy from rival corporate, civic, and political interests.
All viewed natural gas as the new wonder fuel – cheap, efficient, and
pollution free. While the producers of natural gas were vigorous free
enterprisers, pipelines could not be. They were monopoly common
carriers where the pressures of the marketplace were replaced by
government regulation. But there were strong incentives to invest in
such operations. The profit levels, while regulated, were steady through
good and bad times, creating a secure cash flow that could be invested
in related energy activities where the profits were not regulated. Trans-
Canada Pipeline, Alberta Gas Trunk Line (Nova), and Westcoast
Transmission have grown into huge conglomerates spawned from
their original pipeline base, so it was only natural that tough corporate
struggles to secure the initial franchise and later to control these
companies would be part of the process. Arctic Gas or Foothills inevitably touched important vested interests of both the state and private
corporations. Of necessity the federal bureaucracy took a *very* close
interest in the details of the application and the criteria for planning
a northern pipeline. In addition were the unprecedented challenges
to technology in confronting permafrost or other Arctic constraints,

and with the 2,500-mile length this would be the granddaddy of all pipeline systems in North America. To engineers such as Bob Blair and Vern Horte this challenge was a compelling attraction, for the project would have historic importance for both the industry and the science of gas transmission.

Early in 1969 the first of the contenders for an Arctic pipeline began to gear up. Two years earlier three major pipeline companies – Michigan-Wisconsin of Detroit, Natural Gas Pipeline of America (Chicago), and Trans-Canada of Toronto – had studied the feasibility of a pipeline to tap reserves found in the southwest corner of the N.W.T. The reserves proved insufficient to justify a major new line but two years later this consortium expanded the study to consider a line all the way to the Mackenzie Delta and Prudhoe Bay. In the process they acquired three more partners: Atlantic-Richfield (ARCO), Standard Oil of Ohio (SOHIO), and Humble, a subsidiary of Exxon, all of which had producing properties at Prudhoe. This new consortium[1] took the corporate title of the Northwest Project Study Group. The motive of each of the six parties was very clear. The first two were American gas utilities seeking to line up future gas supply; the third, Trans-Canada, wanted to ensure that no new rival pipeline system would erode its monopoly position as the transporter of Alberta gas to eastern Canadian markets; and the last three wanted to see the pipeline planned to reflect their production and profit priorities in Alaska. With a projected forty-eight-inch line, larger than any then in existence, the group hoped to be delivering gas to eastern markets in the U.S. and Canada by 1976. To demonstrate their seriousness they planned to spend $12 million on feasibility studies, including what was vaguely referred to as "ecological investigations." With Humble being involved with the *Manhattan* voyages, the public image of the group suffered a little in Canadian eyes. Behind the scenes, personnel from Natural Gas of America and Exxon chaired the key executive, finance, and engineering committees, leaving Trans-Canada, led by Vern Horte, very much in a minority position. According to Bob Blair, Alberta Gas Trunk applied for membership in the study group but was refused entry.[2]

Not all the oil and gas interests in Canada were prepared to turn over this strategic project to American-dominated interests, especially Alberta Gas Trunk Line of Calgary. This company was a curious hybrid of the private and public enterprise traditions of Canada. Back in 1954, Alberta's Social Credit government had decided to bring the gas-gathering systems and trunk pipelines into a single Alberta-controlled company and formed Alberta Gas Trunk with the province as part-owner. This initiative was most unwelcome among the multinational oil companies, which were accustomed to getting their own way.

In December, 1969, Bob Blair came to AGTL as executive vice-president and nine months later was president. He was a chemical engineer out of Queen's University in Ontario who went west and had risen to become president of Alberta and Southern, a subsidiary of Pacific Gas and Electric of California. Blair had resented the controls exerted by the parent and when he moved to Alberta Gas Trunk he brought with him a nationalist philosophy that was a rather uncommon phenomenon in the oil and gas business. In eight years Blair changed AGTL from a provincial gathering system into a huge, diversified energy and energy-related corporation. One subsidiary was the leading force in the development of a petrochemical industry in Alberta and another produced pipeline valves in the U.S. and Italy; AGTL purchased controlling interest in Husky Oil, a significant producer with extensive heavy oil reserves for the future; it was involved with planning projects for a pipeline from Montreal to the Maritimes and for LNG tankers from the High Arctic islands. Thus the Arctic pipeline was only one of the schemes planned by the ambitious executives of Alberta Gas Trunk Line Limited.

From the beginning, Blair saw the Arctic pipeline as a magnificent opportunity to expand AGTL northward to tap a whole new hinterland and funnel Alaska resources through his Alberta system to markets further south or east. In this way, his company would control one of the largest and most powerful energy transmission systems in the world with a clear strategy to counter the eventual decline of Alberta reserves. By April, 1970, the Trunk North Project had been born with some different goals from those of the Northwest Project Study Group. One of their principal aims was to keep the equity control of the Canadian portion of the project primarily in Canadian hands. Blair also wanted to see full utilization of existing facilities (including AGTL) and the right to purchase gas from the line for local customers and industries along the route. Northwest and its backers wanted a totally separate "express line" through the country so that they would be free of entanglements with Canadian companies or provincial regulations.

One of the first barriers Blair faced was that AGTL was authorized under provincial regulation to operate only within the Alberta borders. The provincial authorities were worried that if it expanded outside Alberta it would become subject to federal regulatory control when the principal reason for its existence was to keep control within Alberta. The solution to this problem was for Alberta Gas Trunk to establish a separate federally chartered subsidiary that would bring the gas up to the Alberta border and then deliver it to the provincially incorporated parent. With the blessing of the provincial government, the project was publicly announced in June, 1970, about two weeks before their rivals in the Northwest Study Group formally unveiled their plans.

A third group, the Mountain Pacific Pipeline project, was also at work devising plans for extending the Westcoast Transmission system of B.C. north through the Liard field in the N.W.T. to Prudhoe Bay. Although Westcoast had powerful American partners in El Paso Gas and Bechtel Construction, the project never really got off the ground. It proposed to bypass Alberta to the west through the mountains and the Alaska Highway route.

In each of the three projects the routing was determined by the vested financial interests of the study group partners. Northwest was dominated by eastern American oil companies and gas utilities who wanted the most direct route from Alaska to hit the U.S. border at Emerson, Manitoba. The Trunk North Project wanted a central route through Alberta to serve either eastern or western American markets. Mountain Pacific, dominated by B.C. and California interests, wanted a direct route through the mountains to Washington State. Vern Horte, president of Trans-Canada, was determined to get frontier sources of supply out of the hands of Blair and the Alberta government because his company was already upset with the AGTL monopoly position as supplier from Alberta. Blair, for his part, shrewdly saw the tremendous potential for Alberta to become the energy corridor between the large Arctic reserves and southern markets in the United States and Canada. In May, 1970, he wrote to the premier of the province: "If the route . . . passes centrally through Alberta, the Government and private citizens and companies in this province will be involved to a great extent and their public and private policies and investment desires will be reflected in the Alberta portion and throughout the entire development."[3]

For Blair, though, this argument was a two-edged sword. What was economically stimulating to Alberta was a loss to the eastern business establishment in Toronto and their political friends at the provincial and federal levels. With incredible optimism, Blair hoped that his application would be filed in the fall of 1970; construction would begin in 1971; and gas would be coming on stream in 1974. Within a few days of the public announcement, the Alberta Mines Minister had officially endorsed the project. When Northwest unveiled its project a few days later at a press conference in Toronto, the group emphasized that their line was 300 miles shorter and therefore cheaper for eastern and midwestern consumers. They felt that the Alaskan reserves were inadequate to service California as well, but if they increased with further drilling they would be prepared to build a spur to join the existing Canadian export lines into the American Northwest. The battle lines were now drawn and the action was about to begin.

During 1970, the Trunk North Project underwent a metamorphosis and re-emerged as Gas Arctic Systems Study Group with five new partners to share costs. The five were Canadian National Railways and four large American gas transmission companies – Columbia, Northern Natural, Texas Eastern, and Pacific Lighting. These companies had been excluded from Northwest but were all critically interested in potential Arctic gas supply. Through 1971 and into 1972, each of the two rival study groups went their separate ways with field research and pipeline planning. Northwest built a test facility at Sans Sault on the northern Mackenzie, and Gas Arctic operated smaller test facilities at Prudhoe Bay and Norman Wells. In addition, Blair established an independent environmental research group at Winnipeg called the Environmental Protection Board, which was funded by the study group but free of any influence on its work. Both groups began regular VIP trips to the western Arctic to try to woo key corporate, government, political, and media figures; after all, who could turn down a free trip to the Arctic when so few Canadians had ever seen the area.

The emergence of the two rival study groups had sparked interest and consternation within federal government structures. Although the government presence in the North had been established with the Department of Northern Affairs in the 1950's, the Prudhoe Bay discoveries caught Ottawa unprepared for large northern development projects. Ottawa, as a result of the *Manhattan* voyages, took a hard line on the issue of northern sovereignty and pollution control in Washington; but at the same time, the government tried to entice the Americans to accept a route across Canada for the northern natural gas pipeline. These were the two poles of their carrot and stick approach to Canadian-American energy relations.

In addition, significant background research and analysis were undertaken by a complex series of interdepartmental committees under the Task Force on Northern Oil Development. Most of this policy work was done out of public view and without any discussion by Parliament. As Edgar Dosman has argued: "The key therefore to understanding northern policy lies in these secret internal discussions within the elite [civil servants] and between it and the business community."[4] A number of major decisions relating to the pipeline were made in this way. They decided that a northern pipeline *should* be built from Alaska across Canada and if need be they would *not* wait

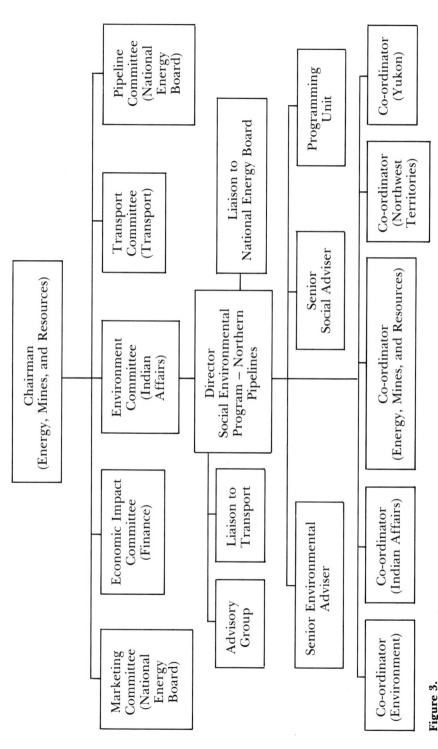

Figure 3.
Task Force on Northern Oil Development.

80

for a native land claims settlement before commencing construction. In some important ways this was predetermining the National Energy Board's role in judging "the public convenience and necessity" of the project and Berger's scope for recommendations on native land claims. Neither matter was of great concern to a government determined to appear in Washington as being able to deliver any joint project in a speedy and efficient manner. Diplomatic fears spurred bureaucratic secrecy and arbitrary action.

As a partial blueprint for the corporate planners, the government tabled in the House of Commons in June, 1972, its "Expanded Guidelines for Northern Pipelines." This document, hastily prepared and ambiguously worded, was far more a sermon on good intentions than a technical directive on the terms and conditions to construct a pipeline. However, as will be shown later, even the very listing of a whole series of environmental and social concerns and goals was to prove very useful for Berger. Also, the government wished to see the first pipeline as part of a transportation corridor so that they had to do their planning as a package, not with the gas pipeline in isolation. In the guidelines no mention was made of public hearings, only that the public were "invited" to send their comments to a government office in Ottawa. By law, the NEB had to hold public hearings, but these would hardly be adequate to handle the environmental and social concerns involved in the land permit for a right-of-way. At this point in 1972, the public interest groups beginning to emerge had no clear idea what opportunities there would be for input and public discussion of the issues.

One of the political realities facing the rival study groups was that only one of them could be successful and it was clear that the federal authorities wished the two groups to merge.[5] A long, drawn-out battle through the regulatory hearings might give victory to the all-American El Paso project for LNG tankers down the West Coast; if Washington feared that there would be long delays in Canada, El Paso might win by default. In addition, for Blair the arguments for an Alberta route appeared to be getting stronger as California markets strengthened their interest.

Meetings between Blair and Horte on the possibility of a merger began in August, 1971, and continued through the next ten months. The main issues in debate were the level of Canadian equity ownership, the route for the line, and the role if any for the existing AGTL system. Horte felt that Blair was less than committed to a merger and it was evident through the course of the meetings that Blair was worried his Alberta interests would be swamped by the U.S. partners. In the final analysis, the willingness of the U.S. partners of Gas Arctic,

Figure 4.
Canadian Arctic Gas System Map. From NEB, *Reasons for Decision: Northern Pipelines*, I (Ottawa, 1977), appendix.

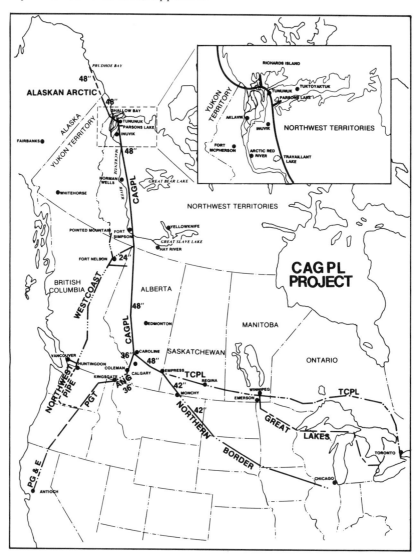

who were prepared if necessary to abandon Blair, forced him into the merger. The details of the merger were thrashed out in an exhausting all-day meeting of sixteen companies on June 8, 1972, in Houston, Texas.[6] Out of this shotgun marriage the two sister companies of Canadian Arctic Gas and Alaskan Arctic Gas emerged to be *the* applicant for a northern pipeline. Shortly after, William Wilder, president of Wood Gundy, Canada's largest stock brokers, was appointed chairman and chief executive officer while Vern Horte was named president. These appointments, along with those of a number of other senior executives, gave the new company a powerful and able group of experienced executives with strong expertise in the financial and engineering sectors. Many in the business community saw it as an unbeatable team.

The achievement of the merger, however, in no way implied that Arctic Gas was in for smooth sailing. Many policy decisions had not been resolved and there was a year of fierce wrangling on the route and the structure of ownership issues. The final compromise was for the pipeline to be a separate express-line system but to follow the route of AGTL through Alberta. Also, the company would be a single corporate structure, not fragmented as Alberta Gas Trunk had wished. After completion of the main line, consideration would be given to utilizing the unused capacity in AGTL provided undue engineering and operations problems were not created. Alberta Gas Trunk now faced the prospect that the new system would be a competitor, not a funnel into the AGTL system. Blair's sensitivity on the Canadian ownership and control issue made some of the other partners uneasy, although the Canadian government had made it plain it expected majority Canadian control of the Arctic Gas system in this country.

With a basic *modus operandi* for Arctic Gas finally in place by the end of June, 1973, the consortium could begin preparation of the detailed filings required for their applications to the National Energy Board in Ottawa for a certificate of "public convenience and necessity," to the Department of Indian Affairs and Northern Development for the land permits, and to the U.S. Federal Power Commission for approval in Washington. As those documents were being prepared, international events intervened to improve their chances of success. In November, 1973, with the devastating impact of OPEC price increases becoming steadily more evident, frontier sources of oil and gas became more economic as prices rose and the U.S. became more vulnerable to foreign policy blackmail from Arab states.

In December, 1973, when the issue was raised in the House of Commons, the Prime Minister clearly committed the government to supporting the principle of building an Arctic pipeline. He stressed that "it would be in the public interest to facilitate early construction by any means which do not require the lowering of environmental standards or the neglect of Indian rights and interests." Several days later, Donald Macdonald, the Minister of Energy, warned that because there was not a need for Canadian domestic supply, any immediate

TABLE ONE

The Corporate Sponsors of Canadian Arctic Gas (March, 1974)

American Companies	Foreign Subsidiaries in Canada	Canadian-controlled Companies
1. Atlantic Richfield (ARCO)	1. Alberta Natural Gas	1. Alberta Gas Trunk
2. Colorado Interstate	2. Canada Superior Oil	2. Canada Development Corporation
3. Columbia Gas Transmission	3. Canadian Utilities Limited	3. Canadian National Railways
4. Humble (Exxon Corporation)	4. Gulf Canada	4. Canadian Pacific Investments
5. Michigan-Wisconsin Pipeline	5. Imperial Oil (Exxon)	5. Consumers' Gas
6. Natural Gas Pipeline of America	6. Shell Canada	6. Numac Oil & Gas
7. Northern Natural Gas		7. Pembina Pipeline
8. Pacific Gas Lighting Development		8. Polaris Pipeline
9. Panhandle Eastern Pipeline		9. Trans-Canada Pipeline
10. Standard Oil of Ohio (SOHIO)		10. Union Gas (of Ontario)
11. Texas Eastern Transmission		

start on the pipeline would entail exports of Delta gas to the U.S. in order to provide the through-put to finance the project.[7] These two statements appeared to be policy commitments to Arctic Gas, indicating that the government had already made up its mind before any hearings opened and even before the applicant had filed all the details of the project. It was little wonder that the public interest groups were discouraged: they felt any hearings would now be a *fait accompli* used to justify what had already been decided.

When the Conservatives moved a motion of non-confidence in the minority government due to its "incompetent, inconsistent, and vacillating energy policy which is bringing economic loss to Canada and hardship to the consuming public," Stanfield included the Liberal pipeline policy as part of his indictment. Ottawa had lost the oil pipeline and now the government was downgrading the environment and native rights in its haste to get the project. Trudeau and his colleagues were preparing "to make the Americans some offer that they cannot refuse." David Lewis, in his reply for the NDP, seemed to be mainly concerned with making sure that the Delta gas was used to supply Canadian customers. His other comments were more general ones about the energy corporations and their ownership pattern. The NDP did not take Stanfield's challenge for support and sided with the government on this energy vote.[8] The overall impression from Lewis's comments was that the pipeline was not a serious enough issue at this time for his party to defeat the government and fight an election on it.

As with many shotgun marriages, Blair and Horte found their relations strained in carrying through the merger. Blair never trusted Exxon and some of the other U.S. partners, who exhibited little concern for Canadian, let alone Alberta, priorities. Majority Canadian equity ownership and control as a goal gradually receded from the horizon as Morgan Stanley, the financial advisers from New York, gained the upper hand. Horte and Wilder were prepared to work with and accept the wishes of the American interests to secure financing for the project. Blair was not. All the committees were headed by Americans and the key finance committee was chaired by an Exxon representative. This was hardly surprising, for it represented the clear voting majority of the U.S. oil and pipeline companies. Blair was helped partially by the pressure from the Canadian government for extensive Canadian content in the engineering and design work on the project. This stand forced a Canadianization of the American firm of Williams Brothers into Northern Engineering Services, which provided the bulk of the design work for Canadian Arctic Gas. Surprisingly, the Americans apparently did not take very seriously the other requirements in the Expanded Pipeline Guidelines of 1972 for Canadian financing and ownership. Had Vern Horte emphasized this it would have made Blair's task a little easier. Consequently, Blair felt isolated and to be losing at every turn to the American voting majority in the consortium.

At the Berger Inquiry in August, 1975, Blair was asked to explain the reasons for his company's withdrawal from Arctic Gas. He responded with a long answer that was not overly illuminating, but he did emphasize a couple of points. At the root of the decision was his belief that Arctic Gas had come to reflect the aims of the old Northwest Study Group "to create an internationally known and wholly new express line across western Canada" and that the group "was doing too much for the special purpose and under the influence of the United States companies."[9] When Blair had entered the merger he had been promised that there would be a thorough study of utilizing existing pipeline systems like Alberta Gas Trunk or Trans-Canada. When the report came down, Blair was bitterly disappointed – its main recommendations attacked the very concept of shared facilities that was central to the future expansion of his company within Alberta.

On the financial structure of Arctic Gas, he appeared also to be losing out, as well as in his concerns about Canadian control. Horte welcomed the large American companies because he saw them as buttressing the credit rating of Arctic Gas, which to him was more important than their national perspective. In addition, he was committed to the single corporate unit concept, which left no room for an Alberta section separately owned by Alberta interests. When Arctic Gas filed the first volumes of its formal application at the National Energy board on March 21, 1974, Blair clearly had lost most of the boardroom battles. If he left, no other partners would leave with him. Horte must have been sure that he had now won, for it looked on the surface that Blair would lose if he remained in or lose if he tried to start a new project of his own.

Two months later Blair informed his colleagues at Arctic Gas that AGTL was looking into an alternative system of a forty-two-inch line from Alberta north to tap only the Delta. In the summer of 1974, while Blair was considering his options, Kelly Gibson, the chairman of Westcoast Transmission, let Blair know that he was prepared to join with AGTL in a new venture providing it left the Arctic Gas consortium. This was exactly the stimulus that Blair needed to cut the final links to Horte and his colleagues, which he did formally at the September management meeting. Foothills Pipeline Company had been a small subsidiary of AGTL since 1964 and it now became the vehicle for the formal challenge to Arctic Gas. Most industry observers

Figure 5.
Foothills (Maple Leaf) System Map. From NEB, *Reasons for Decision: Northern Pipelines*, I (Ottawa, 1977), appendix.

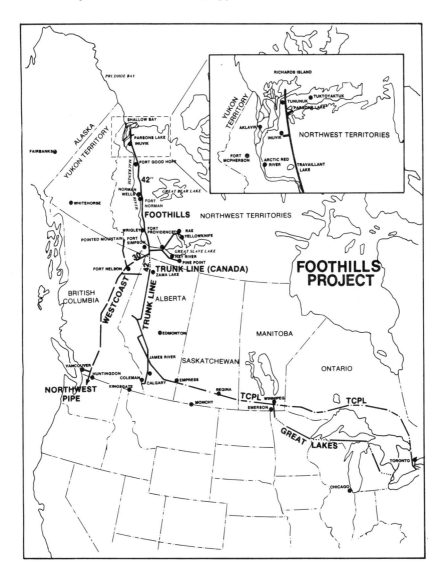

dismissed the new competitor as without the slightest chance of success. How could two Canadian companies like Westcoast and Alberta Gas Trunk challenge a consortium backed by some of the most powerful companies in the world. Blair was accused of wasting AGTL money to soothe his wounded pride. As one oil executive remarked to me at the time, "It was like David facing Goliath without even a slingshot."

CHAPTER 5

The Berger Commission: The Public Inquiry Process and Northern Policy

In the political evolution of Canada, public inquiries have enjoyed a lengthy but less than distinguished record of achievement. The first inquiries act was passed in 1846 amid the battles for responsible government. As an institution to complement Parliament it can probe failings within government or contentious and complex policy issues. Generally there have been two types of inquiries: those designed *to advise* on a general area of policy (i.e., railways) and those established *to investigate* some weakness or scandal within a specific department (i.e., the Gerda Munsinger affair). For a variety of reasons, Canada has resorted to formal inquiries more frequently than the Mother of Parliaments in the U.K. Since 1867, Ottawa has appointed about 400 advisory policy tribunals and close to 1,500 investigatory ones. Some of these were commissioned under the Great Seal of Canada and hence were Royal Commissions; others were authorized only by Orders-in-Council; and still others appear to have emerged without formal authorization.[1] Too often their real purpose was to delay or to defuse a highly controversial issue, especially on the eve of an election. Others that produced imaginative recommendations have seen them pigeonholed by cabinets reluctant to take the political risk. Some have had so little impact on public affairs that there remains no record of their activities or conclusions. Some appointees as commissioners clearly failed to achieve the goals of their terms of reference, while for others the terms of reference frustrated their efforts to run a comprehensive inquiry. Each commission must devise its own machinery and acquire the necessary personnel to do its job. Many commissioners have complained about the *ad hoc* nature of the arrangements that made it difficult for them to achieve their goals. With this *modus operandi* it is little wonder that their record of achievement has been so uneven. While the theory of inquiries was to open up the process of government, the practice often involved more mundane considerations.

When Justice Thomas Berger was appointed he was well aware of this past history. He stated in his report: "It is often said that commissions of inquiry have little or no impact on public policy in Canada."[2] However, he liked to cite the work of the Rowell-Sirois, Rand, and Hall inquiries as examples of major contributions to public policy. Part of their strength and their weakness lay in the fact that these inquiries operated outside the three traditional areas of government – Parliament, the ministries, and the courts. They can probe into questions the parties are reluctant to face and recommend controversial solutions; but they do require parliamentary action to achieve any results. A great responsibility rests on the shoulders of those who are heading the inquiry to ensure the fairness of the proceedings, for there are not the checks and balances of an elected assembly. Berger was clearly aware of these potential pitfalls and was determined to ensure that his inquiry would achieve a thorough airing of the issues and concrete public policy results.

To understand the dynamics of the Berger Inquiry, it is essential first of all to look at Thomas Berger himself, for he put a very personal stamp on the inquiry. In his intellectual development, Berger had been deeply influenced by Frank Scott, one of the great figures of Canadian law and politics. Scott above all had articulated the problems facing minorities and dissenters within the Canadian body politic from the point of view of a civil libertarian, a social democrat, and a federal centralist. Berger even served as junior counsel to Scott before the Supreme Court in 1962. In a tribute to Scott in February, 1981, Berger stated that in our pluralistic Canadian society "the history of minorities and dissenters is the history of Canada" for they are at the centre of our institutional arrangements and our political life. The victories and defeats of minorities demonstrate the success of our institutions and the will of our majorities. Native claims were the oldest question of human rights in Canada and the most recent. "We may reject the claims of the native peoples but if we do we will be turning our backs against the truth of our own beginnings as a nation."[3] In addition to Scott, Berger talks about Justices Ivan Rand and Emmett Hall as the other great influences on his thinking.[4]

Berger brought to the inquiry a clear philosophy of law as a vehicle for social change and a deep concern for the historic forces and the social fabric of the nation. His social conscience became evident in his brief tenure as NDP leader in British Columbia and his legal work as counsel for the Nishga Indians. Had he operated in the U.S., one would have seen him in the line of progressive jurists like Holmes and Brandeis. This school viewed law as a living, evolving organism that reflected the social conditions of the time and was not confined to a static commitment to past precedents. Good law was that which reflected the collective social needs. From his speeches and his report, it is clear he possesses a deep reverence for history, not as a justification for the status quo, but as a means of understanding the dynamics of change from one era to the next. This came out clearly in his concern for the social and cultural shocks of an industrial society on the traditional communities of the Mackenzie Valley.

Berger saw public inquiries as an important part of the political handling of the dynamics of change. As the Rowell-Sirois Commission had opened new paths for federalism, or the Hall Commission for Medicare, Berger hoped his commission would set the pattern for northern development and contribute to the settlement of native land claims. But in addition to charting new policy initiatives, Berger was anxious to devise more effective means of public participation, for he believed that public inquiries offered great scope for this. In his report he wrote:

They have brought new ideas into the public consciousness. They have expanded the vocabulary of politics, education and social science. They have added to the furniture that we now expect to find in Canada's storefront of ideas. And they have always had real importance in providing considered advice to governments. This is their primary function. But in recent years, Commissions of Inquiry have begun to take on a new function: that of opening up issues to public discussions, of providing a forum for the exchange of ideas.[5]

In a period of social tension and change, they could as well provide a safety valve for the stifled frustrations of ethnic or ideological minority groups, such as the Dene or the environmentalists, and give them an opportunity to influence wider opinion in the country. At a time of ever-expanding government structures, it was important to the system that there be a means of direct consultation so the public could experience a sense of involvement and not have their views filtered and translated through the normal bureaucratic and political processes.

While the Berger Inquiry was under way, the federal government's Law Reform Commission embarked on a special study of commissions of inquiry. In his report Berger quoted their conclusion that "Today the need for other avenues of expression and influence is often focussed in greater demands for public participation. Increased participation allows those individuals and groups to express their views to public authorities."[6]

Public input into Parliament was inadequate when the politicians sought to judge complex socio-economic and environmental questions. Government decision-making suffered from a serious flaw in impact assessment. It had failed to develop "a methodology that is sufficiently comprehensive to encompass a wide range of variables, a variety of conflicting interests, and a realistic span of time." With only one member representing the Mackenzie Valley, the House of Commons was hardly in a position to take the time to weigh the conflicting claims. "If you are going to assess impact properly, you have to weigh a whole series of matters, some tangible, some intangible." Inquiries provided "more representative opinion to decision-makers" free of the partisan rhetoric and strategies inherent in the House of Commons. Commissioners of inquiry have an advantage that ministers and senior public servants do not enjoy. They can go out to the people "to hear all the evidence, to reflect on it, to weigh it, and to make a judgment on it." Under cross-examination conflicting viewpoints can be assessed and the evidence weighed.[7] Parliament is supreme, but it requires good advice. In this sense, an inquiry was both an extension of the political process and a catalyst to promote the necessary changes in public opinion, which in turn would bring pressure to bear on those who have appointed the inquiry.

On the surface, the appointment of Berger seemed a surprising choice for a Liberal government; but Trudeau had been impressed by the Nishga case, which Berger had assembled and argued. If the Trudeau government lacked credibility with the native groups as a result of the White Paper and its court actions, then the inquiry had to be headed by someone who did command their respect. This was not merely idealism – there were strong pragmatic reasons. If the native groups participated fully and with some faith in the commissioner, they were more likely to abide by his recommendations in authorizing the pipeline. In its careful negotiations with the Americans, Ottawa wanted no native militancy that might scare off the Americans from accepting the Canadian route.

In addition, with a minority government, the NDP enthusiasm for the former B.C. leader would help to solidify votes in the Commons on northern and energy issues. For once, idealism and political expediency could be combined. Setting up a special northern inquiry had a further advantage to the administration. It would divert to Yellowknife the main environmental and native rights hearings where fewer southern activists could participate and the media would return south after the first week. Thus the NEB hearings, where the government felt more comfortable, would remain front and centre in Ottawa and prepare public opinion for acceptance of the project while most of the critics, hopefully, would be lost in the wilds of the Northwest Territories.

When the inquiry was first being considered by cabinet, Jean Chrétien, the Minister of Indian Affairs and Northern Development, phoned Berger to offer him the job if he was interested. He indicated that this initiative was the product of discussion between himself, Trudeau, and Donald Macdonald, and they wished to take Berger's name to cabinet for approval.[8] When Berger's appointment was announced in the House of Commons on March 22, 1974, it did not receive prominent news coverage. The next morning, the Toronto *Globe and Mail*, which had given very prominent coverage to the Arctic Gas application earlier in the week, buried the Berger appointment in a small two-column item on page ten. At this time the significance of the inquiry was not fully realized, although in the business community there were a few quiet rumblings about the "socialist" judge.

During the hearings and after, Berger has been accused of ignoring his terms of reference and expanding the scope of the hearings. In 1977, Don Peacock wrote: "The Berger staff, evidently inspired by a messianic fervour, went at once beyond the mandate of the inquiry, which was to examine the impact of a pipeline."[9] Therefore, it is a matter of some importance to review the terms of reference and their interpretation. Berger was ordered under Section 19(h) of the Territorial Lands Act to inquire into and report on the terms and conditions for granting a pipeline right-of-way under two specific headings: "the social, environmental, and economic impact regionally of the construction, operation, and subsequent abandonment of the proposed pipeline" and "any proposals to meet the specific environmental and social concerns set out in the Expanded Guidelines for Northern Pipelines" of June 28, 1972. The first part was directly related to the specific application of Arctic Gas; the second opened up the inquiry to the general concerns about northern development and its impact on native society.

This last part must have infuriated the lawyers for Arctic Gas, who wished to keep the Berger Inquiry under wraps, limit the opportunities for social and environmental "doomsday speculation," and complete the hearings quickly to defeat El Paso in Washington.[10] In addition to the impact of its own project, the applicant was expected to provide evidence on the suitability of the route chosen for later pipelines and other transportation facilities that would constitute a transportation "corridor."[11] With this type of open-ended instruction, Berger was free to range widely over the nature of development in the western Arctic and its impacts on the traditional hunting and trapping society. Few commissions of inquiry in Canadian history have been given such ambiguously wide terms of reference; in the ensuing years, a few Ottawa officials learned to regret the hasty wording of the 1972 pipeline guidelines[12] and even more their inclusion in Berger's terms of reference.

In developing procedures for the inquiry, Berger took great care to consult the potential participants through a series of preliminary meetings in Ottawa and the North from April to September of 1974.[13] Berger demonstrated from the start that he put the highest priority on achieving rapport and credibility with the native organizations and he made it clear that he would hear their arguments about land claims as background to the pipeline issue in spite of the opposition from Arctic Gas. He was also flexible in terms of timing, allowing them and the other public interest groups nearly a year to review the evidence before the commencement of the hearings. He devised a relaxed set of procedures that did not turn the inquiry into an exclusive forum for lawyers and expert witnesses but allowed natives and others to speak their mind.

In addition, he established two different types of hearings: the formal hearings of expert evidence in Yellowknife and the informal community hearings designed to measure local opinion. At the formal hearings, legal cross-examination of the experts was essential in trying to establish the truth between conflicting positions. In the community hearings, the people were allowed to speak in their own languages and in their own way to the judge. As Chapter 9 will show, this made it possible for local residents to show their continuing relationship to the land and their fears about development. As Berger himself emphasized: "Even at the formal hearings, we did not insist upon a too rigid observance of legal rules of admissibility, for that might have squeezed the life out of the evidence." A public inquiry investigating social, environmental, and local economic impacts has separate needs from those of a criminal or civil trial.[14] It must come to grips with the *nature* of the society and the way of life, which in this case were a very different set of assumptions than those dominating the legal system imposed on the Dene and Inuit from without. Thus the community hearings were a crucial part of the inquiry, and a good deal of their success came from this careful planning by Berger himself and his staff, led by Professor Michael Jackson on leave from UBC Law School.

Although Berger was sympathetic to the native position, there were tensions between the inquiry and native leaders who remained suspicious of all government activities. James Wah-Shee, president of the Native Brotherhood of the N.W.T., challenged the basic legal status of the inquiry. "It is clear to us that the legitimacy of these hearings is highly questionable in so far as you are to deal with matters of a right-of-way over our lands. We have consistently opposed the notion that these are Crown lands as specifically referred to in the Privy

Council Order initiating the inquiry." If the federal government did not have clear title to the land until the native land claims were settled, what right did Ottawa have to appoint a commissioner to determine the terms and conditions for disposing of a portion of that land to a private developer? Berger was also warned that the past treaty practices in the south were not an acceptable format for negotiating the northern land claims. As George Manuel, president of the National Indian Brotherhood, bluntly stated, they were not prepared to have their way of life "legislated out of existence."[15] With this intensity of feeling it was clear that very great skill would be required on the part of the commissioner to keep the hearings from turning into a repetitious catalogue of the historic grievances of native people.

Michael Goldie, the experienced senior counsel for Arctic Gas, quickly realized the threat the native land claims issue raised for his client. Because of Berger's background, he desperately wanted to confine the hearings to the specifics of the project, where his engineering and financial experts were on their home ground; but if the hearings formally considered land claims then the latter might emerge as part of the terms and conditions delaying or prohibiting a pipeline. At the very least, he believed that the claims would bog the hearings down in fruitless speculative discussion about a matter that could only be resolved by Parliament. He made a distinction between land use and land claims; the former, including hunting and trapping, was clearly a concern of Arctic Gas in determining the route – any disturbance of existing land use would be covered by compensation.[16] On the other hand, the land claims were a private matter of negotiation between the government of Canada and the individual native groups. They were bound to honour the settlement whenever it was completed. "The pipeline company would then negotiate fair compensation for the right of way, and if no settlement could be reached, then that compensation would be determined in accordance with procedures that apply to all owners of land affected by a pipeline."[17]

Despite all the care and diplomacy in his wording, Goldie's comments could not avoid the hated spectre of expropriation. Because the pipeline only required ownership of a slender slice of land and would be buried in the ground, Goldie argued that construction would not be "prejudicial" to those claims and the claims were not relevant to the hearings.

Goldie fiercely resisted the request for delay in the start of the hearings, for any lengthy delay could remove Arctic Gas from contention in Washington. Its competitor, the powerful El Paso corporation, had argued that the Americans could not wait for the serious delays involved in Arctic Gas getting regulatory approvals in Canada.

Figure 6.
El Paso LNG system map. From a Foothills Pipelines circular.

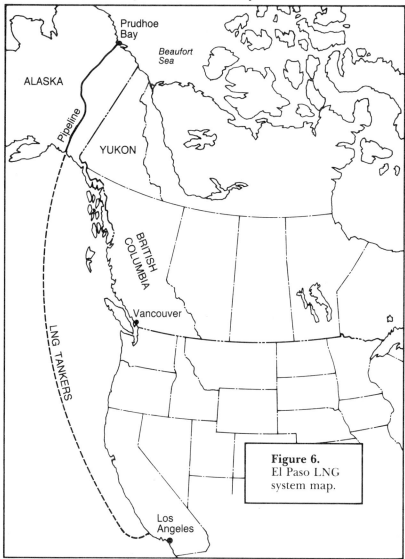

Figure 6.
El Paso LNG system map.

A year's delay in commencing the hearings would be taken in Washington as proof of the El Paso allegations and the weakness of the Canadian resolve on the pipeline. Berger could force Arctic Gas to lose by default and the nation to lose the economic benefits of the project. Goldie's strategy was very clear: to get the hearings under way as soon as possible and to restrict the debate to the terms and conditions for a pipeline. Everything else should be left up to the government or to the National Energy Board hearings where Arctic Gas was more at home.

The preliminary hearings brought out many groups and individuals concerned to have a say in the format of the inquiry. There were the Canadian Arctic Resources Committee and its allies, such as Pollution Probe, from the environmental sector; there was the Committee for an Independent Canada, reflecting nationalist concerns; and there were the Mental Health Association of the N.W.T., the Association of Municipalities of the N.W.T., and such individuals as Tom Butters of Inuvik. Thirty-seven submissions were presented in the eight days of hearings. There was general unanimity on a few points, such as special local community hearings, northern locale for all the main hearings, and flexibility in the rules of cross-examination. In such areas as the disclosure of documents, however, there were profound differences of opinion between the public interest groups and the applicants. Everyone was aware that Berger's decisions on these procedural matters would go a long way to determining the type of hearings to follow.

The Berger Inquiry incorporated a number of novel features that helped it to accomplish its goals. The government of Canada, from northern expertise within the civil service, established the Pipeline Application Assessment Group under Dr. John Fyles, on loan from the Geological Survey of Canada. Initially, the task of this group was to review the application filed by Arctic Gas and to prepare a detailed report on its deficiencies. When published this would constitute a useful background tool for all those involved with the Berger and National Energy Board hearings. Once the inquiry was under way, Dr. Fyles and some of his associates were transferred to the inquiry staff, where they did excellent work in areas such as permafrost. Their analysis supplemented that of Carson Templeton and the Environmental Protection Board, whose work was also freely available in published form.

The Canadian Arctic Resources Committee (CARC) played a major role in the preliminary hearings in presenting the public interest point of view on procedures. While supporting the native position, they moved on to articulate their own environmental concerns. Arctic Gas had emphasized the parallel hearings at the NEB, but CARC reminded Berger that the NEB's past record and lack of environmental staff meant that his inquiry had to be the main arena for ecological concerns. On timing the opening of the hearings, they believed that it would take at least a year to evaluate the complex technical filings of the Arctic Gas application. Andrew Thompson, the chairman of CARC, expressed a feeling common among public interest groups that the applicant determined the timetable for consideration of the project. Berger resented this implied criticism of his own independence of action and bluntly interrupted: "I decided that this hearing would be today."[18] With some of the filings of Arctic Gas still being prepared and the report of the Pipeline Application Assessment Group not due until the fall of 1974, CARC argued that there was no way the public interest groups could be ready before the summer of 1975. They believed that Berger must use a broad interpretation of his terms of reference if the social and environmental impacts were to be properly assessed. They were also concerned that sufficient monies would be made available to them to do a competent professional job during the hearings.

Following the preliminary sessions in Ottawa in May, the public interest groups held a series of private meetings to plan strategy for the main hearings. There was a clear feeling among the participants that they had to provide an umbrella organization to unify the research plan and avoid duplication of effort or wasting public funds. CARC agreed to organize a detailed technical review of the application under a wider aegis to be known as the Northern Assessment Group (NAG). This group would seek funds from the inquiry and the results of its work would be freely available to all public interest groups in the hearings. The groups involved showed a certain geographic concentration: Pollution Probe, the Federation of Ontario Naturalists, and the Canadian Environmental Law Association, all out of Toronto; CARC and the Canadian Nature Federation, of Ottawa; and only one group, the Canadian Scientific Pollution and Environmental Control Society (SPEC) of Vancouver, being from west of the Great Lakes. It was understood that the environmental research of NAG would be coordinated with the socio-economic research undertaken by the various native organizations. NAG would not be a party to the hearings, but would operate through CARC in presenting its evidence.[19]

At the private meetings the Committee for an Independent Canada formally announced its decision to withdraw from any official involvement in the Berger hearings as its policy concerns were more appropriate to the national economic terms of reference of the National Energy Board hearings. It did, however, retain close ties to CARC and the Native Brotherhood so activities could be co-ordinated between the Berger and NEB hearings. The CARC executive met in Edmonton in August, 1974, to hammer out the final details of the NAG structure, which was formally approved by Berger and his staff later in the month.[20]

One of the key issues for the public interest groups was the funding of their efforts. Berger persuaded the federal government that it was important to the commission that their case be properly and thoroughly presented. As Berger stated: "They do not represent the public interest, but it is in the public interest that they should be heard." Any group wishing to apply for funds had to meet five criteria: (1) it had to represent a clearly ascertainable interest that ought to be represented at the inquiry; (2) it had to be capable of making a necessary and substantial contribution; (3) it had to have an established record of concern for the interest it sought to represent; (4) it did not possess sufficient financial resources; (5) it possessed a clearly delineated and sufficiently well-organized proposal so that it could account for the funds.

Once Berger's criteria were met, the groups were allowed complete freedom as to how the funds were spent in preparation of their cases, provided an audited statement of expenditures was filed with the inquiry. In his final report, Berger noted that he did not believe that the funding of intervenors is appropriate in all inquiries. "But I can speak to its usefulness in this instance." As Arctic Gas spent in excess of $150 million on its application, it seemed only appropriate that the counter case should have serious funding. Berger supplied the native, environmental, municipal, and northern business organizations with about $1.8 million, or about 1 per cent of the funds available to Arctic Gas.[21] Money was a continual problem for the public interest groups, all of whom underestimated the length, complexity, and cost of the hearings in much the same way that the applicants did. A number of requests for funding were refused, including Tom Butters (Inuvik, pro-pipeline councillor), the Vancouver Voice of Women, and the Canadian Labour Congress.

Another important area of debate was the issue of public information. When the application was filed in March, 1974, it appeared that both Arctic Gas and the federal government had done much more research than had been released to the public. The CIC and Pollution Probe both charged that Arctic Gas had withheld consultants' reports if unfavourable to its project.[22] In the age of Watergate the term "cover-up" had come into common usage and was easily applied to this situation. There was growing dismay among public interest groups that research critical to their own cases before regulatory boards would be withheld by government because of its commitment to the pipeline.[23] Several government reports leaked to these groups seemed to substantiate the charges.

Many critics of the pipeline feared that unless all of the relevant studies were out in the open, the Berger Inquiry might fail to accomplish its purpose and accept the subjective evidence of the applicants.

Although he possessed the power to subpoena evidence, Berger wished to avoid this awkward procedure. He therefore ordered all the intervenors to submit a list of all studies and reports in their possession. These lists were then distributed to all parties. Any of these could be requested by other intervenors and the procedure was sufficiently successful that subpoenas were avoided. In fact, by the end of the hearings all the intervenors were so swamped with the flood of paper that it required a full-time librarian to keep them under control. Yet, access to information was an important public issue of the 1970's. All the rhetoric about public participation was virtually meaningless unless it allowed access to all objective technical information from which informed judgements could be made. The public had paid for government research and it expected access to those reports whether they reflected government policy or not. For many officials this concept had profoundly disturbing implications, which would be embarrassing to any government in power and might needlessly promote opposition to official policies.

Prior to the opening of the hearings, Berger had a clear strategy in place to maximize media coverage of the proceedings. His staff carefully contacted radio, television, newspapers, and even the National Film Board to ensure that they would be there. In fact, no royal commission in Canadian history received such sustained media attention in spite of its remote location. The CBC became indirectly a part of the hearing process. Berger wanted daily radio reports to go out in the six native languages to all areas covered by the hearings. He recognized that such service would be costly, even suggesting that the inquiry could subsidize the CBC Northern Service by $20,000.[24] Berger hoped that with such coverage the issues would be known in each settlement before he arrived to conduct the local community hearings. The second major purpose was to ensure that the inquiry would not be lost from public attention in the south. There were fears that the media would all go home after the first week, once the novelty wore off; if this occurred Berger could never make the impact on the Canadian electorate he felt he needed to have political leverage on the cabinet. In the end the government came through with $500,000 in special funding for the CBC Northern Service, and the multilingual coverage became a daily feature at the hearings.

In addition, extensive coverage by Whit Fraser and others was featured frequently on southern airwaves. Several newspapers, including the *Edmonton Journal* and the Toronto *Globe and Mail*, assigned regular reporters to cover the proceedings; others depended on the Canadian Press wire service reports. Diana Crosby of Berger's own staff worked tirelessly to keep this flow of information going and, incredibly, the hearings remained a media event throughout their eighteen-month duration. When, late in the hearings, Berger toured the southern cities, from Vancouver to Halifax, the media exposure brought great dividends in terms of local interest and participation. The coverage helped to swing public opinion into a generally supportive attitude to the environmental and native rights concerns of the inquiry. The reporters were generally caught up in the mystique of the hearings, and their general suspicion of oil companies came out in their attitude to Arctic Gas. This media slant effectively countered the slick and expensive public relations campaign of the pipeline company to sell its project. Arctic Gas frequently complained that its critics got much better coverage than its own spokesmen.[25] On the corporate side only Bob Blair seemed to possess the flair to capture attention in the media.

Berger was fortunate in having a very able commission counsel in Ian Scott of Toronto, and he used him in ways not traditional for Canadian inquiries. He split off Scott and the inquiry staff from his own office and made them an independent party to the hearings. Scott was free then to take a participatory role in the hearings with vigorous cross-examination and production of his own witnesses in areas where he felt this was needed. Normally, the role of commission counsel was a more neutral one to clarify the record. As a result of this "independent party" status, Scott could have no private advisory role to the commissioner but could only speak to him through the public proceedings of the inquiry. At the end of the hearings, the inquiry staff presented their recommendations formally to Berger in a huge document that all other parties were given the opportunity to comment on. The commissioner, in turn, was in no way bound by their recommendations, although obviously they had influence on the final report. Here, Berger had resorted to American-style counsel and staff and the system worked well. Scott and his staff played a crucial role throughout the hearings and were far more involved and effective than their counterparts, the counsel for the NEB. However, for some on the corporate side this interventionist approach was a disturbing deviation from the norm, for it increased their problems in protecting their witnesses.

When Berger came to issue his rulings on the nature of the inquiry, he rejected the two main contentions of Arctic Gas on the timing and scope of the hearings. Although there would not be "any undue delay" in beginning, all parties would get a fair opportunity to prepare for the hearings; Berger refused to recognize that he had any responsibility to Arctic Gas in its battles with El Paso in Washington. On the scope of the hearings, he was even more emphatic. "I take no narrow view of my terms of reference." The inquiry was not confined to consideration of a pipeline application but related "to the whole future of the North." Such directions gave the hearings a magnitude "without precedent in the history of our country."[26] Berger left no one in doubt about the wide vision he had for his commission, and he made this at a time when parties could still protest his interpretation in the final sessions of the preliminary hearings.

Another of the key areas Berger had to rule on was native land claims, which Goldie wished to see excluded. Once again, Arctic Gas saw its arguments rejected. Berger acknowledged that the inquiry was not to decide the extent of native land claims, but he insisted that the native groups should be allowed to present the evidence on traditional land use and occupation, which is the basis of those claims. This would provide an "essential focus" for considering the impact of the pipeline on native society and would also help to ensure that Arctic Gas would be able to meet its commitment that the pipeline could be built without prejudice to the land claims.[27] This would hardly be possible unless Arctic Gas knew the nature and extent of the land claims. With language like this, Michael Goldie could be in no doubt as to what lay ahead for Arctic Gas in the Yellowknife hearings. Berger did, however, reject several of the public interest group arguments to broaden the hearings further. He refused to include provision for the consideration of corporate revenue that would flow to the Delta producers or the macro-economic questions of national economic impacts to be covered by the National Energy Board. He also dismissed the native arguments for assessment of the Great Bear Hydro Project at least until more concrete evidence could be presented that it was under serious consideration as a support system for the pipeline.

Never before had a commission been appointed with such a wide mandate to search out the future impacts of a large development project. Traditionally in Canada, we have avoided systematic analysis of the social costs of economic development. This field of study requires a long-term data base often covering social indicators that are difficult to quantify and impossible to evaluate in dollars. The money has seldom been available for such studies, except in a superficial fashion by the applicant for a project. Following construction there has been little interest from government or the corporate sector to raise doubts about the success of projects in place. As a result, Canadians have been largely ignorant of the social costs that result from economic development. Also, these social costs are often borne by low-income Canadians who are least able to protect their interests or communicate their problems to the country as a whole. In addition, the evidences of social cost have a tendency to disappear – through death and migrations from the original site. For instance, some of the casualties of the James Bay Project will flee from the watersheds of the Rupert, Eastmain, and La Grande to become additional statistics for welfare, alcoholism, and crime in Montreal. As a result, there has been a built-in tendency to underestimate the social costs and damage of major development projects.[28] This fundamental problem Berger helped to address directly in his hearings because of the background of his staff, the structure for the inquiry, and the personal philosophy of the commissioner.

When Mr. Justice Berger formally opened the Mackenzie Valley Pipeline Inquiry on March 3, 1975, in the glare of television lights, it was nearly a full year since his appointment. The scene was set in the ballroom of the Explorer Hotel (nicknamed Exploitation Hotel by the public interest groups who could not afford its rates), which was jammed by several hundred intervenors, supporters, journalists, and curious locals. The contrast between the cold and dry Arctic air and the overheated and packed hearing room was only equalled by the contrast between the immaculate three-piece suits of some of the corporate brass and the jeans and beads of native groups and their white advisers. Before a word was spoken, the tension between the two conflicting cultures was clearly evident. Berger's own opening comments seemed too vague and low key for the excitement of the moment. Ian Scott, commission counsel, more properly caught the mood of the moment when he admitted his own "trepidation" in commencing an experience unique in Canadian history. On the behalf of the inquiry staff, he promised that the process would be long, detailed, and arduous, and above all "it will be open." Then, in words reflecting his own aspirations and those of the public interest groups: "Sir, it is our hope that by this effort the Inquiry will be a model for the planning of great national developments in the future."[29] In that electric atmosphere, there was an intense feeling of excitement and of uncertainty because no one was sure what lay ahead.

Following Scott was Pierre Genest, the able and amiable counsel for Arctic Gas who had replaced Michael Goldie, whose ponderous style was more appropriate for the more formal National Energy Board hearings on the pipeline. Genest was an excellent choice: he was one of Canada's most distinguished corporate lawyers and his charm and bubbling sense of humour lulled targets of his cross-examination into a false sense of security. To the critics of the pipeline, Genest's well-rounded figure and less formal dress did not fit the image of a Bay Street lawyer. His opening address centred on two themes basic to the Arctic Gas case: Canada required the pipeline to meet energy shortages that would be with us by 1980; the "north as a whole needs a sound and stable economic base which will provide wage employment for those who wish to seek it" and leave traditional patterns for those who choose them.[30] This was the standard Arctic Gas argument; all appeared to be proceeding according to form.

Reg Gibbs, the counsel for Foothills Pipelines, followed Genest. Gibbs, with a slightly deceptive manner, was also a notable choice for counsel. His slow speech, his moustache, his intense manner, and his tall, slender frame gave the outward appearance of a small-town lawyer confronting the Bay Street tycoons. This fitted perfectly the overall Foothills strategy of underdog, of the small *Canadian* company confronting the Exxon-backed multinational consortium of Arctic Gas. Gibbs shrewdly played that role throughout the hearings. This morning he opened on a strongly nationalist theme.

He stressed that Foothills as yet was merely a participant in the hearings; but he advised Berger that they would be filing as applicant to build the smaller "Maple Leaf" line from Alberta north to the Delta. He argued that this project would get Canadian supply on stream at a lower capital cost and free of foreign entanglements. He warned that the Arctic Gas application, stripped of its rhetoric and detailed technology, constituted "a threat and danger to the whole of the Canadian people and the Canadian nation." How can there be Canadian control when only five of the twenty corporate sponsors are genuinely Canadian? In addition, he raised the spectre of a possible U.S. government intervention. "I am sure that we are all sufficiently familiar with world politics to know that nothing will be permitted to interfere with the sustenance which that gas flow will represent." Gibbs felt it was incredible, after the history of the CPR and so many other systems that followed all-Canadian routes, that we should succumb to building "the equivalent of a Panama Canal across western and northern Canada." This type of sharply nationalistic attack infuriated Arctic Gas, even though it was largely irrelevant to Berger's terms of reference. Gibbs also tried to make use of regional prejudices to attract support. He spoke: "I grew up in an area secure in the knowledge which I am sure is shared by northerners that the road to Toronto is paved with good intentions."[31] Needless to say, the Arctic Gas head office was in Toronto. Foothills, whose application was still months from being completed, had to play for time; its strategy was to attack the basic "foreign" structure of Arctic Gas because it was not ready to debate the nuts and bolts of the rival projects. From the opening day there was no love lost between Foothills and Arctic Gas.

Following Gibbs came Russ Anthony for CARC, who continued some of his earlier arguments and concentrated on public access, public participation, and public accountability. In the development of northern policy during the 1968-72 period "conscious efforts were made to exclude the public. Not even Parliament was informed." Berger was entering an area where there was considerable cynicism of government intentions, especially with the NEB helping to plan the pipeline. Anthony charged that the government had not co-operated with the inquiry. The list of government reports was not filed until well after the November 30, 1974, deadline, and when CARC requested production of the documents, the government had not complied. In addition, the government list of reports was incomplete. Thus, the inquiry had been launched without the benefit of this promised research.

In the last few days, Anthony noted, newspaper reports had stated that the Department of the Environment had been instructed (apparently by cabinet order) not to intervene in the Berger hearings; hence, the one group of scientists who had done field studies but were not in the pay of Arctic Gas would be unavailable to testify on their work. The apparent attempt of the government to exclude this evidence rekindled suspicion that the government had made up its mind on the pipeline and was not interested in a full public inquiry. CARC appeared to be suggesting that this alleged conspiracy of government and applicant could subvert the good intentions of Berger and his staff. These charges did nothing to improve the already tense relations between the government and CARC. CARC had every intention of using subpoena to get this government evidence before the Commission.

In closing, CARC attempted to protect its virginity; it claimed to be neither for nor against a Mackenzie Valley Pipeline: it was involved to assist in a "full and complete study of the issue."[32] From its opening statement, CARC clearly was determined to force full public disclosure of federal research, which must have created a few problems for Berger, who had no assurance that Ottawa would co-operate.

Glen Bell, who acted as a unified counsel for the Brotherhood and the Métis Association, next moved to the podium to address the inquiry. He repeated some of the concerns voiced in the preliminary hearings, especially the belief that the hearings were the best way of getting their position on the land claims before the wider audience of the people of Canada. They resented the Prime Minister's comparison of the pipeline with the building of the CPR, which was "a disaster" for southern native people. To avoid a similar fate for northern natives, they must have their land claims settled before any pipeline, for the project would "have an intolerably prejudicial effect" on the negotiations. Bell was obviously annoyed with Genest's professed concern for the native people, which he believed was "hypocrisy." In the thousands of pages of filed evidence from Arctic Gas, only eleven related to the socio-economic concerns of native people, including the "hollow promise of jobs" that will disappear with the end of construction, and even these jobs are really for non-natives imported from the south, Bell insisted. This line of argument, which was clear and emphatic from the opening day, remained one of the great weaknesses of the Arctic Gas case through the whole hearings.

John Bayly followed as joint counsel for COPE and the Inuit Tapirisat of Canada (ITC), whose position on the land claims was very similar to that outlined for the Dene. They rejected the Arctic Gas position on compensation because their concern was not for cash but to retain the use of the lands themselves. Also, the Inuit of the Delta were particularly concerned that Berger investigate thoroughly the impacts of the gas gathering and processing facilities to be located there, not just the trunk pipeline as in his terms of reference.[33]

With all the publicity for the native and environmental activities, it was often forgotten that other serious "public interest" concerns were represented to Berger through the Northwest Territories Association of Municipalities and the N.W.T. Chambers of Commerce. Murray Sigler for the Association of Municipalities painted a dark picture of the problems of municipal government that could be intensified by major development. They desperately needed the time and fiscal base to provide in advance the services for any major influx of people to work on the pipeline, he said, and they had to prepare serviced land for new buildings, the social services for human casualties, and so on. They did not want the incredible problems of Fort McMurray repeated north of 60°. It was fine for the federal officials to make all their grand pronouncements but it was the local municipalities "who will be responsible for picking up the pieces and dealing with the social and economic aftermath."[34] With the end of the first day, it was already evident that there were deep-rooted differences between the parties and tensions on some of the key issues. All seemed reasonably happy with the format Berger had devised and with his own independence to consider the case on its merits. Berger must, however, have had a few worries about his ability to deliver a fair settlement, especially in light of the government's clear commitment to northern development. All in all, however, it seemed to be a good beginning in Yellowknife. Unfortunately, political storms were brewing further south.

On the very day of the opening of the Berger Inquiry, Tommy Douglas of the NDP rose in the House of Commons and asked the Acting Prime Minister whether he could assure the House that the government would wait until Berger's report had been received and considered before making any decision on the pipeline. Mitchell Sharp refused to give such an undertaking and the fat was in the fire.[35] The news was wired to Yellowknife, where it seemed to raise doubts about the government's commitment to Berger and his hearings. Within the public interest groups, there had always been doubt about the government's sincerity; now it seemed to be confirmed. Ottawa might not wait for Berger to report. The *News of the North* concluded that Berger and the inquiry staff were "confronted with the strongest evidence that the federal government does not intend to take it seriously." Now it was "becoming increasingly reasonable to suspect" that the inquiry was "simply a fraudulent public relations gimmick staged by the federal government." NDP leader Ed Broadbent, who was in Yellowknife, made the most devastating comment of all: "Judge Berger will have to ask himself whether it is morally legitimate to carry on with the Inquiry."[36] Although Berger never made any official comment on this matter, later in the week when one of the witnesses apologized for taking a great deal of time, the commissioner said with a firm tone but a twinkle in his eye, "My time isn't running out."[37] Although it was obviously meant as a humorous aside, it appeared to be his reply to those who might clip his wings or hurry his proceedings.

For the rest of the first week of March, the inquiry heard "overview" evidence of the history, geography, economics, and peoples of the Mackenzie Valley. All of these "expert" speakers were invited by commission counsel to give background papers to introduce the various topics to the intervenors and staff. It was an interesting comment on Canadian scholarship that some of them were from outside the country, such as June Helm from Iowa. Most of this was factual and relatively non-controversial until Thursday afternoon, when Dr. Stewart Jamieson presented his economic overview. Berger had intended and the various counsel had agreed that the overview evidence would be presented without cross-examination. Jamieson's evidence was such a clear attack on the economic assumptions implicit in the Arctic Gas application that Pierre Genest demanded the right of cross-examination. Berger readily agreed to the right of recall of witnesses for cross-examination at the appropriate point when the hearings were dealing with that area of evidence.[38]

While the overview evidence was being presented, CARC raised serious objection to the absence of Department of the Environment witnesses and the difficulty in getting government documents. It warned that it would not be ready to commence Phase II of the hearings on schedule. CARC was also facing added costs, for any public interest group using the subpoena powers of the inquiry would have to pay the expenses of these witnesses, which was beyond its financial resources. CARC requested commission counsel to telex the Minister of the Environment requesting that departmental experts be made available to the inquiry at government expense or for commission counsel to arrange for them to appear and cover their costs. CARC argued that the people of Canada would be shocked to learn that the agency of government responsible for protecting the environment would not appear and that the public interest groups would be left to bring forward the expertise and research financed by public funds. If this failed, CARC might ask for adjournment "until this information can be available to the Inquiry."[39]

Ian Scott contacted directly Jeanne Sauvé, the Minister of the Environment, and even flew off to Edmonton on the weekend to talk to ministry officials to ensure that the logistics for government witnesses were all arranged. The Department of the Environment then agreed to make available in Yellowknife published and unpublished material relevant to the pipeline. However, it warned that this material was to be "available to the Inquiry only, and for no other purpose."[40] Clearly, the ministry had been prodded into this disclosure policy by the political prominence of Berger and it wanted to emphasize that this decision did not constitute a precedent for any future requests. Nor did it apply to government agencies such as the National Energy Board or Crown corporations like Petro-Canada.[41] Although CARC had achieved significant progress toward public disclosure, its victory was limited in scope and confined to these hearings alone. It had failed to achieve any basic change in federal policy on public information.

On March 11 the Berger Inquiry began its main task of the detailed assessment of the Arctic Gas application, commencing with geotechnical and routing questions. The number of curious onlookers rapidly dwindled as the tedium of detailed cross-examination became the dominant feature. Few could get very excited about brittle fracture probability rates and crack arrestors. Engineering jargon was another of the linguistic barriers within the inquiry. On the technical questions Berger was fortunate to have strong competence in the Environmental Protection Board, his own support staff under Dr. John Fyles, and the witnesses brought forward by the inquiry counsel. The work of assessment was also greatly assisted by having two applicants who delighted in showing any weakness in the other, providing it did not raise doubts about its own project. The content of the next year and a half of hearings broke down into four general areas – geotechnical, biological, social, and economic. As these subjects were being probed simultaneously at both the Berger and the NEB hearings, they will be dealt with in separate thematic chapters later in the book.

In spite of all the public relations efforts, the inquiry proceeded only with the sullen acquiescence and even some open hostility of pro-development northern whites. They believed that their own prosperity was dependent on the pipeline providing a powerful economic stimulus for small business and professional services. Many of these people had come north in expectation of a resource boom that always seemed to be delayed for some reason beyond their control. For some of these people, the pipeline was a symbol of unrealized ambition, including an inflated view of its economic benefits to the North as a whole. Development was like a mirage on the horizon. They were not opposed to land claims; they only wanted a speedy settlement to clear the way for development. In addition, the royalties from gas production and the taxation from the pipeline would bring significant new territorial revenues to support local services and strengthen the movement for provincial status. To this segment of the northern population, Berger was perceived as a threat to their future prosperity.

The publisher of *News of the North*, Colin Alexander, in his book, *Angry Society*, denounced the inquiry: "Judge Berger has permitted his hearings to become the sounding board for radicals of all kinds" while the views of elected officials are ignored. In an emotional outburst David Searle, Speaker of the Legislative Council, stated: "We must cast out the socialists. We must call out their names loud and clear – Mr. Berger, Mr. Watkins, to mention only two – and tell them they are not liked, they are unwanted and ask them to leave." These individuals believed that only one side of the story got presented before Berger and the grievances of the native people had been blown out of proportion by southern bleeding hearts and do-gooders. "It has extended in some instances to a 'hate-the-white-man' campaign; it has promoted racism, apartheid, and even a form of secession from the established Canadian constitution." Even the churches had jumped on the bandwagon "to revitalize their flagging membership in the South" and without properly consulting the northern clergy.

In this view, the Brotherhood leaders were only a small elite who had manipulated their own members and were now doing the same to the federal officials. Dick Turner wrote: "I feel that the Brotherhood leaders represent no more than a few individuals who have learned to exploit the guilt-ridden southern do-gooders to help the Brotherhood obtain federal subsidies. Payments designed not only to fund their lives but also to fund a host of legal battles aimed at further extending the funding." Some of these reactions were extreme in their wording, but they were based on a widely held fear that if the Dene won their battles, northern whites would be relegated to second-class citizens. As *News of the North* stressed: "Citizen plus (special status) implies the existence of citizen minus."

With the news of major oil and gas strikes, northerners had hoped that their area would no longer be an economic backwater of the country dependent on handouts and subsidies from Ottawa. They particularly resented the southern advisers, for they argued that these people would not have to stick around and live with the consequences. Most frontiers breed a class ideology of entrepreneurial individualism; many northern whites reflected those feelings and aspirations. They also saw the southern media as a further aspect of the conspiracy to "freeze" the North. In their eyes, these writers exhibited the worst aspects of yellow journalism, being "naively and simplistically sympathetic to every new extremist outburst."[42] Given the nature of the hearings and the economic dreams of many northern whites, these feelings of frustration were understandable. The hearings heightened the tensions between the white business community and the native organizations, but the experience was part of a maturing process for both.

As has already been indicated, the CBC acquired a semi-official role with its extensive and multilingual local coverage. But in the process some of the CBC staff became emotionally involved with the ongoing debate. At the Norman Wells community hearings, Whit Fraser, the voice of the CBC to southern listeners and manager of the crew, spoke out against the pipeline as an official witness to the inquiry. He had heard with a growing sense of frustration some of the white opinion at this Imperial Oil town, which in his view was ignoring the lessons from Alaska.[43] Fraser recognized that his action was a breach of normal professional conduct but was prepared to accept the consequences for what he believed in. Several prominent northerners protested all the way to the Prime Minister that Fraser must be removed because he had abandoned any commitment to objectivity. The incident led to extensive correspondence in official channels between CBC management and the inquiry, for Berger was concerned that the controversy not lead to a cutback in CBC coverage. Although Fraser received a reprimand from Andrew Cowan, the head of the Northern Service, in a later letter to Berger, Cowan noted: "Personally I support everything which Whit Fraser said."[44]

The incident showed the problems for the media in retaining their neutrality covering this type of hearing where feelings ran deep. However, for many northern whites it was merely further evidence of their own firm belief that the southern media were committed to the native/environmentalist position. They resented the image they were given of reactionary rednecks, for they believed that the liberal idealism of some reporters led them to simplify the very complex social problems of the North. As southern attitudes and Ottawa politicians would be influenced by these reports, they feared they were locked into a "no win" situation in which whatever they said was bound to be misunderstood. As a result, many whites never bothered to participate in the public hearings of the inquiry.

A unique feature of the Berger hearings was the work of the Environmental Protection Board (EPB) headed by Carson Templeton of Winnipeg. The organization had been created originally by Bob Blair and Alberta Gas Trunk in 1970 as an independent environmental assessment body paid for by the pipeline company but operating at arm's length from it. When Alberta Gas Trunk entered the Arctic Gas consortium, it brought the EPB along. However, when Blair left the consortium in 1974, the terms of reference of the EPB were radically changed. The Toronto-based Arctic Gas management wanted no consultants who were not subject to the normal corporate accountability. He who pays the piper calls the tune.

In November, 1974, the EPB was advised that funding would be restricted to attendance at the hearings, thus eliminating any further research. This precluded its evaluation of the cross-Delta lateral or any of the other route changes, which now totalled over 450 miles. Yet the EPB participated vigorously in the hearings with its engineering and scientific expertise and produced an impressive four-volume report, which, in addition to specific analysis, called for the development of an environmental code and a single government "super agency" to oversee the project. In January, 1976, about halfway through the hearings and with its funding exhausted, the EPB withdrew and formally dissolved, although Carson Templeton remained active.[45] Later, Blair reconstructed the board for studies of the Alaska Highway project. This experiment demonstrated Blair's own belief that his company would profit from independent assessment and could afford public airing of weaknesses in the project. His idealism was just about unique in the North American oil and gas business. It did, however, give him greater credibility with environmentalists who recognized the usefulness of this initiative. The materials produced by the EPB were used widely at both Berger and the NEB and even found their way into university curricula across the country.

Another of the unique features of the Berger Inquiry was the community hearings held in thirty-five settlements potentially affected by the pipeline. All local residents were encouraged to express their own views in their own language and in their own way, free of the threat of lawyers and cross-examination. Counsel for the applicants were confined to general factual statements that might clear up misunderstanding about their clients' projects. The judge always stayed until everyone had his chance to speak. About 1,000 people contributed to the record at these various stops. In some communities a sizable percentage of the residents presented their views; at Old Crow, with

Figure 7.
Communities Visited by the Berger Inquiry. From Berger Report, vol. 2.

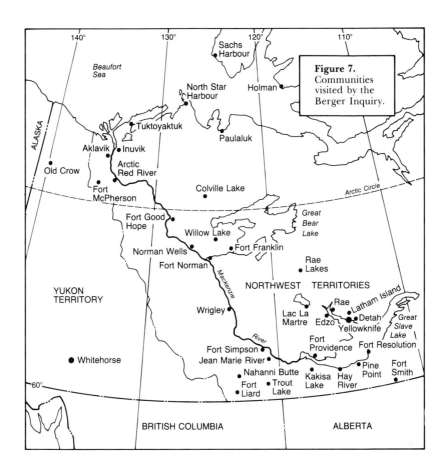

Figure 7.
Communities visited by the Berger Inquiry.

the summer heat at close to 90°F, about eighty of the 200 local residents spoke. The testimony was often rambling and anecdotal in nature, very different from the more formal presentations of expert witnesses in Yellowknife.

Professor Michael Jackson, special counsel to the inquiry, organized these settlement hearings and timed them to avoid conflict with local activities on the land. Staff members tried to prepare the communities in advance for the judge's arrival, and due to the extreme premium on accommodation the inquiry entourage was strictly limited. The wide degree of participation and the relative unanimity of views allowed Berger in his report to generalize about native opposition to the pipeline without having to rely solely on the comments of the activist leaders.[46] The people's intense commitment to the land emerged clearly and eloquently while details from hunting and trapping gave Berger biological insights unknown to the expert witnesses. On the social impact questions, these hearings were invaluable because, as Berger stressed, "Their thoughts were not filtered through a screen of jargon. They were talking about their innermost concerns and fears."[47]

Berger's own approach and manner also contributed to the success of these community sessions. Above all, he showed immense patience in sitting for twelve or fourteen hours a day to hear the people's views in spite of the high degree of repetition even within individual statements. The respect he achieved in spite of the cultural chasm is best summed up in the frequent use of the term "our judge" in referring to the commissioner. This was a great mark of respect from a people who felt alienated from the normal processes of government. At some of the settlements, the sessions lasted for twelve hours from early afternoon until after midnight. Then Berger would adjourn the proceedings to join the local people in a baseball game or drum dance. For those familiar with the racial and social tensions in the North, it was an amazing achievement to see this rapport between the commissioner and the community.

As the northern hearings approached conclusion, Berger did a quick trip through the major southern cities from Vancouver to Halifax, holding hearings and offering the local media an opportunity to see the inquiry in action. These southern hearings brought out very little that was new, but they did demonstrate the intensity of feelings on the issues the inquiry was addressing. The majority of the participants presented motherhood statements that were sympathetic to the native rights and environmental causes, but a few of the spokesmen reflected the profound misgivings of some from the corporate sector with the whole approach of Berger. These feelings were particularly strong in Alberta and the oil industry, where pipeline critics were equated with communism. Their strongest and most articulate spokesman was Mayor R. Sykes of Calgary, who appeared at the hearings in his city. Although his views were extreme, they represented a small but financially influential segment of Canadian society.

Sykes attacked what he termed the misguided attempts to preserve under the meaningless title of culture a "primitive life of insecurity and hardship." If they knew a better life, they would hardly wish it on their children. When the romance and the rhetoric are stripped away, Sykes claimed, the basic facts show the native peoples have existed below the poverty line or on welfare. All Canadians have an equal interest in the North and its resources. Ottawa should not sterilize the North to expand the mistaken Indian reserve system and chain Canada to a rate of energy progress of "a square stone wheel." We are all equally descended from immigrants, Sykes stated, the only difference being the timing of arrival. Sykes was "amazed that Canadians have tolerated" and even financed all the talk about land claims from people "who would in many cases rather talk than work," but "many Canadians have had enough of this nonsense and are not prepared to tolerate much more." They had had "enough of the politics of blackmail" and "threats of terrorism and violence" from domestic or imported troublemakers. Government must "deal decisively with this intolerable situation." Project delays were far more damaging to Canada than any of the other factors under scrutiny by Berger. If there had been a similar commission for the CPR or the Trans-Canada Pipeline, neither of them would ever have been built. "Let's get on with the job," Sykes implored, "build the line and build it now."

Mayor Sykes claimed that while he did not question the "integrity and good faith" of Berger and his inquiry, he had profound misgivings about the process. Public participation should not be "a pooling of ignorance or a process of intimidation." The Commission has provided a "platform for troublemakers attacking the territorial unity of Canada, threatening the energy resource supplies of all Canadians, and setting up claims that some Canadians have more rights" than others.

He identified four main areas where the inquiry had done harm. The consultative process had been used consciously and unconsciously to exploit the fears of ignorant and simple people. Second, the process could destroy public confidence and faith in the ability of science and technology to cope with the construction problems of the North. In Calgary, where so much of the engineering and research work had been done, technology was a basic article of faith not to be questioned. Next Sykes moved on to an equally fundamental ingredient in the Canadian way of life. The inquiry was in the process of undermining public confidence in the "good faith and integrity of private enterprise in a country which depends upon private enterprise for survival." Finally, he believed the process will "create distrust of the principle of consultation." Simple, unsophisticated people, when consulted, will come to believe that their views will have some "identifiable effect on decisions" even if their comments have "little of rational value." They will come to believe that sheer numbers, sheer emotion, the head count system "can conquer fact and reason." This seemed to be a basic comment on the shortcomings of democracy.

"The inevitable result will be shocking disillusionment and great bitterness, which will be exploited politically." The Berger Commission, according to Mayor Sykes, was "a disastrous and costly mistake" that has eroded Canadian unity by pitting the special rights demanded by one group against the interests of all Canadians. Such a prospect was an economic threat to those Canadians "who work and save and stand on their own feet."[48]

Although many would strongly disagree with some of these comments, they are important for understanding the corporate response to the inquiry. Mayor Sykes had the honesty to say in public what many corporate spokesmen believed and discussed among themselves in the privacy of the Petroleum Club or the coffee alcove at the National Energy Board. Berger was seen as a dangerous revolutionary because he did not accept the primacy of corporate development. He was part of the wider movement to press social and environmental concerns that were a threat to business in their own right but in addition became the rationale for increased government intervention. These concerns were also policy areas where most petroleum executives, trained to concentrate on cash flow and the bottom line, were ill at ease. They had trouble distinguishing the relative seriousness of the issues or else dismissed them as an unproductive use of capital. Many of these executives were hindered by the weakness of their own public affairs departments in analysing and assessing these ideas and their public support. One of the great strengths of Blair and the Foothills' approach was that they recognized the profound changes under way within society and tried to meet Berger on his own ground, taking seriously the criteria he had defined for his inquiry. Arctic Gas assumed that his terms and conditions were an aberration from reality, which Ottawa decision-makers did not take seriously. To this thinking, the Berger Inquiry was a sop to the cranks. This attitude reflected the traditional approaches and the effectiveness of the powerful oil and gas lobby. But with public attitudes changing in the 1970's, the political process was influenced by those changes. The failure of Arctic Gas to perceive those changes cost the consortium dearly in the final decisions.

In October, 1976, prior to hearing final argument, commission counsel presented its formal summation and recommendations to Justice Berger. This 800-page loose-leaf printed volume was distributed to all intervenors for their comments before the hearings closed,[49] which demonstrated a further aspect of Berger's "open process." He stressed: "I felt they should be made public so that all participants at the Inquiry would have the fullest opportunity to challenge, support, modify, or ignore their proposals."[50]

Their advice to the commissioner could be rebutted in the same fashion as the evidence of any other party. This Staff Report was largely a compilation of the key evidence under topical headings; it bore little resemblance to the final report in its format although it drew attention to areas that turned out to be central to Berger's own argument.

One of the huge issues the Staff Report attempted to address was the problem of how government would handle a project of this magnitude. The jurisdiction of about fifteen ministries, from Health and Welfare to External Affairs, would be involved. The report recommended, as had the Environmental Protection Board, that the federal government should establish a single super-agency to regulate all the technical, environmental, social, and economic aspects of the project; this would increase the speed and efficiency in meeting hundreds of government regulations. Rather than have to deal with dozens of government bodies, the pipeline company would only have to work through one co-ordinating body. This would require important switches within bureaucratic jurisdictions, but it attracted wide support as a means to cut red tape and ministerial delays.[51]

When released, the Staff Report attracted little media attention because of its awkward organization and ambiguous wording. Only Jeff Carruthers recognized its significance in weakening the Arctic Gas application and as a hint of what was to come.[52] However, it did evoke worries within the Arctic Gas consortium even though they were expecting criticism from the Berger staff. One of their consultants, botanist Larry Bliss, attacked the report for its failure to consider properly terrain and vegetation questions.[53] However, this volley was really only a continuation of some of the battles from the hearings.

Following completion of final argument in November, 1976, Berger returned to Vancouver to ponder the wording of his report. With the NEB bogged down in tedious infighting between the applicants, it turned out that he had more time than he had expected. Berger was desperately anxious that his own report would be out in time to influence the final deliberations at the NEB, but he was also aware of many critics waiting to pounce if there were any weaknesses in it. With a herculean effort, he and his personal staff had the report completed in April for release in early May. With the NEB still in session, he had kept to his schedule and the Board would have to take notice of his analysis and recommendations.

The report was shrewdly divided into two separate parts for separate audiences. The first volume, which he rushed into print, covered the basic commentary on the public policy issues, while the second, which came six months later, dealt with the technical questions of the terms and conditions for a pipeline. For most people, volume I *is* the

Berger Report. As a royal commission report, it is unique for its hundreds of photographs, its maps and diagrams, and its clear, eloquent prose. It was written with a clear sense of conviction for the environment and the social problems of the North. In many places, Berger lets the people's own words speak for themselves, and their words carry the ring of conviction. In reading the report today, it is timeless in its analysis. The issue was the Mackenzie Valley Pipeline but the themes are relevant to every northern project of the 1980's, for the clash between the industrial frontier moving north and the traditional societies already there will continue for many decades.

A detailed analysis of the report would hardly be to the point: it is best to read it in the original and not in someone else's summary form. At $5 it remained the best book bargain in Canada. Berger saw the North as occupying a position of economic dependency; its own fragile society could be overwhelmed by projects like the pipeline. While omitting any ideological terms, his report was a further contribution to the staples thesis. Mel Watkins noted the Innis influence on the structure of his economic analysis. "It is clear that Berger understands Canada much better than do most of our historians and social scientists" and has created a report "with intellectual credentials that have not been in evidence for almost forty years, since . . . the Rowell-Sirois Report."[54] The report was strongest in its presentation of the complex interrelationship between technical, environmental, social, cultural, and economic factors. It was weakest in its presentation of the way in which renewable resources could meet the future demands of a growing native population.

Much of the controversy surrounding the report involved its two principal recommendations: that pipelines should be permanently prohibited from crossing the environmentally fragile North Slope of the Yukon and that any pipeline in the Mackenzie Valley should be delayed for ten years to allow for settlement and implementation of the native land claims. In the first of these points he was severing the Arctic Gas system from its main source of natural gas at Prudhoe Bay, which, needless to say, was not received with indifference by the project sponsors. But it also enshrined the principle that projects could be stopped by environmental veto, which astounded many business organizations.

Berger openly attacked this point of view in his report. "There is a myth that terms and conditions that will protect the environment can be imposed, no matter how large a project is proposed." There is the assumption that when enough studies and reports have been done "all will be well. It is an assumption that implies that choice we intend to take. It is an assumption that does not hold in the North."

A few mitigative measures were not enough to protect critical habitat; if areas essential for caribou calving were cut through with a pipeline, the impacts would be too great a price to pay. The only solution he saw was that development had to be excluded.[55] For many Canadian businessmen, this environmental veto was a dangerous precedent that could easily be applied to other projects. They also felt it was unfair to Arctic Gas, which had spent so much money on environmental research.

The second major recommendation involved the ten-year moratorium on pipeline construction in the Mackenzie Valley. Business found this provision equally offensive, for business had no responsibility for the delays in the negotiations. If settling the land claims was a necessary precondition for development, why had the government wasted the decade since 1968? Once again this recommendation affected the applicants very unequally. It was crippling to the Arctic Gas proposal, because the United States would not wait a decade for the moratorium to be lifted; Foothills, on the other hand, could live with the consequences merely by delaying the Dempster lateral until 1987. The business community was upset with these two recommendations because they went beyond the "terms and conditions" for constructing a pipeline to the more basic issue of whether the pipeline should be built. For some in Toronto and New York, the recommendations involved a built-in bias against the multinational consortium and in favour of the smaller Canadian alternative; yet the main component of the Foothills proposal, the Alaska Highway pipeline, had not been examined by the inquiry. Business critics suspected that behind the social and environmental rhetoric of the Berger Report were clear socialist and nationalist motives. Following the release of the report, they did not abandon their belief that Arctic Gas would win out. They continued to believe that the NEB and the cabinet would not be swayed by Berger's type of arguments.

Arctic Gas had expected trouble from the Berger Report and had tried to plan counter-moves. It had carefully arranged in advance to have the *Globe and Mail* publish a major article by the company chairman on the page opposite the editorial page on the day the Berger Report was to be released. It was a strident, alarmist article: without Mackenzie Delta gas, Canada faced energy shortages equal to twenty-one new Syncrude plants or forty-two new Pickering nuclear power plants.[56] But the strategy to pre-empt Berger misfired completely when Jeff Carruthers scooped the country for the *Globe* with the details of the Berger Report twelve hours before its release. As a result, the Carruthers story provided the headline and feature story on page one in the same issue as the Arctic Gas article. Later in the day, when the report was formally released, all the other papers gave it equally prominent treatment. Then that evening, when CBC did an hour television special on the report, the network chose one of the prime critics of the project to co-host the show out of Toronto, while Vern Horte, the president of Arctic Gas, was cut off after twenty seconds when he attempted to present the company's position. The whole day was a public relations nightmare from which the company never recovered.

In addressing the land claims issue, Berger was well aware of the political minefield he was entering. Yet he faced the issue with a clarity and determination that officials in Ottawa had scrupulously avoided. In his view, the settlement must be part of a "fundamental re-ordering" of the relationship between white and native, in order to entrench their rights to the land and to lay the foundations for "native self-determination under the Constitution of Canada." The claims were a means of establishing a new "social contract" based on the concept that they constitute "distinct peoples in history" and enjoy special status under the British North America Act, the treaties, and the Indian Act. Alien political models, he said, have been imposed on them, rather than their being given the opportunity to adopt their own Dene and Inuit models reflecting their traditions of consensus and local decision-making.[57]

For some of the policy-makers in Ottawa this analysis was profoundly disturbing. It appeared to be vague and dangerous idealism, arousing native expectations that could never be fulfilled. The report appeared to be adopting some of the phraseology of the Dene Declaration, such as "self-determination," without any clear definition of what this meant or how it could be fitted into a viable constitutional framework. In Ottawa, the Dene Declaration was understood by few but feared by many as a separatist and Marxist document. Anthony Westell reflected some of these corporate and government fears when he wrote: "It is not surprising when native leaders in the first flush of ambition put forward such fanciful ideas but it is regrettable when a man of Berger's experience and prestige endorses them."[58]

Yet Berger was correct in his direct approach to the land claims issue – there were too many in Ottawa who wished to postpone a settlement indefinitely. He drew attention also to the comprehensive nature of the claims and the continuing importance of the land-based activities that many were unaware of. New approaches were certainly needed if the dismal failures of southern reserves were not to be repeated. As the Dene and the Inuit were still groping to define the political institutions needed to entrench their cultural goals, it would have been presumptuous of Berger to spell out what they should be.

Figure 8.
Financial Post Cartoon of Berger, May 21, 1977.

As expected, the reaction to the Berger Report was as varied as the opinions about northern development. Native leaders, environmentalists, and the media were generally in support, but there were exceptions in each group. Rick Hardy of the N.W.T. Métis Association complained that the moratorium "dooms the Mackenzie Valley south of Fort MacPherson to a welfare economy for a long time" and the N.W.T. territorial assembly censured the report in an 8-1 vote. While many southern commentators recognized the legitimacy of the environmental and native claims, they had lingering doubts about the adequacy of northern energy supplies. Richard Gwyn caught some of these feelings of ambivalence when he wrote: "The point to be decided, though, is whether, even if Berger is right, we southerners can afford his ideals." Alastair Gillespie, Minister of Energy, Mines, and Resources, warned the press that the Arctic Gas proposal was still very much alive; renegade Tory Jack Horner snorted: "If Berger had been around a hundred years ago, we would still have the buffalo herds in the West and the CPR wouldn't be built." The Toronto Stock Exchange largely ignored the report for there was little movement in the share prices of Imperial, Gulf, and Shell, the Delta producers. The market was already well aware of the small size and marginal economics of Delta gas production.[59]

With the damage of the Berger Report clearly evident, Arctic Gas attempted to mount a counter-attack with all the means at its disposal.

To fight Berger openly in public was clearly not practicable given the attitude of the media. Instead, Arctic Gas quickly assembled a volume of just over 100 pages to counter his arguments and revive morale among the project supporters. This anti-Berger Report was designed for a select audience of corporate and government officials. The company claimed that he had exaggerated the environmental dangers and assumed the construction of other projects for which they were not responsible. The Alaska Highway route he seemed to favour was 375 miles longer and had not been examined in any detail in the hearings. Copies of this counter-report were quickly distributed to the NEB and others in high places in an attempt to discredit Berger and his recommendations.[60] In addition, the two top executives, Bill Wilder and Vern Horte, toured the country speaking to selected audiences, as did executives of Imperial Oil, who now for the first time began to worry that their great northern project might be in doubt. Intensive lobbying took place on Parliament Hill to try to keep political allies in line. However, key figures were now clearly wavering because of the public response to Berger. Gillespie went off on a private flying trip to view the Alaska Highway Pipeline route for himself and when he returned he sent a private note to the U.S. Energy Secretary, James Schlesinger, emphasizing that the Foothills Alaska Highway Pipeline was now under serious consideration.[61]

At this critical phase, the Arctic Gas consortium was hurt politically by its image of being the creation of the multinational gas companies. With an election expected within a year, no party wished to be seen as the protector of Exxon and opposed to the idealism Berger had come to represent. Consequently, most of the public relations efforts of Arctic Gas were unproductive. As Ron Anderson wrote in his business section column of the *Globe and Mail*: "Arctic Gas has lost a great deal of its credibility in the eyes of the public, in terms of its methods and its motivations."[62] This result was a product of its failure to cope with the new demands of corporate social responsibility it had faced at the Berger Inquiry. In the two months following the release of the report, while the NEB was in the final weeks of its deliberations, Arctic Gas was unable to reverse this loss of momentum.

The Berger Inquiry remains one of the classic case studies of a successful royal commission in Canadian history. It got the government off the hook politically by suggesting a less controversial alternative whereby the Americans could get their gas to market. The inquiry commenced operations in the spring of 1974 and Berger completed the second volume of the report late in 1977. The total cost of the inquiry was approximately $3.5 million, with a further $1.8 million in payments to intervenors.

Was it worth all the money and effort? As the first of the great northern mega-projects, the Mackenzie Valley Pipeline required a thorough appraisal of the geotechnical, environmental, and social problems and this was certainly accomplished. However, Berger tried to do far more – he tried to develop a philosophy for northern development that put a higher priority on social and environmental considerations than on non-renewable energy projects. Royal commissions are invented to provide bold and imaginative answers to politically loaded questions. Berger attempted to fulfil this expectation. He also produced a report that was unique in the history of royal commissions or special inquiries: it became a best-seller overnight. It is ironic that the government could have recouped a portion of the costs of the inquiry had it not signed away the publishing rights to a private company. The huge sales of the volume and its use in many university courses gave it a wide influence on public opinion and some influence on public policy. The readership of volume 1 became nearly global. Several years later Berger got off the plane to visit a remote settlement in the northern territory of Australia and there to greet him were the local aboriginal leaders clutching their copies of the Berger Report. His fame spread to the United Nations, where he was approached to head a new commission for the conservation of whales, but the project failed to muster sufficient support in the complex politics of that organization. This offer was hardly surprising, for Berger had attempted to address universal social issues, not just the specifics of a pipeline.

In the final analysis the inquiry broke new ground in several important ways. In the area of public policy process Berger set new standards for: achieving wide levels of public participation; devising a successful formula for funding public interest interventions; increasing the effectiveness of commission counsel; making the Staff Report a public document subject to debate within the hearings; and separating the hearing process into formal and informal phases. On the content side Berger accorded a new significance to the environmental and social evidence even to the point of an environmental prohibition of development on the North Slope of the Yukon and a ten-year moratorium to protect social priorities in the Mackenzie Valley.

But the report also had to be viewed in a wider context. It assumed standards of corporate social responsibility that executives planning future northern mega-projects will have to study carefully for their own good. It prodded the federal government into taking more seriously its responsibility as trustee for the native people. To be sure, many of these strengths of the Berger Inquiry provoked serious controversy that will last for decades. The bulk of the controversy surrounded the values Berger brought to his interpretation of the evidence and in forging his conclusions. Clear alternative policy directions are surely one of the main reasons for appointing a special inquiry or royal commission; here the Berger Inquiry emphatically fulfilled its mandate. In spite of the controversy generated, it will be remembered as one of the half dozen most important public inquiries since Confederation, which is high praise. Above all, Berger exploited the special inquiry format to range broadly over the policy issues in a way the parallel regulatory hearings at the National Energy Board could not.

CHAPTER 6

The National Energy Board:
The Politics of Pipeline Regulation

The National Energy Board was born out of the controversies and scandal involved in the famous pipeline debate of the 1950's, which focused on the Trans-Canada natural gas system. The Borden Royal Commission on Energy investigated these events and recommended the establishment of a new independent energy regulatory board to remove such complex matters from the partisanship and emotional bickering of the House of Commons. Since its establishment in 1959 the Board has quietly carried through the complex job of regulating interprovincial and international energy transmission.

Often there have been profound differences of opinion between the regions or between producers and consumers. In the early days, before the establishment of the Ministry of Energy, Mines, and Resources in 1966, the Board played a key advisory role in major initiatives such as the National Oil Policy of 1961 and the easing of restrictions on electric power exports in 1963. Through the 1960's most of the decisions, such as marketing surplus oil and gas in the United States, were relatively straightforward. However, since 1972 the Board has been in the centre of vigorous public controversy over its export policies, its pricing decisions, and its pipeline hearings. Most recently there has been a strong industry lobby to emasculate the NEB as part of a wider pattern of deregulation similar to American efforts. The Board has not been the subject of much scholarly analysis. The northern pipeline hearings, the longest in its history, are a useful case study of its strengths and weaknesses and their relationship to the overall energy decision-making in Canada. As a nation we greatly depend on this Board for the independence and the accuracy of its judgements.

The responsibilities of the National Energy Board involve two basic tasks: one as the private adviser to government and the other as the regulator of the industry. As the adviser to the Minister of Energy, Mines and Resources the NEB monitors and reports on virtually all aspects of federal energy policy. Under its act of incorporation, the Board enjoys broad powers to force public disclosures and to recommend action "in the public interest." It has used these powers with great care and caution. In its operations it has tried to avoid confrontation with industry or controversy that could raise embarrassing questions in the House of Commons for the minister. Above all, it has sought to operate within government policy, not striking out with bold initiatives where it might be overruled by cabinet. In their advisory role, members of the Board serve on many interdepartmental committees and task forces – no less than forty-four at the time of the opening of the northern pipeline hearings.[1] They are thus part of the web of government policy formulation, not an independent regulatory board in the American sense of the term. Also, these advisory functions are carried out behind the scenes, out of the view of journalists or public scrutiny.

The major regulatory functions of the Board consist of granting certificates of "public convenience and necessity" for construction of interprovincial and international pipelines and international electrical transmission lines; issuing licences for the export of power, oil, or natural gas or the importing of natural gas; and approving federally regulated tariffs and tolls for pipelines. In the 1970's its public hearings on pipelines, exports, and oil/gas supply became a focus for the national debate on energy policy. It was accused of accepting uncritically data and arguments from multinational oil companies that led to a number of mistakes, such as exporting oil that should have been reserved to supply the domestic market. Thus, the NEB attracted the public attention it had tried to avoid. Originally, its greatest challenge was trying to market surplus oil and gas as an extension of the needs of the industry; then, following the OPEC revolution, oil shortages and sharply rising prices created demands for a much more interventionist role to protect the public interest. Neither its staff nor its philosophy was designed to meet these new challenges.

The 1970's opened with the Board approving large new export contracts, which pleased the Alberta producers anxious to increase their cash flow. However, public criticism began to emerge from those convinced that Canada would now face long-term domestic shortages and evidence seemed to demonstrate that they were right. By 1974 the same oil majors who had pushed for natural gas exports in 1971, based on their figures of a huge surplus in reserves, were now telling the Canadian public that gas shortages by the end of the decade would necessitate the construction of the highly expensive Mackenzie Valley Pipeline. Public interest groups attacked the NEB for its failure to apply rigorously its own rules for a twenty-five-year domestic supply before approving exports. They charged that this indicated a subservience to the multinationals. In addition, in 1974 the NEB suffered the indignity of three court challenges to its procedures or decisions[2] and the resignation of Donald Morgan, a senior official of the NEB Energy Allocations Board, after CBC disclosures that he was financially involved in international petroleum contracts.[3] Clearly, the Board was losing its credibility and meeting increasing opposition, and its structures were in need of overhaul. All these problems were emerging at the very point when the Board was facing its greatest challenge with the northern pipeline applications.

Although there was clear pressure to adopt a more demanding and interventionist approach in dealing with applications before it, changes occurred only slowly in its procedures. The corporate sector was joined by the producing provinces in urging the NEB to keep to its traditional ways. Alberta in particular wanted as little federal regulation as possible. The Board was in a vulnerable position because the Lougheed government was withholding increases in the gas supply needed for industrial expansion in Ontario until domestic prices were increased.[4] As the dozens of volumes of the Arctic Gas application arrived at the NEB late in 1974 and in the early months of 1975, gas policy was already a complex and controversial area where the Board was on the defensive from public criticism.

In a number of important ways the gas supply hearings from November, 1974, to March, 1975, were the preliminary skirmishes in the main battle over the northern pipeline. The Arctic Gas consortium and the Mackenzie Delta producers were well aware that they had to establish that Canada required frontier gas in order to justify the huge expense of the project while the public interest groups were attempting to demonstrate that additional gas in Alberta could delay the need for a pipeline for a decade or two.[5] Following these hearings, the NEB concluded that Canada was facing serious supply/demand shortages by late in the 1970's or early in the 1980's. "If export commitments are to be met, frontier gas if available is needed as soon as it can be connected. Even if export commitments were abrogated, frontier gas would still be needed, for Canadian use, by the mid-1980's."[6] The drastic change in the supply picture from 1970, when large new exports were approved, was blamed on poor drilling results and unforeseen deliverability problems, especially in the new fields of northern British Columbia. In commenting on the report, the minister endorsed its conclusions while urging Canadians to conserve so export commitments could be met "to the greatest extent possible." Earlier in the year Canada had been warned that it would face serious retaliation if the gas contracts to the United States were broken. Two possible actions suggested were cutting the flow of American coal to Ontario and rejection of the Canadian Arctic Gas Pipeline.[7] Such pressures made the gas export issue a sensitive one for both the National Energy Board and the Trudeau cabinet.

Some of the public interest groups were sceptical of the whole scenario being presented to justify the pipeline. They pointed out that subsidiaries of American energy companies had large reserves in Alberta for which they did not as yet have export contracts. Alberta and Southern Gas, a wholly owned subsidiary of Pacific Gas and Electric of California, had 9.7 trillion cubic feet (Tcf) under contract: export licences for 5.1 Tcf, with the remaining 4.6 Tcf being held as a future reserve for California consumption. At this point in 1975 the locked-in reserves of Alberta and Southern alone were roughly equivalent to the total proven reserves found in the Mackenzie Delta. To the public interest groups it seemed only rational that these Alberta reserves should be allocated to the domestic market before Canadian consumers should be forced back on high-cost Arctic gas. Because export prices were higher than domestic, Alberta and Southern had an edge in lining up Alberta reserves.[8]

John Helliwell, an economist from UBC, had been the only non-corporate intervenor to do detailed computer analysis of future deliverability of Canadian natural gas. With a different set of assumptions, he presented a much more optimistic forecast showing that conventional southern reserves would be adequate for many years.[9] Helliwell's work was assailed by many industry spokesmen as technically naive but he defended his position vigorously under fierce cross-examination. The Board, in making its own projections, ignored Helliwell's contentions and presented a very conservative supply scenario. After its mistakes in 1970 with overly liberal supply estimates, it now went to the other extreme.[10] With projected shortages only five or seven years away, the NEB was clearly implying the need for a quick start on the Mackenzie Valley Pipeline. The public interest groups were sceptical of the industry figures because they became too convenient an argument for the higher prices the producers demanded as a necessary condition for further exploration. Also, the arrival of Mackenzie Delta gas in southern Canada would require significant further price increases to allow it to be competitively priced. Thus, there was industry-wide support for the Arctic pipeline because it offered a convenient means to improve profit margins. The NEB gas supply report seemed to be an endorsement of the need for the Arctic Gas system and the price increases that went with it. Arctic Gas appeared to be over the first hurdle at the National Energy Board and running well.

While the gas supply hearings were proceeding, the Board was gearing up for the northern pipeline hearings. Following the receipt of the application, there were six steps it had to follow.

1. In-house assessment of the filed documentation.
2. Deficiency letters issued by the NEB and the written response of the applicant to them.
3. Board order for public hearings and the filing of intent by interested parties.
4. Public hearing.
5. NEB report and recommendation to cabinet.
6. Cabinet approval, modification, or rejection.

The in-house assessment is carried on by Board staff members who over the years have built up considerable expertise on technical, legal, and economic aspects of regulating pipelines. Within the NEB a coordinator is responsible for guiding each project application through the various stages and maintaining liaison with the applicant. The deficiency letters help to alert the applicant to potential problems prior to the public hearings, which may be delayed until the application is in an acceptable state. The letters and the written responses become part of the public record for the hearings. At the Berger Inquiry, the Pipeline Application Assessment Group report provided the same kind of early warning system to all parties.

When the public hearing phase is announced, copies go to all citizens and corporations on the NEB mailing list and advertisements are placed in key newspapers across the country. Any individual or group may apply for intervenor status by explaining the nature of its interest in the case. The Board has the power to reject such applications but has not done so since the early 1970's. Once granted intervenor status, the individual or group is supplied with a copy of the application, including supporting documentation, and has the right to cross-examine witnesses and to present its own written and oral evidence. Evidence presented in the hearings must be sent in advance to all other intervenors. In the northern pipeline hearings this meant the cost of producing and delivering 150 copies. Hearings of any serious matter involve a panel of three drawn from the eleven Board members. The length of any hearing may extend from a day or two to the record set by the northern pipeline hearings of one year and nine months. As a quasi-judicial regulatory agency, the NEB proceedings are more formal and legalistic than the free-wheeling Berger Inquiry. Normally the Board operates beyond media attention since its sessions are dominated by the technical detail of engineering and financial witnesses confronted by the adversarial semantics of corporate lawyers. The language problems at the NEB often have little to do with either official language of the country. Technical jargon is the first line of defence for the harried witness.

After completion of the hearings, the Board usually takes several months to complete its report, which is then sent on to cabinet. The bulk of the report is usually written by staff members, with the exception of the section containing recommendations and conclusions, which is written by the presiding panel. The report will often include deficiencies or requests for further information so approval may be conditional. In a case like the Norman Wells Pipeline Report (1981), the list of deficiencies may be very extensive. Cabinet may reject a project approved by the Board; but any project rejected by the Board cannot be rescued by cabinet for political or any other reasons. If cabinet amends or changes the NEB decision, this must be sanctioned by a bill through Parliament. Normally, however, reports approved by cabinet receive no scrutiny in the House of Commons, which is a political advantage for governments wishing to avoid controversial debate. Often there is no public announcement until after the cabinet decision. Appeals against an NEB decision lie through the Federal Court of Appeal, but appeals can be made only on the basis of questions pertaining to law or jurisdiction.[11] From the above it is evident that the legal and political position of the NEB as a regulatory board is far stronger than the advisory role of a public inquiry such as that headed by Berger. The Board, through its membership in the committee system of government, is within the power structure and a part of the process of formulating policy.

As a result of this intimate relationship within government many of the public interest groups were sceptical of the objectivity of the Board. Yet they were determined to mount an effective opposition because of the weaknesses they perceived in the project. From statements in the House of Commons it appeared that the government was already committed to building the pipeline. When challenged on this point by Eddy Goodman, chairman of the CIC, Donald Macdonald retreated to the extent of claiming that there was no commitment "at this stage." This appeared to be at odds with the earlier statement of Jean Chrétien, Minister of Indian and Northern Affairs, that he had no doubt that a pipeline would be built even if the final decision might take a few months. These comments increased the worries that the government had already made up its mind before the opening of the hearings. Also, it appeared from Macdonald's statements that Canadian gas exports would be used to facilitate the financing of the pipeline irrespective of the projected future shortages for domestic supply.[12]

In the election campaign of 1974 pressure was brought to bear on all three parties to issue northern development policy statements acceptable to the public interest groups. All but the Liberal Party put forward such statements, but some Liberal candidates, such as Mel Hurtig in Edmonton, were outspoken in their opposition to the project.

During 1973, while the NEB was gearing up for the hearings, discussions continued with Donald Macdonald about funding for groups at the NEB. The minister appeared to be sympathetic but unwilling to commit himself at this point. There were even signs that the NEB itself was beginning to soften its opposition. Fred Lamar, general counsel to the Board, in addressing the annual meeting of the Canadian Bar Association, stressed that environmental groups deserved financial support to present "legitimate points of view" before regulatory boards.[13] In June, 1973, the Ministry of Consumer and Corporate Affairs began yearly grants to the Consumers Association of Canada for its consumer advocacy work before regulatory boards such as the Canadian Transportation Commission. The Privy Council Office investigated various schemes for funding or the appointment of a "public defender" to argue public interest points of view.

In 1974 the pressure for funding increased with the submission of the Arctic Gas application. Efforts to prod Macdonald failed when proposals were stalled at cabinet; the minister's office explained that the Ministry of Justice opposed any contributions until a scheme applicable to all regulatory boards was in place. Oral assurances were given that at least some of the costs would probably be covered through a joint package to cover funding for both the Berger and the NEB intervenors. Efforts were made to gain the support of Robert Stanfield and the Conservatives during the 1974 federal election campaign. A statement favourable to the public interest groups and their funding was approved by Stanfield but suddenly withdrawn by the party on the eve of its presentation at a press conference. When the election produced a Liberal majority, that party cooled to the idea of public funding except for the Berger Inquiry, which the government could claim was no precedent for a general funding policy.[14] By the opening of the NEB hearings in October, 1975, no funding had been secured. As a result, the CIC lost the ongoing presence of Hugh Morris, its experienced counsel. This was a serious blow because it weakened CIC cross-examination of the corporate applicants as well as the presentation of its own evidence.

In October, 1975, in preparation for the NEB hearings, all the public interest groups came together to form the Public Interest Coalition (PIC) to co-ordinate their efforts. With no money, it was a corporal's guard of volunteers who mounted the intervention over the next year and a half. Under the chairmanship of Professor Ian McDougall from Dalhousie Law School, François Bregha, Nydia McCool, Bruce Willson, and Bob Page were the main participants, with John Olthuis and John Robinson playing a major role in the later stages. The main organizations involved were the CIC and the Canadian Wildlife Federation, both of whom supplied money and services through their Ottawa offices. The organization and mobilization of witnesses were tied together by personal friendships across the country and between various groups. This work was also carried through at considerable financial cost to those involved.

When the NEB finally got to its pre-hearing conference of counsel in July, 1975, it was already well behind the parallel hearings of Berger in Yellowknife and the Federal Power Commission in Washington. This meeting was convened by Board counsel to discuss the procedures for running the hearings with the other parties. The board was clearly concerned with the prospect of nearly 100 intervenors, about fifteen of which were public interest groups.[15] They feared that the hearings would become chaotic and repetitious even if only a quarter of this number chose to participate seriously. The Board, therefore, tried to herd all the public interest groups into one consolidated group, but this scheme failed because of the differing interests they represented.

One of the issues raised by these groups was the costly problem of transcripts. To limit the expense involved with running its hearings, the NEB had contracted out the production of the transcripts, the official record of each day's proceedings. The company involved recouped its costs and made a profit by selling the printed transcripts back to the intervenors at the rate of sixty cents per page. For the northern pipeline hearings the cost of these documents, essential for cross-examination, totalled over $20,000, which was clearly beyond the means of the public interest groups. After some discussion the Board agreed to purchase two sets that would be available for the exclusive use of these groups at the hearings. This system worked well, thanks to the careful efforts of the NEB registry staff.

Some of the issues raised at this pre-hearing conference, such as the disclosure of public documents, continued as matters of dispute through the duration of the hearings. With no Freedom of Information Act in Canada until 1982, the public interest groups had no leverage to gain access to government research on the pipeline.[16] When the head of the CIC met with cabinet minister Judd Buchanan to attempt to arrange a flow of research reports similar to that arranged by Berger, he was curtly informed that all he needed could be purchased through Information Canada, the government bookstore in Ottawa. Ian Blue, on behalf of the Board, promised that the Board would contact the relevant government departments asking for a list of pipeline-related documents and research. He stressed: "Presumably if they would list them, they would make them available."[17] As far as can be determined nothing ever came of this commitment, even though it was merely repeating what Berger had done for the northern hearings.

There were also questions about the scope of the NEB proceedings. The CIC sought unsuccessfully to get the gas plants and the gathering system (feeder pipelines) of the Delta producers included in the hearings. These had serious social and environmental implications and had been excluded from Berger's terms of reference. As this area was linked to the Board's mandate, it could not refuse the request formally. However, this would have produced delays in the hearings because the producers did not have the necessary documentation available nor were they sure what they were going to do. The Board, therefore, deferred any decision on the matter and then it was quietly transferred to the Environmental Assessment and Review Office. Especially for the Inuit of the western Arctic (COPE) this left a serious gap in the analysis of the overall project, which they bitterly resented. It certainly appeared that the representations of Imperial, Gulf, and Shell carried more weight with the panel than the concerns of the local people. In dealing with southern projects the Board was used to confining its assessment to the main trunk pipeline; production facilities were under provincial regulation. It used the same approach in the North despite the fact that there was no provincial authority but rather total federal jurisdiction. The Board made no attempt to exclude any of the public interest groups or individuals from intervenor status; however, it did request further information from two of them, which seemed to be a gentle reminder that the Board retained its right to exclude even if it chose not to exercise that right on this occasion. Most of the debate at the pre-hearing involved the unrelenting battle between Gibbs for Foothills and Goldie for Arctic Gas to devise procedures that would put their clients' cases in the best possible light and hinder their opponents. Watching these two match wits and semantics was a useful introduction to the strategic chess game between rival applicants that continued every day of the hearings.

The opening of the NEB hearings on the pipeline in October was designed as a media event to strengthen the Board's public image. Up to this point it was Berger who had been attracting all the attention. With the television cameras present in the Château Laurier's ornate ballroom, Ottawa hoped to divert attention from native rights and caribou to the hard reality of future energy shortages. On this morning the future path of the NEB seemed very clear: the speedy approval of the Arctic Gas application, for at this point no one took Foothills very seriously. In the friendly surroundings of the NEB, the immense technical and financial expertise behind the $150-million application of Arctic Gas, so the conventional thinking went, would quickly overwhelm Bob Blair and his colleagues who had the temerity to challenge both New York and Toronto. Yet the first of many surprises came before the opening formalities had been completed.

Leading the impressive entourage into the room in the glare of the television lights was Marshall Crowe, the scholarly looking chairman of the National Energy Board. Crowe had enjoyed a distinguished career mainly in the public service of Canada. Born in Manitoba in 1921, he had entered the Department of External Affairs in 1947 after service in the armed forces. In the mid-1960's he had left the public service briefly to work as an economic adviser to the Canadian Imperial Bank of Commerce, returning to Ottawa in 1967 to become assistant secretary to the cabinet. In his work in the Privy Council Office he participated in detailed government planning for a Mackenzie Valley Pipeline. For instance, he chaired a meeting on May 12, 1970, of representatives from a number of ministries from which a consensus decision emerged that the construction of a pipeline was deemed to be in the "national interest." In 1971 Crowe moved on to become president of the Canada Development Corporation (CDC), a federal Crown corporation holding shares in various industrial and resource companies.

Arctic Gas, as an American-dominated consortium, was a prime target for the economic nationalism implicit in the CDC. As president, however, Crowe led the CDC into the Arctic Gas consortium and was named to its management committee. Ottawa viewed the involvement as a means of keeping an eye on the project; for Exxon and other members it appeared to be a means of cementing government support. If it was a party to the planning, it could hardly reject the application at a later date. Crowe attended a number of Arctic Gas meetings in 1972 and 1973 in which key decisions were taken, including the route and ownership structure.[18] Later in 1973 Crowe left CDC and soon thereafter assumed his new role as chairman of the NEB, which received the Arctic Gas application in 1974. After completing its preliminary assessment and issuing the usual deficiency letters, the Board in 1975 announced that hearings would open later in the year before a panel yet to be named.

In the United States the Alyeska Pipeline had suffered three years of delays through court challenges from native and environmental groups. Arctic Gas feared that Crowe's involvement would open the way for legal action if Crowe sat on the panel judging the application. If the hearings became locked in a lengthy legal battle in Canada, its rival El Paso might win by default in Washington.[19] Vern Horte and Bill Wilder had taken up the issue directly, warning Crowe privately of their fears. Their lawyers drafted an official letter outlining the legal impediments as they saw them.[20] After the pre-hearing, Michael Goldie saw Board counsel as a further warning. Copies of the documentation were supplied privately to the public interest groups by Arctic Gas in case they might wish to act. Some of those within Arctic Gas who were pressing to keep Crowe off the panel were not motivated by fears that Crowe was biased in their favour; rather, the reverse.[21] As a strong economic nationalist Marshall Crowe had little reason to love the multinational oil companies behind the Arctic Gas project. When the NEB announced on August 20, 1975, that Crowe would chair the panel hearing the northern pipeline applications, the whole issue spilled out into the open. It was announced that Crowe, in opening the proceedings, would read a statement outlining his CDC involvement, after which the panel "would hear objections if any." After consulting legal opinion, Crowe had decided to take the plunge; he desperately wanted to be involved in the greatest project application in the history of the National Energy Board.

Thus there was a sense of drama as Crowe, Jacques Farmer, and William Scotland, the three panel members, trooped into the Château Laurier ballroom. After the opening roll call, Crowe carefully read his statement on his CDC activities; a forty-five-minute adjournment followed, after which each party had to state its objections or else waive its rights to raise them. All the corporate intervenors in turn announced that they had no objections. Arctic Gas was by now aware that others would object, sparing it the stigma of questioning the objectivity of the chairman of the panel hearing their application. In the minutes that followed, the Canadian Arctic Resources Committee, the Consumers Association of Canada, and the Committee for Justice and Liberty all raised objections. Although the Board was aware that objections would be raised, the members appeared to be dumbfounded and seemed to lack any plan of action. Hyman Soloway, the Board counsel, requested adjournment until nine the next morning to "get some additional information."[22] The great media event had turned into a great media disaster. The Board appeared to be incapable of running its own affairs, for if there was any serious issue of bias it should have been referred to the federal court in the months before the opening of the hearings. By failing in their effort to bluff their way through, the Board and its panel had been made to look incompetent, and on national television at that.

The next morning the large number of intervenors and spectators was once again present but this time the panel did not appear. Soloway, looking a bit haggard, read a brief statement that the adjournment would continue for another twenty-four hours; everyone trooped out again, mumbling a few obscenities about the Board getting its act together. Finally, on Wednesday morning the panel reappeared with Crowe announcing that the case would be referred to the Federal Court of Appeal and that, in the interim, the Crowe panel would proceed with the hearings.

The Marshall Crowe case was filled with irony and intense cross-currents of opinion. Crowe was certainly one of the members of the Board most sympathetic to the concerns of the public interest groups. Yet the clear feeling of those who challenged was that the principle of bias within regulatory boards was a structural weakness widespread within the Canadian regulatory system. Therefore, a case with such clear legal evidence could not be allowed to drop – not because Crowe was committed to Arctic Gas but because he was committed to building *a* pipeline. In fact, he had helped to commit the government to the idea long before the Arctic Gas application was submitted. It was clear in their minds that he had already decided the basic issue of "the public convenience and necessity" for such a system. Yet, for some, his strong nationalist assumptions were needed to face the pressures from the multinational phalanx of the Arctic Gas consortium. Representatives from Foothills tried to get the public interest groups to drop their case, arguing that their application would not get a fair hearing unless Crowe was on the panel. There was also some truth in Jeff Carruthers' comment that "the public interest groups are falling into the inexcusable trap of doing the dirty work for Canadian Arctic Gas" when the Board desperately needed its nationalist backbone.[23] Thus, not surprisingly, there was a lack of unity among the public interest groups on the advisability of the court challenge.

For Ottawa mandarins the Marshall Crowe case constituted an impertinent challenge to one of the government's most respected senior figures. The integrity of the civil service was on the line with Marshall Crowe. Consequently, the Ministry of Justice and the NEB counsel were rushed into the breach to defend the chairman. Many in Ottawa had grown to dislike the activist tactics of the public interest groups, including the media attention their biting criticisms always seemed to receive. Public servants felt deep frustration, for they could not reply in public even when the charges were totally unfounded. At the same time elsewhere in Ottawa, Robert Bryce, another respected senior mandarin, was under attack for pro-corporate bias in chairing the Royal Commission on Corporate Concentration.[24] In addition, Ottawa faced serious practical problems in staffing regulatory agencies if service with Crown or private corporations in the same field excluded them from appointments. So the Ottawa establishment was in a fighting mood to protect Crowe, not only for his own sake but as a symbol of the integrity of the Canadian public service.

While Arctic Gas, Foothills, and the government lawyers combined to support Crowe in the federal court, the three public interest groups attempted to raise money, hire experienced counsel, and prepare their case. At the same time, a few blocks away at the National Energy Board the daily battles continued with two other public interest groups operating under the stern gaze of Marshall Crowe.[25] The federal court moved swiftly to consider the case, ruling unanimously on December 12, 1975, in Crowe's favour.[26] Unsatisfied with the judgement, the public interest groups led by the Committee for Justice and Liberty sought legal opinions on the advisability of an appeal to the Supreme Court. The seriousness of this step was obvious to all, for if they lost and were assessed the costs, the bill could be in excess of $25,000. Early in January agreement was reached to spread the potential liability beyond the three original groups, thus allowing the appeal to proceed. On February 2 the Supreme Court granted leave to appeal and three days later the NEB finally decided to adjourn further deliberations pending the court's decision. For the first time it now seemed to recognize the seriousness of the challenge to the chairman.

In March the Supreme Court heard the appeal and announced its decision almost immediately. In an historic split decision, the Supreme Court reversed the lower court's ruling. Chief Justice Bora Laskin, speaking for the majority, stressed that the Board's function was "quasi-judicial" like a court, hence it must reflect the rules of natural justice. The issue was not one of actual bias but "reasonable apprehension, which reasonably well-informed people could properly have, of a biased appraisal and judgement." The justices were concerned that there should be no lack of public confidence in the impartiality of adjudicative agencies with a mandate to protect the public interest. The minority report rejected the concept that the NEB was quasi-judicial and stressed that the rules of natural justice must be tempered by the needs of the tribunal to be staffed by persons of "experience and expertise."[27]

Involved in the case were a number of issues relating to the law and the organization of government in Canada. First were the facts of the case, that Crowe had participated in the management decisions concerning a project whose merits he later had to judge. Second were the more general questions of the background of individuals appointed to regulatory agencies. The court could have phrased its judgement in such a way that any other member of a regulatory board who had previously served a company operating in that field would be open to legal challenge – such as Harry Boyle, then chairman of the CRTC, who had worked for the CBC for twenty-five years. The case brought many of the worries about this problem out into the open. As one of the feature writers for the *Financial Post* observed: "The Crowe case also touches on some of the least attractive aspects of the way we are being governed. The federal cabinet has shown a disturbing lack of sensitivity in its dealings with, and appointments to, what are supposed to be apolitical regulatory agencies."[28]

Flowing out of this was the third question relating to the conflict between the advisory and the regulatory functions of the Board. Here the public interest groups hoped to show that Crowe, as part of the Privy Council Office, had been involved with government planning that had decided a northern pipeline should be built. Not only had the NEB participated in those deliberations but Crowe was now its chairman. This created a type of structural bias. The judgement of the Supreme Court was a narrowly legal one, based on the specific facts of this case. Therefore, it had relevance only for the second area and none for the third. Even so, it was a landmark decision that sent shock waves through official circles in Ottawa, especially the NEB. The outcome was a great tribute to Ian Binnie, the thirty-six-year-old Toronto lawyer who had taken on some of the most prestigious legal talent in the country and won. Within the public interest groups there was a great sigh of relief because they were freed of the financial worries.

Disqualified by the highest court in the land, Crowe and the other two members of his panel were forced to step down from the case, thus aborting five months of hearings. A new panel had to start from scratch. While the public interest groups were jubilant in their belief that they had achieved an important legal precedent, Arctic Gas was furious – nearly six months had been wasted. Each month gave Foothills precious time in its efforts to put a satisfactory pipeline application together. In the light of Foothills' annoyance with the Crowe challenge, it is ironic that without this delay it would never have got its successful Alaska Highway 48″ Express Line into the NEB before the closing of the hearings. Also, Arctic Gas had the discouraging prospect that the court ruling had not really eliminated Marshall Crowe; he remained as an embittered figure in the background, still chairman of the NEB and influencing events.

On April 12, in the less than elegant surroundings of the NEB hearing room, the whole process began all over again. The new panel was chaired by Jack Stabback, with Geoff Edge and Ralph Brooks.[29] In some ways it was a better panel. Stabback's cool, detached manner, scrupulous patience, and quiet courtesy set a clear tone of judicial impartiality. The addition of Geoff Edge was to be of major significance because he possessed the sharpest mind and fired the toughest questions of anyone on the Board. In the following months he showed his impatience on occasion with unresponsive answers from witnesses who were trying to avoid the questions. In his opening statement Stabback dismissed the delay as "minimal," for some of the evidence in such areas as reserves had to be updated anyway. Once again the ritual of each intervenor accepting the Board format and procedures or stating objections was followed. This time CJL sought to withhold its answer until the written argument of the Supreme Court had been handed down. The panel, being in no mood to tolerate any gamesmanship or delaying tactics, ruled that this constituted an objection and rejected it. Very quickly the hearings got down to business on the very first morning.

The general strategy of both applicants was clear. Arctic Gas stressed its wide research, its technical competence, and the economic benefits of a single delivery system for Alaskan and Delta gas; it quietly ignored the environmental and native rights issues. Foothills argued that its smaller system would be more manageable, easier to finance, and could be timed to meet Canada's needs rather than being tied to an American timetable.[30] Arctic Gas wanted to see the deliberations move with all speed; Foothills was quite happy to move only as fast as prodded by the Board. In spite of the ingenuity of some of its arguments, Foothills was hardly a serious competitor at this time, for the Delta reserves would not as yet justify the huge capital investment. Arctic Gas still viewed El Paso as its principal opponent and speedy approvals in Canada were the key to defeating that challenge.

The Arctic Gas opening argument looked at alternatives to pipelines for the transmission of frontier gas. To no one's surprise it concluded that pipelines were best. However, there were some interesting moments when Arctic Gas came to deal with some of the more exotic schemes, such as LNG aircraft and huge submarine tankers. There were even rumours that Richard Rohmer would make a dramatic entrance from the sky to draw attention to his ideas about the feasibility of natural gas dirigibles. Some of the alternatives formally discussed seemed closer to science fiction than science. The railway alternative, which was a serious contender, did not get an airing when the Institute of Guided Ground Transport from Queen's University withdrew at the last moment. A private citizen, Mr. R.A. Bradley, appeared to champion his own design for an LNG conveyer-belt delivery system. But all in all, the opening sessions went smoothly for Arctic Gas, which was now delighted to be finally under way and defending evidence.

At this point the main protagonists were well familiar with each other's tactics. Each day Goldie for Arctic Gas and Gibbs for Foothills played the complex tactics of their clients. Each tried to force as much information as possible out of the other while giving as little as possible in return. They went through these rituals with all the skill and semantic dexterity they could muster. Michael Goldie from Vancouver was a seasoned veteran of the corporate wars. Day in and day out, he went at his job with a relentless and dry professionalism. Heading a staff of about ten lawyers, he intervened frequently while leering over his glasses at Gibbs or other parties. He could lecture the Board or any other party on technicalities of the law, the importance of which was not always evident. He was tough, able, rigorous, and thorough to a fault. For Foothills, Reg Gibbs created a very different public image. Representing the underdog he could at times radiate the innocent sincerity of a small-town lawyer. Especially in the early going, Gibbs' efforts and careful strategy kept Foothills in the battle until all the components in its application were in place. The absence of key parts to begin with and then the substantial changes in the application in the course of the hearings necessitated a high degree of verbal dexterity. Without Gibbs' skill, it would have been easy for Foothills to have lost its credibility and appeared as the opportunist that its critics charged it to be.

The other leading figure in the lineup at the hearings was Hyman Soloway, counsel to the Board. Because of the time and the demanding nature of these hearings, the Board had gone outside the ranks of its own legal staff. Soloway was a veteran member of the Ottawa bar with close connections to the Liberal Party. Silver-haired and a little overweight, Soloway was a benign father figure trying to keep the warring factions under control. Staring out from under broodingly thick eyebrows, he was content to try to keep things running smoothly. Unlike Ian Scott for the Berger Inquiry, there was no sense of crusading zeal in probing the issues. In addition, at times he had trouble keeping up with all the manoeuvring between Gibbs and Goldie. He was accustomed to representing corporate clients, which made him uncomfortable with the public interest aspects of the hearings with all their social, environmental, and native rights questions. Yet his own outside interests, such as being chairman of the board of governors of Carleton University, meant that he was not unsympathetic to some of these interests. Throughout the hearings his relations with the public interest groups were tense but correct – neither side fully trusted the other.

The remaining cast of characters in the NEB drama included some fascinating individuals who deviated from the normal stereotypes. John Ballem, representing Imperial, Gulf, and Shell, was not only an accomplished Calgary lawyer but well known for his dramatic novels and plays; some of the characters in these stories appear to have come from the real-life drama of those hearings. Jack Smith, another Calgary lawyer, presented delightfully irreverent cartoons to other parties depicting some of their obvious failings. Then there was John Hopwood of Alberta Gas Trunk, whose soft, cultured English accent seemed out of place for his Alberta client, and Jerry Paschen, a private individual from Edmonton whose buckskin jacket made him look like Davy Crockett among all those drab three-piece suits. Finally there was Bruce Willson, the ex-president of Union Gas of Ontario, who aroused great animosity when he used his detailed knowledge of industry practices to embarrass witnesses during cross-examination for the CIC.

Generally there were very good relations between the different intervenors, with all co-operating for the scheduling of witnesses and the filing of evidence. Arctic Gas and Foothills both dealt fairly with the public interest groups and they turned out to be much more co-operative in releasing information and supplying data than government departments. Both the applicants felt that they were on home ground in these hearings and appeared more relaxed than at Berger. In the last two months of the hearings, however, the general tone of cordiality eroded as most parties experienced total exhaustion. Arctic Gas was aware by that point that its fortunes were changing, but even so, on the last day it threw a party for all the intervenors who had survived the year and a half ordeal.

As the hearings progressed in 1976 it became increasingly evident that Foothills' "Maple Leaf" line from Alberta to the Mackenzie Delta was not attracting serious support. The reserve base in the Delta was inadequate to provide sufficient gas to finance the system, and the 1975 drilling results led to a decrease in the proven reserve estimates. Arctic Gas, with its access to the huge Prudhoe Bay reserves, was not hurt by these changes. In Washington the Federal Power Commission hearings were showing that while the El Paso system of LNG tankers was technically feasible, it would be more expensive to the American consumer and would deliver gas to California instead of the Midwest, where the greatest need existed. Besides, the Trudeau government wanted the industrial and commercial spinoffs for Canada of the larger joint line. The government saw Arctic mega-projects as a catalyst for economic growth and increasing R & D. Unless Blair could offer something more to both countries, Foothills would not become a serious contender.

In the Foothills entourage were several individuals who believed that the Alaska Highway route was a superior corridor for the delivery of the Prudhoe Bay gas. Carson Templeton of the Environmental Protection Board had always believed that it was less disruptive for wildlife than the route across the North Slope, which was still a wilderness area. Prior to joining Foothills, Westcoast Transmission had looked at a route north from B.C. for the Prudhoe Bay gas but this Mountain Pacific project had never been seriously studied. In doing its cross-examination of Arctic Gas at the Berger Inquiry, Foothills had updated some of the Mountain Pacific data and had even tried to convince Arctic Gas to opt for the highway route, thus leaving the Delta gas available for the Maple Leaf project. As a result, the Berger staff became seriously interested in the route as an alternative even though they had no mandate to investigate it formally.

In October, 1975, Bob Blair and Ed Phillips, the president of Westcoast, met with Senator Ted Stevens of Alaska, a strong supporter of El Paso in Congress. Many Alaskans objected to Arctic Gas and its North Slope route not only for environmental reasons but because none of the gas would be available for industrial purposes in the urban areas located in the southern portions of the state. In November, 1975, in Washington the Federal Power Commission released its draft environmental statement followed a month later by the Department of the Interior's report on alternate routes. Both favoured the Alaska Highway/Fairbanks corridor for environmental reasons. Foothills, however, was hesitant to jump in with a new project when it lacked the key component, an American partner to handle the construction in that country.

While the Marshall Crowe case was dragging on, key negotiations were going on behind the scenes. When the new hearings opened in April, 1976, the partnership of Alberta Gas Trunk, Westcoast Transmission, and Northwest Pipeline in the United States was finally in place.[31] Northwest already purchased B.C. gas from Westcoast and was a natural ally for construction of the Alaskan system. However, it was a relatively small and politically weak partner to take on the giant El Paso corporation or the Exxon-backed Arctic Gas. Ed Phillips wanted to jump in immediately and abandon the Maple Leaf project while Blair, with his nationalist concerns, wanted to blend both projects together. After Gibbs' opening tirade to the Berger Inquiry, Blair was sensitive to the political importance of a nationalist image as well as the matter of consistency. However, everyone involved in Foothills recognized that it had to move quickly if the project was to be considered by both governments.[32]

The three companies signed a letter of intent on May 5, 1976, but there was serious doubt they would be allowed into the Federal Power

Commission hearings, which were well advanced at this point. When Northwest threatened litigation it was allowed into consolidated hearings on July 23, only two weeks after its sketchy application was filed. In August, Foothills filed a companion application with the NEB to cover the Canadian segment of the project; and on September 10, Foothills (Yukon), as the Alaska Highway Pipeline came to be known, was formally added to the two other applications under consideration. This forced the NEB to go back and repeat for the new project the phases of the hearings already covered for Arctic Gas and Foothills (Maple Leaf). The entry of this eleventh-hour application had been an amazing piece of executive stickhandling to get the new project in the door for regulatory consideration; but it still seemed unlikely that it could overtake the tremendous head start Arctic Gas enjoyed.

The application was a curious patchwork of new pipe and the utilization of existing systems. As originally proposed in the summer of 1976, it was a 42″ line running south from Prudhoe Bay to Fairbanks along the existing right-of-way of the Alyeska Oil Pipeline. From Fairbanks it followed the Alaska Highway corridor through southern Yukon into northern British Columbia, where it joined the Westcoast system and then a new link eastward to join the Alberta Gas Trunk mainline near Zama Lake. The Alaskan gas would flow south through the expanded Westcoast Transmission and Alberta Gas Trunk systems, intermingling with the local provincial gas. The whole system, it was claimed, could be constructed as cheaply as the Arctic Gas system and could be in operation in 1980, a year earlier than its rival. From the American point of view there were two major criticisms – the mingling of the gas and the fact that the existing Canadian systems were subject to provincial regulation, not the NEB. Earlier in the 1970's when Westcoast had encountered serious reservoir flow problems in its most northerly field, all the necessary cutbacks were assigned to the export contracts, not pro-rated between Canadian and American customers. The United States was still smarting from that experience when Westcoast appeared in Washington as part of the Foothills consortium. El Paso did everything in its power to refresh memories in Congress, emphasizing that foreign jurisdictions could not be trusted with such a vital energy artery for the American economy.

One of the most difficult problems the Board faced with the northern pipeline hearings concerned the extent of northern public participation. Obviously the NEB had no intention of duplicating the community hearings of Berger, but, in political terms, it had to do something to assess public opinion. In the end the Board chose to visit the main white settlements – Inuvik, Whitehorse, and Yellowknife – and ignore the native settlements. Also, Yellowknife was hundreds

Figure 9.
Foothills' Original Alaska Highway Pipeline Proposal. From NEB, *Reasons for Decision: Northern Pipelines,* I (Ottawa, 1977), appendix.

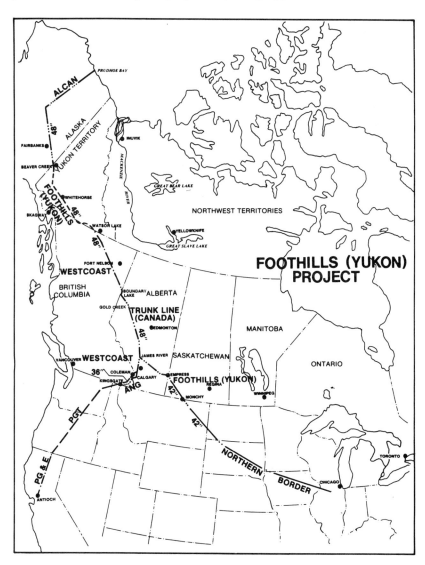

of miles from the pipeline right-of-way. When the hearings opened in Inuvik the presentations were almost all from pro-development white representatives; only Sam Raddi of COPE appeared to present a conflicting view.[33] It was clear that the native organizations, absorbed with the final weeks of the Berger hearings, placed a low priority on the NEB's appearance. As far as could be determined the Board had made little effort to ensure it got a representative sampling of northern opinion.

Next the panel moved on to Whitehorse in the Yukon, where the presentations began with Commissioner Art Pearson speaking for the territorial government. He expressed the government's concerns about the potential damage from the Arctic Gas proposal and its support for Foothills (Yukon), which had been endorsed by a unanimous resolution of the Yukon assembly. Pearson stressed that "utilization of the Alaska Highway would have fewer potential social and environmental impacts" with more long-term benefits from increased energy supply for the populated portions of the southern Yukon. The business, native, and environmental groups that followed all opposed Arctic Gas and supported Foothills in varying degrees. The Chamber of Commerce claimed also that because Yukon native organizations were a "much more responsible force" there was a better chance of a native land claims settlement there than in the N.W.T. In the months ahead this view was repeated frequently, but never by Yukon native groups, who felt that it gave them an "Uncle Tom" image. There was also a general demand that the NEB return when the specifics of the Foothills application were being considered. Foothills had to be delighted with this official endorsement from the elected assembly and the federally appointed commissioner; these were northern allies that the National Energy Board could not ignore.[34]

If Foothills appeared to make progress in Whitehorse, it encountered new opposition when the hearings switched to Yellowknife. The announcement of the Alaska Highway project created fears in the Mackenzie Valley that the Maple Leaf line would be delayed for many years. By the time the NEB panel arrived, the Arctic Gas public relations staff had moved in to exploit those fears among business and municipal leaders. From the start there had been a fierce rivalry between the two applicants to sign up local allies as a demonstration of support. In the early months Foothills won friends with its promises to subsidize gas supply laterals to the main valley communities and to locate its headquarters in Yellowknife. Then came the Alaska Highway announcement. In August, 1976, Blair had made a special trip to the Berger Inquiry to try to counter the Arctic Gas campaign. When the NEB panel arrived six weeks later it was evident that Blair's efforts had been far from successful. The Association of Municipalities of the N.W.T., led by the mayors of Hay River, Yellowknife, and Inuvik, passed a resolution formally endorsing the Arctic Gas project to the clear consternation of the Foothills' representatives at the Board hearings.[35]

As the NEB panel flew south to resume the Ottawa hearings, they must have had mixed feelings about the success of their northern swing. With the exception of Whitehorse, they created little local interest and they heard mainly from a narrow business-oriented segment of society. The Dene Nation and CARC made no appearance, as they were absorbed at Berger. The attitude of the Board was that they had made the gesture for northern input and that was all, politically, they were expected to do. However, it did weaken their ability to talk authoritatively about environmental and social impacts when they failed to consult the people most directly affected.

While the panel had been in the North, another Arctic trip had aroused considerable media comment. The *Globe and Mail* broke the story that Marshall Crowe had accepted a free fishing trip to Baffin Island courtesy of Panarctic Oils; also present were the president of Polar Gas Pipeline (then preparing an application for the NEB) and the president of Union Gas, one of the sponsors of Arctic Gas.[36] These revelations led to a series of stinging editorials and criticism from opposition spokesmen in the House of Commons. The Conservative energy critic, Jim Gillies, complained that this was further evidence that senior government and regulatory officials were becoming too close to the industries they were supposed to be watching.

When questioned by reporters, Crowe rejected any hint of impropriety in accepting such expensive favours. After all, he noted, he had contacts, including social lunches, with people opposing the pipeline, such as representatives from the CIC. When the press contacted the CIC, they were informed that not only had there been no social lunches but its official request for a meeting at the chairman's convenience to discuss procedural problems had been refused by Crowe.[37] Obviously, the public groups resented these comments as well as the continuing fraternization of Crowe and oil and pipeline company executives. They were surprised after the Supreme Court judgement that the chairman was not more careful in such matters. In April and May, 1977, when the hearings were at a critical stage, Crowe spoke to private meetings of financial executives in the U.S. and Canada in a manner that might have appeared to favour the Foothills position. In 1978, after he had resigned from the Board, he joined a small consulting/exploration firm controlled by the U.S. partners of Foothills.[38] Crowe, like a number of other senior civil servants at this time, followed the path of early retirement and corporative consulting in the field that he had been regulating.

In retrospect the fishing trip was not a major scandal, but it does show the temptations available to senior public officials. They are not offered as bribes but as a means of improving friendships and an opportunity for corporate views to be conveyed informally at a time of relaxation and fun. Hopefully for the companies involved, this would influence attitudes when later the officials would have to deal with projects in regulatory hearings. In 1973 the Trudeau cabinet had tried to come to grips with the problem in special conflict-of-interest guidelines for public servants.

It is by no means sufficient for a person in a position of responsibility . . . to act within the law. There is an obligation not simply to obey the law but to act in a manner so scrupulous that it may bear the closest public scrutiny. In order that honesty and impartiality may be beyond doubt, public servants should not place themselves in a position where they are under obligation to any person who might benefit from special consideration or favour on their part or seek in any way to gain special treatment from them. Equally a public servant should not have a pecuniary interest that could conflict in any manner with the discharge of his official duties.[39]

Crowe was not in a legally defined conflict of interest by accepting the hospitality of the oil company. However, he was certainly defying the spirit of the guidelines. As the critics of the pipeline were in no position to offer him exotic fishing trips, they were at a disadvantage. Through this whole episode Crowe appeared to be curiously insensitive to public concern about receiving gifts from parties to the hearings. That he had done so was serious enough; that he defended his actions after the fact seemed even worse. The minister, Alastair Gillespie, was reported to be furious with the chairman of the NEB and his aides leaked the story that Crowe would be forced out quickly.[40] This seemed to be a rather harsh reaction as Gillespie, his son, his wife, and his deputy minister were all on the same fishing trip. The only difference was that the minister informed the *Globe and Mail* that he had asked to be billed for the cost of the trip.

In the course of the hearings Professor Ian McDougall attempted to challenge the Board on a number of procedural questions to try to improve the effectiveness of the public interest interventions. He argued that the lack of adequate funding limited the evidence that they could bring to the Board, the staff they could use to prepare cross-examination, and their overall ability to cope with the massive filings of the applicants. Meaningful interventions required comparable computer simulations programmed with different assumptions than those employed by the oil industry. Basic principles of natural justice were violated, McDougall argued. The Board uses an adversary format but one side was in no way comparable to the other in its

146

resources. The public interest groups did not even have proper legal counsel to defend their witnesses and argue the points at issue. Public participation was of little consequence on such complex matters unless expert advice could be brought to bear to support consumer or environmental points of view. Scientific studies, not raw opinion, were what the Board required to base its opinions on. If the only such studies were from a corporate standpoint, they would have undue influence on the final decisions of the panel. At every point the Board refused to consider any funding support. It appeared that they did not want to encourage "public interest" intervenors. Public participation could be limited by ensuring that it took place at a heavy cost to those involved.

One of the concerns of the public interest coalition was to bring out into the open the informal advisory functions of the NEB to show just how deeply involved it was in government policy-making structures. On April 26, 1976, McDougall addressed a written request to the Board secretary for a list of the interdepartmental committees on which Board or staff members served. In the hearings proper he attempted to find out if the Board was in receipt of any directions from the minister or the cabinet in connection with the northern pipeline hearings. The issue he was trying to illuminate was the degree of independence under which the NEB actually operated. Many believed that it was very restricted in spite of the terms of the National Energy Board Act. Under such circumstances the decision to proceed with the northern pipeline might have been taken by the government long before the hearings opened. The Board refused to discuss either request. The Board secretary curtly replied: "it is not Board policy to provide such information."[41]

National Energy Board Representation on Interdepartmental Committees and Task Forces (1974)

Ad Hoc Interdepartmental Committee on Manpower Requirements for Northern Pipelines
Advisory Committee on Northern Development:
 a) Policy Committee
 b) General Committee
 c) Transportation Subcommittee
Bank of Canada – Northern Gas Pipeline Study Group
Canada/U.S.A. Emergency Planning
Capital Requirements Committee:
 a) Task Force on Capital Requirements
 b) Macro-Economics Projections Subcommittee

Energy Conservation Committee
Engineering Review Committee for Tidal Power
Federal/Provincial Committee on Noise
Federal/Provincial Committee on Oil and Gas Statistics
Foreign Investment Review Agency:
a) Task Force on Ownership of Canadian Natural Resources
b) Committee to Study Hypothetical Foreign Takeovers in the Oil and Gas Industry
Initiating Committee on Price Survey of Petroleum Products
Interdepartmental Committee on Candide – Candide Users Group
Interdepartmental Committee on the Disposal of the Haines-Fairbanks Pipeline
Interdepartmental Committee on Energy Statistics:
a) Executive Committee
b) Subcommittee on Coal and Coke
c) Subcommittee on Oil and Gas
d) Subcommittee on Special Projects
Interdepartmental Committee on the Environment; and Subcommittee on OECD Environmental Activities
Interdepartmental Committee for Metric Conversion
Interdepartmental Committee on Oil
Interdepartmental Committee on Rehabilitation of the Alaska Highway
Interdepartmental Committee on Socio-Economics of Pollution Abatement
International Joint Commission – Standing Committee on Health Aspects
NATO – Petroleum Planning Committee
National Advisory Committee on Petroleum Statistics; and Ad Hoc Working Group in LPG Statistics
National Design Council
National Gas Advisory Committee
OECD:
a) Ad Hoc Group on Natural Gas
b) Interdepartmental Energy Panel
c) Oil and Energy Committee
Petroleum Resources Committee – Subcommittee on Economic Analysis; Task Force on Energy Research and Development; and Transmission Panel Task Force on Northern Oil Development:
a) Economic Impact Committee
b) Market Subcommittee
c) Pipeline Engineering Committee
d) Social and Environmental Subcommittee
Technical Advisory Committee on Petroleum Supply and Demand; and

a) Subcommittee on Data Needs
b) Subcommittee on Seaway Movement of Oil
c) Subcommittee on Shipping
Technical Advisory Committee to Hydro-Québec Institute of Research

One of the most controversial procedural matters throughout the northern pipeline hearings concerned the hours of sitting. As a result of the Marshall Crowe case and the late emergence of the Foothills (Yukon) application, the NEB was seriously behind schedule and always trying to catch up. Originally the hearing hours were 9 a.m. to 1 p.m., which allowed afternoons and evenings to prepare cross-examination and review the day's transcripts. This schedule was not easy but it was manageable. Then the hours were increased to 8 a.m. to 1 p.m. and then, in August, 1976, to 8:30 to 12:30 and 2 to 4:30.

The Board had been under public pressure for its slow rate of progress, which some observers had blamed on the public interest groups.[42] However, in explaining the change the Board merely complained of the inordinate amount of time spent in cross-examination on matters of minor importance. As most of the cross-examination had been by the two applicants and Board counsel, it was clear that they were pointing the figure at Goldie and Gibbs. The changes in hours were acceptable to Arctic Gas but opposed by Foothills and the public interest groups. Arctic Gas, with its larger staff, consistently pressed the Board on the need for speed in an attempt to curtail the chances of Foothills completing its application in time. Allies of Arctic Gas, such as the government of Ontario, pressed the Board to speed up the deliberations allegedly on the basis of fears of gas shortages in Ontario. Thomas Enders, the American ambassador in Ottawa, leaked to the press the story that the Ford administration was annoyed with Canada's slow progress in the hearings. In responding to these pressures the Board increased the hours of sitting but refused to limit its proceedings even though, as Michael Goldie sagely observed, it was applying "the well-known principle that nothing expedites cross-examination like exhaustion."[43]

In doing their cross-examination of witnesses, the public interest groups were sometimes subject to oral harassment from protective counsel. In November, 1976, when a financial witness for Arctic Gas tried to avoid admitting the commitment of the Canada Development Corporation to Canadian ownership and control, the CIC brought forward the minister's statement in introducing the bill to incorporate the CDC, which contained a clear commitment to that goal. Counsel for Arctic Gas protested that ministerial statements were inadmissible, citing a Supreme Court ruling, when it was a well-known fact that the rules of evidence were different. Interestingly, it was Reg Gibbs, not Board counsel, who jumped to his feet to set the matter straight. The purpose of the original interjection was clearly to try to test the knowledge, intimidate, and disrupt the flow of questions.[44] These are standard tactics for lawyers trying to protect witnesses whose testimony is dubious. Without legal counsel it made the job of the public interest groups all the more difficult.

Throughout the hearings, Board staff members were annoyed by criticisms of their work levelled by public interest group spokesmen. The media gave wide coverage to those charges, not all of which were well founded. There was general interest within the Board of devising a way to curb these comments, which were hurting the NEB's public image. Marshall Crowe and others had never forgiven the groups for the court challenge. So it was that in March, 1977, new rules of contempt were established by the Board to cover activities by intervenors both within and outside the hearings. The new rules were specifically designed to cover hearings already under way and to be in force immediately, not when published in the *Canada Gazette*. The public interest phase of the hearings was just starting and Bill Houston, assistant Board counsel, personally delivered copies to the public interest groups present, so it was clear that the Board was trying to discipline its critics. These new contempt rules, like the refusal of intervenor status, were powers the Board wanted to keep in reserve to show there were limits to its patience in allowing activist groups to participate.

While the Board staff members were clearly interested in a thorough airing of the technical and economic issues, they were far less concerned with social and environmental questions. Their staff support in these areas was mainly of a temporary nature brought in to do a specific job. In the chain of command at the NEB there was no senior person responsible to argue these areas in decision-making. Soloway, in his cross-examination, reflected these priorities by resorting to motherhood questions. He asked the president of Arctic Gas: "There has been some concern recently expressed in so far as any problems with water pollution as a result of siltation and other similar matters. Will all necessary steps be taken to ensure there is no risk of pollution as a result of the construction of your pipeline?" This type of question allowed for the simple response, "Yes, there will, sir."[45] Soloway explained the Board's position to the author as simply being that they had no intention of "redoing Berger." Yet, under its mandate the Board had to consider all these matters; in this case they were used as the principal reason for rejecting the Arctic Gas application.

One of the significant differences between Berger and the NEB was in the production of evidence. In cross-examining the Arctic Gas environmental panel, the CIC made reference to the published volumes of the Environmental Protection Board, which had been financed by Arctic Gas. When Arctic Gas challenged the use of this material, Board counsel suggested it was the responsibility of the CIC to demonstrate its relevance and to supply the Board with copies, which seemed ludicrous given the source. At Berger these documents had been part of the record from the start because the Commission counsel had actively sought relevant materials. In this case Board counsel was unaware of their existence and felt no responsibility to arrange for copies as public documents. As Board counsel never led evidence, they were dependent on the intervenors to bring outside documentation to their attention. The corporate applicants, of course, had no interest in bringing forth such material and so it was up to the public interest groups. This was true of a wide range of materials from government, academic, and independent sources.

In the final weeks, in April and May of 1977, the NEB sat morning, afternoon, and evening in its efforts to complete its task. The exhaustion factor was clearly apparent in the performance of all parties. Tensions and personal animosities now surfaced, for it was clearly apparent that Arctic Gas was losing momentum. During these lengthy and tense closing sessions it was the genial good humour of the chairman, Jack Stabback, that kept the hearings on the rails in spite of the incredible hours everyone was working. The transcript recorders worked all night to have the volumes ready for the morning start. Exhausted witnesses made basic mistakes and no one seemed to notice. Counsel for the Board were reviewing chapters of the report while the testimony and the cross-examination proceeded. In those last weeks the knowledge that the hearings were coming down the home stretch kept everyone going. Final argument came in through June, and with a frenetic effort the report was released on July 4, 1977. The rush had been so great that only the first of the three volumes was available in French.

In a strongly worded decision the Board rejected the Arctic Gas project and gave conditional approval to Foothills provided that: it did further environmental and social impact studies; it shifted the route north through Dawson; and it applied to build a Dempster lateral north from the Alaska Highway to the Delta by the summer of 1979. The report cited environmental and social factors as being the critical reasons for its decision. A route across the North Slope of the Yukon and the Mackenzie Delta was "environmentally unacceptable" because of the impacts on the Porcupine caribou herd, the snow geese, and the beluga whales. The Arctic Gas project suffered from "incompatible time constraints" between the urgent American need for Alaskan gas and the Canadian requirements for time "to resolve socio-economic concerns" in the Mackenzie Valley. The Board rejected also the legitimacy of the financial backstopping requested by Arctic Gas from the government. Under the provisions of the NEB Act any project rejected by the Board could not be rescued by cabinet except by special legislation. For Arctic Gas it appeared to be the end of the line, even though company representatives tried to keep a bold front in comments to the press.[46]

In the years between 1977 and 1985 the Board continued on, mainly with oil and gas supply, export, and southern pipeline hearings. The Norman Wells Oil Pipeline and the Arctic Pilot Project were the only two northern matters during this period. These hearings, which will be discussed later, raised many of the same problems the Board had faced with the pipeline hearings of 1975-77. These hearings were a watershed for the Board in a number of ways. The Marshall Crowe court challenge forced it to be careful about the background of its members. The public interest groups had mounted their greatest effort in terms of intervention. They had helped to defeat Arctic Gas but they had lost their battles to change procedures, secure public funding, and increase the flow of public information at the hearings. As a result, public participation at the NEB has declined since 1977; in the 1982 hearings on the Arctic Pilot Project only CARC and the Inuit organizations were left from the fifteen public interest groups involved in 1977.

By its very nature the NEB must view procedural matters in a more restricted fashion than a "one-shot" inquiry like that of Berger. Concessions made to fit the circumstances of one hearing become a precedent for all future ones. Yet a number of provincial regulatory boards in jurisdictions such as Alberta have gone further in procedural reform, public information, and funding for public interest intervenors without creating the administrative chaos that some Board members fear. Under its mandate it must consider a broad range of consumer, environmental, social, native rights, and national concerns that are currently inadequately represented in the hearings and within the NEB staff. At the root of its dilemma is the emerging concept of the public interest, which is in conflict with the normal tendencies of a regulatory board to enforce procedures reflecting its own concerns for administrative convenience. The NEB is happiest when it can operate quietly behind the scenes without public controversy or media attention. It is best on narrow technical questions and worst on broad policy issues where it could be accused of leading government policy.

The political context in which it must operate should never be forgotten. Many of the appointments of Board members in the last five years have reflected political criteria. The federal-provincial tensions of the early 1980's reflected back on the Board's own operations as a federal institution. The rapid increase and then gradual erosion of world energy prices made economic projections of project viability extremely difficult, especially given the long lead times to completion. Frequent changes in federal energy policy between Conservative and Liberal governments forced radical shifts in the NEB's own perspective. The drive in the 1980's for new gas and even light crude oil exports tended to erode the Board's traditional formula for ensuring future domestic energy supply. With the election of the Mulroney government in 1984, there was a rising chorus of demands from industry groups for oil and gas deregulation following similar moves in the United States. All of these forces combine to make the job of the Board a complex and difficult one where the theory of regulation has to be sharply curbed by the practical reality of the business and political climate in which it has to operate.

Since the conclusion of the northern pipeline hearings in 1977, the NEB has experienced a number of changes. Jack Stabback, who carried so much of the administrative load for the Board during those hearings, succeeded Marshall Crowe as chairman and then took early retirement, moving west to head up the energy department for one of the chartered banks. He was replaced as chairman by Geoffrey Edge, who by all reports appears to be running the NEB very tightly. At this point of writing in 1985, the Board has survived many demands for basic reform and even abolition. Its job remains a complex and difficult one, given the political and economic problems of the 1980's. As a result of the efforts of neo-conservatives for deregulation in the United States and Britain, the Board is facing similar challenges in Canada, some of which originate within the Mulroney cabinet. Also, it has lost some prestige as changes in export pricing and policy have clearly been a product of cabinet pressure. Thus far, however, it has avoided the fundamental structural changes that have been seen in Washington. Given the ideological differences between Canada and the United States this is hardly surprising. There is no question that successive Canadian governments have found the Board's advisory role a useful component in policy-making and in helping to keep a unity and coherence in the overall federal energy process. With no great price increases or potential energy shortages in the mid-1980's, the NEB is sailing through a calmer period in its history with the media and Parliament less interested in its operations and decisions. In retrospect the most trying years were those between 1974 and 1977, when the world energy scene was undergoing fundamental changes, the public interest groups were vocal critics, and the Board was facing unrealistic deadlines for the northern pipeline decision. Now that some of the questions of process have been considered with the above analysis of Berger and the NEB, we can turn to an assessment of the specific issues of northern development in thematic chapters on technology, biology, social impacts, and economics.

CHAPTER 7

The Physical Environment and the Limitations of Technology

Like Alaska and Siberia, the Canadian Arctic has provided some of the most difficult engineering problems known to man. All construction must be based on a firm foundation; yet in the Arctic regions, because of permafrost on land and ice scour under the water, permanently stable foundations are much more difficult to design and maintain. The accumulated southern experience on which the engineering profession was built is often invalid in the North. As a result the engineers that were involved with creating the design for a Mackenzie Valley Pipeline were continuously breaking new ground with the technical details required for the project. Many of the physical problems they were confronting remain today as unresolved issues confronting all future mega-projects in the Arctic.

In addition, there is the wider problem of the uncertainty of untried technology; in many cases there were no models in operation to test theoretical assumptions. This type of scenario makes the job for the regulatory board all the more difficult. In our age we have had basic faith in the invincibility of technology. This belief, which flows out of the Industrial Revolution, has made it all the more difficult to appreciate properly the power of some of the physical forces we are wishing to confront. However, in the hearings one came to recognize that ice can be tougher than steel.

At both Berger and the NEB the most basic issue for this phase was the question of language; the hearings were dominated by the engineers and their technical vocabulary, which could always be resorted to by witnesses in trouble. The real advantage therefore rested with the applicant and its team of hired expert consultants. They were on their own home ground for they had done the original research and design work; lawyers in cross-examination could often be confused and led off the scent unless they were well briefed on the technical background. Yet even here the public hearings uncovered major design flaws through perseverance and even repetitious probing by a variety of parties. It was never an easy or straightforward process for it often involved disputes on procedural rules for the presentation of evidence. The issue was at the heart of the nature of the hearings.

Early in the Berger hearings Ian Scott, the Commission counsel, tried to sort this issue of language and comprehension. At what level of technical detail should the hearings be conducted? Scott complained that the initial Arctic Gas oral testimony consisted of repeated assertions that they had confidence that their design was sound, which would be fully proven by further field work to be carried out between now and the commencement of construction. Scott argued that the inquiry was entitled to more detailed design analysis, including the assumptions on which decisions had been made. Otherwise they would hardly be in a position to assess the adequacy of the technology.[1]

Scott was well aware that witnesses are directed to say as little as possible on the witness stand and to say it in as imprecise a way as they can get away with. This limits the empirical data on the record from which lawyers can try to find weaknesses in the project or inconsistencies between witnesses. In essence, Arctic Gas was keeping the technical discussions at such a trivial level, it was difficult to visualize the design planning, let alone subject it to serious scrutiny. The day following Scott's criticism Arctic Gas reversed its tactics by presenting such complex technical detail that the explanations were incomprehensible to the other parties. Berger made it clear that he wanted all evidence presented in language that could be understood by laymen; witnesses who really knew what they were talking about could accomplish it without destroying the scientific validity of their comments.[2] Berger was particularly concerned that the daily broadcasts in the native languages should convey to the local people some meaningful idea of the nature of the project so their own comments in the community hearings would be informed and accurate.

In the initial planning of any pipeline project one of the most critical decisions is the choice of route. First comes the primary or strategic decision about the general route or corridor (i.e., the Mackenzie Valley vs. the Alaska Highway), followed by the specific local issues involved in the exact location of the right-of-way within that corridor. Decisions on routes inevitably involve political influences for the economic benefits, and, in this instance, the gas supply would be attractive to municipal and provincial governments. In addition, the choice may involve trade-offs between technical, economic, environmental, and social considerations. To what extent do you lengthen the route (and increase the cost) to avoid environmentally sensitive areas? These were difficult judgements that inevitably were going to be controversial. Under cross-examination, however, it was conceded that the route was "essentially fixed" before the Expanded Pipeline Guidelines of 1972 were consulted, before any consultation with native trappers, and before the reporting of the social, environmental, and archaeological consultants. The decisions were made primarily on available economic and engineering data. Second, the key individuals making the decisions were professionally trained as engineers or corporate financial planners and therefore not able to assess properly input on social or environmental matters. Philip Dau of Arctic Gas had to admit that since he was not an expert in the field, he had been asked to make an "impossible judgement" and that the company had never given any instructions on the scale of values or priorities to be accorded to environmental considerations.[3] Hence the timing of inputs and the structure of the decision-making tended to determine the priorities for the choice of route.

Once the main geotechnical aspects of the hearings were opened, it quickly became evident that permafrost was the most critical and controversial issue facing both applicants. Permafrost as a phenomenon stretched all the way from northern Alberta to the Arctic Ocean.

Location	Depth of Permafrost	Description[4]
Keg River, Alberta	5'	scattered patches
Fort Simpson, N.W.T.	40'	discontinuous
Norman Wells, N.W.T.	150 to 200'	nearly continuous
Inuvik, N.W.T.	300'	continuous

As long as it remained permanently frozen there would be no problem but if air or water penetrated, erosion and collapsing land forms could follow. The builders of the Alyeska Oil Pipeline in Alaska had finally resorted to elevating one-half of their whole system on piles to avoid heat transfer in the permafrost sections. Arctic Gas hoped to avoid the problems of melting the permafrost by keeping the gas in the pipeline chilled below freezing. When the hearings opened most of the experts felt that they understood the nature of the problems; only as the hearings progressed did their faith begin to erode.

The physical properties of permafrost are important in trying to understand the pipeline construction problems. In some areas ice crystals can constitute as much as three-quarters of the volume of permafrost soils; if heat is transmitted by air, water, or construction into the permafrost, it can lead to the melting of the ice crystals and collapse of the land form. Permafrost is insulated on top by the "active layer," which is a soil and organic mat ranging normally in depth from six inches to three feet. This layer melts every summer and freezes again every winter. It sustains all vegetative growth while shielding

Figure 10.
Permafrost Profile. From Berger Report, I, p.18.

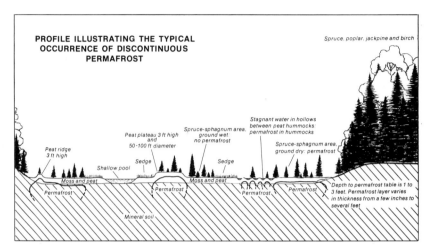

the frozen ground below from any heat carried by air or water. In summer, this active layer creates the ponding on the surface that gives the tundra the appearance of all-pervading wetness; any disturbance of this layer by nature or man will allow air or water to penetrate into the permafrost below, causing further ponding and melting and a cyclical pattern of erosion that will continue through each successive summer. Permafrost has been described as land floating on frozen water, for ice-rich soils have the composition of ice cream with some sand and gravel mixed through. The key to preserving the stability of the land forms is to keep the permafrost locked in its frozen state through techniques such as a gravel pad for roads or piles to keep buildings above ground.

From a construction standpoint, the basic problem is that any building is subject to frost heave in winter and thaw settlement in summer. Because of the underlying permafrost conditions, the destructive potential of both of these is very much greater than in southern portions of the country. As highway construction in the North has shown, it is difficult to estimate in advance the measures required to control heave or prevent erosion on slopes or at river crossings. Northern pipeline construction presents two further threats to the thermal regime. The digging of the trench cuts through the active layer and penetrates four or five feet or more into the permafrost. If the pipeline operated at normal temperatures it would radiate heat into the surrounding frozen ground. Both could lead to serious ponding and erosion along the right-of-way. Arctic Gas, when it approached this problem, was well aware of its seriousness; because of the heavy cost it quickly rejected the most obvious solution, which was an elevated pipeline through the permafrost areas. In the end, Arctic Gas chose to attempt to avoid the consequences of trenching by constructing in winter through the permafrost areas and to overcome the heat transfer problem by chilling the gas.

This bold, innovative design reflected the experimental philosophy of the Arctic Gas team. They wanted to make an important new contribution to northern engineering and they did not lack confidence in their own ability. Chilling the gas, however, created a serious new problem for the 550 miles of discontinuous permafrost from the Alberta border to the southern edge of the Mackenzie Delta. There were also unfrozen areas under the major rivers and lakes. The problem arose because the chilled pipeline would freeze any moisture in the surrounding soil and draw further moisture to it, increasing the ice lensing. As the ice layers thickened, upward pressure from frost heave would increase under the pipeline. This pressure was partly a product of the 10 per cent expansion factor of converting water into ice. But in addition, in fine-grain silt or clay, successive layers of ice would accumulate as moisture was drawn in. This frost bulb would act as a wall, stopping the flow of ground water across the right-of-way, adding to the available moisture through ponding on the surface. The upward pressure from this frost heave would not be constant but would vary with the moisture content and soil conditions; this differential rate of heave increased the possibility of pipeline fracture; and if the pipeline cracked there was a significant probability of a fire that would burn until all the gas was consumed. If Arctic Gas chose to stop chilling the gas in discontinuous permafrost, frost heave in the unfrozen areas would be eliminated but the resulting heat transfer would lead to thaw settlement in the frozen zones. For the pipeline engineer this constituted the basic dilemma of discontinuous permafrost.

The Soviet Union had attempted to cope with some of the same conditions through using a variety of techniques in constructing a smaller line. In ice-rich soils they had elevated the pipeline rather than chill the gas; in well-drained, sandy soils they had successfully buried it; and in soil conditions between the two they had placed the pipe on the ground with a soil mound or berm over top of it. The Russians had attempted to limit the potential physical forces involved; Arctic Gas chose to challenge them directly. Because of the differences in the projects and in local conditions, the Soviet experience was of limited usefulness to the Berger and NEB hearings;[5] yet it constituted the only related experience anywhere in the world. As the hearings progressed the uniqueness of both the challenge and the technological response gradually sank in to all parties. The engineers and scientists who had created the Arctic Gas design showed a justifiable sense of pride in their work, which was breaking new ground in the history of pipeline technology.

The concept of chilling a buried gas line was not universally accepted in spite of the attractiveness of the theoretical model. In order to neutralize frost heave, Arctic Gas proposed deep burial in a trench plus a mound of soil or berm over top of it. The engineers estimated that the extra weight pressing down on the pipeline would equal or exceed the upward pressure from frost heave, creating a "shut-off" point to further ice formation. With elaborate equations and intense faith, they fiercely argued the feasibility of their design. The only experimental evidence brought forward was from their test facility near Calgary where they attempted to recreate the soil and climate of the Mackenzie Valley in the laboratory. In March, 1975, Arctic Gas led off the Berger hearings with an impressive panel of experts who confidently testified under oath that they understood the forces at work and their deep burial design could cope with frost heave pressures of up to 5,000 pounds per square foot.[6]

Arctic Gas had recognized how central the frost heave issue was to their technical design, so they hired some of the most experienced engineering consultants available. Their theory and design went through the hearings of the U.S. Federal Power Commission without serious challenge. Their "shut-off" theory was questioned at the Berger Inquiry and the NEB but initially no flaw could be isolated. Behind the scenes Dr. John Fyles, a government scientist on loan to the Berger staff, suspected both the theory and the design. Working on the basis of these doubts, Commission counsel sought out other witnesses to try to resolve the issue. Finally Dr. Ken Adam, a civil engineer with the Environmental Protection Board and the University of Manitoba, and Dr. Peter Williams from Carleton University directly challenged the Arctic Gas frost heave plans.

Arctic Gas in turn brought back a further panel to contradict the evidence of their critics. They freely admitted that if Williams' contention of greatly increased potential frost heave was correct, the pipeline could not be built. But they dismissed his views as unique and unrepresentative of reliable experts in the field. His theory would even mean some frost heave in areas of continuous permafrost because the moisture would migrate through the frost front into frozen ground that remained just below the freezing point. Hence the potential frost heave would be many times the Arctic Gas estimate. The Berger Inquiry now faced conflicting evidence from reputable scientists. While the company claimed that a two-metre berm would be sufficient, Williams argued that "even the weight of a 60-metre berm might be insufficient."[7] Mr. Justice Berger requested the parties to meet privately to try to reconcile their differences but these achieved no progress because there was considerable tension between the two camps. Each group felt that their professional reputations as scientists were on the line. The whole inquiry seemed to be locked into a serious impasse on the single most important geophysical question.

With about one week to go in the regular hearings, Arctic Gas made a dramatic announcement that there had been a continuing malfunction in its test facility, which now placed its frost heave evidence in doubt. As there was insufficient time for rectification, retesting, and the filing of new evidence, the company advised Berger that he would have to leave the analysis of frost heave up to the National Energy Board, whose hearings would be continuing for some months.[8] The malfunction had been caused by air leaking into test chambers, thus lowering the shut-off pressure. The leaks had been discovered by Edward Penner of the National Research Council when the NRC had attempted to do some tests on the Arctic Gas equipment. After the vehemence with which the experts had defended their work earlier, this admission at the eleventh hour hurt the technical credibility of the applicant.

Later at the National Energy Board, Arctic Gas abandoned its "shut-off" theory as impracticable, for it might require a berm of 100 feet or deep burial of 140 feet. It brought forward a totally new design involving insulation, heat-tracing, and heat probes. In the overland portions through shallow permafrost of less than fifteen feet the pipeline would be insulated and heat-traced (electrical resistance cables along the insulation). In overland portions through deeper permafrost, electrical heating probes or elements would be angled underneath the pipeline to limit the ice lensing. At major river crossings, insulation and heat-tracing would be installed inside special steel casing. Also, the southern limit for chilling the gas was moved north from the Alberta border to the Fort Simpson area.[9] In this area of shallow, scattered permafrost it was now assumed that the problems of thaw settlement would be easier to control than those of frost heave. This new complex design, which was nicknamed "the electric blanket around the refrigerator" approach, raised a series of new requirements, including a power source and power lines along the right-of-way.

The complexities of the design were made all the more difficult because permafrost is not a static phenomenon but expands and contracts with changes in the mean annual temperature. Permafrost may also contract if peat, bushes, or trees are removed in clearing the

161

right-of-way. Thus the Arctic Gas design had to take into account the potential for permafrost migration; they would have to install sensing devices to turn on or off the heating units to reflect changing conditions during the forty- or fifty-year life of the pipeline. In watching the Arctic Gas team grapple with this problem, one had the sense that they were continually in search of the "technical fix" that would solve their problems. But this search led them into more and more complex technology. Each adaptation to solve one problem seemed to open the way for one or two new ones to emerge. They seemed intent on confronting nature rather than adapting to the physical forces at work.

During the course of the NEB hearings Arctic Gas was adding new details orally to its design as the cross-examination proceeded;[10] the experts appeared to be desperately trying to recoup their position but these *ad hoc* additions only made things worse. The absence of any empirical data on heat probes and heat-tracing in permafrost made the whole exercise a study in guesswork. They were well aware the frost heave issue was sufficient grounds for dismissing their application. But, equally serious, it could be used by regulatory boards as an argument for delay that could be fatal for Arctic Gas in Washington. Foothills suffered from the same problem but to a far less degree; it claimed that only the last fifty miles to the Alaskan border would be subject to serious permafrost.

The purpose of this section is not to denigrate Arctic Gas and its consultants, Northern Engineering Services. Their research was probably the most advanced in the world. Any of those who went through the hearings came away with a new sense of the physical power of the environmental forces in the North and the technical challenges presented by huge projects like pipelines. Here Canada was attempting to design a type of facility never attempted anywhere on the globe before. For once we could not just draw on Texas technology. The basic difference was the permafrost environment, the basic science of which was not fully understood. Peter Williams, in his recent book on the subject, concluded: "It may seem surprising in view of all the accumulated evidence, that there is still little agreement about what is actually going on in frozen soils, and in particular, disagreement about the precise, quantitative description of the process of freezing and thawing in porous materials."[11] Williams believed that frost heave must be studied in connection with *existing* permafrost (close to the freezing point in temperature) as well as with the unfrozen pockets of discontinuous permafrost. This conclusion, if substantiated by further research, will increase considerably the area of potential frost heave and complicate the problems for regulatory boards in risk assessment of future applications such as the Polar Gas Pipeline. Until we understand the nature and extent of the physical forces involved in permafrost we can hardly design a technology to cope with them.

Because of the controversies surrounding some of Williams' work, it is important to look to other sources as well in documenting this uncertainty. In March, 1978, an international workshop of civil engineers working in northern areas came to a similar conclusion. "Although a certain amount of data on frozen soil behaviour has been accumulated in recent years, there is still a clear lack of reliable information on several important properties and aspects necessary for the design of structures in permafrost." The minutes went on to list eight areas where deficiencies existed, including ice lensing at near zero temperatures in frozen ground.[12] A number of those attending these sessions had done work for Arctic Gas or Foothills and had testified as to their certainty about the nature of ice lensing to Berger and the NEB.

The frost heave problem was not the only one in which technical design changes were made in the course of the hearings as a result of the growing awareness of the physical and climatic forces at work in the North. All these design changes in midstream make the problems of regulatory assessment all the more difficult; one had to keep track of the hundreds of amendments to the original application in doing cross-examination. One of the great strengths of the Berger Inquiry as opposed to the NEB was that it had the time, the determination, and the available expertise to unravel complex technical problems. Counsel for the inquiry viewed their role as that of active participant and, unlike the NEB, they could bring in their own witnesses to challenge the applicants. On frost heave this evidence was central to the debate because other parties, such as the Environmental Protection Board or the public interest groups, did not possess the technical expertise.

The permafrost issue demonstrates one of the wider problems for environmental assessment, namely, terrain analysis to determine the composition of the surface and subsurface areas. Mapping the distribution of permafrost is essential for virtually all development, yet air photo and remote sensing techniques are not yet adequate. This forces companies back on the very slow and costly drill cores for the soil profiles. For one 250-mile stretch of the right-of-way there were only nineteen bore holes to document the conditions, including bed rock that would require blasting.[13] Yet this data must be available for a comprehensive regulatory assessment. Because of the cost, detailed ground-level terrain analysis for major projects like pipelines is only done *after* regulatory approval as part of the final design phase; yet cross-examination of the design proposal is difficult because no one knows the terrain conditions in which the line will be laid. Once approval for the project is given it is unlikely that serious changes in design or route would be ordered for these would affect the approved financing package. From the company's point of view, it does not wish to spend the huge amounts for terrain analysis until it is assured it will have the green light on the project and a means of recouping the costs.

The extremes of northern climate had a wide variety of impacts on construction equipment and techniques. In the extreme cold, metal becomes more brittle and its properties change. One of the key pieces of equipment affected by this problem was the "Super-Ditcher" required to cut the thousands of miles of trench. In order to keep to the critical Arctic Gas schedule each of these machines would have to cut about three-quarters of a mile per day;[14] trials in frozen rocky ground showed that the existing machines were totally inadequate. Larger, more powerful ones were built but these suffered the same fate. By the end of the hearings Arctic Gas had a design for a new ditcher using a belt of twenty-one buckets with seventeen teeth each. The teeth had been the weak point of earlier models, for they had snapped or worn down very rapidly. Depending on one's point of view this new creation was known as the Super or Phantom Ditcher.

The reliability of machinery for any northern project is a critical component in ensuring completion on schedule. When, as in this case, the prototype had not yet been built, let alone tested to work out the bugs, it was hardly surprising that many analysts were quite sceptical of the applicant's ability to meet the stated schedule. For Arctic Gas the third winter, when it proposed to construct the lateral from the Mackenzie Delta to Prudhoe Bay, was the Achilles' heel. If it failed to complete before the snow roads began to melt in the spring, the whole line would be held up for eight months before conditions would be right again for heavy equipment on permafrost. This meant that the consortium would be carrying the $10-billion-plus financing package without the cash flow from gas sales in the south. The alternative scenario, which Berger believed would happen, envisaged that the pressure on government would be too great and summer construction would be allowed irrespective of the damage to the permafrost and the caribou.[15]

A related problem on scheduling involved worker productivity during the Arctic winter. Arctic Gas was proposing to use artificial light and wind shields to cut down on the horrendous problems along the Arctic coast. In Alaska it was found that equipment could not be operated below −40°F and worker productivity declined toward zero when the temperature or the wind chill factor reached −35°F.[16] Alyeska gave up construction during the winter months because of the combination of total darkness, cold, and wind, which created both physical and psychological barriers to human activity. Yet this was the very time when the permafrost was least vulnerable and the right-of-way most stable for the essential heavy equipment. Winter construction, which initially seemed to be the perfect answer to the problems of permafrost degradation, gradually became less and less attractive as the technical and human problems became apparent. Especially in the extremes of the Arctic coast, winter pipelining appeared to be an insoluble problem for mobilizing southern unionized workers. In the final months of the hearings, Foothills abandoned its proposal for winter work and switched to the more feasible idea of summer construction on a gravel pad for that portion of the Maple Leaf project north of the tree line.

Probably the most fundamental geotechnical issue of all was the integrity and durability of the pipeline itself. Arctic Gas were proposing a 48″ high pressure line to operate at 1,680 pounds per square inch, which was greater than any pipeline system in existence. Increased pressure meant expanded throughput volumes, greater economies of scale, but increased possibility of pipeline fractures. This cracking along the line would spread like lightning for up to hundreds of yards even through welds joining the lengths of pipe; there would be a significant possibility of an accompanying fire. Fractures usually originate from defects in the pipe that should be caught in the factory or in the pressurized hydrostatic tests when the pipeline is laid. However, for a variety of reasons these defects sometimes are not caught. After going into service under high pressure these flaws or corrosion or exceptional external stress can all trigger fractures, especially under conditions of extreme cold. With these circumstances it is easy to see the potential for damage from frost heave.

To try to limit the potential for brittle fracture Arctic Gas introduced another new technical feature called "crack arrestors." The term provided a few Freudian puns during some of the duller sessions of the NEB hearings, where humour is normally an endangered species. The arrestors were four-foot-long sleeves that slid over the pipelines at intervals of about 300 feet. They became snug when the line was pressurized, thus providing a reinforcing collar. Experiments with this new technology showed that it did not always work, while it complicated the coating and the taping of the pipeline so necessary to seal it from corrosion. These bands created new rigid zones of stress when the pipeline was bent into the trench. Foothills, which was planning to run its line at lower pressure, rejected the need for these arrestors, arguing that they were a menace promoting fractures, not retarding them. Once again Arctic Gas, by resorting to new technology to combat the northern environment, ran into increasing difficulties as the hearings progressed.[17] It will probably take several decades of operation of a chilled Arctic gas pipeline before this question will be settled with any degree of certainty.

The Foothills (Yukon) route along the Alaska Highway, while avoiding the worst of the permafrost problems, did face other risks in cutting through an earthquake zone. Tremors in the area could threaten the physical integrity of the line itself as well as pose indirect dangers such as landslides. Fault lines crossed the proposed right-of-way at several points and special design features were proposed to allow for some ground movement without fracturing the pipeline. However, there was no doubt that a serious quake centred in the area would destroy the line. Up until very recently it was assumed that the Mackenzie Valley was a safer route to avoid any chance of tremors. However, in October, 1985, an earthquake registering 6.6 on the Richter scale struck between Fort Simpson and Wrigley to the west of Great Slave Lake. This event surprised seismic experts and will force reconsideration of our risk assessment assumptions for the valley corridor.

The Mackenzie is one of the truly great river systems of the world. Its power is so great that those who live along its banks have learned from experience to respect its churning waters and unruly spirit. Some native legends have even given it supernatural powers. Like the great rivers of Siberia it possesses a south-to-north flow pattern with the spring flooding in the upper reaches in Alberta before the ice has broken up in the sections below Great Slave Lake. This restriction of the exodus increases the velocity and the violence of the ice breakup when it finally comes on the lower Mackenzie. In the narrow Ramparts sections near Fort Good Hope ice can pile up as high as eighty feet above normal river level. With ice jams, the potential for ice scour is increased; there are deep holes in the floor of the river of up to 100 feet for which there are no sure explanations in terms of our existing knowledge of channel hydraulics. To counter the threat at river crossings and the cross-Delta section, Arctic Gas proposed to twin the pipeline with parallel lines several hundred yards apart. The theory was that if one line was cut the other would remain to divert the gas through. If the line was severed during the spring breakup the system could be out of commission for anywhere from thirty to 150 days if there was no alternative pipeline lateral. They had even considered overhead crossings, which would be extremely difficult given the width of the Mackenzie in most sections.

Ice scour is a fundamental problem for marine aspects of the petroleum industry in the western Arctic. Imperial, to maximize its

166

Figure 11.
Beaufort Sea Drilling Zone. From Berger Report, I, p. 58.

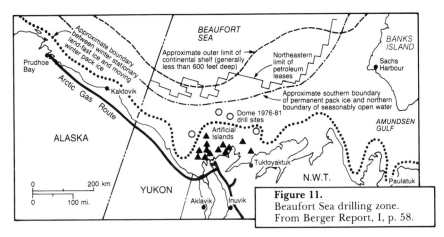

Figure 11.
Beaufort Sea drilling zone.
From Berger Report, I, p. 58.

production at Norman Wells, has now built special island platforms in the Mackenzie; north of the Delta, Dome, Gulf, and Imperial have to design special artificial islands to house their production facilities in the Beaufort Sea. Most of the proven reserves are under the river or the ocean. Stable shore-fast ice can be a great help for drilling, as has been the case in the High Arctic islands; however, in the Beaufort Sea moving pack ice challenges anything in its path. In the summer the pack moves north to open a zone for drill ships but the return of cold weather in October brings the ice back to the coastal zone.

Spring breakup on the Mackenzie or multimillion-ton ice islands in the Beaufort can destroy submarine production facilities or pipelines even if they are sunk into the river or ocean floor. For instance, in sixty feet of water off the Delta it is estimated by engineers that the pipeline would have to be sunk as deep as fifteen feet to avoid potential ice scour. Needless to say, this adds to the costs of construction. Submarine production facilities in particular must be carefully protected, for in the event of a blowout in the pack ice areas cleanup must await the retreat of the ice the following summer. It could be up to eight months before a relief well could be started. Since failsafe blowout preventers have failed elsewhere in the world under less extreme conditions, one cannot rule out the chance of it happening in the Beaufort. There is not as yet any technical means of cleaning up a major oil spill in pack ice because the normal skimmers and booms would be inoperative. In the year it could take to stop a blowout, the crude oil would flow out under the ice and be carried westward by

167

Figure 12.
Ice Scour in the Beaufort Sea. Courtesy Department of Fisheries and
Oceans.

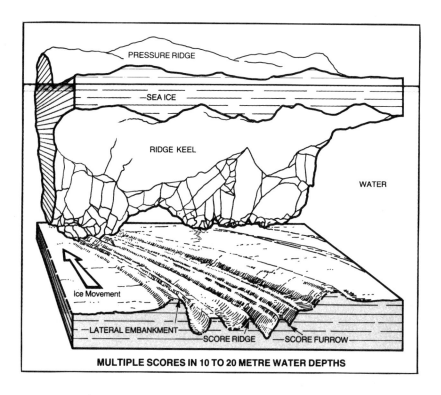

MULTIPLE SCORES IN 10 TO 20 METRE WATER DEPTHS

the winds and currents across the outer fringes of the Delta, across
the north coast of the Yukon, and then into Alaskan waters. The
biological consequences of such an accident will be discussed later.

With the oil reserves now found in the Beaufort at Atkinson Point,
Issungnak, Koakoak, Kopanoar, and Tarsiut[19] by the summer of 1985,
there is no question that this area will become a major oilfield. However, there is considerable doubt when these reserves will come on
stream and in what fashion the oil will be transported out of the
Beaufort. Imperial Oil wants to extend the Norman Wells Pipeline
north to the Delta or construct a whole new pipeline system south to
Alberta. Imperial is actively at work through the facilities of Interprovincial Pipeline. Dome Petroleum, on the other hand, is pushing
ahead to develop its tanker technology to ship out future oil production via the Northwest Passage or the Bering Sea. The Norman Wells

Figure 13.
Oil Tankers through Arctic Waters. From Dome Petroleum, *Beaufort* (December, 1982).

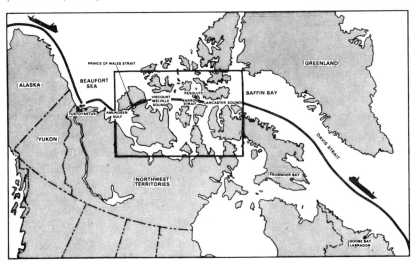

crude is exceptionally light, thus allowing it to flow through the pipeline at temperatures even below freezing. This means technically that the pipeline can be buried with little problem of heat transfer to melt the permafrost. The Beaufort Sea oil is heavier and would probably have to be elevated to avoid permafrost problems such as those faced by Alyeska, which pumped its crude oil through at 60°C.

The technology required for this system was pioneered in the 1970's by the Alyeska line. Even though it is elevated there are still permafrost problems because the poles into the terrain must remain permanently bonded to the surrounding frozen soil. Any heat transferred through the post can lead to a gradual weakening of the structure. To counter this thermal problem, each of these vertical support poles in the permafrost areas will contain a cryoanchor within each pole. The cryoanchors are metal tubes filled with ammonia as a refrigerant. Liquid ammonia absorbs heat from the surrounding ground and rises as a vapour to the top of the tube where above-ground facilities cool it, thus causing it to drop down below ground where the cycle begins anew. In this way heat from the surrounding soil is drawn into the system, thus permanently cementing the pole into the frozen ground.

Because of the wide range of temperatures along the route of the pipeline (−60°C to +40°C), expansion and contraction is a serious engineering problem. In the elevated sections the pipeline will be

Figure 14.
Proposed Dome Oil Arctic Tanker. From Arctic Pilot Project.

secured to the poles through a movable "saddle and slide" assembly that can move either way. Also, the compressor stations built on permafrost will have to be constructed atop gravel pads and in some cases with additional refrigeration probes down into the gravel to ensure the stability of the frozen ground underneath. In the southern portions of the line, as it enters Alberta, the permafrost problems are ended but there are other geotechnical concerns that have to be handled carefully. In some of these muskeg areas the water table is very close to the surface and the pipeline creates its own upward buoyancy pressure. Concrete or other weighty anchors must be used to keep the line in place. The pipe also requires a protective coating against corrosion, and in some cases strips of zinc serving as "sacrificial anodes" will be laid parallel to the pipe to protect the line from electrolytic corrosion caused by electric currents between the pipe and the soil. The oil pipeline has a number of other engineering problems already discussed in connection with the natural gas line.[20]

While Imperial has been at work with Interprovincial in planning the Mackenzie Valley Oil Pipeline, Dome Petroleum has purchased a major shipyard and has begun design work on VLCC (very large crude carriers). Here they are extending the known technology of icebreakers, including their own *Canmar Kigoriak*, along with that of the great new supertankers. The total displacement weight of these tankers will be about 300,000 tons; they will be 1,280 feet long, 170 feet wide, and draw 65 feet of water. They will be designated Arctic class-ten vessels capable of smashing through ten-foot-thick ice while proceeding at three knots; it is estimated that they would be capable of operating year-round anywhere in the Arctic. The two independent engines will produce up to 150,000 shaft horsepower (about three times that of a conventional supertanker) with enclosed twin screws and twin rudders for greater manoeuvrability. The propellers will be shrouded in steel rings to maximize the thrust and give greater protection from the ice. The tanker will possess a special spoon-shaped bow allowing it to ride up onto the ice, where the tanker's weight will split and separate the ice as the ship pushes its way through. The reamers in the bow will ensure that the channel cut is wider than the ship itself, thus improving its turning capability. Switching of ballast will allow the tanker to heel over if required. To reduce ice resistance along the hull, two seawater jets will pump a lubricating stream of water back from the bow. Should the sides of the vessel be pierced a compressed air system is designed to force oil out of the damaged compartment into empty side tanks before significant volumes could escape into the sea. To facilitate navigation through difficult ice, the steering bridge will be forward not aft. On the bridge will be dials to monitor the levels of ice pressure around the sides, which may allow for evasive action before damage is done to the special double-skin hull.

Dome's strategy for oil production from its deep-water wells is totally dependent on the technical viability of these tankers and the development of the even more expensive loading atolls for them. These are major barriers yet to be overcome for engineering and matters of economics as well. To what extent they will work, given the power and strength of Arctic multi-year ice and pressure ridges, has yet to be determined. Certainly the technology of Arctic shipping has improved in the last decade; but past experience would indicate that one can expect extensive and expensive experimentation before these tankers will be able to cope with all-year navigation in the High Arctic ice conditions. Also, from tanker accidents elsewhere, it is clear that human error often plays a significant role irrespective of the quality of the engineering design.

The above planning is based on the assumption that there will be several major producing oilfields in the Beaufort Sea by the mid-1990's. But the history of drilling in the area makes this anything but a certainty. The offshore exploration has gone through three distinct phases, each utilizing a different technology.

In the early 1970's Imperial Oil began the process with drilling from artificial islands constructed from fill in the shallow waters north of the Mackenzie Delta. Soil was dredged up from the bottom; sand bags, rock, and filter cloth were used around the edges to stop erosion; and the drilling surface was surrounded by gently sloping contours designed to break the waves or allow the ice to ride up on it. During the winter drilling, the island was locked in by the surrounding shore-fast ice as a stable platform. But after the drilling was completed the "sacrificial beach" concept allowed it to be eroded by wave action. Imperial Oil has constructed more than twenty of these islands in water depths up to twenty metres. In the High Arctic islands differing ice conditions allowed for alternative methods of drilling. Here the ice was shore-fast but the water usually too deep for artificial islands. So water was poured on the ice to create a strengthened ice platform five metres thick, more than sufficient to carry the weight of the drilling rig. The seawater was cheap and readily available, unlike dredged sediments and gravel required for the artificial islands. This design has proved to be safe and efficient and has been used by Panarctic each winter since 1974.

The second phase commenced with deep-water drilling in the Beaufort in the summer of 1976. Dome brought in two converted cargo vessels and a regular drillship, all of which were reinforced to withstand the scattered summer floating pan ice. These drillships with the supporting vessels were very expensive to own and operate, especially as they were confined to the short drilling season of from eight to fourteen weeks when the floating pack ice retreated north in the mid- and late summer. Canada was the first country in the world to attempt marine drilling in such ice-prone areas and its decision was protested by the U.S. State Department because winds and currents could carry the oil from any blowout westward into Alaskan waters. Dome has monitored its drilling very carefully to avoid incidents, but even so there have been water and gas discharges from Dome wells. The technology employed is the state of the art and Dome, through its subsidiary Canmar Drilling, has spent hundreds of millions on equipment, including triple blowout preventers (BOPs), which are installed in the glory hole below the floor of the Beaufort Sea.

Out in this deep water in depths up to sixty metres, the largest geological formations were found and Dome desperately gambled that oilfields equivalent in size to the Middle East would be found. Here, small and medium-sized fields were uneconomic. The results to the mid-1980's have been mixed. There have been significant finds, such as Koakoak and Kopanour, but a huge elephant on the scale of Prudhoe Bay has eluded them. Yet only such a massive field will justify the enormous costs of developing a unique oil production system that can survive the ice of the Beaufort Sea. In the 1980's Dome has been operating four drillships mainly in farm-outs or rented to other oil companies because of the precarious financial condition of the company.

The drillships can operate only in open water or in the thin early fall ice when their anchoring system and supporting tugs can keep them in position. Once the serious pack ice begins to move in they must leave or be pushed off position, possibly with ice damage. At this point the well is suspended and the vessel moves to winter quarters at Tuk or McKinley Bay. On average it takes 150 days to drill and test a deep well; many years they get no more than ninety days of actual drilling, hence the two-year time frame for results. The drilling in the Delta/Beaufort area can also be complicated by areas where the geological strata have been badly faulted or where methane hydrates (frozen natural gas) are found in permafrost. Either can create uncontrollable pressure up the drill stem.

To try to overcome the short drilling season of the Canmar fleet, Imperial, Gulf, and Dome all began experimenting with new technical designs that could allow the extension of the artificial islands into deeper water. The major problem lay in the low gradient of the sides, which required rapidly escalating amounts of fill for each foot of depth. Yet the erosion factor from wave action at the surface required such gentle slopes. The end result was that artificial islands rapidly became uneconomic in water depths greater than twenty metres. Research showed, however, that the sides of the island could be much steeper if they did not have to cope with erosion from wave action at the surface. Therefore, with a concrete or steel structure on the top to deal with the waves, the fill requirements would only be a fraction of the sacrificial beach design.

One of the first efforts to apply this technology was the Gulf-operated Tarsiut N-44 well. Here a caisson-retained island was built in twenty-two metres of water. The four outer walls of this structure were composed of hollow concrete chambers. They were towed to the Beaufort and sunk into place on an undersea berm. The centre of the structure was then filled with dredged sand that gave it the weight and stability to cope with early winter ice. Modified designs were developed by Imperial and Dome. Each of these can be pumped out and moved to new locations and each has powerful walls to resist ice pressure. The Esso Caisson Retained Island is an eight-segment steel

Figure 15.
Molikpaq – Moblile Arctic Caisson. From Dome Petroleum, *Beaufort* (1984).

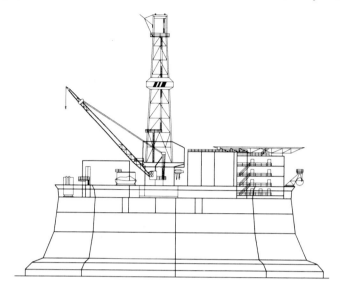

PROFILE

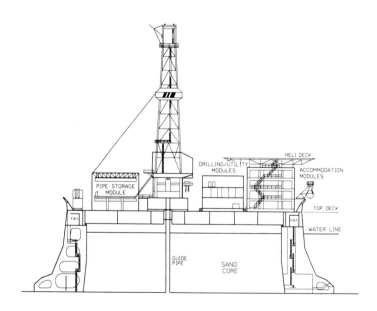

SECTION VIEW

Figure 16.
Beaufort Discovery Wells. From National Research Council, *Science Dimension*, 3 (1985), p. 21.

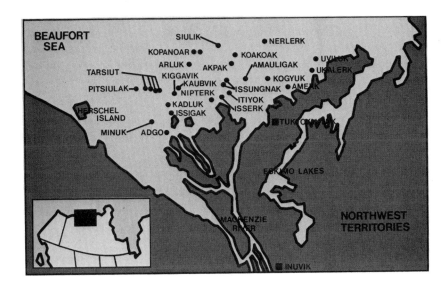

ring, 100 metres in diameter; the Dome Mobile Arctic Drilling Vessel (SSDC) is quite different in design. It is a converted oil tanker with a reinforced double hull, filled with more than a metre of concrete, and can operate in water depths up to forty-five metres. Towed into position and then sunk on a berm, it contains more than enough storage area for a whole winter of drilling; its length is the equivalent of two football fields.

In the 1980's Gulf replaced Dome as the bold innovator in technology. In June, 1982, Gulf announced a $674 million program to develop a new design for both drillships and caisson retained islands. It assumed that its expensive new equipment would attract Canadian companies as partners and would be eligible for the special federal program of PIP grants, which could cover up to 80 per cent of the drilling costs. Many analysts were sceptical of the economic viability of this new equipment, especially now that the PIP grants are being phased out by the Mulroney government. Gulf, on the other hand, wanted more efficient means to drill longer into the winter. The first of the new units was *Kulluk*, a floating conical drilling platform. With its ice-deflecting circular hull, it can get on station earlier and leave later than Dome's drillships. However, it did not meet all the expectations of its designers and was put up for sale in the summer of 1985. The second new unit was the caisson *Molikpaq* designed to drill in depths between fifteen and forty metres. This is a far more substantial facility than the earlier caisson retained islands, with a solid deck on which are mounted the drilling rig, crew quarters, copter pad, power generator, water purification system, sewage disposal system, recreation facilities, huge storage area for pipe, drilling fluids, etc. There is also a very elaborate alarm and evacuation system so people can be moved quickly if weather or heavy ice threaten the stability of the structure. Following the large loss of life with the *Ocean Ranger* disaster off Newfoundland, all the oil companies are very sensitive on the safety issue.

Thus far the technical challenges from Beaufort drilling have been confined to exploration, not production, facilities. As yet no field of commercial size (one billion barrels) has been found but there are several with proven reserves of 100 million or more. There is a great jump in the complexity of the technology required for production drilling and production platforms, which require fixed positions confronting the offshore mobile pack ice. With multi-year pressure ridges and ice islands, there can be serious danger of ice scour down to 100 feet. Imperial, which operates in the shallow offshore waters, is considering a 400 to 500 millimetre oil pipeline up the Mackenzie Valley to Zama Lake, Alberta, with a series of small feeder pipelines cut into the floor of the Beaufort Sea to link up the various fields. Dome's discoveries are in the deeper waters where such a system would be more difficult. It is proposing to develop special production and loading atolls where tankers could shelter while loading. The Beaufort EARP (Environmental Assessment and Review Process) panel in its report recommended proceeding with a small-scale oil pipeline if and when sufficient oil is discovered. Both the Imperial and Dome production facilities are still in a rough conceptual stage, making detailed analysis of their feasibility difficult. Like the chilled natural gas pipeline in permafrost, oil production facilities in pack ice require that Canada be a world pioneer. We must pay the heavy economic cost of the design and development of this technology. Currently, it would appear that Beaufort Sea oil will be the most costly conventional oil produced anywhere in the world.

Northern development has provided a tremendous stimulus to Canadian engineers and scientists probing the challenges of the Arctic. Although much time, money, and expertise have been put into re-

Figure 17.
Glomar Beaufort Sea I. From Exxon, *Offshore Resources*, 3 (Spring, 1985), p. 10.

search in these areas, we still lack adequate technical answers in a number of areas. In addition, the Arctic can always surprise you: Imperial had been using artificial islands for a decade and a half when it lost one in a storm in September, 1985. Most of our planning has been based on design concepts and computer simulations that still have to be tested under operating conditions fundamentally different from those anywhere else. The most experienced pipeline engineers in the world made basic errors in estimating the moisture migration, the ice lensing, and the potential for frost heave in the Arctic Gas design. Often, southern experience is of little help in confronting the problems of the North. Too often we have untried technology being assessed within the context of unprecedented geophysical forces such as permafrost or ice scour. Arctic Gas, in its engineering philosophy, attempted to attack the forces of nature by creating even greater forces to control frost heave in its "shut-off" theory. Generally, it is sounder engineering practice to try to avoid the impacts rather than to create them and then attempt countervailing forces. The impact can create a chain reaction of related effects that make the overall process unsound. In simple terms, it is better to go along with nature than to challenge it directly.

Canada should be proud of the achievements of its engineering profession; on northern questions we are as advanced as any nation. But engineers are born optimists because they have a professional commitment to the ideology of the technical fix – namely, that with adequate funding there is no challenge that they cannot overcome with new technology. Yet in the North that faith is being severely challenged by the power and the subtle interaction of the physical forces involved. Some observers expected that the northern experience would breed a new conservatism in their belief in technology, but there is little evidence that it has. Only low world oil prices and slack market demand have slowed the pace of development. Technology often assumes it is its own justification when in reality it must be measured by the net worth, the costs weighed against the benefits. It is here that many engineers in management find their greatest frustration. Superb engineering can still create unacceptable impacts. Nowhere is this comparative analysis easy, but nowhere is it more difficult than in the North. It is now necessary to turn to the biological sphere to see another of the facets of northern development.

CHAPTER 8

The Living Environment and the Challenge of Northern Development

The natural ecosystems of the world have suffered from the gathering momentum of industrial impacts over the last 200 years, but the real crisis has only emerged in the last quarter century. With an ever-increasing number of toxic chemical compounds, the proliferation of nuclear wastes, the relentless destruction of habitat, and declining air and water quality standards, man seemed incapable of combining industrial "progress" with environmental protection. Yet the one area of North America that remained relatively unspoiled was the Arctic wastes of Alaska and northern Canada. In many eyes this was the one region where there was some chance of preserving wilderness values and essential habitat. In many ways it became a symbol of what we had lost. This concept of preservation evoked a strong response among southern environmental groups, especially following the Prudhoe Bay oil discoveries of 1968, when the exploration focus of the petroleum industry moved north to exploit the last frontier. The major battle in the United States took place over the Alyeska oil pipeline between 1969 and 1975 and in Canada over the Mackenzie Valley Gas Pipeline during the years 1971-77. This chapter proposes to investigate the Mackenzie Valley example to try to establish how serious was the challenge to the Arctic environment, then proceeds to consider some of the current areas of controversy in the 1980's.

When the Mackenzie Valley Pipeline debate began only limited baseline data were available on the western Arctic, and there was a good deal of general but rather nebulous concern about the fragility of Arctic ecosystems. With relatively few species resident in the Arctic, such simplicity made it more vulnerable to disruptions and the extremes of climate were claimed to make ecosystems more fragile. Usually, little scientific evidence was presented to document these environmental generalizations. As yet there were serious gaps in the extent of our biological knowledge about life cycles, animal behaviour, habitat, as well as weaknesses in our ability to synthesize such data into overall environmental impact statements. Early in the 1970's we had neither the knowledge nor the scientific methodology. As Max Dunbar wrote about Arctic ecology in 1971: "We have been caught in a state of scientific near-nudity both in terms of environmental impacts and the means necessary to conserve and to protect."[1] No one was sure how far Arctic species could withstand increased disturbance, stress, and decreased habitat from industrial impacts.

Related to this were general worries about the survival of endangered species, some of whom, like the peregrine falcon, had their last refuge in the inhospitable northern wastes. In addition, even if the knowledge was available, many doubted the will of the federal government to protect the environment. The Ministries of Indian and Northern Affairs and Energy, Mines, and Resources were committed to a development philosophy that the weak and newly created Ministry of the Environment was in no position to challenge at the cabinet table.[2] The environmental research for the Mackenzie Highway was done after the project was announced during the election campaign of 1972. Thus, for many environmentalists the Mackenzie Valley Pipeline appeared to be a *fait accompli* and potentially the greatest ecological disaster in Canadian history. Their fundamental worries were surfacing through CARC[3] and other organizations long before Arctic Gas had released any of the details of its project.

These public criticisms sparked an extensive response within government and corporate circles. From 1970 onward there was a sizable increase in sponsored biological research related to a pipeline corridor along the Mackenzie. With the Expanded Pipeline Guidelines of 1972 it was clear that any pipeline applicant would have to produce extensive biological and socio-economic data on its project. Hence, no project in Canadian history received so much attention from professional biologists and no project contributed so much to their prosperity. Academics suddenly became consultants and small firms emerged from the woodwork all over the country. Arctic Gas alone spent over $30 million on its main forty-one-volume Biological Report Series, which was a major contribution to our knowledge of northern species. The federal government produced several hundred smaller studies, many of which were published under the auspices of the Task Force on Northern Oil Development. The Environmental Protection Board and CARC also made significant contributions, which tried to look at the process of environmental impact assessment as well as basic data. Yet, after all the research studies, the public hearings, and the millions of words of debate, the issues and the answers were not clear. Science alone did not provide a resolution. Not only were the population statistics for caribou at issue; the value perceptions of human beings in weighing the relative importance of preserving those caribou or getting on with development were equally involved.

This central question – environmental integrity or technological development – lies behind all the biological issues dealt with in this chapter and every other environmental decision facing mankind. This chapter is meant as an introduction to the problems of environmental impact assessment rather than a definitive statement on northern biology, which I gladly leave to those professionally trained in the field.

Another of the factors complicating the interpretation of biological evidence was the social ramifications that flowed from wildlife questions. Biological evidence was not just an end in itself but the means for sustaining the native way of life. This inevitably brought further value judgements and emotion into some of the scientific debate. For the purpose of this chapter it would be clearly impossible to try to summarize all the problems with so many different species of mammals, birds, and fish involved. Thus, to demonstrate the nature of the problems, the analysis will concentrate on three species – caribou, snow geese, and beluga whales.

The unique nature of Arctic ecosystems makes it imperative to probe some of the biological circumstances so that one can properly weigh the agonizing trade-offs often involved in development. With a limited number of species present in the North, the food chain from mosses and lichens to large mammals is much more limited than in the south. Of the 3,200 known species of mammals, only nine are found in the High Arctic; of the 23,000 varieties of fish, only twenty-five inhabit Arctic waters.[4] Hence, any particular stage in the food chain may be dominated by one or two species; for instance, lemmings provide the herbivore "links" for foxes, snowy owls, and weasels. Loss of one species can cause starvation further up the food chain; in the south alternatives often would be available. Some species in the North are late maturing sexually and therefore take longer to recover if their numbers are depleted. The cold water limits food production, and even though huge trophy fish can be caught, overfishing can rapidly decimate numbers. Many northern lakes are already suffering from this problem. Monitoring of wildlife population trends can be difficult because of wide oscillation from natural cycles – lemmings can decline drastically in an area only to rebound via reproduction and migration. Severe weather can also play its part. A very severe ice storm one fall in the 1970's on Victoria Island coated all the vegetation and killed off most of the local muskox. In such cases it could require decades before the numbers are recouped or before migrations from other islands replenish the local stock. Northern ecosystems suffer from a shaky equilibrium and are acutely sensitive to disruptions or pollution by man.

In the process of environmental assessment it was inevitable that caribou would play a central role, for in so many ways they are the essence of the northern environment. Through many millennia they have evolved to be able to flourish in the harsh extremes of climate. They exist on the meagre vegetative cover of the barren lands through which they are the means of converting the limited energy bestowed from the sun into a protein supply to sustain human and other animal life. The migration of the massive herds in the North is one of the great spectacles of the earth, which few can witness without a deep sense of emotion. George Calef in his recent book on caribou caught with poetic eloquence the sense of exhilaration in observing these awkward beasts:

> To follow the caribou is to experience every facet of the northern environment, for the caribou are the central creatures of the North, the pulse of life in the land. They quicken the country not merely by adding animation and excitement themselves, but also by carrying along a host of other creatures; the wolf, the fox, the raven. The empty tundra may appear a drab and barren place, but let one caribou trot onto the skyline of an esker and the land comes alive.[5]

One of the last of the great herds, with over 100,000 animals, is the Porcupine herd of the North Yukon. The herd winters in the central Yukon in an area recently penetrated by the Dempster Highway and the route for the proposed Dempster Lateral of the Foothills Pipeline system. In late March or early April the caribou begin their migration north and west. The migrations would appear to be triggered by growing daylight, changing snow conditions, and the advancing pregnancy of the adult females. Wolves will follow the herd, attacking stray animals or those weakened by disease or injuries.[6] The herd will keep to open country where their speed and mobility will not be checked by deep snow. Along the migration route are many swift-flowing rivers, which the caribou do no hesitate to cross in spite of the risks involved.

By late May or the first days of June the cows and the yearlings will have reached the coastal plain adjacent to the Beaufort Sea, where local conditions are optimum for the calving to take place. If the migration is delayed, then calving will take place prior to arrival with increased mortality from wolves, river crossing, and the like. In the first weeks successful bonding is essential for survival of the calves,

Figure 18.
Caribou Herds of the North. From George Calef, *Caribou and the Barren-lands* (Ottawa, 1981), p. 16.

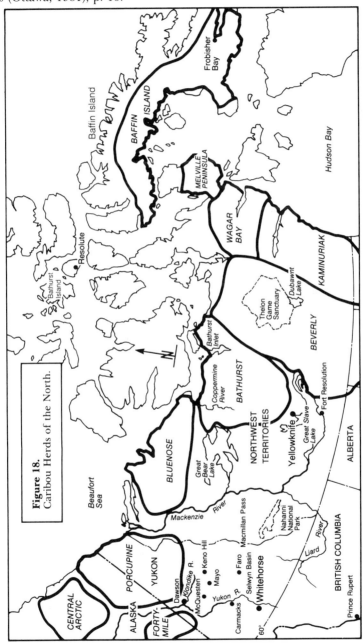

183

Figure 19.
Porcupine Caribou Herd: Winter Range. From Foothills Pipelines (Yukon) Ltd., 1978.

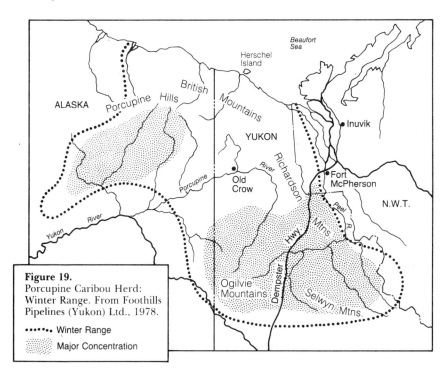

Figure 19.
Porcupine Caribou Herd: Winter Range. From Foothills Pipelines (Yukon) Ltd., 1978.

••••••• Winter Range

Major Concentration

for if a calf gets separated from its mother, no other cow will sustain it. In this selected habitat the cows will be relatively safe from predators, but late-season blizzards can take their toll of fragile, newly born calves. With calving, the females lose their antlers and the yearlings are sent on their independent way.

Caribou have to be three or four years old before pregnancy and then they bear only one calf per year; thus, their reproductive potential is limited. Because of the stress involved in pregnancy and calving, the habitat must be undisturbed or mortality will increase. At birth the calf does not instinctively know or follow its mother. It will eagerly follow a human if confronted and has no fear of intruders. In the first days it must learn the sight, smell, and sound of its mother, just as the cow must become acquainted with her calf. This is the critical bonding process which, if interrupted by some intrusion such as a low-flying plane, may lead to separation and starvation for the calf. The early period is crucial for building the strength and mobility

Figure 20.
Porcupine Caribou Herd: Calving Grounds, 1972-74. From Arctic Gas
Biological Report Series, Vol. 32, 1975.

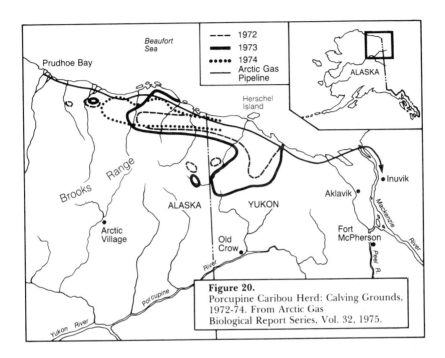

Figure 20.
Porcupine Caribou Herd: Calving Grounds,
1972-74. From Arctic Gas
Biological Report Series, Vol. 32, 1975.

of the young before the cows move off to join the mature bulls on the summer range further inland.

The calving grounds are critical habitat because they are unsuited for wolves, who require underground denning for their own young. The few predators who do get into the calving grounds (wolves, grizzly bears, or golden eagles) have a relatively easy time killing calves and weakened cows. Also, by travelling north the caribou postpone the onslaught of the massive clouds of blood-sucking insects that constitute such a stress and drain on the herd until after the calving and early nursing. On the rocky coastal plain the new growth of cotton-grass provides the concentrated nutrients when the energy demands of calving and nursing are the greatest. All of these environmental factors are of great importance in giving the young some chance of survival.

In mid-June, following the calving, the herd congregates and moves west into the post-calving aggregation where the warm weather brings the onslaught of mosquitoes and other insects. As the summer proceeds the herd turns inland and eastward in Alaska by which point the mature bulls, who migrate later, finally catch up to the cows, the yearlings, and the new calves. The summer is spent grazing across the North Slope where attacks from bears or wolves can be outdistanced by the speedy caribou. The main torment, however, is the mosquitoes that breed everywhere in the moist pockets on the tundra. The harassment can be so great as to stampede the herd, and such stampedes can trample infirm members of the herd and separate young calves. River crossings are another menace, especially for calves who may drown or be killed by wolves that corner reluctant swimmers. In August the great herd begins to disperse, with some heading west across the Old Crow flats toward Arctic Village in Alaska and others south to the central Yukon. In the early fall the annual great hunt of the caribou takes place as the herd crosses the Porcupine River. Archaelogical evidence indicates that natives have killed caribou at the crossing points of the Porcupine River for at least 30,000 years.[7] Here native hunters from Old Crow stock up for the approaching long winter by taking about 500 animals, or about ten per hunter. The remaining herd continues south to the area of the Ogilvie Mountains and the Peel River.

By mid-October the bulls are moving into an aggressive pattern of behaviour for the coming rut or mating season. With necks swollen to double their normal size the big bulls attempt to assert their dominance over potential rivals by lowering their heads and charging. Some injuries and a few deaths can result, including instances where horns become permanently locked. In the third week of October, as the cows come into heat, the formal rut begins with frenzied activity from the dominant bulls, who move on from one conquest to another. When the week is over they are exhausted from fighting and rutting and their stored fat from the summer and fall has been expended. Following this the bulls lose their antlers and move off from the cows and the calves to separate winter range.

From November through April the caribou are absorbed in their primary struggle for survival. The only available food consists of mosses and sedges that have to be cleared of snow by their well-designed hooves. If the snow is crusted or the vegetation covered by ice from freezing rain, then it may take more energy to procure the food than is contained within it. No other grazing mammal can exist on such low nutrient intake and the animal's whole system has evolved to cope with these conditions. In the extreme the caribou will curl up, using the snow cover as a shield with the cows protecting the calves. Yet through the whole winter they must remain alert to the threat of wolves, which shadow groups of caribou always looking for stragglers.

The caribou, except when feeding, try to keep to open spaces like lakes where they can see the approach of predators. However, this behaviour, developed as a defence mechanism against wolves, makes them a sitting target for hunters who can easily spot their prey.

By spring even the most vigorous caribou are showing the signs of fatigue from the winter ordeal; luckily, the pregnant cows retain their antlers, which helps them in fighting for the meagre food supplies. In late March or early April with lengthening days and increasing warmth of the sun, the caribou become restless; then the females begin to move north, thus starting the yearly migration cycle all over again. For thousands of years the losses to wolves and native hunters have been balanced by the reproductive powers of the herd.

In the 1970's the issue quickly became clear: could this equilibrium continue with the arrival of major developments like a pipeline? When the Porcupine caribou herd came to be considered by the Berger Inquiry, there was distressing evidence regarding other herds just across the line in Alaska. The Forty-Mile herd, whose range was just south and west of the Porcupine, had shrunk from an estimated 568,000 in 1920 to 6,000 in the mid-1970's.[8] The great fear was that the northern caribou were headed for the same fate as the prairie buffalo. It was not easy to explain the scale of the decline in numbers, but increased access and hunting and disruption of habitats by development were obviously involved. Caribou, although fearless in swimming raging streams, could be upset by roads or railways, which could become severe barriers physically or psychologically. For instance, in northern Manitoba, they abandoned all the range to the south of the Hudson Bay Railway some years after the line had been built. Hence it was not easy to predict in advance how caribou would react or how serious the impact would be in terms of maintaining the numbers in any given herd.

The Arctic Gas proposal forced the debate on caribou into a clear focus because it sought to construct the pipeline straight through the coastal calving zone of the Porcupine herd. Although the main construction would take place in winter, the compressor stations and some auxiliary functions would have to be done in summer. In addition, overflights by helicopters or fixed-wing aircraft would be required to monitor the right-of-way and because the visibility on the North Slope was often poor, this would require low-level observation. Such disturbance would have a serious impact on the pregnant cows or the bonding problems for newly born calves. Most of the biological evidence concluded that this North Slope route was a major problem except for that from Arctic Gas, which rejected any such conclusion. When the Berger Report appeared, Arctic Gas rejected it as biased against its project. Yet the NEB and the U.S. Department of the Interior came to exactly the same conclusion.

> Increased access, disturbance by aircraft and ground vehicles on the calving ground, summer borrow activities, and shipping activities all will act adversely on the herd. Disturbance factors associated with material staging, construction and operation of the compressor stations will add to the adverse, long-term impact. . . .

The herd could lose its size if it abandoned this traditional habitat and moved to less suitable adjacent areas of its summer range.[9] Arctic Gas proposed to keep its flights at 2,000 feet to limit disturbance, but this seemed impractical given the nature of the task: they had to pick out potential erosion problems from spring runoff or pipeline leaks evident only from vegetation discolouration.

Arctic Gas rightly recognized the critical nature of the North Slope habitat for many varieties of flora and fauna. It promised unconditionally a whole series of mitigative measures that supposedly would control negative effects. There would be no permanent road from Prudhoe Bay to the Delta; the company would shut down construction if the caribou approached; aircraft would be restricted to a 2,000-foot minimum; any trench areas would be filled or fenced to avoid injuries; construction workers would be prohibited from bringing firearms; and permanent sites, such as compressor stations and airstrips, would be fenced.[10] These assurances were not considered enough.

Berger rejected the evidence of the Arctic Gas witnesses, who with one exception supported the coastal route for the pipeline.[11] Among the Arctic Gas consultants was Dr. Frank Banfield, one of the leading authorities on caribou. Berger instead chose to accept the analysis of public interest witnesses that the potential impacts were too great, regardless of proposed mitigative measures. In addition, he did not believe that they could keep to the construction schedule because of lower worker productivity and the difficulties of constructing snow roads on the frozen tundra for their heavy equipment. Berger also concluded that any pipeline would inevitably bring further pipelines or roads along the route. He found the evidence supporting the arguments for no pipeline in the area "complex and circumstantial but . . . compelling."[12]

This conclusion, which had not been proposed by the Environmental Protection Board or his own Staff Report, was one of the most important in the whole report. In one stroke of the pen Berger had severed the pipeline system from its Prudhoe Bay source of supply. After the event Arctic Gas was particularly bitter about this recommendation, claiming that he had deliberately ignored Arctic Gas evidence and commitments regarding construction while introducing the prospect of a further pipeline and road, which had nothing to do with the application.[13] It even argued that because of his socialist or even Marxist political views he was just looking for an excuse to prohibit its application.

Since the appearance of the Berger Report there has been great concern expressed about the decline of the great caribou herds of the Canadian North. Sensational media reports have been followed by firm denials from officials and native elders. The Dempster Highway opened in 1979, increasing the disturbance and the hunting in the winter range of the Porcupine herd, which some suggested was a greater threat than the Arctic Gas pipeline. By 1985 there was no clear evidence of any significant decline in the herd. In 1981 there were reports from territorial game officials that the Kaminuriak herd to the east of Great Slave Lake had suffered a drop from over 100,000 in 1955 to 36,000 while the Beverly herd has been cut in half to 100,000.[14] The latter had suffered from over-hunting in the southern portions of its range where caribou had been slaughtered for the tongue and prime cuts. News stories reported that caribou meat had been bartered for liquor. In his 1981 study of the barren ground caribou herds, George Calef predicted that the three main caribou herds could be virtually wiped out within a decade if the existing trends continued.[15] Yet, mysteriously, in the years since 1981 the caribou numbers have appeared to rebound to the amazement of many wildlife biologists.

For centuries the herds have coped with the assault from wolves, the extremes of weather, the danger of ice-choked fast-flowing rivers, and the native hunters, but now snowmobiles, four-by-four trucks, high-powered rifles, and hunting from aircraft have led to an alarming increase in the rate of kill. Normally no more than 5 per cent should be taken in any one year and the kill should be confined to bulls. Curtailment of hunting has been weakened by the inability of federal, territorial, and provincial wildlife officials to co-ordinate their efforts. Politically, it is easier for each to blame the other for the situation than it is to enforce unpopular hunting regulations.

Also, hunting restrictions are resisted by native groups as inconsistent with their aboriginal or treaty rights; recent court decisions have tended to give native people the right to hunt on public lands without restrictions. For obvious internal political reasons native leaders are reluctant to give up these rights, expecially prior to settlement of their land claims, because hunting and trapping are the basis of their cultural identity as well as their physical well-being. Some northern native leaders reject the idea that there is a crisis. Michael Amarook, vice-president of the Inuit Tapirisat of Canada, has said, "There's no over-hunting. Most of the older people believe the caribou are increasing, not declining." Raised as hunters, many of them are determined not to be denied their way of life by white bureaucrats. Some of the white bureaucrats in turn claim that "The native people have no concept of conservation and there is no precedent for it in their culture." Within some native circles, however, there appears to be a growing realization that there *is* a problem and native people have the most to lose. Peer group pressure has begun to mount to stop merely wasteful slaughter or the practices of bootlegging meat for liquor or other considerations.

Even more important is the development of joint government/native boards to oversee the herds. In October, 1981, the Dene Nation, the Inuit, and the territorial wildlife officials approved plans for a joint body, composed of eight native and five government representatives, to manage the Beverly and Kaminuriak herds.[16] If George Calef's grim prophecy is to be avoided this body will have to move to curb over-hunting, which is a tough task given the local circumstances. This group is also a partial recognition of the Dene political structures, which some in Ottawa had hoped to avoid. Still, it is difficult to believe that serious progress will be made on management of the caribou herds until the native land claims have been settled and implemented.

In considering the environmental impact of development on large terrestrial mammals such as caribou, moose, doll sheep, muskox, and grizzly and polar bears, four general factors emerge. Protection of *key habitat* is essential, especially during critical parts of the life cycle. Yet the very conditions that can make the area attractive for caribou may be the same conditions needed for constructing pipelines, i.e., stable terrain with local gravel. One of the great ironies of the North is that with such huge expanses of territory there are strategic areas like the North Slope, the Mackenzie Delta, and Lancaster Sound where environmental concerns clash directly with the aspirations of the oil and gas industry, making co-existence so difficult. Industrial facilities can also have impacts on habitat. Sulphur dioxide from burning coal or smelting ores can destroy the lichens so essential for the caribou in winter.

Second, all wildlife is affected by human hunting. The equilibrium between reproduction rates and natural predators can leave little surplus for increased rates of take from hunting. With many northern species being late maturing, the net decline from hunting can be increased.

The third general factor is disturbance, which can take a wide variety of forms: aircraft, highways, tanker traffic, railways, or even human activities. Caribou at calving time are under stress with all the demands of this part of their life cycle. Added stress from external disturbances can lead to loss of calves or gradual abandonment of the key habitat.

The final general factor is that of man-made barriers, which can disrupt migrations. Snow fences, railways, elevated pipelines, even highways can divert animals from their normal patterns. Caribou who will swim a raging stream can sometimes balk at crossing a railway track or be diverted along a road. The psychological aspects of barriers, real or perceived, are sometimes difficult to predict. The study of animal behaviour is an imprecise science.

Because of these factors, Berger concluded that there were areas like the North Slope where there should be no development, otherwise "it would entail irreparable environmental losses of national and international importance."[17] While Berger's pipeline recommendations appeared to be accepted by the Trudeau government, the latter was completing the construction of the Dempster Highway cutting through the winter range in the central Yukon. This was judged to be less sensitive than the calving grounds, but it does open up the area for serious white hunting.

The social significance of caribou is clearly evident in those areas of the North frequented by the major herds. In times past the caribou could provide the alternative to cloth. The soft calf hides were used for underclothes or boot lining; the bull hides for sleeping skins and tents; and the tough lower leg skin for footwear. Meat was cut into strips, dried, and smoked. Sinews were extracted and twisted for thread. Tallow from bull rumps was used as fuel in stove lamps. Fat was mixed with dried meat to make the infamous pemmican.[18] Some of the uses have been phased out, depending on the region, but for many areas the caribou remains the most important source of protein, especially for the difficult winter months. The Porcupine herd supplies a number of Delta and Alaska native settlements as well as Old Crow, situated in the centre of its range. The caribou are the greatest renewable resource, an irreplaceable asset because of the prohibitive cost of meats imported from the south. Since 1975 the Alaskan Fish and Game Department has imposed rigorous restrictions on hunting caribou while promoting the hunting of wolves. As a result some of the depleted herds have experienced significant rebounds – the Western Arctic herd from 65,000 in 1976 to 140,000 in 1980. So the situation is not hopeless, but it does require more political resolve than has been demonstrated thus far in Canada.

As is clear from the above, it is insufficient merely to stop development to preserve the natural heritage of areas like the northern Yukon. Since the 1950's momentum has been building for an international wilderness park to protect the northeast corner of Alaska and the adjacent areas of the Yukon. Following pressure from the Sierra Club, the Wilderness Society, and other American organizations, the Eisenhower administration in its final weeks withdrew 8.9 million acres to create the range. Conservation lobbyists then turned to the Canadian side of the border where they had allies in the federal Canadian Wildlife Service. After approval by the Ministry of Northern Affairs and Natural Resources, the project was stalled in the Diefenbaker cabinet by opposition from the Yukon territorial council.

The political scenario changed drastically with the Prudhoe Bay discovery in 1968. Suddenly the threat to the area became very real, resulting in stepped up pressure on Ottawa to withdraw the area. In 1973 Jean Chrétien presented the proposal to cabinet but pressure from development interests again caused the cabinet to back off. The issue was complicated by the Yukon's drive for provincial status, after which it would control all land policy. Not only would the wilderness designation eliminate oil, gas, and mineral exploration but it would close off the Yukon from a northern outlet to the sea. Therefore, the territorial politicians resisted any basic decisions until the power was in their own hands.

Berger, however, was clearly unhappy with this political impasse, which put the future of the herd in jeopardy. In his report he stressed: "In the North, certain ecosystems and certain migratory populations can be protected and preserved only by recognizing the inviolability of wilderness."[19] He proposed a multimillion-acre wilderness park as the Canadian portion of the Arctic International Range. This was an important statement of principle as there was not a wilderness designation within federal parks policy. With the Dempster Highway through the winter range, the development pressures would increase regardless of the pipeline decision. The issue was further complicated by the Western Arctic Inuit (COPE) claims to lands along the north coast of the Yukon and the Council of Yukon Indians claims for the people of Old Crow. Thus there emerged a four-way struggle to influence policy between the territorial council, federal wildlife officials, the native organizations, and the Ministry of Energy, Mines, and Resources, which wished to promote development.

In the summer of 1977 the Arctic Gas application was rejected but none of the specific recommendations of the Berger Inquiry were formally endorsed. Ottawa merely opted for the more politically acceptable alternative, the Foothills line. In July, 1978, Hugh Faulkner, the Minister of Indian and Northern Affairs, decided to act unilaterally by withdrawing the 9.6 million acres from the Porcupine River north to the Beaufort Sea, including Herschel Island. Six months earlier Parks Canada had begun planning six new national parks, of which the northern Yukon was one. Faulkner stressed that the conservation value of the area was greater than the development potential; the natives would retain full rights to hunt and trap in the area; existing permits for oil, gas, and mineral exploration would be honoured but no new leases would be issued.[20] This proposal created a storm of controversy, especially in the Yukon where the cries of "colonialism" were raised once again.

In 1978 and 1979 Canadian and American wildlife officials produced a draft "Convention . . . for the Conservation of Migratory Caribou and their Environment." These negotiations have also reached an impasse, for both countries appear uncertain about the direction of future policy; in Washington environmental affairs have been accorded a low priority by the Reagan administration. However, unless both countries work together to preserve the area of the North Slope, the future for the herd would appear in doubt. Within Canada the Parks officials finally won their battle in 1984 and an area was designated for a wilderness park along the Beaufort coast, which would still allow a development corridor through to King Point.

One of the key questions that emerges from all of this concerns the reasons for pure wilderness as opposed to multi-use parks. George Calef summed up his own views in these words: "In the northern Yukon Territory lies a land richer in wildlife, in variety of landscape and vegetation, and in archaeological value than any other in the Canadian Arctic. Here, high mountains, spruce forests, tundra, wide 'flats' of lakes and ponds, majestic valleys, a major river delta, and the arctic seacoast come together to form the living fabric of an arctic wilderness."[21]

Wilderness is more than merely an absence of development. It is a basis for research into the changing ecology of our planet. The maintenance of pristine or undisturbed ecosystems provides baseline data or a control from which changes elsewhere can be measured. Second, wilderness provides a refuge for some endangered species to allow them to survive, thus maintaining species and genetic diversity as an essential part of the viability of nature. A.R.E. Sinclair has argued that "The establishment of unexploited baseline or control areas is an insurance policy for the ecological viability of a country."[22] Third, an increasing number of Canadians find spiritual and aesthetic fulfilment in the wilderness experience devoid of expressways, television commercials, and the throwaway society. In addition, in the north Yukon it may be the only means of ensuring the future protein supply for native people.

A further reason for the wilderness range is the archaeological significance of the area. The northern Yukon is just about the only area of Canada that is unglaciated and therefore with early artifacts still in place. During the last ice age sea levels were lowered and a land bridge linked Siberia and Alaska. The interior of Alaska and parts of the Yukon, being free of ice, provided a means for the migration of Asian peoples as the first settlers into the Americas about 25,000 to 30,000 years ago. The artifacts from this and later waves of migrations can be found in the area, which makes it truly significant in our efforts to learn the pre-Columbian history of North America. Digging in the Old Crow area has already uncovered artifacts dating back beyond 25,000 years. In spite of the growing antagonism between native people and archaeologists who are accused of being grave robbers, there is great need for a slow and orderly investigation of this area, potentially so rich in Dene heritage.

Adjacent to the North Slope of the Yukon is the Mackenzie Delta; while the former showed some of the problems of terrestrial ecology, the latter demonstrated aquatic concerns. The Mackenzie Valley is one of the great flyways of the world for migrating ducks, geese, and swans that breed each summer in the Delta or in the adjacent coastal areas to the east and the west. The Delta itself is habitat for a number of mammals while the surrounding shallow seas are prime habitat for beluga whales, polar bears, and seals. Yet these same areas are the focus for Arctic oil exploration. As in so many cases in the North, the vegetation, the wildlife, the people, and the oil potential are all crowded into relatively small areas of the barren North where they inevitably must clash.

In early summer the Mackenzie Valley is alive to the sight and sound of a multitude of over 100 species of migrating birds, some of which have come all the way from South America and even Antarctica. The Delta itself is a myriad of small lakes, lagoons, bays, and winding channels so perfect for hiding the nests and protecting the young. The relatively warm waters of the river provide ample nutrients for many fish species and other organisms essential for the birds' diet. As a result, for many ducks and geese going on to the High Arctic islands or the Alaskan coast, the Delta is the staging area to replenish depleted food levels in the body at the end of migration or in the early fall to store up for the long flight to the winter habitat. Others stay the whole summer in the Delta itself or on the surrounding lakes or coastal areas.

The level of development activity in the Delta was already significant at the time of the hearings, with dozens of exploratory wells and thousands of miles of seismic survey lines. Arctic Gas proposed to construct its pipeline straight across the Delta and then down the east bank of the Mackenzie. In addition there would be smaller feeder pipelines to tap the individual gas fields. Imperial Oil had built artificial islands in the shallow waters offshore, while every summer since 1976 has seen the Dome drillships in the deeper waters offshore. Tuktoyaktuk and McKinley Bay have now become the base for these drillships with all the necessary ancillary facilities. Imperial, Gulf, and Dome all have large-scale drilling and production plans costing billions of dollars planned for the next decade. The federal government clearly appears determined to press ahead, which makes some of the 1970's analysis from Berger and others all the more relevant for the 1980's.

It is against this background of development and anticipated development that the biological questions have to be assessed. In the late spring the open waters of the Delta provide ideal habitat for feeding and staging recent arrivals such as snow geese from the south when surrounding areas are still frozen. Small leads or openings in the outer fringes of the Delta are crammed with various species. Later in the spring some of these sandy spits provide the kind of protective isolation for nesting, breeding, and moulting. During the thirty- to forty-five-day moulting period, ducks, geese, and swans lose their flight feathers, are incapable of flight, and are extremely vulnerable to predators or oil spills. If a bird is coated by oil it will try to clean its feathers with its beak, thus injesting lethal quantities of the toxic substances contained in oil. This type of pollution also destroys the amazing insulation properties of feathers; an oil spot the size of a quarter can kill a bird in the frigid Arctic waters. With all the oil and gas exploration in the Delta region since 1969, disturbance is a serious biological factor in the local habitat. Disturbance could take a number of forms. Low-flying aircraft, for example, could flush the parents from the nest, opening the way for predators such as jaegers or arctic foxes. While in the Delta, the birds are subject to an incredibly tight timetable during their summer stay. Birds such as snow geese are driven by a relentless sense of urgency to nest, lay, incubate, hatch, and rear their young in preparation for the fall migration. "So great is the sense of urgency that the birds will have already mated before even choosing a nesting site. There is no time for leisurely courtship and pairing . . . the birds have mated while en route northward, on gravel bars and islands in the Mackenzie River." Their overriding concern is to get the brood underway and then to get them strong enough to leave before the plunging fall temperatures destroy the food supply. Disruptions and delays, which in the south may be only inconvenient, can be fatal in the North. Snow geese must have the stored energy to sustain them for the long flight to California or Mexico.

The stress experienced by birds from disruption is something only now being studied directly. Arctic Gas carried out extensive tests under Dr. William Gunn on the effects of noise and aircraft on snow geese. Gunn was an independently-minded scientist who deviated on occasion from his client's position; he refused to sanction the coastal route across the North Slope because of its impact on his beloved snow geese. In one of Gunn's tests snow geese would not feed any closer than 1.5 miles from the equivalent of compressor station noises while birds overhead could be diverted in their flight path by 90 degrees or more. In another test small aircraft flushed geese out of their nests at 1.6 miles; large aircraft at 2.5 miles; and small helicopters at 2.3 miles. They even flushed when the aircraft were as high as 5,000 to 10,000 feet, while deliberate low-level harassing of the geese could clear them right out of the area.[23] It seemed impossible to conceive of the construction of production facilities, the gas-gathering system, and the trunk pipeline without frequent aircraft disturbance. The greatest potential problems would occur if delays from human disturbance combined with nature (such as early winter) to cut off, prematurely, essential aspects in the life cycle.

The problem of preparing good biological analysis of the applications is compounded when radical changes are made in the technology or the route. Both Foothills and Arctic Gas made basic changes in their routes while the hearings were in progress. For instance, Arctic Gas at the opening of the Berger hearings announced that it was going to abandon the route skirting around the Mackenzie Delta and replace it with a new route straight across it. By cutting nearly 200 miles of pipeline they expected to save over $100 million in capital cost and lower the charges for transporting the American gas.[24] The economic rationale for the changes was clear; but it put the government and public interest group analysts at the disadvantage of having prepared for the wrong route. Also, Arctic Gas refused to fund additional work by the Environmental Protection Board. Yet the biological significance of the changes was massive for a wide variety of species. More recently, the Polar Gas Pipeline and the Arctic Pilot

Project have also undergone basic changes. This structural problem seems to emerge frequently in connection with the huge northern mega-projects, and it creates further problems in all areas of assessment but most acutely with environmental assessment, which requires carefully collected baseline data from several years' work in the field.

In the Delta the problems are complicated by the way the proposed production facilities, the feeder pipelines or gathering system, and the main trunk pipeline are all interacting to multiply the total environmental impacts. Imperial Oil's development of the Taglu gas field will require gravel pits within and production facilities surrounding the Kendall Island bird sanctuary, a critical habitat for snow geese and other species. Rising activity in exploration and future production facilities for onshore and offshore fields like Adgo and Issungnak on the outer fringe of the Delta and the shallow waters beyond will affect staging areas where large numbers of swans, cranes, and ducks congregate. Dr. Gunn, in his report, *The Need to Preserve the Integrity of the Mackenzie Delta*, directly challenged the production plans of Imperial, Shell, Gulf, and other oil companies. The aircraft and vehicular and even larger traffic for on-site and support activities would create serious disturbance and pollution threats. "Although the environmental effects of any one of these plants might individually be acceptable, we are particularly concerned with the combined and cumulative effects. Because we believe that they would unquestionably result in deterioration of the Delta as a viable ecological unit."[25]

In addition, the prime route for the trunk pipeline down the east bank of the Delta ran through or close by a number of International Biological Program (IBP) sites such as the Campbell Lake area, where falcon sites are already under stress from the disturbance of the Mackenzie Highway. In response to the criticisms Arctic Gas moved its planned compressor station to the mainland, but the producers have continued on with their plans for production facilities within these critical areas of the Delta habitat. In 1980 and 1981 the planning was expanded to include an oil pipeline to link the Imperial proven reserves offshore with those from Atkinson Point on the Tuktoyaktuk Peninsula.

When confronted with biological evidence the oil and pipeline companies made clear promises that construction would cease if wildlife entered the area. Alex Hemstock of Arctic Gas testified that the arrival of snow geese on the cross-Delta lateral would halt work. Yet under cross-examination it was admitted that when the ornithologists recommended such a move during test work at Shallow Bay, the company ignored the recommendation.[26] In making such decisions there were problems in the chain of command. The biologist would be reporting to an engineer who might not recognize the importance of the issue involved. The construction schedule was a tight one with a limited season when heavy equipment could work. Delays to avoid environmental impacts could result in heavy additional costs, especially if the pipeline took an additional winter to build. Many critics believed that, given the time constraints and the financial pressures, the environmental commitments would probably be abandoned as impractical.

Also, the problems of disturbance did not end with construction. As the United States Department of the Interior concluded: "The entire population of snow geese could be adversely affected if repeated aircraft overflights, such as might be expected with a major repair of the pipeline system, were required to cross critical staging habitat areas while the geese were present." The geese would probably seek less suitable habitat with a resulting decline in numbers.[27] Later, after the conclusion of the Berger hearings, Dr. Gunn was still at work behind the scenes trying to modify the cross-Delta plans. In the spring of 1977 he gave his approval to the Arctic Gas project but it was not unconditional. In final evidence to the NEB he warned of serious adverse impacts on the bird population unless his recommendations were "strictly adhered to."[28] Such admonitions were rather exceptional for corporate consultants, most of whom followed the party line much more carefully.

Another biological concern raised by the cross-Delta route was the beluga whale habitat on the west side of the Delta. In late June or early July about 5,000 beluga or white whales enter the shallow waters of the Mackenzie estuary to calve in the warm, food-rich area. The calves require the shallow, warm water for surface breathing and to maintain their body heat until they can develop sufficient blubber; disturbance or noise may frighten the belugas into deeper water, to the detriment of the calves. The whales can penetrate into the network of channels in the Delta where some have even become trapped. They exit the area about mid-August, dispersing into the expanses of the Beaufort or the Pacific until the next June.

The belugas constitute an important food source for the local Inuit, who take 170 to 200 per year, which appears to be fully sustainable through natural reproduction. Summer construction would create some direct harassment in the Shallow Bay area from dredging, underwater blasting, boat traffic, pipe laying, and other related activities. Air cushion vehicles that were considered for use because of their ability to traverse water, ice, marsh, and land turned out to be particularly disturbing. Yet, like the calving grounds of the Porcupine caribou, this small beluga calving area is essential for the whole beluga population of the Beaufort Sea. Arctic Gas argued that its late summer construction would take place after whales were gone but this was contradicted by local residents from Tuk. The stress on the whales is currently on the increase, for although Arctic Gas was rejected, the offshore oil and gas exploration has now speeded up with Dome, Imperial, and Gulf all active in the Delta offshore area.[29]

With such mounting pressure on the beluga calving zone, Berger proposed the establishment of a whale sanctuary in west Mackenzie Bay from which development would be excluded (see map earlier in this chapter). The proposal came from Dr. David Sargeant of the Department of the Environment but Berger scaled it down to avoid direct conflict with Imperial Oil's artificial islands. Berger argued that native hunting of whales should be allowed to continue until it could be proved that the hunters were a threat to the herd. Because the main calving areas were further west than the main drilling areas, it appeared that this recommendation might have a greater chance of success than the Kendall Island bird sanctuary, which was in the centre of the drilling action.

Marine drilling involves a serious risk factor, as the blowouts in the Gulf of Mexico and the North Sea have dramatically demonstrated. Three of the first ten wells drilled by Dome in the Beaufort experienced water discharges but the oil strikes have been carefully contained. Some of the geotechnical aspects of ice scour were discussed in the last chapter as well as the long delays of up to a year for a relief well to be drilled to check a blowout of crude oil. The greatest scour, however, takes place in the shear zone between the shore-fast ice and the moving pack-ice fields. This zone is biologically the most productive as well as the location for the Dome drillships. The concentration of these factors makes the offshore drilling such a serious environmental question.

The most toxic elements in crude oil are also the most volatile; in tropic and temperate climates they disperse into the surrounding water and air but in the cold environment of the Arctic this would be a much slower process. Crude oil contains sulphur compounds, acids, phenols, and heavy metals such as nickel, mercury, and lead, which if injested by lower forms of life will be concentrated in the higher forms of life that prey on them. Some forms of micro-organisms that can metabolize hydrocarbons will flourish on crude oil but the damage will emerge further up the food chain.[30] Also, the growth of micro-organisms that break down the heavier components is severely restricted in the near freezing waters. As a result it would probably require more concentrated use of chemical dispersants, which in turn would have serious toxic impacts on marine life.

In the shear zone there are open leads in winter providing critical habitat for seals, polar bears, and many species of marine life on which the Inuit depend for food. The sea floor here contains the necessary conditions for the vigorous growth of benthos, the bottom-dwelling plants and animals on which the larger species depend, while zooplankton are tiny marine animals found drifting near the surface. Both can be poisoned by components in crude; heavy oil blobs will separate out and sink to the bottom; on the surface dissolved aromatic compounds will kill off these tiny forms of life.[31]

The full consequences of a major oil spill on the individual species as well as the overall viability of the food chain are still a matter of conjecture until there is a major blowout or spill. With the ice sealing in the most toxic hydrocarbon components, the effects would be worse than in warmer climates. It is therefore not surprising that, in addition to environmental groups, the United States government protested to Ottawa in 1976 when the decision was announced to proceed with drilling. For some Americans the earlier Canadian rhetoric about the *Manhattan* voyage and Canada's new 100-mile pollution control zone appeared now as hypocrisy in the light of the dangerous policy of drilling in conditions where neither the Soviet Union nor the U.S. would sanction drilling at that time. Canada, the United States, and Russia shared the clockwise currents moving around the Beaufort Sea. Pollution from one sector would eventually end up in the others. But oil production, it would appear, had a higher priority than our international obligations to the environment.

From the statistics it is clear that blowouts, although infrequent, do occur. They can be the result of unforeseen circumstance, geological pressures, equipment failure, or human error. One consulting firm estimated the chances of blowout at one in 200 while another put it at one in 100,000. However, there are doubts about the value of such risk analysis statistics when the drilling is in such totally new conditions. The drilling thus far in the Beaufort has been exploratory wells, not production wells where most blowouts have occurred. They are also deep wells, which tend to be safer than shallow ones. However, the fact remains that a blowout or major tanker oil spill could occur irrespective of the care and concern of the personnel involved.

With this possibility clearly in mind the federal government in 1973 established a special Beaufort Sea Project at the same time that cabinet approved in principle the offshore drilling by Dome. This project was a special study group jointly financed by government and industry to investigate the means of containment and cleanup of a major blowout or spill in the Beaufort. They found that counter-measures such as containment booms and skimmers were totally impractical in ice-festooned waters. Even burning was difficult because it was hard to get the oil temperature up high enough to ignite even the volatile components.[32]

In view of these disturbing conclusions and Dome's ongoing drilling, Ottawa established the Arctic Marine Oilspills Program (AMOP) to try to come up with solutions. The program consists primarily of engineering design and testing involving containment devices, combustion systems, chemical dispersants, remote sensing equipment, oil removal equipment, and shoreline cleanup techniques. Much of the work thus far has been conducted in southern laboratories, with small test spills in the North. And they have encountered difficulties with funding; in 1978 the budget was cut in half. But it is clear they are still a long way from any solutions. In June, 1980, S.L. Ross, manager of AMOP, stressed his own feelings: "It is universally recognized that the general state-of-the-art for dealing with major oil spills is inadequate and unsatisfactory. The low level of countermeasure capability and the environmental damage of social dislocation that can result from major spills have been demonstrated time and time again."[33]

With offshore drilling now proceeding in the Beaufort Sea, the High Arctic, and Hudson Bay there are profound hopes that no major blowout will take place. Even the events surrounding small oil spills from ships do not give one much confidence for the future. When the *Edgar Jourdain* ran aground in September, 1980, in Foxe Basin, the hull was badly punctured, allowing 3,100 gallons of diesel oil to spill out. With internal wrangling among Transport, Environment, and Indian and Northern Affairs, the winter was allowed to set in. Nine months later, in June, 1981, the cleanup began, thus provoking strong protest from environmental groups and questions in the House of Commons.[34]

The Mackenzie Valley Pipeline proposals were environmentally assessed by the Berger Inquiry but all subsequent northern projects are covered under the Environmental Assessment and Review Process (EARP), which was established by cabinet order in December, 1973, and amended in February, 1977. Each federal ministry is responsible for initial "in-house" assessment of projects under its jurisdiction, screening each into one of four categories.

(a) No adverse impacts and no action required.
(b) Environmental impacts are known and judged to be within the control of mitigative measures. Initiator is responsible for taking the appropriate action but there is no further reference to EARP procedures.
(c) Environmental impacts are not fully known and a detailed Initial

Environmental Evaluation (IEE) must be produced. When the initiator has reviewed the project IEE it is moved into either the (b) category above or the (d) category below.

(d) The initiator recognizes that significant environmental impacts are involved and requests the chairman of the Federal Environmental Assessment and Review Office to establish an EARP panel to review formally the whole project.

Under the EARP system, a project put forward by a private company (the proponent) would operate through the ministry with jurisdiction over the area in question. This ministry would carry through the initial screening of the project under guidelines supplied by the EARP office and the project would then follow one of the three streams through the process (see diagram). If the initial assessment finds serious potential impacts, an EARP panel is established that may include members from outside government service. This panel establishes the guidelines for the Environmental Impact Statement (EIS), which is prepared by the project applicant. When the EIS is completed the panel will hold public hearings on its validity, after which the panel will recommend acceptance, modification, or rejection. In turn the minister can accept or reject the panel's recommendations and then cabinet can do the same.[35] Thus it is important to stress the discretionary and the advisory nature of the process. The ministry may decide there are no serious impacts, thus eliminating the appointment of an EARP panel and the holding of public hearings, and, as noted, the minister or cabinet can totally reject recommendations coming from any panel. The panel's power is *only* that of moral persuasion; they are not a regulatory board with the power to stop any project on their own.

The establishment of EARP has been a major step forward but it has by no means ended the controversies with environmental groups. Unlike the American equivalent NEPA,[36] it is not established by statute and therefore is not enforceable through the courts. No project has to be subject to EARP; the Dome offshore drilling in the Beaufort was exempt in spite of the obvious environmental hazards. The normal procedures of EARP may be abbreviated if there are serious time constraints, such as in 1977 with the decision on the Alaska Highway Pipeline. In 1979, in connection with Dome's application for a dredging permit at McKinley Bay, north of Tuktoyaktuk, the local advisory committee's recommendation for an EARP panel was not accepted by Indian and Northern Affairs, presumably for the fear of delay to the Dome drilling program.[37]

In other instances the power may be transferred to other bodies. While the Alaska Highway Pipeline was subject to EARP, the special

Figure 21.
Environmental Assessment and Review Process.

Schematic Diagram of the Federal Environmental Assessment and Review Process

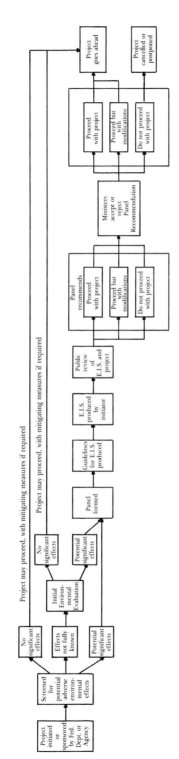

powers granted by statute to the Northern Pipeline Agency allow it to override any existing piece of environmental regulation.[38] In general, the number of northern projects subject to EARP public hearings has been increasing and at least in one case, that of Lancaster Sound, drilling approval was not granted. The 1981-82 EARP panel on the Dome production facilities for the Beaufort saw increased non-government involvement on the panel and substantial government funding for the public interest groups. However, government restraint then cut the funding and the public interest groups withdrew in protest. These hearings also showed another of the procedural problems for EARP. Dome presented only stylized drawings and very general preliminary plans, which made precise assessment very difficult indeed. These problems and inconsistencies have raised doubts in the minds of environmentalists about the legitimacy of the EARP process and adequacy of environmental regulation in the Canadian North.

Environmental Impact Assessment (EIA) is still an adolescent science, groping its way toward adequate theory and methodology. It has also suffered from a lack of government will to apply what is known to the immediate problems at hand. EIA has approved some second-rate science by individuals whose entrepreneurial instincts were greater than their scientific qualifications. The individual's title, "the mass of the report, the author's salary, and his dress and bearing often carry more weight with the commission . . . than either his scientific competence or the validity of his scientific investigation." This has produced a "travelling circus" of scientists with dubious credentials. "As a result, impact statements seldom receive the hard scrutiny that follows the publication of scientific findings in a reputable scientific journal."[39]

One of the fiercest debates in this branch of science revolves around the objectivity of corporate-funded research studies presented to support project applications. The researcher knows in advance the conclusions the sponsor wants and he knows that further contracts will only come if the anticipated results are produced. The scientist can prostitute his science by becoming merely a hired gun for the company. Some of the environmental witnesses at places like the NEB are clearly not in this category. Bill Gunn for Arctic Gas is a good example. But it is hard for a struggling scientist on his own or working for a consulting firm not to be influenced by these pressures.

Environmental Impact Assessment is now something much more than merely applied biology – it must involve input fom disciplines ranging from the physical sciences to sociology. In theory it seeks to give authoritative and scientific answers to guide the decision-making of government. Yet in practice it seldom reaches this objective. Most of the volumes in the massive Biological Report Series of Arctic Gas consisted of descriptive reports of individual species in a particular area. It was left to the policy witnesses of the company, often not biologists, to make the overall environmental judgements. There was only very limited analysis of interactions between species as well as of the actual impact of the pipeline on those species. Yet these internal dynamics of an ecosystem are central to understanding environmental impacts. It is becoming evident that the integrated whole of these effects is greater than the sum of the effects on individual species. Scientific analysis of these synergistic effects on such aspects of life as food chains is only now getting serious attention. Environmental Impact Assessment assumes that you can take knowledge of the existing state of an undisturbed ecosystem and then *predict* the impact of industrial technology on it. Such predictions are difficult in the south, where the data base is extensive while the existing methodological tools are limited. However, EIA becomes only very rough guesswork in the North, where the data base is so thin and where there is no experience of previous mega-projects to draw on.

Environmental Impact Assessment is being put forward as a new type of interdisciplinary science attempting to integrate and collate the disparate data from many fields of the sciences and social sciences. It includes quantitative data with those which are only descriptive. As each of these different disciplines operates with profoundly different theory and methodology, the development of overall environmental or ecosystem analysis becomes incredibly difficult. How can trade-offs among wildlife survival, permafrost degradation, and added costs for consumers be decided? Too often in business and government, these decisions are made on the basis of traditional cost/benefit analysis in which all the factors are translated into dollar terms. The simple fact is that it is far easier to quantify the benefits (additional energy supply) than the costs (cultural erosion, wildlife decline, or social alienation).

In addition, the discipline of mainstream economics contains a built-in bias against proper consideration of environmental factors. They are relegated to the background category of externalities, and because they involve government intervention they are viewed as a distortion of normal market forces. The monetarist philosophy of President Reagan's policy initiatives has involved a very basic attack on environmental regulation.[40] If the standard Harvard Business School approach is followed, capital invested to meet environmental considerations is an "unproductive" use of the company's resources because it in no way contributes to product sales and profitability.

Partly as a result of the "science" issues raised above, environmental experts often have difficulty presenting their evidence effectively to regulatory boards. In the last decade there has been a continuous search for new methods of presenting data so the full impact will be evident to non-environmentalists. Danger areas needed to be highlighted through codifying the relative levels of environmental impacts. One such effort was the attempt to develop environmental indexes that would include many variables in much the same way as the Consumer Price Index monitors the rate of inflation. Using a base figure of 100 for the level on the month it was instituted, each month's figure would show graphically the decline or improvement in some component in the environment, such as air or water quality, in the following manner:

January, 1980	100
July, 1980	96
January, 1981	91
July, 1981	93
January, 1982	75
July, 1982	76

Some scientists, such as Dr. Herbert Inhaber of the federal government, wanted to take the system much further by combining individual indexes to create overall models that would monitor all the different factors, including social and aesthetic impacts.[41] This type of ecosystem modelling to include social and other factors quickly became very controversial and the subject of considerable sarcasm from many scientists, who argued that the numbers would be meaningless by the time they finished. While the concept is attractive, the methodology is not yet in place.

The Environmental Protection Board out of Winnipeg developed another approach using the matrix method. A matrix is a huge chart with hundreds or thousands of individual boxes with the main components in a project along one axis and the environmental/social factors along the other. If you wanted to check the relative level of the impacts of constructing gravel pits for pipeline construction on Arctic char, you found the former on the side axis and then ran your finger across the chart until you came to the column for Arctic char running down from the top. Each of the boxes could be colour-coded to show the level of the impact (i.e., bright red for severely negative to bright blue for highly positive). One matrix for the Mackenzie Valley Pipeline had 25,344 boxes to summarize all the environmental impacts of the Mackenzie Valley Pipeline.[42] The matrix, however, could only show direct bilateral relationships between one environmental component and one facet of human activity, not complex interrelationships. Also, the final decision on each individual box involved subjective human judgements on the acceptability of the impacts. What one corporate observer might define as moderate, another outside analyst might consider as severe.

With environmental impact statements there is as yet no way of excluding these subjective factors. In the North it is wrong to expect definitive and objective science when the whole discipline is at such an early stage. When we are still uncertain about the forces at work within a given habitat it is hardly possible to be certain about what constitutes an acceptable level of impact. EIS is not a science in the full sense of the word, because the human element cannot be eliminated from the judgement involved. It is important to recognize the transitional nature of the discipline in order not to expect definitive answers where they do not exist.

Although the great mega-projects have not yet begun, environmental change is already under way. The outcome of this process is a matter of intense scientific debate. Some have argued that even the current level of oil, gas, and mineral exploration will lead to severe environmental degradation through a process of "insignificant increments."[43] Others have countered with the claim that the Arctic is not as fragile as previously assumed, for many northern species would be capable with time of adapting to changed habitat. This bitter, ongoing debate will continue for some decades. To determine the level of impacts, there must be careful monitoring of species on a long-term basis because of the wide fluctuations of numbers from natural causes.[44]

Generally, northern scientific research has been too closely tied to meeting the immediate needs of development projects and hence not particularly influential in government decision-making. In the environmental area there is still a great deal to be accomplished to improve the process of assessment. There is a need to fill in the gaps in our knowledge of northern species and, even more, in the internal workings of Arctic ecosystems; there is need to improve the scientific methodology involved in environmental impact statements; and we need to improve the structures of environmental decision-making within government to give biological considerations a higher profile. Either the political processes of government have remained too divorced from scientific input or the scientific input has tended to be too politicized. M.J. Dunbar summarized his own long experience in the following manner.

Industrial development in the North has brought into focus two things: the scientific neglect of the North and the attitude of government to science. The first can be put right by basic scientific investigation, long overdue; the second calls for continued education of government, including many of the senior public servants [who], though perhaps once trained in science, have forgotten what it is all about. . . . The belief that science can be turned on and off like a tap, as required, is at the bottom of much of our trouble.[45]

A basic problem – the corruption of science – lies at the heart of much of the weakness in northern policy formation. Currently there is a lull in the pressure of mega-projects, which in turn has led to a decrease in research. Yet within a short period a whole series of northern projects will be pushed ahead for approval once world oil and mineral prices have become firm. Now is the time to do this type of basic research, before the decisions have to be made and when the political atmosphere will allow for greater objectivity. Not only the wildlife is "under stress" during regulatory hearings but scientists seeking to endure their own future existence are as well. In the long term it is essential to maintain the northern environment and wildlife, for these provide the basis for native survival.

CHAPTER 9

Social Impacts and Native Rights

Social and socio-economic impacts constitute a challenging new field for corporations and governments. Of all the areas within the mandate of regulatory boards, it is probably the least understood and least consistently applied. Social science expertise has tended to be limited within their ranks. In the 1970's with the public debate surrounding the James Bay Project and the Mackenzie Valley Pipeline, social impact assessment (SIA) has finally emerged and been recognized as a legitimate component in project assessment.

Until the last few years the corporate concept of social responsibility was essentially a legalistic one. Compensation would be paid for land acquired or direct physical damage verifiable in court. Everything else was assumed to be covered by government. To consult with the local population was to invite opposition and promote complaints that otherwise might never emerge. The standard approach was to wine and dine the local municipal politicians, emphasizing the additional tax assessment the new project would bring and the potential new jobs for local citizens. An influential member of the party in power was usually appointed to the board of directors to facilitate representations to government and neutralize public complaints if and when they materialized. Yet by the final years of the 1970's times were changing, including the environment in which business had to operate. New standards of corporate social responsibility were being demanded, such as the National Energy Board Guidelines for Regional Socio-economic Impact Assessments for Pipeline Projects (1979). These regulatory changes were largely a product of northern events earlier in the decade.

"Social impacts" is a very wide term, which for the purposes of this study has been defined to include social, socio-economic, cultural, and related questions such as native land claims. In the North it is exceedingly hard to separate out these elements, which overlap and are interrelated to a great extent.

Most of the communities of the Northwest Territories are small, isolated, and predominantly native; the exceptions, like Hay River, Yellowknife, and Inuvik, seem to be of another world. In such circumstances the potential social impacts of industrial development are very much greater than for comparable projects located in the south. The isolation of these scattered communities has been the basis for their social stability and cultural survival. Now, however, the largest development projects in Canadian history are on the horizon and northern society is already suffering from the shocks and disruptions of social change, which is evident in the statistics for alcoholism, crime, and welfare. This social change will continue even without development; however, with massive development it will accelerate and intensify the stresses and strains between the white and native societies resident in the North.

Will it be possible to keep these tensions within tolerable limits or will the social costs be too high? These are fundamental questions that only time and events will answer. The human spirit is remarkably adaptable, but history has shown that there are clear limits to the rate of change that can be tolerated, especially where civilizations with profoundly different values are confronting each other. The Dene culture has flourished for tens of thousands of years in the Mackenzie Valley, from before the time of recorded history in the British Isles. This society has been remarkably successful in adapting to the physical challenges of one of the harshest environments on the globe; yet it is now facing its greatest challenge in the social onslaught of Western industrialized society. For whites it is all too easy to underestimate how fundamental the crisis is for native peoples.

Traditionally in Canada we have neglected systematic analysis of the social costs of resource development. For instance, few Canadians are aware of the human toll exacted from the Irish and Chinese navvies who built the CPR and other rail lines in the nineteenth century or the social cost to the prairie native people when the great buffalo herds were decimated as the white agricultural frontier moved in. The current northern energy projects are comparable to the CPR in the sense that they will "open up" huge areas of the North, isolated thus far from the rigours of the industrial economy. Also, they are a logical extension of the basic concept of Confederation; the East-West system of resource exploitation is now expanded along a new North-South axis. Prime Minister Trudeau, in talking of the Mackenzie Valley Pipeline, even used the same CPR imagery when he referred to it as part of "Our National Dream." Implicit in this romantic rhetoric is the idea of "progress" and civilization flowing west and now north through the vehicle of economic development. Social casualties were a regrettable but inevitable part of the march of progress. Social Darwinism explained that there would be some who would successfully adapt to changing circumstances and others who would fall by the wayside in the social struggle for survival.[1] This evolutionary process had given the Western democracies their entrepreneurial spirit and their economic growth. To question the process and the values behind it was to question one of the most basic articles of faith in our economic and political system.

Yet this was precisely the nature of the debate that rocked the Berger Inquiry. The northern pipeline was merely the latest example of the successive frontiers of industrial expansion central to the free enterprise philosophy. The debate that had been raging for some time was put into a new, sharper relief by the northern context, which evoked a strong, idealistic response from many southern middle-class Canadians. This popular response had its effect on government, which made new demands in terms of corporate performance. The appointment of Berger and the definition of his terms of reference should have been a signal to corporations like Arctic Gas of the changes under way.

When the Berger Inquiry opened the social tensions were clearly evident, as has been described earlier. Many of the expert witnesses and native leaders who appeared in the main hearings in Yellowknife were accused by corporate spokesmen of being politically motivated and unrepresentative of native feelings. It is useful, therefore, to go to the transcripts of the community hearings, which could not be stage-managed. They are an invaluable primary social record of the fears and aspirations uncluttered with social science jargon or white assumptions. Too often the writings on the North are exclusively the words of those who see the country through the filter of white cultural assumptions.

For many of the witnesses who came forward the *land* was the central focus of their existence, and this focus ran through their social, economic, cultural, and even spiritual activities. "The Land is seen as Mother because she gives life, because she is the provider, the protector, the comforter. She is constant in a changing world, yet changing in regular cycles. She is a story teller, a listener, a traveller, yet she is still, and when she suffers we all suffer with her. . . . She is a teacher, a teacher who punishes swiftly when we err, yet a benefactress who blesses abundantly when we live with integrity, respect her, and love the life she gives."[2]

The great concern was that the land was a sacred trust and legacy handed down to them by their ancestors; it was the basis of their wealth, their social life, and their identity. Now all this appeared to them to be in jeopardy. There was an incredible sense of ecological continuity and timelessness in their world view and their individual concerns. "We are like the river that flows and changes, yet is always the same. The river cannot flow too slow and it cannot flow too fast. It is a river and it will always be a river, for that is what it was meant to be. . . . We are human. That is what we are meant to be. We are not meant to be destroyed and we are not meant to take over other parts of the world. We were meant to be ourselves, to be what it is our nature to be."[3] The great Mackenzie became not only a symbol of life but it took on a mystical and even spiritual overtone through its power and majesty. The relentless surge of its waters symbolized the laws of nature, which must be understood and obeyed.

Their cultural traditions and way of life dictated that they preserve their relationship to the land. The river of time had taught them lessons they could not ignore if they were to understand their society. Whites who have seldom thought about losing their way of life had difficulty comprehending the traumatic significance of such a change: "I wonder how people in Toronto would react if the people of Old Crow went down to Toronto and said, 'Well, look, we are going to knock down all those skyscrapers and high rises . . . blast a few holes to make for lakes for muskrat trapping, and you people are just going to have to move out and stop driving cars and move into cabins.'"[4] Involved in a way of life was the pride of knowing that you belong and your values are reflected in the shared sense of community. The social structures of the Dene and Inuit grew out of this shared experience, the lessons of which through thousands of years of hunting and trapping had shaped their culture. If Europeans are proud of their philosophic and political traditions, which have evolved over the last 500 years, then we can appreciate the Dene pride in their society and roots, which have been evolving in the Mackenzie Valley for so much longer than Europeans have been in the Americas.

For many native witnesses, the decline of their society began with the treaty ceremonies conducted in 1921 following the discovery of oil at Norman Wells. "Now at the time of the treaty . . . 55 years ago, it was mostly with the government, they said 'As long as the river runs, as long as the sun goes up and down, and as long as you see that Black Mountain up there, well you are entitled to your land.' The river is still running. The sun goes up and down, and the Black Mountain is still up there, but today . . . the government is giving up our land . . . to the seismic people and the other people comin' up here. . . ."[5] This historic sense of grievance the Dene have from the experience of Treaties 8 and 11 was documented repeatedly during the Berger hearings. As participants in the treaty ceremonies, the clergy felt that their own integrity was involved when the promises of medical help and other support were not fulfilled.[6] Their protests were a natural extension of their concern for the welfare of their flocks. Not surprisingly, the legacy of those treaties is contributing to much of the current militancy complicating land claims negotiations for the federal government. Native groups argue strongly that they were given no indication the treaties involved extinguishment of their land rights and that they naturally interpreted them as treaties of friendship. As mentioned earlier, when Mr. Justice Morrow interviewed some of the survivors of the signing ceremonies he came to the same conclusion. In his judgement, "notwithstanding the language of the two Treaties [8 and 11] there is sufficient doubt on the facts that aboriginal title was extinguished" that a caveat could be put forward on the land.[7] Although this decision was later reversed by the Alberta Court of Appeal, the net result was to strengthen in native minds the firm belief in the legitimacy of their interpretation that their aboriginal land rights had not been extinguished by the treaties.

Closely tied to the treaties question is the historic perception of the destruction of native society by the pattern of events in the south. "We are being destroyed. Your nation is destroying our nation. What we are saying today, here and now, is exactly what Louis Riel was saying roughly a hundred years ago. We are a nation. We have our own land, our own ways, and our own civilization. We do not want to destroy you or your land. . . . your Prime Minister is willing to say that Louis Riel was not all wrong. He is willing to say that, a hundred years later, but is he willing to change the approach that destroyed Louis Riel? And his nation? And is now threatening to destroy us?"[8] Reservations under the treaty system had proved to be a disastrous mistake for native people. Now they were seeking to create new political forms sensitive to their own concerns. As one chief noted: "It was not too obvious that the territorial government programs were set up so that the native culture, the native identity, and the native language would be eliminated."[9] This comment was directed particularly at the school system, which they saw as a vehicle for assimilation. Church and government schools made native youth dissatisfied with the language, culture, and traditional hunting and trapping society.

A number of those who spoke at the community hearings had bitter memories of their school days. "At the time I was eight years old the mission over at Aklavik opened up a school . . . some of us were told to go for a ride and you'll be back, some of us were told you are going down to the fish camp, so my brother and I, we jumped in and went to that Aklavik school. Before I went to the school the only English that I knew was 'hello' and when we got there we were told that if we spoke Indian they would whip us until our hands were blue on both sides. And also we were told that the Indian religion was superstitious and pagan. It made you feel inferior to whites. . . . We all felt lost and wanted to go home and some cried for weeks and weeks and I remember one Eskimo boy every night crying inside his blanket because he was afraid the sister might come and spank him. . . . Today I think back on the hostel life and I feel ferocious. I feel a lot of anger inside me. Between the ages of 12 and 17 I spent that in hospital, TB, over in Aklavik. . . . It wasn't fun either. Five years. I decided to stay home and forget about education and tried to see how I make out in the bush, living the way my mum and dad did."[10] The end result was social alienation and cultural erosion, including a tragic generation gap between children who had gone to white schools and their parents who had not. As a result, it is hardly surprising that control of the education system is one of the firmest demands of the Dene Nation.

When the pipeline proposals emerged in the early 1970's they acted as a catalyst in bringing into focus these wider feelings of frustration and uncertainty already present in northern native communities. Settlement of their land claims became the means of slowing down or reversing the social and cultural erosion under way. They had to regain some power over the events that were critical to their lives before those forces of social change overwhelmed them. As one Aklavik resident stressed: "I would like to see a land settlement between the government and the people of the Northwest Territories, a land settlement where the native people will control their land and development. We are not against development but we want to control it. In every movie about the Indian wars, the Indian people always lose. I now ask the government, the southern people of Canada, to let us win this one."[11] They could see the creeping encroachment on their lands of the activities of the oil companies and other development projects. If they did not take a stand on the principle of no pipeline until the land claims were settled they would weaken seriously their own bargaining position. They would end up like the James Bay Cree, negotiating about lands where the bulldozers were already at work.

Some of the early efforts of the oil companies to consult with native people were poorly designed to meet their goals and only led to further feelings of distrust. "When representatives from the oil companies came in for meetings, they sometimes bring us some free movies in and then when we go to the meeting they talk to us about things that they want . . . they use all those great big words (I call them $80 words) you know, that the people don't understand; and when we say 'No' to what they want, they go ahead and do it anyway."[12] To the Dene and Inuit this type of paternalism was degrading: to appear to canvass people's opinions when you had already decided what you were going to do. In addition, they believed that they, not the oil companies or the Crown, controlled access to the land pending the settlement of their aboriginal claims.

The intensity of the native opposition to non-renewable resource development was annoying to some who spoke at the community hearings in Hay River, Norman Wells, and Inuvik, which were the centres for the oil industry and support services. "It hasn't been a one way street for the native people of the North. It hasn't been all bad . . . . How many people in the North really want to live in the past and live off the land? Those who really want to live off the land are already doing it. Those who think they want to live off the land, nothing but themselves is stopping them. To the rest I say they are dreaming."[13] Some whites were concerned that the entrenchment of native rights would restrict their rights. They were also frightened that the land claims settlement would seriously inhibit development projects and thus harm their own economic future in the North.

Some of this white frustration came out in the charges that the inquiry was a sounding board for native radicals who were outside the mainstream of moderate opinion among the Inuit and Dene. This view is impossible to sustain, given the clear consensus that emerged in the community hearings. Many whites did not understand the social roots of the land claims movement; they saw it rather as an expression of communism or socialism. These charges in turn brought fierce denials from the native leaders who resented these "Red scare" tactics. "When we stand up to speak we're called down. We are called radicals, leftists, communists, socialists. Why is that? In the past when the Indian people fought for their land they were called pagans, savages, today they are called militants . . . I don't understand these things."[14]

For some of the corporate observers, such as the head of public affairs for Canadian Arctic Gas, the Dene Nation was led by a radical elite determined to "establish a separate Marxist state in the north."[15] Such analysis failed to understand or recognize the nature of the movement and helps to explain why Arctic Gas had such a poor working relationship with native organizations. The communal aspects of native society naturally made them sceptical of the competitive individualism of free enterprise capitalism, especially when it was evoked to support the efforts of the multinational oil companies. The primary purpose of the land claims movement was essentially a conservative one: to protect and preserve their own society at a time of crisis. It did not seek to change the economic and political system of Canada.

Yet the pressures of the moment brought out very strong expres-

TABLE TWO

Public Participation in Community Hearings
(sampling of fourteen native communities and Norman Wells)

Community*	No. Witnesses (non-corporate)	1971 Pop. (CAGPL estimate)	Witnesses as % of Total Pop.
Ft. Simpson	40	1,004	4%
Ft. McPherson	58	841	7
Aklavik	27	660	4
Ft. Providence	15	647	2
Tuktoyaktuk	21	627	3
Ft. Franklin	41	434	9
Ft. Good Hope	77	375	21
Norman Wells	24	363	7
Ft. Norman	23	260	9
Old Crow	42	216	19
Wrigley	19	191	10
Arctic Red River	23	95	24
Jean-Marie River	6	50	12
Trout Lake	7	40	18
Total	423	5,803	7%

*Inuvik and Hay River excluded.

sions of opinion in only a few cases. The president of one of the pipeline companies was assailed in the following terms: "You are the twentieth century General Custer. . . . You are coming to destroy a people that have a history of 30,000 years. Why? For twenty years of gas? Are you really that insane?"[16] While most of the individuals who appeared before the Berger Inquiry referred only to peaceful means of redress, a few did issue veiled threats concerning what native people might be driven to in order to protect their only possession, the land. "If your nation becomes so violent that it would tear up our land, destroy our society and our future and occupy our homeland by trying to impose this pipeline against our will, then we will have no choice but to react with violence. I hope that we do not have to do that, for it is not the way we would choose. However, if we are forced to blow up the pipeline . . . ."[17] In the age of the American Indian Movement, the violence at Wounded Knee, and the armed occupation of a Canadian park near Kenora, these comments were hardly surprising, especially given the historic sense of grievance the Dene had inherited.

In negotiating land claims there are a number of problems for both sides. On the government side, delay allows resource exploration to proceed, which increases federal knowledge of the areas where oil or minerals are most likely to be found. As the picture becomes clearer each year, it reduces the chance that valuable resources would be lost to an area of exclusive native control under the land claims settlement. Just as Ottawa kept control of land and resources for twenty-five years after Alberta and Saskatchewan achieved provincial status, so in the North the federal authorities want exclusive control of resource development in spite of the rising pressure from native and white northerners for provincial powers and control of the resource revenues. Part of the reason for this lies in the billions of dollars in future oil royalties that Ottawa desperately needs to combat its chronic deficits. Also, if Ottawa controls major oil and gas reserves on federal lands it is less susceptible to energy blackmail from the producing provinces. The land claims and native rights tend to take second place to such strategic considerations in the politics of Confederation.

The second reason for procrastination is cost in land and dollars. The northern native land claims of Inuit Tapirisat of Canada, Committee for Original Peoples Entitlement, the Dene Nation, and the Council for Yukon Indians will involve a cash outlay of several billion dollars, which the Treasury Board is in no hurry to pay. Also, with regional land-use planning still in its infancy, Ottawa is still uncertain about its own priorities for many of the geographic areas under claim. Parks Canada, the Canadian Wildlife Service, the Department of National Defence, Transport Canada, Energy, Mines, and Resources, and Indian Affairs all have different interests to be reconciled. So from the vantage point of money, power, and planning, Ottawa has a vested interest in delaying the process of land claims settlements. For native people, however, the old adage that "justice delayed is justice denied" is clearly relevant.

Native organizations have also had reason for caution in approaching land claims negotiations. Above everything else is the sombre realization that all future generations will have to live with the bargain struck. Future circumstances must be anticipated if future problems are to be avoided. Lands given up will be lost permanently, yet control of land is the basis for the federal wish to achieve a land claims settlement. When both parties want a settlement in order to control land use and development, it would appear that some conflicts will be inevitable.

In approaching the negotiations the native leaders are well aware of the legal ambiguities involved with some of the basic terms, such as "aboriginal rights"; this situation has made it exceedingly difficult to define even the principles involved, let alone the details to be negotiated. All they could do was to research and document the areas that each band had traditionally occupied and habitually used for hunting and trapping. This evidence was not easy to come by and was subject to widely differing interpretations. For example, did one trap line through an area constitute occupation? For reasons mentioned above the native groups are searching for a settlement based on land, not cash; yet, how do they entrench their land settlement so that future governments cannot expropriate areas or pass a bill through Parliament to override the land agreements? This type of guarantee is anathema to many federal planners because it will be a serious restraint on northern development.

Equally as important as the settlement itself will be the new political forms to implement and carry through the settlement. The Inuit and the Dene are only slowly clarifying their thinking on political structures, but there is no way that this issue will not result in basic disputes with Ottawa. The federal authorities are clearly opposed to separate, ethnic-based Dene or Inuit political forms and are less than enthusiastic about three-, five-, or ten-year residency requirements for white voters. These are tough areas for the negotiations that lie ahead; and whatever their result, they will break new ground in the constitutional history of this country as well as of native affairs.

On a more pragmatic level there have been other problems in coordinating land claims negotiations. The political split between the Dene and the Métis Association (1977–80) has already been mentioned. Currently, most of the native groups in the North are desperately short of funds for their research efforts and legal interventions. Much of the documentation for the land claims is found in the oral traditions of the people, which white legal systems are reluctant to accept even though they may be the only source in non-literate cultures. There is genuine distrust of the white lawyers and legal system through which the settlement must be negotiated, for many of the concepts are alien, such as individual land ownership. All this stalling and caution, however well founded, has tragic overtones for the native people desperately in need of new financial resources that a land claims settlement might bring. The settlement may also bring new approaches to wildlife management, which is equally critical for future native welfare.

Closely related to these issues was the question of eligibility for land claims benefits. This issue triggered considerable controversy within native circles, especially among non-status Indians and Métis who feared that they might be excluded. Does an individual whose ancestors were primarily white still qualify? If so, where does one draw the line? By the spring of 1982 general guidelines for the Dene appeared to be on the verge of approval. Any status, non-status, or Métis normally a resident of the Northwest Territories who could demonstrate some family ties to one of the five Dene tribes would be eligible. Children adopted legally or by custom into a Dene family would qualify, as would children of mixed marriages. In the latter case only the non-Dene spouse would be excluded. Any who qualify for benefits under the Dene settlement would be excluded from any land claims settlement elsewhere in the country. Borderline cases could be presented to a local enrolment committee whose decision could be appealed to a central committee and if need be into the courts.[18] The above provision on mixed marriages was designed to avoid the sexist discrimination implicit in the federal Indian Act. The wide definition of eligibility had important political ramifications within native circles. The Métis, if they were going to merge with the Dene Nation, had to be sure that all their members would qualify for benefits, including enfranchisement for Dene elections. This was a concession on the part of the Dene, some of whom saw the Métis as too deeply influenced by white ways. There was also concern that the attractions of the land claims settlement might lead to some impostors trying to enter Dene ranks via the Métis Association.

Native concerns about land claims intensified with the James Bay agreement signed in the mid-1970's. This document became the subject of intense scrutiny and then criticism by the late 1970's. Native critics argued that the land base was inadequate and that provisions in the treaty, such as those for sanitation and health facilities, were never implemented. In the latter case the deaths of a number of Cree children added emotional fuel. In the government's view these promises had been conditional upon existing levels of funding within the budget of Indian Affairs; when financial restraint cut the funds available, Ottawa no longer felt obliged to provide the facilities promised. Within native circles the explanation was neither understood nor accepted. This settlement had been negotiated in haste. Some of its clauses were open to differing interpretation, but this cannot explain all the controversy aroused. A nine-month review of the situation by officials of the federal Justice and Indian Affairs ministries concluded: "The review team discovered several significant areas" in which "there have been serious problems of implementation, unresolved disputes, and in some cases, a failure to fully implement the agreement in both its spirit and letter."[19]

There has been serious questioning, too, that the land base secured in the James Bay agreement will prove adequate to sustain the traditional hunting and trapping society of the James Bay Cree, while the cash payments of $231 million spread through to 1997 are rapidly losing their value through the ravages of inflation. Years after the signing of the agreement conditions within these settlements remain deplorable, while the multibillion-dollar James Bay Project is pumping low-cost power into the Quebec and New York State grids. The native people who gave up their lands to make this scheme possible appear to be the net losers in the whole exercise. This lesson is hardly an inducement for other Indians or Inuit to settle land claims; in fact, the James Bay agreement has only added to the historic sense of grievance.

Government structures and bodies seem in so many cases to be alien to native input even when there is no hostility involved. At the Berger Inquiry these tensions were eased by the careful planning and patience of the inquiry staff. But at the NEB hearings the tensions were continually present, especially as a result of the adversarial approach to evidence. The Board was concerned to get native input and it went north with its hearings to get it. But the results were profoundly disappointing because most of the native leaders would not appear. They believed that their appearance would be legitimizing a process where the cards were stacked against them. The Board appeared impervious to the problems of public image it had with native people. Back in Ottawa, George Erasmus of the Dene Nation did appear, but an unfortunate event seemed to confirm the worst fears of the Dene about the Board. The chairman of the Board panel, in excusing Erasmus at the conclusion of his testimony, noted: "You have described yourself as a product of that system [colonialism] and I can say it cannot be that poor."[20] Although I think Jack Stabback meant it as a compliment to Erasmus, it came out as a challenge to the validity of his evidence and a belittling of the problems faced by the Dene. Under such circumstances it is hardly surprising that native organizations in Canada retain such a low regard for federal regulatory bodies like the National Energy Board. Yet the Board itself felt that it had done a great service to the native people when its report supported the main contentions of the Berger Report.[21] Out of this experience, however, it did not come to appreciate the cultural barriers to meaningful participation faced by the Dene and the Inuit.

Northern development presents immense problems of coping with social change for northern native groups. The social tensions can intensify feelings of alienation and cultural disorientation, which in turn promote the search for an escape through alcohol. During the Berger Inquiry the Department of Social Development of the government of the N.W.T. did a special study on "Alcohol Availability" that documented the growing social cost of booze and drugs. Per capita alcohol consumption was the highest in Canada with the sole exception of the Yukon. Violent crime in the Northwest Territories was almost eight times higher than the national average; assaults almost ten times; and murder 8.8 times. In the oil exploration boom of the early 1970's, when disposable income was at its height, welfare payments, alcohol consumption, and anti-social behaviour increased alarmingly. In 1968-69 welfare payments in the western Arctic stood at $495,294; by 1972-73 they had risen to over $1 million. The social and cultural erosion appeared to be a product of the increasing industrial impacts and urbanization in the North. There also appeared to be a link between the rising levels of disposable income and the increasing alcohol consumption. A nurse in Aklavik testified that 60 per cent of the cases she was treating were directly related to drugs, alcohol, and the effects of alcoholism.

For many who feel secure, there are social barriers to excess drinking: it may hurt their chances for promotion or their social standing in the community. For those who feel that they have no hope on either score there is not the same constraint on behaviour. For some northern natives there is a curious dichotomy in their thinking about liquor. This type of conspicuous consumption becomes a way for the individual to demonstrate that he has the money to make it in the white man's world; at the same time, it provides a means of escape from the social alienation that made it impossible for him to function in that same world. By 1982, fifteen northern native communities had attempted to tackle the alcohol problem by voting in local prohibition; however, with the frequency of visits by planes and boats it has proved hard to stop the flow of bootlegged beer and liquor.[22]

In this unsettled social environment, the links between disposable income, alcohol, violence, and even mental health can be clearly established. At the Berger Inquiry all the doctors and nurses who testified expressed their fears about mental health problems if the pressures of development were increased. Dr. Wheeler expressed his own feelings this way: "The solution to these problems and with it the survival of the Dene, lies within the Dene. They must be allowed to develop these solutions within a time frame of their own choosing before we get stampeded into a social disaster from which the North may never recover."[23] Within so many northern native bands there is a desperate search for the time to devise the means to cope. Time is needed to negotiate a land claims settlement; time is needed to create a strong native educational system to revitalize the cultural base of this society under stress; and time is needed to prepare native people for a meaningful economic role in the economy of the North. Yet, if serious energy shortages re-emerge in the late 1980's, there may be a rush of mega-projects to upset the fragile social equilibrium.

One of the important aspects of the land claims is the relationship to the wider economic system of Canada. Each of us is forced to base his position in our system on the strength of possessing one or more of the critical economic components in demand – skills, capital, property, or political influence. Whether one is a farmer, plumber, entrepreneur, professional, or unskilled labourer, one has one's income determined by the economic value in the marketplace. Without the land claims settlement native people would be without the leverage to gain the skills, the capital, and the other ingredients they require to compete. They would remain divorced from the means of production and pushed to the margins of Canadian society. Many native leaders have high hopes that these agreements will be the basis for a new start and a proper entry to the mainstream of Canadian society.

Thus far the dual economy of the North combines the traditional sector (hunting and trapping) with the industrial sector (non-renewable resources). Both are subject to instability from fluctuation in world prices. Fur prices reflect the whims of the North American and European fashions; oil and gas exploration follows seasonal patterns as well as huge changes from year to year in the level of activity, depending on profits available for reinvestment. In bad years exploration budgets can be cut to the bone. Even when completed, the great mega-projects will not change this uncertain employment pattern; for instance, the Alaska Highway Pipeline will provide only about 300 permanent jobs in the North, with native people qualifying for few of these. Aware of these problems, the pipeline companies established the Nortran native apprenticeship program in the early 1970's. However, the dropout rate has been very high and few natives have completed all the required training for skilled positions.[24] The cultural and social barriers have not been easy to overcome. To many natives, the oil and gas industry is seen as a serious disruption of their land-based economy without compensating opportunities in which they can participate. They see that the real beneficiaries of the projects will be the transient workers, the corporate shareholders, and the federal treasury.

Arctic Gas tried to counter this image of the native as victim by pushing the pro-development model of Charles Hobart, a sociologist from the University of Alberta. Hobart argued that the traditional native culture had been largely destroyed by the collapse of the fur market, the white curriculum in the schools, television, the highways into the North, and so on. The native peoples had been "socialized" away from the former lifestyle toward the wage-labour economy. With the demographic explosion of the 1960's and 1970's increasing numbers of young native people were coming out of the school system with expectations of a consumer economy that could not be met unless rapid development took place. If their hopes were frustrated there could be a powerful backlash against the system. The root cause of the social tensions in the North was not pipelines and the industrial system but poverty, welfare, and the chronic lack of jobs. Increased opportunities for employment would cut into that demoralization, welfare dependency, and alcoholism. According to Hobart's view, everyone should avoid the romanticism and accept that the traditional hunting and trapping economy was on its last legs.

Hobart admitted that there would be some social costs and tensions involved in completing the transition to the wage economy – including further alcoholism and violence. But he argued that the process of cultural erosion had gone too far and the population explosion now meant the land could not support future generations even if they wished to live off the land. Not only would they profit from wage labour, but with the cash from the land claims settlement they would have capital for entrepreneurial activities of their own. New jobs would be a socially stabilizing force. In brief, Hobart's model was the American Dream applied to the Canadian North. He assumed that industrial capitalism, which had evolved over 400 years in the West, could be adopted successfully by a communal and non-industrial society in a generation. At the root of his model was the assumption that the material inducements of the white economic system would overcome the cultural and social shocks. Every man has his price.

In the hearings and after, no love was lost between the Dene and Hobart, who was viewed as the "hired gun" of the oil companies. In return, Hobart aggressively attacked Mel Watkins and the white advisers, hoping to drive a split between them and the Dene. He argued that their socialist ideology was attempting to isolate the North as a "museum piece" divorced from the economic benefits enjoyed elsewhere in North America. The Dene were being used to further the political ends of these left-wing intellectuals; they were the *real* enemies of native people, not the pipeline companies: "I must confess it seems rather presumptuous to me for whites to tell them [native people] what they should or should not want for themselves, for their communities, and for their children." The comments infuriated the elected leaders of the Dene, who had chosen their staff and resented the implied criticism. They believed it was Hobart who was guilty of the very presumption he denounced. This war of words continued on through the hearings and beyond to intensify the tensions between the camps.

Behind the scenes, too, Arctic Gas claimed that the opposition to its project was a product of the white advisers who had misled the Dene from their normal moderation, thus quietly ignoring the almost unanimous views expressed by individual native people against the pipeline in the community hearings. It was even alleged that they forced the removal of James Wah-shee and had him replaced by the more radical George Erasmus as president of the Indian Brotherhood of the N.W.T. (later the Dene Nation). This line of attack was resented bitterly by the Dene, who did not see themselves as puppets on a string being manipulated by the white advisers.[25] They employed consultants exactly the same way that the applicants did. The point was settled once and for all when the white advisers were fired immediately on the conclusion of the hearings, as a clear demonstration of where the power lay.

Hobart's work was central to the Arctic Gas case because he was striking at the core of the native contention that the net impacts of the pipeline would be negative. While Hobart provided the overall social model, consultants such as Gemini North tried to provide the socio-economic data to flesh out the Arctic Gas application. This group of consultants, made up of journalists, proved to be a major embarrassment to their clients. Even Hobart felt constrained to dissociate himself from the simplistic assumptions on the cash value of native country food and other analysis. Even the normally judicious Berger noted that their evidence "could not be relied upon."[26] Arctic Gas, embarrassed by these superficial efforts, quietly dropped the Gemini North evidence before they presented their case to the NEB. Like many corporations in the early 1970's, Arctic Gas had only limited in-house expertise and it was burned by entrepreneurs passing themselves off as experts. As a result, it fell back on Hobart's work, which might be controversial but no one could challenge his professional credentials. After the collapse of Arctic Gas in 1977, Hobart moved on to provide the social analysis for other northern projects, such as Polar Gas Pipeline, whose application may come before regulatory hearings late in the 1980's.

A great deal of the evidence led by native groups to counter Hobart focused on the intangibles of a way of life, which made cross-examination by the corporate lawyers virtually impossible. The few times that they attempted it, they retreated in some disarray. Native spokesmen also drew attention to the fact that during the period of heaviest oil and gas exploration (1968–73) there were increasing welfare and alcohol problems. Jobs had not stabilized social problems in the way that Hobart had argued.

Behind the scenes there were deep social tensions with racial overtones between some of the parties to the pipeline debate. In spite of the millions of words being uttered, there was little communication between some of the corporate groups and the native organizations. In the hearings everything was quietly correct; but in the bars after hours the veneer peeled back and the real antagonisms emerged.[27] In public it only came out in more subtle ways. While promising jobs for native people, Arctic Gas did not employ Dene or Inuit in presenting its social impact evidence to Berger or the NEB. Foothills, on the other hand, had spokesmen with native backgrounds. This avoided the appearance of a colour bar and lent more credibility to Foothills' social and cultural analysis. Foothills' president was also exceedingly careful in his own statements to recognize the legitimacy of native concerns. In the long term this paid immense dividends to the company, for it helped to convince Ottawa that the Alaska Highway Project would create fewer tensions, which was a major political advantage for the Trudeau cabinet.

In the northern pipeline debate the Dene Nation was the most controversial of the native groups. Their use of the term "genocide" always raised emotions in government and corporate circles. While the Dene used the term to mean the gradual destruction of their way of life, most whites remembered the term as applied to the Nazi death camps. Midway through the hearings they released the Dene Declaration, a document filled with ringing rhetoric but with few specifics concerning a land claims settlement. Their use of such terms as "self-determination" led some in the south, including the Minister of Indian and Northern Affairs, to denounce it as a separatist document. Given the intense preoccupation in Ottawa about Quebec separatism, this was not surprising. However, the declaration allowed many who were generally opposed to native rights to try to use it to influence opinion against the Dene. Again the white advisers were accused of trying to direct the North into a socialist revolution. The declaration is certainly an ambiguous document, which emphasized the need for new political forms to meet the circumstances of the North. Yet the rhetoric and even the wording was no more revolutionary than that of some of the provincial premiers of the day. In a period of critical debate on the constitution, the native people were determined to have a spot at the bargaining table; but given the fragile nature of Canadian unity, their intervention was often misunderstood. It was difficult for many Canadians, who had only slowly come to accept that there were two founding nationalities, to recognize that there were three.

Another controversial aspect of the Dene case was the economic and socio-economic evidence put forward by academics from a variety of backgrounds and ideological perspectives. Most of the evidence clearly reflected the Innis tradition of staples analysis from either a liberal or Marxist perspective. But it was Mel Watkins' own evidence that most clearly articulated the opposition not just to the specifics of the pipeline but to the whole economic system of which it was a part. Governments and the multinational companies had combined to promote the export of raw staples from the region to service the American industrial empire. Unlike Hobart, he tried to trace where the profits or economic rents from northern development went – the evidence was clear that it was outside the North. The main *raison d'être* of Arctic Gas was to serve the Alaskan gas producers and the American gas distributors. The main economic benefits from the project would be siphoned off to U.S. interests. Even the development of the Mackenzie Delta gas would benefit the foreign owners of Imperial, Gulf, and Shell. Native people, in Watkins' analysis, were divorced from meaningful participation in this colonial economy. If one had to make a choice between the interests of non-Canadians and the interests of native people who are Canadians, "Surely it is of the essence of the nature of the nation-state that it should be biased in favour of its own citizenry." Because of the power and influence of Exxon in a consortium like Arctic Gas, the project inevitably involved a degree of erosion of Canadian sovereignty and a rejection of Canadian priorities. With an emerging surplus of gas in Alberta, the timetable for developing these resources should reflect Canadian needs and hence be delayed. Until the native land claims settlement was in place the Dene should have a veto over resource projects, for the revenue from such projects normally accrues to the landowner. In addition, the current pattern led to the exporting of raw staples with little or no economic linkage to trigger the spinoff of other economic activity. The North was a typical resource hinterland exporting raw resources while importing capital and manufactured goods.

Watkins argued that this outward draining of economic surplus locked the North into a "staples trap." It had neither the capital nor the political power to control its own destiny. A few seasonal construction jobs would do nothing to change this cycle of dependency; native people would lack the skills, the capital, and the opportunity to reach the promised land Hobart had portrayed. They would be a permanent proletariat divorced from the means of production.[28] Watkins' testimony constituted the opposing model to Hobart's and was an important contribution to Canadian political economy, extending the liberal staples thesis into a northern and Marxist perspective.

Whether or not one accepted all of the ideological assumptions, the work presented the economic dilemma of the North with a stark and compelling logic. The colonialism and the dependency of the Northwest Territories economy were nearly as great a problem for small business as for native people. The boom/bust cycles of non-renewable resources meant that the uncertainties were ever present for all except government employees. Yet his testimony, because of its socialist assumptions, became a type of lightning rod, attracting all the bolts of the corporate critics, although when the pipeline companies had Watkins in the witness box, they were reluctant to cross-examine him seriously. The issues he raised were ones they had trouble addressing; besides, few of the lawyers had training in economics or political economy so they were ill-equipped to challenge his assumptions.

The northern pipeline debate raised a whole series of social and ethical questions that were unsettling for business and government. Within corporate circles, it was part of the wider debate about "social responsibility" that enlivened many annual meetings of shareholders in the 1970's. For some companies these new issues were allocated to be handled by the efforts of the public relations departments; for a few there was a genuine effort to rethink the usual assumptions concerning the corporate role in society. Arctic Gas tended to follow the first philosophy and Foothills the second. Profits still remained the crucial bottom line, but the new political and social assumptions had to be recognized in public hearings before regulatory boards. Also, social or environmental disasters could seriously harm the corporate image, increase public opposition and project costs, and delay approvals. Much of the new corporate social responsibilty was enlightened and pragmatic self-interest by executives wishing to avoid political controversy. Yet many old hands in the oil patch failed to perceive the changing social attitudes and their influence on the regulatory climate.
Many in government were troubled as well by the ethics of a northern development policy. Combined in the mandate of the Ministry of Indian Affairs and Northern Development were conflicting responsibilities for the trusteeship of northern native people, protection of the northern environment, and promotion of northern economic development. Many believed that the first two were incompatible with the third, and development priorities dominated the overall policy decisions. During the northern pipeline debate there was confusion in the ministry as the competing factions struggled for control of policy while frequent ministerial changes weakened the control from the top. Both cabinet and the bureaucracy were trying to come to grips with the newly emerging concepts of social responsibility and

their political implications. This confusion helped to open the way for Berger to have a greater impact than normally would have been the case. The bureaucracy had been put on the defensive as a result of Ed Dosman's *The National Interest*, the court challenge to Marshall Crowe, and continuous criticism from public interest groups.[29]

The debate on ethics was brought into sharp focus through the intervention of church groups in support of native peoples, especially Project North and the Committee for Justice and Liberty. The Anglican and Catholic churches had a long history of involvement in the North in providing spiritual, educational, and medical services through the work of their missionaries. They were joined by social activists – both clergy and lay – from other denominations concerned about the plight of the Dene and Inuit. The Northern Initiative was similar to those involving Third World issues raised by the Task Force on the Churches and Social Responsibility. The churches' entry into the pipeline debate aroused fierce opposition from business leaders within these denominations who tried to argue that the church should stay out of "politics." Led by John Olthuis of CJL and Hugh and Karmel McCullum of Project North, there were strong efforts to mobilize the churches against the pipeline, including a book these three produced through the Anglican Book Centre in Toronto.[30]

The churches involved themselves directly in events in the North, which evoked further comment. When the Métis Association of the N.W.T. withdrew from the united front with the Dene on the land claims negotiations, the federal government withdrew its funding. The Dene were dependent on those funds to hold their assembly in October, 1975, at Fort Simpson. The Dene appealed to their church allies for aid, and the Anglicans and Catholics provided a grant of $100,000. A similar request from the Métis Association was turned down on the basis that this assembly was not dealing directly with the land claims issue. Even so, it gave the appearance that the churches were siding with the more radical party in an internal battle within the northern native community. Not surprisingly, this grant sparked more controversy within the churches. Project North's criticisms were not confined to the specifics of the pipeline but broadened into a general attack on the unjust economic system. The group argued before Berger: "Most of us live in and benefit from a socio-economic situation which is sinful. By social sin we mean that we create and sustain social and economic patterns of behaviour that bind and oppress, give privilege to the powerful and maintain systems of dependency, paternalism, racism, and colonialism."[31] The church, Project North insisted, could not be true to Christ's teachings if it silently acquiesced in this subordination of the northern native people. Many in Project North were upset with the materialism and possessive individualism that industrial capitalism had injected into Western values and were attracted by the non-materialist and communal sharing implicit in the Dene and the Inuit way of life.

In April, 1977, a number of the church leaders appeared personally at the NEB pipeline hearings. Bishop Remi De Roo of Victoria represented the Conference of Catholic Bishops. As he put it bluntly: "we feel that we cannot remain silent on this ethical issue when we see people literally being destroyed." The Board members, especially Stabback and Edge, appeared to be annoyed by the implied criticism that the Board's policies and procedures were not in accordance with ethical considerations.[32] Some of the industry representatives were even more outspoken in denouncing the appearance of the churchmen. As one commented sarcastically to the author after the NEB session: "Next they will be saying that God is opposed to the Mackenzie Valley Pipeline." Although no one likes to be challenged in terms of his ethics, there was no question that many were uncomfortable with the churchmen's comments.

The leading witness among the church leaders was the head of the Anglican Church of Canada, Archbishop Ted Scott. His keen intellectual mind and broad knowledge made his testimony an interesting statement of social philosophy. Scott stressed: "I believe that this issue of aboriginal rights is so crucial an issue that our response to it will be central in determining the inner meaning of Canada as a nation." Justice demanded that there must be a moratorium on northern development as recommended by the Anglican General Synod. On the one side were the basic ethics of the land claims negotiations and the ecological viability of the land for future generations; on the other side were the short-term corporate profits from energy exploitation and exports. Archbishop Scott believed that some of the most fundamental issues involved in the pipeline debate came back to ethical questions of first principles.

Scott also saw projects like the Mackenzie Valley Pipeline as part of a wider pattern of "social and moral chaos" emerging in Western society. Canada "can no longer avoid the reality that a whole range of our present day societal problems can be traced to this obsession with economic growth rates." While two-thirds of the world's population suffers from poverty and starvation, man continues to promote policies reflecting high energy consumption and materialistic, hedonistic lifestyles. The end result is affluence for a few and poverty for many. We must learn from the native people a deeper reverence for nature, Scott said, for "their integrated concept of stewardship of natural resources" will help to lead Canadians toward a new lifestyle.

Our most basic gift, the land, must not be despoiled for the profits of a few. If we are going to live in a sustainable society, Scott insisted, we must abandon this commitment to the present philosophy of economic growth. Otherwise our civilization will crumble. Man was instructed in Genesis by his creator to replenish the earth, not just have dominion over it.[33]

The overall impact of the churches' efforts in the pipeline hearings is very difficult to estimate; however, they certainly strengthened the case of the public interest groups, who had attempted to raise some of these broader questions earlier in the hearings. For the Board it was obviously an unsettling experience. Even if the Board could not accept the ethical perspective of the church leaders, obviously they could not ignore it because it represented wider social concerns of the electorate in general.

Following the defeat of the Arctic Gas application in the summer of 1977, other projects came forward that continued the pressures of social development for the Dene and Inuit. Progress toward a native land claims settlement remained agonizingly slow. There was little progress with the Dene Nation and ITC; only COPE and the Council of Yukon Indians appeared to be close to a settlement and the agreement in principle with COPE was allowed to lapse during the brief Clark administration. When various interest groups mounted an attack on the agreement, there were few spokesmen prepared to defend it.

Late in 1980 and early in 1981 the focus for development swung back to the Mackenzie Valley when Imperial Oil and Interprovincial Pipeline proposed a new twelve-inch line to run north from Alberta to an expanded Norman Wells field on the Mackenzie. The announcement rekindled Dene fears that had eased since 1977. Both the NEB and the Environmental Assessment and Review Process held public hearings and then approved the project, with the former allowing for an immediate start and the latter calling for a one-year delay. Both reports catalogued a number of deficiencies in the project that the applicant would have to overcome before construction could begin, and both reports challenged Mr. Justice Berger's ten-year moratorium to allow for settlement of the land claims in the Mackenzie Valley. At the same time, though, the NEB report quoted Berger on the importance of a land claims settlement:

Their claims must be seen as a means to the establishment of a social contract based on a clear understanding that they are distinct peoples in history. They insist upon the right to determine their own future, to ensure their place, but not assimilation, in Canadian life. . . . Their concerns begin with the land, but are not limited to it: they extend to renewable and non-renewable resources, education, health and social services, public order and overarching all of these considerations, the future shape, order and the composition of political institutions in the North.[34]

After endorsing this statement, it seemed rather contradictory for the Board to recommend an immediate start on the project regardless of the fact that the proposed pipeline cut through the key areas to be considered under a land claims settlement. However, it was clearly a central feature of Board policy that under no circumstances could land claims hold up development projects.

When the cabinet came to consider these reports they also faced a dilemma. Their own policy called for maximizing oil production, especially on federal lands, to ease their dependence on the producing provinces and increase federal revenues. The Berger recommendations, including the ten-year moratorium, had never been adopted as government policy. Yet there was a strong moral obligation on Ottawa to make concessions to facilitate the land claims negotiations. After the Dene denounced the NEB and EARP reports, the minister, John Munro, went north seeking to negotiate a solution. For a variety of reasons, including pipeline security, Ottawa wanted to get agreement so the Norman Wells project could proceed amicably.

The economics of the project were a particular bone of contention for northern residents seeking a revenue base to fund local activities. Imperial Oil had estimated that the new production at Norman Wells of just over 25,000 barrels per day would gross about $250 million per year ($27.50 per barrel). With the one-third federal ownership of the field, federal corporate income taxes, and royalties Ottawa would receive about $40 million per year. With this revenue at stake the conflict of interest for federal policy-makers was very clear. Territorial officials estimated that they would receive about $6 million per year in local taxes; yet they would have to absorb so many of the social and environmental costs. The shortcomings in the economic deal for the North helped to bring natives and whites together in fighting a further example of southern colonialism.

To try to overcome native opposition, Munro tried to get native involvement in the project through jobs and equity investment. Ottawa promised an extensive retraining program so that the Dene could qualify for skilled jobs when construction began. Interprovincial offered a 10 per cent equity stake for $10 million, which the Dene rejected; their proposal to purchase equity in Esso Resources pro-

231

Figure 22.
Norman Wells Oil Pipeline. From National Energy Board, March, 1981.

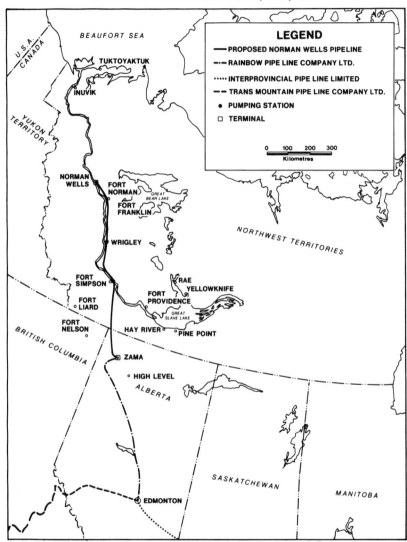

INTERPROVINCIAL PIPE LINE (NW) LTD.

duction facilities was in turn unacceptable to Imperial Oil. The oil company was only prepared to offer the Dene a joint venture involving one drilling rig, one service rig, and one construction camp. The Dene complained that this was mere tokenism that excluded them from any

232

share in the real profits. In a billion-dollar project (oilfield expansion and pipeline) they could bid on only $8.5 million worth of construction (less than 1 per cent) and they had no assurance that their bids would be successful.[35] Thus the claims that oil development would bring prosperity to native people were a sham. The age-old economic exploitation policies were once again being imposed on the North.

If the economic benefits would be limited, the social costs could potentially be quite serious for the Dene and the territorial government. The NEB report documented that there would be significant social impacts flowing from the project. The pipeline would "physically impinge" upon the traditional hunting and trapping economy and because of accelerated inflation increase the cost-of-living for northerners. The Dene would be diverted from their own economy during the construction phase but these jobs would end after two winters. The permanent pipeline jobs would be few in number – sixteen at Norman Wells, nine at Fort Simpson, and four at Zama Lake in Alberta – and would be of a highly skilled or professional nature. Interprovincial did not plan any special training for northern natives except for the construction phase.

The NEB report seemed to accept that there would be a net loss from the project for the Dene in the area: "Since this sector is sensitive to inflationary pressures and since the magnitude of losses is difficult to predict and determine, it would appear virtually impossible to mitigate or compensate for all project-induced impacts upon this sector."[36] In addition, the pipeline right-of-way is so close to Fort Norman, Wrigley, and Fort Simpson that the social environment of these communities will be affected by migrant and off-duty workers. Judging from the Alaskan experience, increased alcoholism, violent crime, mental illness, prostitution, venereal disease, and racial tensions can be expected.[37] Small, isolated native communities are ill-equipped to deal with a large worker influx, which creates social tensions within these communities and trap-line destruction outside. The EARP report, which recognized these social problems, suggested the establishment of a special trust fund from federal revenues to counter some of the criticism that Ottawa and the resource companies were siphoning off the wealth of the North while putting very little back to cushion the social disruption that resource development caused.

In the early summer of 1981 the Trudeau cabinet worked to hammer out a compromise between its development priorities and the native concerns. On July 30, John Munro flew north to Yellowknife to brief native leaders and territorial assembly representatives on the government's decision. The trip came a few weeks after the federal court had thrown out the legal challenge of the Committee for Justice and Liberty to the NEB report.[38] The cabinet decision was to approve the project but to impose a two-year delay in the start of construction to allow time for the negotiation of a land claims settlement. A number of economic inducements were also contained in the package. Two-thirds of the 350 construction jobs were to go to northern residents while northern business should be allowed to tender on $100 million in local contracts. For native entrepreneurs, Ottawa offered $1 million in start-up capital for launching a $9 million joint venture with Esso Resources for a drilling and service rig to be used in the expansion of the Norman Wells oilfield. No agreement was reached on Dene equity investment in the project although there was clearly some interest on both sides to see this accomplished.

This time schedule was based on the huge assumption that the land claims could be settled, even in principle, within two years. Past history and the complexity of the issues involved would tend to cast doubt on its practicability. In the past ten years neither the government nor the native groups have appeared to be working vigorously in this direction. However, in 1981 and 1982 there was some progress. The Dene and the Métis Association were back together in a united front, which had been a government precondition to negotiations. Their response to Munro's Norman Wells announcement appeared to be positive. George Erasmus, leader of the Dene Nation, hailed the two-year delay as "a major victory for the people of the North" that will create "the kind of climate needed for successful negotiation of our land claims." This was in marked contrast to earlier statements following the release of the NEB report that Ottawa was "programming genocide." James Bourque, president of the Métis Association, was equally supportive of the cabinet announcement. He stressed that they were particularly pleased by the $10 million retraining program: "That alone is a tremendous breakthrough. The delay itself would not have been any good if we did not have the necessary skills to compete for jobs and contracts."[39]

This stand indicated the Dene and Métis were prepared to relinquish their commitment to Berger's ten-year moratorium. The reasons for this are complex. Since 1977 there had been growing interest within native circles in seeing more economic development in the N.W.T. to complement the traditional trapping economy. This change in turn helped to ease the tensions between the Dene and the Métis, who tended to be more pro-development. It also eased the tensions with the white community and the territorial assembly. Their new unity increased their bargaining position on land claims with the federal authorities, who had long used the excuse of native disunity to justify their own wishes for procrastination.

As this volume goes to press the Norman Wells Oil Pipeline had just been opened, with the first Arctic crude reaching Zama Lake, Alberta, on April 9, 1985. As promised, many native people did receive jobs in the construction phase while northerners constituted 43 per cent of the overall work force. Shehtah Drilling Limited, the Dene/ Métis joint venture with Esso Resources, was responsible for drilling sixty of the new wells to expand the field production, which provided important experience for native workers in skilled jobs. Northern companies did procure over $100 million in contracts as federal policy had directed. But not everyone was satisfied with the procedures or even the project itself. The Dene Nation and the local chiefs boycotted the formal opening ceremonies on May 15 at Norman Wells. The previous Liberal government had promised to negotiate partial native ownership of the Norman Wells field before oil would begin to flow south. When the Mulroney government failed to do so, the Dene chose to boycott as their only means of protest. David Crombie, the federal Minister of Indian and Northern Affairs, went on to Fort Simpson after the opening ceremonies to assure the native groups that the federal government wished to negotiate. It currently holds a one-third ownership in the field.

The Dene also had strong environmental concerns from watching the construction of the project. Their president, Stephen Kakfwi, stressed these concerns in a letter to the Toronto *Globe and Mail*: "Certainly the IPL pipeline has been built, but the Dene, who live in and use the surrounding land and water, are concerned that all is not well with the environment and the processes involved in environmental management. We have concerns with contaminated fish downstream of the oil-field development, inadequate water quality standards and insufficient and untested oil-spill contingency planning. It is only slowly that government and industry are starting to recognize and address our concerns." He demanded that there be a five-year delay before any new pipeline proposals would be considered for the western Arctic because of the time delay before some of the environmental impacts would be evident.[40]

The Norman Wells project, despite the environmental worries, did represent an important shift in terms of Dene attitudes to the white economic system of free enterprise. At the Berger Inquiry they appeared to be strongly critical of non-renewable resource development and the multinational oil companies. Now they appeared to be willing to allow such development to proceed even before the political restructuring of the Northwest Territories, which had always been an integral part of their land claims package. Also, they had shown an interest in participating with capital investment in the oil and gas industry dominated so long by the multinationals. The scale of this investment could change dramatically if the land claims settlement included cash and oil royalties, as had been the case in Alaska. This seemed to represent a shift ideologically in their attitude to the free enterprise economy. The new pragmatism may have been the product of political shifts within the Dene movement or merely the acceptance of the inevitability of the project and the desirability of maximizing the economic benefits available to native people. Although it does not assure a speedy resolution of the land claims issue it does appear to be a step in that direction. If the past is an indication, these future negotiations will be tough, volatile, and filled with many more surprises. However, the environment for negotiations appears better now than at any point in the last decade.

In January, 1982, the Dene released a draft document outlining the structure of government they wished to see for the western Arctic.[41] The proposal, developed jointly by the Dene Nation and the Métis Association, constitutes the most concrete attempt yet to define into a workable constitution the complex relations between native and white society in a type of province profoundly different from any other within Confederation. There would be a basic charter of founding principles to entrench the aboriginal rights of the Dene and the collective and individual rights of the non-Dene. The territory would be split into two parts following the native land claims settlement. In addition, there would be separate and parallel school systems and social services for each group. English and the native languages would be entrenched constitutionally as official languages in their new province, which they wished to be known as Denendeh. A provincial national assembly would be established to rule non-Dene areas composed of local chiefs, elected community members, and elected constituency members. The Dene would hold a minimum of 30 per cent of the seats in the assembly. To be eligible to vote, there would be a residency qualification, possibly as high as ten years (but more likely three or five). As George Erasmus put it bluntly: "the principle that some period must be set to give people an opportunity to acquaint themselves with life in Denendeh is not negotiable."[42] Besides the assembly there would be an Upper House or Senate composed exclusively of Dene, which would have a veto power over legislation passed by the Lower House that adversely affected aboriginal rights as defined in the final land claims settlement. Present property ownership would be respected but in future only long-term leases, not freehold tenure, could be acquired. Native collectives for Dene lands and the government of Denendeh in the other areas would maintain and administer land and resource ownership questions.

The regulations for resource development contain a number of unique and interesting features that deserve to be quoted in full to give a proper perspective of Dene resource planning.

The remaining land and resources in Denendeh (with the exception of private property) will be owned and managed by the Government of Denendeh.

As subsistence users of wildlife, the aboriginal right of the Dene to hunt, fish and trap in these lands will take precedence over all other use of the resource. The Government of Denendeh will manage these lands and resources according to conditions which are consistent with the Charter of Founding Principles.

Government decisions about the development of non-renewable resources will be based on the following conditions. These will also help to make cooperative decisions between the institutions set up to manage resource development on exclusive Dene lands and the Government of Denendeh.

(a) The resource is surplus to Denendeh's own needs, determined on a reasonable basis of present and future consumption.

(b) The southern Canadian need is determined on the basis of "a conserver society" level of usage and a firm commitment to renewables.

(c) Exploration, development and transportation will not create undue social dislocation in Denendeh or any of the communities most directly affected.

(d) Preparation, construction and operation of the facilities will not damage the environment of Denendeh or any of the communities most directly affected.

(e) The project is judged to be technically sound.

(f) The project has been determined to be financially feasible and economic benefits will accrue to the Government of Denendeh.

(g) The project is consistent with the economic development plans of the Government of Denendeh.

(h) Ten per cent of all resource revenues collected by governments will be paid into an Aboriginal Trust Fund (a Dene Heritage Fund) controlled by the Dene.

(i) The remaining resource revenue accruing to the Government of Denendeh from the sale of non-renewable resources will be distributed in the following way:
   • first to cover the costs of government in Denendeh at both the community and "provincial" levels;
   • in the event that revenues in any given year are less than the costs of government, the Government of Canada will make up the difference;
   • in the event that revenues exceed the costs of government

in Denendeh, the excess money will be first used to pay the Government of Canada for direct federal assistance going into Denendeh, such as unemployment insurance benefits, children's allowances, etc.;

- in the event that there is enough revenue to provide for the above, the rest will be divided 50% to the Government of Denendeh and 50% to the Government of Canada.

One of the thrusts of the Dene proposal is to lessen the power of elected officials and place more power and responsibility with the people themselves and their local councils. Major resource decisions would be subject to a plebiscite to ensure that the people's wishes were paramount. The government of Denendeh would assume a number of powers similar to a southern province (education, resources, etc.) and some of the powers normally shared by the provinces with Ottawa (fisheries, environment, etc.). The Dene also claimed some areas of exclusive federal jurisdiction, including communications and external relations with other aboriginal peoples. This document is an interesting and complex attempt to divide and share political power and responsibility. It limits the normal processes of democracy to try to protect the communal rights of the Dene and Métis. As a draft document, it is designed to further the process of negotiation that now lies ahead. Many parts of it are highly controversial and likely to be strongly resisted by some white northerners as well as Ottawa officials. The Dene do not underestimate the tough and complex negotiations ahead. In fact, they provide a flow chart on how they might proceed, which is itself instructive as to their strategy and tactics.

The federal government and the resource companies will have trouble living with some of the provisions of the above document. The main negotiations must now begin on the critical issue of land claims, especially relating to the areas for the exclusive use of the Dene, and the compensation (cash, resource royalties, etc.) to be paid to the Dene for relinquishing the remainder of their lands. But this document is now down on the table and Ottawa will have to respond with counter-proposals much more advanced than the timid efforts of the Drury Report on the future government of the N.W.T. This task is complicated by Ottawa's determination to keep control of resource policies and maximize federal revenue from territorial lands. The one over-riding issue is that serious bargaining must now begin before the next wave of energy shortages creates tensions that will destroy the bargaining climate.

In the eastern Arctic, activity, interest, and controversy have increased in the early 1980's. Oil and gas exploration proceeded steadily in the central High Arctic, north and east from Melville Island. The bulk of the drilling was offshore in winter from reinforced ice pads. Unlike the Beaufort, the ice here is shore fast and provides a stable platform. After EARP hearings, offshore drilling moved into the southern part of Davis Strait opposite Frobisher Bay. Further north in Lancaster Sound, after a vigorous battle during EARP hearings, the government chose not to allow drilling pending completion of regional land-use planning. In mining, the Navisivik mine at Arctic Bay on north Baffin was joined in 1982 by the Cominco Polaris Mine on Little Cornwallis near Resolute. Nearby, on Bathurst Island, a major battle was under way, for mining and oil interests were determined to stop the creation of a wilderness park at Polar Bear Pass, an area of critical habitat for a number of species. All these events and controversies brought the Inuit of the eastern Arctic onto centre stage in a way that had not happened in the 1970's when the media focus was on the Mackenzie Valley.

The chief Inuit concern was the Arctic Pilot Project, which underwent public hearings in 1981 and 1982. This project, with cost estimates of $2.3 billion (1981 dollars),[43] proposed to ship approximately 320 million cubic feet of natural gas per day from the Drake Point field on the northern end of Melville Island by pipeline south to Bridport Inlet on the south coast. Here, barge-mounted liquefaction facilities would convert the gas to LNG for tanker shipment east through Lancaster Sound and then south to either Gros Cacouna downstream from Quebec City or Melford Point on the Strait of Canso. Initially there would be two Arctic class-seven icebreaking tankers,[44] each containing 140,000 cubic metres of LNG, making sixteen round trips per year. About 19 per cent of the gas would be used up in transit before entering the Trans-Quebec and Maritime Pipeline system. The project was sponsored by Petro-Canada, Dome, Nova, and Melville Shipping and, it was hoped, would be on stream in 1987 if all approvals were granted by the end of 1982.

With capital cost estimates of over twice that of Norman Wells, this project immediately aroused strong statements of concern from the Inuit leaders because the tankers would open up Lancaster Sound to year-round navigation. The pressures for development had been building up from the Pan-Arctic consortium (led by Petro-Canada), which had been carrying the heavy costs of drilling since the early 1960's without any production revenue. Originally it had been expected that the Polar Gas Pipeline would be built in the early 1980's but southern gas surpluses had eliminated the market. As a result, Polar Gas wisely chose not to press its application forward at the NEB.

TABLE THREE

Dene Scenario for Land Claims Negotiations

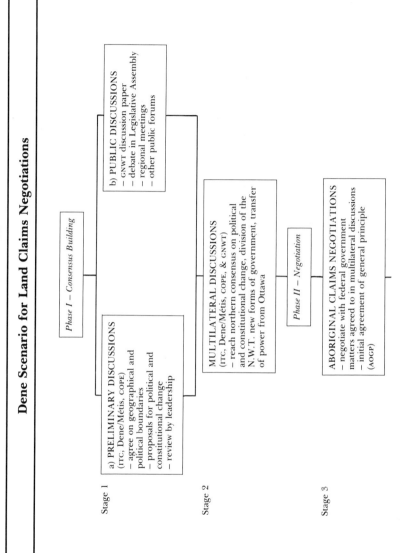

Stage 1

a) PRELIMINARY DISCUSSIONS
(ITC, Dene/Métis, COPE)
– agree on geographical and
  political boundaries
– proposals for political and
  constitutional change
– review by leadership

b) PUBLIC DISCUSSIONS
– GNWT discussion paper
– debate in Legislative Assembly
– regional meetings
– other public forums

Phase I – Consensus Building

Stage 2

MULTILATERAL DISCUSSIONS
(ITC, Dene/Métis, COPE, & GNWT)
– reach northern consensus on political
  and constitutional change, division of the
  N.W.T. new forms of government, transfer
  of power from Ottawa

Phase II – Negotiation

Stage 3

ABORIGINAL CLAIMS NEGOTIATIONS
– negotiate with federal government
  matters agreed to in multilateral discussions
– initial agreement of general principle
  (AOGP)

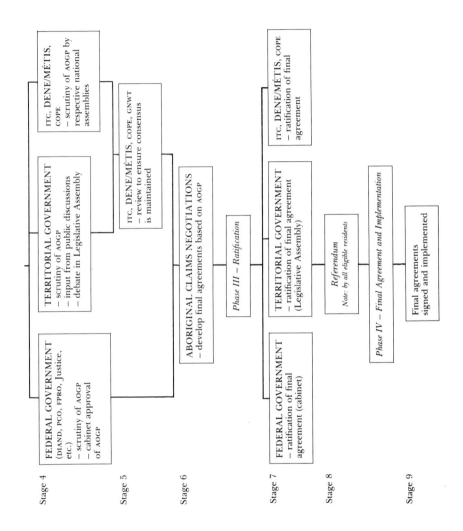

Stage 4

FEDERAL GOVERNMENT
(DIAND, PCO, FPRO, Justice, etc.)
– scrutiny of AOGP
– cabinet approval of AOGP

TERRITORIAL GOVERNMENT
– scrutiny of AOGP
– input from public discussions
– debate in Legislative Assembly

ITC, DENE/MÉTIS, COPE
– scrutiny of AOGP by respective national assemblies

Stage 5

ITC, DENE/MÉTIS, COPE, GNWT
– review to ensure consensus is maintained

Stage 6

ABORIGINAL CLAIMS NEGOTIATIONS
– develop final agreements based on AOGP

Phase III – Ratification

Stage 7

FEDERAL GOVERNMENT
– ratification of final agreement (cabinet)

TERRITORIAL GOVERNMENT
– ratification of final agreement (Legislative Assembly)

ITC, DENE/MÉTIS, COPE
– ratification of final agreement

Stage 8

Referendum
Note: by all eligible residents

Phase IV – Final Agreement and Implementation

Stage 9

Final agreements signed and implemented

241

Figure 23.
Arctic Pilot Project (LNG). From Arctic Pilot Project.

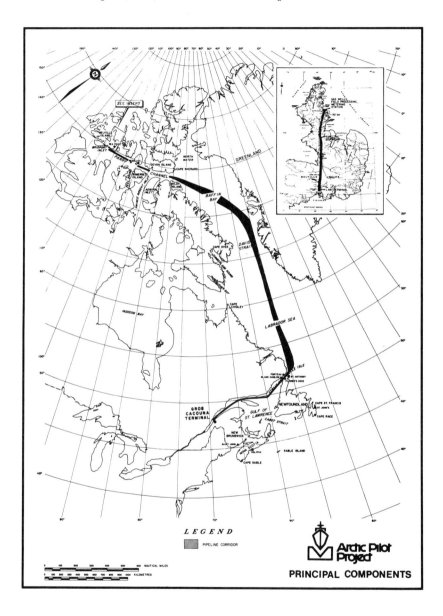

In its place the smaller, less costly Arctic Pilot Project (APP) for LNG tankers was devised, which required daily markets of only 10 or 12 per cent of the pipeline. Even so, the per-unit cost of the gas delivered in the south would be extremely high; hence, Alberta gas would have to be diverted into the export market to open eastern domestic markets and provide additional revenue to subsidize the project. Other problems, as well, made the project awkward for potential purchasers. The southward flow of APP gas would slow with the winter ice conditions when peak demand occurred. This would require huge storage facilities or alternative Alberta supplies held in reserve. Overall, to outsiders the APP appeared to be a very costly and inefficient means of partial supply for eastern Canadian markets.

Unlike projects in the Mackenzie Valley, the federal government provided the corporate leadership in the APP through Petro-Canada and its links to a variety of related companies. It owned just over 50 per cent of the equity stock in Panarctic Oils, the major petroleum exploration company in the High Arctic islands. Panarctic had spent $320 million and discovered significant quantities of gas but had no cash flow from production. If some of its proven fields could be tapped by the APP, this would help to lessen the government's role as the main source of risk capital to keep Panarctic going. Consequently, Petro-Canada, as the project manager for the APP, pressed forward in 1982 when some of its partners were having second thoughts. The other partners were involved for less obvious reasons: Dome, for example, wanted access to the experimental data on Arctic navigation for its own future designing of oil tankers to operate out of the Beaufort Sea; Nova saw it as a further aspect of its diversification from pipelines. In spite of the government's involvement the social and environmental planning appeared to be little different from that followed by Arctic Gas, which was not very reassuring to the local residents of the North.

In the public hearings in 1981 and 1982 opposition emerged from CARC, the regional and national Inuit associations, and the newly autonomous government of Greenland. The critics concentrated on the environment, native rights, and the argument that this scheme would open the way for the even more dangerous oil tankers to navigate through Arctic waters.[45] The regulatory hearings tended to politicize the Inuit into a formal confrontation with the applicant and the government, with some of the issues different from those debated in the western Arctic.

One of the significant differences was the Inuit concern for protecting the integrity of the winter sea ice. John Amagoalik of the Inuit Tapirisat of Canada (ITC) stressed this forcefully in his presentation at the NEB hearings: "We have been saying for a long time that sea-ice is like land. Year round traffic will dismember it and there will be environmental chain reactions if the ice is being constantly opened up."[46] Sea ice was the platform from which Inuit winter hunting could take place. As seals must surface to breathe, Inuit hunters will wait at their breathing holes in the ice or at open leads along cracks in the ice. In turn, polar bears prey on the seals and provide additional targets for the Inuit hunters. To sustain life, large areas of sea ice must be canvassed (several thousand square miles usually) to find the necessary areas of cracks or open leads. With the introduction of snowmobiles Inuit hunters can now range further afield; however, snowmobiles cannot do some things that dogs can, that is, get them home in a blizzard or judge in advance the stability of the ice ahead. The ice ridges from the tanker traffic would create a barrier to Inuit mobility as well as unstable areas where snowmobiles could break through. If the shipping became frequent enough that passages through the ice were being kept open then they would become a serious barrier to hunters or caribou migrating between islands or in search of scarce vegetative cover.

Possibly the greatest environmental problem of all is sound radiated underwater by high-powered ice-breaking tankers smashing their way through the ice. The serious study of sound as an environmental impact on Arctic marine mammals has only been recently undertaken and is still the subject of controversy within the scientific community.[47] Propeller cavitation in heavy ice could cause sound levels as high as 197 decibels, which would reverberate under the ice to drown out and interfere with the low-frequency sounds that whales, seals, and other mammals use to communicate and navigate. According to one Danish biologist the sound shadow from these ships could stretch 100 miles on each side of the vessel. In narrow bodies of water, such as Lancaster Sound or Barrow Strait, the effects could be serious for some species. Bearded seals use sound to stake out their breeding and feeding territories while some species of whales use sound as a type of sonar navigation. Fin whales, when they find concentrations of plankton, emit sounds that bring other members of their species into the area. As food is scarce this is a critical feature in their ability to survive. In Lancaster Sound and east Davis Strait are located areas of open water called polynyas, which are usually kept open by winds or currents. These are areas of intense biological activity providing critical habitat, especially overwintering for many species (seals, narwhals, white whales, shore birds, etc.).[48] In turn, the Inuit are dependent on these areas for their hunting and nutrition. However, the absence of ice in these areas also makes them the prime route for tanker traffic trying to avoid the worst problems of ice.

For many Inuit, protection of these marine mammals and their habitat is *the* most important issue for their future welfare, just as the caribou are vitally important to the people of Old Crow. The one tool they possess to try to enforce vigorous environmental controls is the land claims negotiations and their relationship to regional land-use planning. Some progress has been made in this direction with the government's adoption of a land-use planning format for Lancaster Sound. Yet it is hard to expect the Inuit to accept this process at face value given the selective way in which environmental regulations have been enforced in the past. Also, the only federal efforts to regulate Arctic shipping are confined to pollution control under the Arctic Waters Pollution Prevention Act, which ignores many other environmental and social impacts of concern to the Inuit. Ships using Canadian waters north of 60° are requested to report speed, position, and course every twenty-four hours to the Coast Guard at Frobisher Bay, but compliance is voluntary. As a result, Ottawa may be unaware of foreign ships in Canadian Arctic waters, let alone any environmental violations. As activity mounts from year to year the federal authorities are encountering increasing problems of monitoring events. This is all background to the Inuit fears and to their calls for increased environmental regulation and enforcement to protect their way of life. For many communities, the land claims are meaningless without this offshore environmental component.[49]

The opposition of the Inuit, who constitute 80 per cent of the population north of the tree line to the Arctic Pilot Project, is clear and unequivocal. They have argued that the land claims must be settled and more research done on the project before they can properly consider the merits of the APP. However, they have also made it clear that they would not hold the country up to ransom if international energy flows were cut off because of a war in the Middle East or some other calamity.[50] The Inuit believe that their claims have never received the attention that they deserve, hence are now determined to force the termination of Ottawa's procrastination. While the federal negotiators may be unhappy with the Inuit offshore demands, it is difficult after Canada's aggressive extension of its own offshore jurisdiction through the Law of the Sea Conferences to deny the concerns expressed by the Inuit. They are many of the same concerns that External Affairs has pressed at the United Nations and in Washington. In addition, the Inuit occupation of this area for thousands of years is part of the Canadian case for sovereignty in the High

Arctic. Had the Inuit in the nineteenth century signed treaties with any other nation, the nebulous Canadian claims to the far North would never have held up because government or industry had no effective occupation in the area until recent decades.

In their struggle for establishing their aboriginal rights, the Inuit have also argued strenuously for onshore land rights where they are relevant. In the 1970's on the western side of Hudson Bay there was considerable mining exploration in areas such as Baker Lake, where approximately 1,000 Inuit reside. Urangeselleschaft of West Germany was seriously considering developing a uranium property in an area where the caribou appeared to be in decline. The local Inuit in the area surrounding Baker Lake had depended on the caribou for 4,000 years and they petitioned Ottawa to freeze new mining activities in the area pending completion of the land claims negotiations. In April, 1977, Warren Allmand, the Minister of Indian and Northern Affairs, agreed to a temporary one-year freeze while a thorough investigation of the reasons for the decline of the caribou herd could be made. The mining industry vigorously attacked Allmand's action, for it feared this could become a precedent to be applied elsewhere in the North.[51] Allmand, under attack for his sympathy with native concerns, ran into growing opposition in cabinet, which led to his being relieved of his portfolio. The new minister, Hugh Faulkner, received the report on the caribou, which cast doubt on some of the Inuit contentions that mining exploration was the principal cause. Over Inuit objections, Faulkner lifted the freeze in 1978.

The immediate response of the Inuit[52] was to appeal through the Federal Court of Canada for an interim injunction against mining exploration until the full case could be heard. The defendants in the case were the government of Canada and six mining companies, including the two giants, Noranda and Cominco (Canadian Pacific). The central issue was whether or not aboriginal rights were compromised by the mining exploration. Inuit hunters argued that the activities of the mining companies interfered with caribou calving grounds and migration routes, causing a serious decline in the caribou and, of course, in the food supply being brought to the communities. Mr. Justice Patrick Mahoney granted the interim injunction on April 24, 1978, on the basis that: "The minerals, if there, will remain; the caribou, presently there, may not."[53] The case came to full trial in the spring of 1979, during which the government and corporate legal counsel had a huge advantage over the limited funds and legal staff available to the Inuit. The feelings of the mining industry were dramatically expressed in an editorial in *The Northern Miner*: "it is unthinkable that development should be stopped in order to preserve

246

such a rudimentary way of life as to require hunting for one's next meal. Surely, we have all progressed beyond that, especially in Canada. All too often we have the southern do-gooders and environmentalists wanting to keep these people in their basic life style as a sort of quaint museum-piece rather than encouraging them to become a part of the 20th century."[54] Clearly, aboriginal rights were something a modern, industrialized country like Canada should not tolerate.

The Ministry of Justice and corporate lawyers developed four main arguments in their legal presentation against the Inuit contentions. (1) The Inuit had not historically resided in the Baker Lake area; (2) the Inuit did not possess any rights over their land to begin with; (3) even if they did possess any rights they were abolished by Charles II of England in granting the Hudson's Bay Company Charter in 1670; and (4) even if the rights were not abolished in 1670 they were subsequently extinguished by the government of Canada either expressly or implicitly. The first of these was countered by the Inuit through detailed archaeological evidence, which demonstrated their lengthy occupation in the area. The second point was close to being contradictory to government policy and to the fact that actual negotiations of Inuit land claims were then under way with COPE in the Mackenzie Delta. Luther Chambers for the Ministry of Justice put it forward with a legal simplicity that infuriated the Inuit: "There is no reason to proceed upon any fiction . . . of treating the natives as though they had been or had been akin to a sovereign independent nation." William Graham, the lawyer for American Pan Ocean Oil, warned that the resource companies would close down their activities in the Northwest Territories if Inuit aboriginal rights were accorded a legal basis because then the federal government would lose its jurisdictional control.[55]

Mr. Justice Mahoney rejected these contentions while laying down four criteria for establishing whether aboriginal rights exist: (1) the native group had to constitute an "organized society"; (2) they had to demonstrate effective occupation of the area; (3) their occupation was "to the exclusion of other organized societies"; and (4) this occupation must predate assertions of British sovereignty.

On all four points Mahoney found that the Baker Lake Inuit qualified, except for the southwest corner of their area where their occupation overlapped that of the Chipewyans. Further, he ruled that aboriginal rights were not property rights, hence they could not be extinguished by the Hudson's Bay Company Charter of 1670. In nature they were something outside the normal traditions of the common law for these rights were confined to hunting and trapping. On the last issue put forward in the federal case, the judge ruled that

TABLE FOUR

Income Profile – Baker Lake Heads of Households

Income Source	Income Per Head of Household[1]	Per cent of Total Income
Fur sales[2]	$ 250	2.4
Caribou harvest[3]	$ 4,480	42.3
Goose and ptarmigan harvest[3]	$ 50	0.5
Domestic fish harvest[4]	$ 940	8.9
Subtotal – Income from fur, game, and fish harvest	$ 5,720	54.1
Wages and salaries[5]	$ 4,420	41.7
Sales of carvings[6]	$ 450	4.2
Subtotal – Employment Income	$ 4,870	45.9
Total Income	$10,590	100.0

[1]These data describe incomes for heads of 43 randomly sampled households in Baker Lake for the period November, 1976, to October, 1977. Transfer payments and income from commercial fishing are excluded.

[2]From TFRB records, N.W.T. government.

[3]Harvests by 43 heads of household were caribou 1156, geese 114, ptarmigan 766.

[4]Based on a per family fish consumption of 410 kg and the assumption that a head of household harvested half of the fish caught by a family.

[5]From estimates of wages and salaries earned by heads of household we interviewed.

[6]From Sanavik Co-op and Nunamiut Company.

SOURCE: Interdisciplinary Systems. *Effects of Exploration and Development in the Baker Lake Area*, prepared for the Department of Indian Affairs and Northern Development (Winnipeg, February, 1978), Vol. 1, p. 84.

although Parliament had the power to extinguish aboriginal title, his reading of the statutes uncovered no instance where this had been done.[56] Thus, on the first point of his judgement, Mahoney had sided with the Inuit that aboriginal rights did exist and that the Inuit of Baker Lake qualified for such rights. This was the first time in the

Figure 24.
Notice to Developers, Baker Lake.

NOTICE
TO DEVELOPERS IN
THE NORTHWEST TERRITORIES

By judgement dated November 15, 1979 (and whose appeal period expired Feb. 29, 1980), the Federal Court of Canada issued a declaration ruling that aboriginal title to approximately 30,000 square miles of Territory in the Keewatin District "vested at common law in the Inuit".

It is the opinion of Inuit Tapirisat of Canada (ITC) that the circumstances which led to this declaration similarly exist throughout the other lands of Nunavut* which have been traditionally used and occupied by Inuit, and that these areas are similarly subject to aboriginal title.

Any developer who proposes a project which affects the surface or subsurface of such areas is encouraged to contact ITC, for the purpose of arranging negotiations and resolving differences which might arise between the project and the legal rights of the Inuit.

A project which proceeds without having resolved such differences shall be exposed to all recourses under law.

For further information, contact

Marc C. Denhez,
Senior Counsel,
Inuit Tapirisat of Canada,
176 Gloucester St.,
Ottawa, Ontario.
K2P 0A6

*Nunavut is the area of the Northwest Territories extending northward from the treeline, and from Davis Strait westward to the boundary of the COPE area, which follows an irregular line in the general vicinity of 120° longitude.

history of the Canadian legal system that the courts had supplied any definition of aboriginal rights – it was a landmark decision for all native people in Canada.

The next question was an even more difficult one. Were those aboriginal rights to hunt caribou violated by the exploration activities of the mining companies? On the basis of the evidence as he interpreted it, the judge concluded there was little proof that the ground operations of the mining companies harassed the caribou, except for activities at river crossings and low-flying aircraft. As aboriginal title did not involve property rights, it was necessary for the Inuit to prove that the entire caribou population in the area was suffering from "behavioural changes." There had to be a direct causal relationship established between the mining activity and caribou decline. The judge ruled that he had been unable to establish such a linkage; therefore, there was no basis for an injunction against mining exploration in these circumstances.[57]

The results of the Baker Lake case continue to be debated in legal circles. However, a few matters were clarified. The Inuit failed in their immediate purpose of stopping mining activity in the area. On the other hand, they did achieve a more basic goal through the limited definition of aboriginal rights included in the judgement. So each side was able to claim victory. From a long-term point of view the Mahoney decision left the door wide open for further injunctions against other projects if the Inuit could substantiate the linkage between the environmental impacts and the project. The court, by leaving many unanswered questions in the case, was forcing the whole issue of aboriginal rights back into the political arena where it belonged, for only direct negotiations between the government and native groups can properly settle the land claims and related aspects of native rights.

Following the court case intensive negotiations on the Inuit "Nunavut" proposals began in the spring of 1981.[58] This followed about a decade of public and private debate within the Inuit Tapirisat of Canada and between it and the officials in Ottawa. Some progress has been made toward a comprehensive agreement-in-principle on wildlife harvesting and management, which was imperative. In June, 1982, the Barren Ground Caribou Management Agreement was signed in Winnipeg, which established a thirteen-member board with representatives from government and native groups to monitor the restoration and management of the Kaminuriak and Beverly caribou herds.[59] However, the critical areas of land and resource ownership remain outstanding. In the view of ITC any approval by the government of projects like the APP prior to completion of these negotiations would prejudice the outcome and raise doubts about the government's sincerity.

While the outline of the proposed new political structure for Nunavut is still only roughly sketched, there are important differences from the Dene proposal for Denendeh. As the Inuit constitute 80 per cent of the population in the area, they are prepared to accept universal suffrage and democratically elected local and regional councils with an overall central assembly that would progress toward provincial status within Confederation. Ownership of the land and resources would remain under public control until leased to developers. Some of the land, including sub-surface rights, would be under the exclusive ownership of the Inuit as a part of their land claims settlement; some lands surrounding local settlements would be under municipal control; the remainder would be under joint Inuit, Nunavut, and federal ownership.

Within Inuit ranks there has been some controversy about equity involvement in northern mega-projects. When the Arctic Pilot Project offered ITC the opportunity to purchase equity in the project, the Inuit formally rejected the offer because it appeared to be a ploy to soften their opposition. Behind the scenes, however, some cracks have emerged within Inuit ranks on this question. The independent Inuit Development Corporation headed by Tagak Curley was prepared to negotiate for Inuit purchase of equity stock. Curley had been the founding president of ITC in 1971 and was now the MLA for Rankin Inlet in the Baker Lake area. This corporation had already invested in the Cullaton Lake Gold Mines. The ITC leaders were furious with the Inuit Development Corporation for breaking rank on the APP issue and threatened to cut it off from cash generated from the land claims settlement. The ITC was also less than enthusiastic about approaches made to COPE to draw it into a stake in the Beaufort Oil play.[60] Inuit involvement in free-enterprise capitalism will probably remain a divisive issue for many years to come. However, their constitutional proposals appear to be less exotic and more practicable than the Dene structures.

One of the most difficult and controversial aspects of the Nunavut proposal is the contention that aboriginal rights apply offshore to the areas of sea ice where Inuit hunting occurs. The Inuit claim that aboriginal rights are simply their own customary law and practices in existence at the time of the arrival of European jurisdiction. As these have never been abolished by statute they remain in force today via the principles of the continuity of law. They are the basis of the aboriginal rights they seek to entrench in their land claims settlement.

They claim also that precedents in Canadian and international law recognize rights to areas of frozen waters. The White Sea has been recognized as internal waters of the Soviet Union because it is frozen three-quarters of the year; in Ontario during the age of ice-cutting for refrigeration, courts recognized legal rights to areas of ice as water lots similar to the land beneath them.[61] Hence, the Inuit have argued that there is no legal impediment to the type of sea-ice rights they were claiming. At least in principle Indian and Northern Affairs has recognized that the regulation of offshore wildlife is a legitimate area for inclusion in the final legal settlement of their claims.[62] Yet Ottawa has a clear policy commitment to expanding Arctic navigation for oil, gas, and minerals, which the Inuit see as a clear threat to their way of life. Reconciling these two policy objectives will be one of the arduous chores for federal planners in the years ahead.

The issue of Arctic sovereignty continues to plague successive governments in Ottawa. But if Ottawa establishes its capability to maintain year-round shipping lanes through the Northwest Passage, it would be contributing to the case of the shipping nations (especially the United States) that these straits are international waters beyond Canadian jurisdiction. Some analysts have claimed that the most effective way for Canada to entrench its claims to sovereignty would be to recognize Inuit claims to the sea ice between the islands.[63] This action would provide an ironic twist to Ottawa's efforts to extinguish aboriginal rights.

While the land claims negotiations proceed, there now appears to be little likelihood of the Arctic Pilot Project receiving the necessary approvals in the near future. With weak markets and prices for gas in North America, the sponsors are having doubts about the viability of the project. The federal government has been embarrassed by the intensity and the international character of the opposition. The Inuit Circumpolar Conference linking the Inuit from Alaska to Greenland has drawn attention to the wider ramifications for the enclosed Arctic waters. Representatives of the newly autonomous government of Greenland have journeyed to Ottawa to express their opposition directly to the National Energy Board and the cabinet. These groups hoped to try to embarrass Canada internationally by raising the APP issue at the United Nations and the Law of the Sea Conferences. They would be using exactly the same arguments employed a decade ago by Ottawa in protesting the *Manhattan* voyages.[64]

Within government circles the Inuit have some potential allies in stopping approval. The Department of External Affairs is less than happy with the prospect of provoking a major dispute with Greenland. Energy, Mines, and Resources appears to be at odds with Petro-Canada on this project with the ministry wanting the Crown corporation to use its resources for increased oil production rather than more gas, which would only add to the surplus in the south. At the same time, though, the project has received support from quarters the Inuit did not expect. The territorial assembly, starved for new revenue, gave conditional approval and Richard Nerysoo, the territorial Energy Minister, testified to that position at the NEB. This appeared to be opening a split between the Dene and ITC, with the latter more concerned about tankers while the former saw pipelines as the greatest threat.[65] ITC's efforts were also hindered in the spring of 1982 by a shortage of funds, but they had made their points very clearly and with considerable effect. By the summer of 1982 Petro-Canada had switched tactics and was quietly trying to sell Arctic LNG to European customers.[66]

The overall debate over the Arctic Pilot Project had been an important one for the eastern Arctic and the Inuit. It had brought them into the centre of North American energy politics, which gave their land claims a new sense of urgency; it had brought to the surface a whole series of interrelated social, socio-economic, and cultural questions that were fundamental to the Inuit approach to development; it also showed the differing aspects and perceptions of aboriginal rights held by the Inuit and the Dene. Both of these groups are now heading into the critical phase in their land claims negotiations where nebulous concepts have to be put into concrete terminology. The social questions facing both groups are immense and there are no clear and easy answers emerging. The next decade could be the most important for native northerners since the coming of Europeans to northern shores. Great patience and wisdom will be required on both sides for these negotiations to conclude successfully. If settlement is achieved it will be one of the great triumphs of Canadian history and will introduce a new age for Canada's first citizens.

Social impact assessment, like environmental impact assessment, is still in a nascent stage of development where the demands of government are greater than the resources of this social science. Yet it is an essential planning tool if Canada is to proceed with northern development at an acceptable social cost to northerners. Inevitably, given the nature of these assessments, there will always be differences of opinion with regard to predicting social impacts and to assessing what levels of social cost are acceptable. But a great many of the social impact studies presented to regulatory boards in the 1970's were unprofessional and superficial. The prime requirement for a successful SIA is a high level of local community input analysed by social scientists, some of whom must know at first hand the local language and customs.[67] Southern assumptions can so easily creep into social analysis, for the very use of the English language alone carries with it a vast number of our own cultural assumptions. SIA must try to anticipate the problems of social interaction from alcoholism, prostitution, crime, and so on. Workers under tight discipline for long periods of time in northern camps are quite capable of breaking loose with anti-social behaviour after a few drinks. Work camps must be isolated from native communities to limit social disruptions such as rape and other forms of violence.

Some of the tools of the social scientist do not lend themselves easily to the pragmatic problems of SIA. Often, native elders can be of more use than sociological theory, and there are profound ethical questions involved in northern research, which have surfaced gradually from bad experiences. People's trust has been exploited for commercial purposes; the phrasing and explanation of questionnaires must be done with great care for many people will slant their answers to what they think the researcher wants to hear. So far SIA has tended to be on a pre-impact basis, hence we have only limited post-impact analysis that could show the lessons of past major projects. In the past those who have suffered the social costs of development have usually been the least able to express their concerns in public. They end up as welfare, crime, or suicide statistics in our major urban centres with no recorded link to the cause of their social discontent. Finally, many of the past social impact studies have been little more than the listing of occupational and other groups within a community with little or no serious analysis of the social impact of the project on the different components. The assumption is that if x dollars are spent locally, this must be a social benefit irrespective of the means of delivery.

The basic problem for northern native society is attempting to cope with the two conflicting realities of traditional and wage-labour economies. Trapping, hunting, and fishing remain the basis for much of the food supply in the isolated settlements and for some of the cash income. These land-based occupations are the basis for their culture, social structure, and sense of identity. With rising expectations with regard to consumer goods, however, this alone will be insufficient to meet the needs of the growing northern native population.

Movement into wage labour forces individuals into an alien value system where white assumptions and industrial organization erode the values of native society, including the social cohesion of the local band with its informal social support systems. Disposable income can be a new experience and can lead to excesses, especially if it is accompanied by a sense of social alienation from the boss and other workers.

As one study of Old Crow in the Yukon stated: "The existence of wage opportunities . . . leads to economic independence of individuals. This, in turn, can break down the inter-dependence among people, affects the cohesiveness of the family, and may cause personal destruction through gambling and liquor."[68] If the individual then loses his job for any reason, he tends to drift to the urban centres of the North and falls upon welfare dependency to finance his escape through alcohol. Our economic system is based on individualism in an economic and social sense while native society is based on communal values related to the land. A great deal of romanticism about this lifestyle is quite misplaced. Living off the land can be an arduous and at times precarious existence in the North. Those who wish to cling to this do so for reasons of survival, for it is the basis of their social existence. So much of our social analysis of the North has been based on the assumption of the superiority of our system and the alleged benefits of assimilation. This pattern of social evolution has been rejected by many of the Dene and the Inuit.

They are not proposing to return to conditions as they existed prior to European contact. Social change has gone too far. But they do wish, with Denendeh and Nunavut, to explore new forms of political and social organization within Confederation so that their peoples will not suffer the same fate as their southern counterparts. They fear that the social and economic forces of metropolitanism will sweep away their distinctive hinterland culture, as has happened elsewhere. They have been saved thus far only by their isolation, which is now rapidly ending. They wish to have the freedom to pick those aspects of the new technology appropriate to their society and, equally, to reject others. They have successfully coped with Arctic conditions for thousands of years and are determined to limit the rate of future social change to a manageable level.

CHAPTER 10

The Economics of Northern Development

As Innis and others have argued, the history of Canada is the history of the exploitation of a successive series of staples from fur and fish to oil and gas. The source of the capital and the markets served have always been wider than Canada itself. The North is merely the last of a whole series of resource hinterlands for North American and European industrialism. The barriers that have sheltered it thus far from involvement – isolation, climate, and the lack of transportation facilities – have gradually been rolled back in the last quarter century. Now, even the multi-year pack ice of the Beaufort Sea can be penetrated by the new generation of massive ice-breaking tankers on the drawing boards.

The reserves of oil, gas, and many minerals have been proved but the question remains: will it be economically feasible to develop them? This question more than any other will determine the fate of the mega-projects now under consideration. With soft world oil prices and markets decreasing with conservation, Arctic oil is no longer certain of production if it is found. Also, the scale of the capital requirements creates unprecedented problems for free-enterprise capitalism. With many northern projects the mixing of corporate and government sectors creates an end product that would be recognized by neither Adam Smith nor Karl Marx.

The perspective on oil and natural gas exploration in the Northwest Territories changed dramatically with the Prudhoe Bay discoveries of January, 1968. Overnight the focus for drilling switched north from Alberta to areas like the Mackenzie Delta and the High Arctic islands. In addition, huge sums of money were sunk into various study groups seeking the best means of transporting south the massive Alaskan oil and natural gas reserves. Groups of companies came together to share the heavy costs in studying the problems and estimating the capital costs involved. In spite of an offer from Canada to supply a right-of-way for a Mackenzie Valley Oil Pipeline, Washington opted for a trans-Alaskan oil pipeline (Alyeska) and oil tankers down the Pacific Coast. On a barrel-per-mile basis it was cheaper to ship oil by tanker than pipeline. This economic evidence reinforced the producers' desire to keep this major U.S. energy transmission system free of foreign regulatory controls. As the production of natural gas was a less pressing issue, the decision on the route and type of system was delayed. However, because of the question of volume, natural gas can be transported more cheaply via high pressure pipelines. This avoids the costly necessity of chilling the natural gas into a liquid form (LNG), which is one-600th of the volume.[1] So while there were economic liabilities for routing an oil pipeline across Canada, there were economic incentives for the natural gas line.[2]

From the beginning it was clear to the backers of both Arctic Gas and Foothills that project financing would be a difficult hurdle for any multibillion-dollar Arctic pipeline. Any doubts about the seriousness of the issue were ended when the financing problems of Alyeska became apparent. Regrettably, the term "cost-overrun" took on a new meaning with the agony of this project. Originally estimated to cost about $900 million in 1969, this 800-mile line came on stream in mid-1977 at a capital cost of about $8.5 billion. A baffling variety of factors were involved, including court challenges, permafrost, Arctic weather, and technical flaws. It had the appearance of a financial quicksand. The New York money market was profoundly shocked that such an experienced corporate team could run up a cost-overrun of more than 900 per cent. Had it not been for the fact that all the Alyeska debt was guaranteed by a group of the largest oil companies in the world, including Exxon, the whole project might never have been completed. However, the New York financial houses had learned their lesson about Arctic pipelines; any future applicants would have to demonstrate proven geotechnical planning and unprecedented debt guarantees to get serious consideration. It would appear that Arctic Gas understood the lessons of Alyeska while Foothills underestimated the full implications. Arctic Gas attracted a large number of prominent energy companies from Canada and the United States into its consortium to try to lend support to its image of credit worthiness. When the consortium applied to the NEB, there were twenty-seven companies involved. This was important, for it was essentially a "paper" corporation without assets or cash flow of its own until completion.

In the course of the NEB hearings, there were repeated attempts to unravel the reasons for the spiralling Alyeska costs. Although the court injunctions appeared to hold up the project for three to four years, this delay was more apparent than real. During the delay essential design and route changes were made.[3] In particular, coping with the permafrost was an incredible challenge for the engineers involved. They had to develop a very complicated and expensive elevated design that eventually had to be used for almost half the route. Changes continued in the field as construction proceeded and the problems of local terrain became evident.

A number of other difficulties were continually increasing the capital costs. Worker productivity, especially in the cold and darkness so prevalent from October through March, was well below expectations; complete shutdowns occurred when the temperature dropped below $-30°$ F. The extreme cold took its toll of machinery as well as manpower. Metal parts became more brittle and subject to metal fatigue; machinery became difficult to start even with the special "Arctic" packages provided by the manufacturers; and tires would shred much more easily than normal. Alyeska had chosen to construct major river crossings in winter when flow rates were lowest; but this technique created more problems than it solved. Water poured into the trench as soon as it was excavated and froze rapidly before the pipe could be laid. Also, due to negligence or climatic impacts, the welding of the pipe sections became a major scandal, especially when the x-ray inspections were widely doctored to cover up the poor quality of the job. In the end, hundreds of miles of pipe had to be re-excavated and then rewelded. In short, Alyeska had many problems that baffled the company and antagonized the financial backers.

When Charles Champion, the Alaska state pipeline co-ordinator, testified at the National Energy Board he stressed his sense of frustration in trying to keep capital costs under control even though Alyeska had hired the best technical people available. At the planning stage changes were continuous "because we failed to have the base knowledge necessary to do it correctly the first time." He estimated that as much as 95 per cent of their efforts turned out to be wasted time caused by the chaotic and changing design plans. When they came to construction there were further complications from engineering and route changes and the isolated locale for construction. When a part broke down, "often times the crew had to sit in a bus for two or three days awaiting the arrival of that particular part so that they could get back to work." Because it was impossible to plan for every eventuality of machinery, terrain, or weather there was a tremendous wastage of manpower built into "Arctic megaprojects of this nature."[4] There were also psychological problems for employees living and working in the intensely cold winter darkness. During the construction of the James Bay Project in Quebec, the construction companies piped in the morning radio shows from Montreal, including the traffic reports, to dispel some of the gloomy sense of isolation. In such an environment trivial annoyances can lead to work stoppages, vandalism, and even violence from workers who feel a sense of cabin fever. Excellent meals and the exclusion of alcohol are two essential rules for maintaining worker productivity and keeping the project on schedule. Only recently have corporations come to appreciate the importance of industrial psychology as well as no-strike clauses in the planning of northern projects. Construction delays in one area can quickly affect the whole project, for it has to flow with a military precision. Otherwise it is impossible to keep to the cost estimates that potential investors rely on.

The other worry that came from the Alyeska experience was the threat of court challenges and injunctions. If the Canadian route was approved it was important to the New York financial institutions that there be no chance of injunctions to delay or interrupt construction. If there were serious fears of this occurring the Americans might opt for the exclusively American route of the El Paso project. In Canada, environmental regulations were not entrenched in statutes as was the case with the National Environmental Policy Act of the United States. Therefore, environmental injunctions were far more difficult to procure in Canada. However, with the Nishga case, there were concerns that aboriginal rights could be used, and after the Marshall Crowe decision of the Supreme Court the NEB itself realized that it could be the target for legal action.[5] Representatives of the Dene Nation made it plain in the course of the hearings that they were considering court action if the Mackenzie Valley Pipeline was approved. This was something the cabinet and the NEB desperately wanted to avoid. Given the tight timetable imposed from Washington, they wanted to demonstrate that they were firmly in control of events in Canada and that they could deliver the project as planned. This scenario, with the bankers and brokerage houses watching from the sidelines, provided an indirect inducement for the government to opt for the less controversial Alaska Highway project because they believed there would be less chance of court challenges.

It is clear from the sworn testimony that the financial advisers to both projects were concerned about the aboriginal rights issue. Bob Blair testified that the native land claims should be settled prior to construction to eliminate one of the risks worrying potential investors. The vice-president of Wood Gundy, testifying for Arctic Gas, was even more specific. He stressed that the lenders would want "to see what they consider a satisfactory resolution of the problem" of land claims before the project could be financed.[6] This issue, of course, has never been resolved and remains a lingering doubt and an added risk for most of the major Arctic energy projects under consideration in the 1980's. Lenders want not only a settlement of this issue but an amicable one. If, for instance, a settlement was imposed by Parliament it would overcome the legal barriers. But if forced on the native people, it might add new problems of security, for pipelines are impossible to protect from organized sabotage.

The unique financing problems of the northern pipelines led the companies involved into consortiums. Under this format a group of partners come together to plan, construct, and operate the new facility. This allows for the sharing of costs and risks over a wide number of companies, lends the appearance of economic strength, and limits the liabilities in the event of failure. Arctic Gas was a classic case study of the consortium structure. Initially, its twenty-seven members included: U.S. multinational oil companies such as Exxon, ARCO, and Sohio; Canadian subsidiaries, including Imperial, Gulf, and Shell; Canadian pipelines like Trans-Canada and Alberta Gas Trunk; eight leading U.S. gas utilities; two Canadian utilities (Union and Consumers'); leading Canadian resource companies such as Canadian Pacific Investments; and even the government of Canada, through its Crown corporation, the Canada Development Corporation. Any financier had to be impresssed with that list, which included the indirect endorsement of the Trudeau cabinet. Canadian Arctic Gas had a sister organization, Alaskan Arctic Gas, responsible for the American portion of the line.

In determining the economic viability of any northern pipeline, certain fundamentals must be met before the project can get off the ground. With gas, for example, there must be a large enough reservoir of proven reserves that twenty years' supply at least is available to the pipeline. The volume and price of gas shipped must be sufficient to cover all costs of the producers and the pipeline company as well as provide satisfactory profits for both. Second, the pipeline transmission charges (the tariff) must be low enough that the gas is delivered at a competitive price to the intended market. Third, there have to be sufficient signed contracts from gas utilities willing to purchase the gas that there is adequate cash flow for the pipeline to amortize its debts and provide a satisfactory rate of return for its own shareholders. The rate of return will vary with the rate of inflation and other market factors. In 1982 a satisfactory return was a minimum of 20 per cent annually. If serious doubts exist about any one of these three links in the economic chain there will be no project.

Arctic mega-projects are further hindered in financing by the long lead times, the difficulty with cost estimates, and the high overall risks. Therefore, the profit potential must be very great (higher than in the south) to justify this level of risk and exposure. The regulatory process can be long, involved, and costly. Arctic Gas spent over $150 million on its unsuccessful application before American and Canadian regulatory tribunals. The rival consortium, Foothills, spent a good deal less because it was a much smaller operation composed of two partners, Westcoast Transmission and Alberta Gas Trunk, now Nova Corporation. But Foothills suffered from the disadvantage of having smaller capital resources, with less influence in New York, behind it. Any lender to the project would note that the assets of the two parents were only a fraction of the capital required for the offspring.

When Arctic Gas came to choose its senior executives, competence in financing was clearly a high priority. The chairman of the newly formed company was enticed away from the presidency of Wood Gundy, Canada's largest securities firm. Bill Wilder was joined at the top by Vern Horte, who became president. Horte had been president of Trans-Canada Pipelines, Canada's largest pipeline company. Other senior financial executives were drawn from Exxon in New York, the Bank of Canada, and Consolidated Bathurst. The executive team was a formidable group of exceptional talent reflecting the stern financing challenge that was anticipated. This group possessed outstanding links into business, finance, and government on both sides of the border. As one analyst has noted: "No enterprise in Canadian history, with the possible exception of the Canadian Pacific Railway, had ever marshalled such a formidable list of allies."[7]

When Arctic Gas came to put its financial package together, it knew it would be facing a great challenge from the scale of the capital requirements, which totalled $9,350 million (1976 dollars).[8] The equity float would be the largest single private issue in the history of the New York Stock Exchange, while the bond requirements would be roughly three times the equity or common stock requirements. The Foothills' capital cost estimates for both the Alaska Highway and the Maple Leaf lines to the Delta together were marginally higher, at $9,606 million, for the slightly longer system. Both projects also involved additional multibillion-dollar commitments to cover the Alaska, California, and Midwest portions of the overall system. The money would be raised by the purchase of common stock, mainly to corporate backers, bonds sold to U.S. and Canadian institutional lenders, and bank loans from Canadian, American, and overseas banks. Willard Stewart, treasurer of Arctic Gas, had previously been assistant treasurer of the largest corporation in the world, Exxon. Yet he testified that the Arctic Gas financing package was larger and more complex than anything he had ever handled – it was drawing on financial markets from Europe to Japan.[9] The Alaska Highway Pipeline, which was estimated to cost $4.4 billion in 1977, tripled in price to over $15 billion by 1982. The American portions, especially in Alaska, will be even more expensive and their cost estimates were in excess of $25 billion. If the project had got the go-ahead in 1984, then construction would not have begun until 1986 and the first gas would not flow until 1989 or 1990. The debt charges alone in the final year of construction could be several billion dollars. Although the pre-build will ease some of these problems, the interest charges on the bonds and the bank loans will be massive. If there are further delays in approval or delays in construction, the capital costs will probably rise more rapidly than the general rate of inflation or the consumer price index.[10] Thus the capital requirements are not only unprecedented in the history of Canadian business but are greater than those raised by any U.S. company in a comparable period. Some estimates in 1982 were close to $50 billion for the total system. Hence, the scale of the capital requirements alone might be enough to ensure that the project never got off the ground.

When it became evident how massive would be the size of the financing package, Arctic Gas tried to build into the plan a number of guarantees to reassure the potential investors. It attempted to address directly the three basic worries: that the project would not be completed; that it would not be completed on time; and that it would not be completed close to the original cost estimates. It was decided that the level of risk was so great that normal private-sector assurances would not be sufficient to assure the necessary level of investor confidence. Therefore, it attempted to devise a scheme to guarantee the cash flow of the pipeline company regardless of delays in completion or the interruptions of service after operations began. Here the Arctic Gas package was imaginative in its approach but menacing in the implications for the consumer. It proposed to ensure that the lender got his money back by two revolutionary financing techniques – the "all-events" tariff and government "backstopping."

The all-events tariff had never been used in Canada before. Under this type of tariff a gas utility, once it signed a contract to purchase gas on a given future date, was obligated to pay even if the system was uncompleted and no gas was available. The level of payment to the pipeline company was not the total price of the gas but sufficient for it to cover all the financial liabilities to those who had invested in the line. For the financial consultants it was deemed essential to have a means of guaranteeing sufficient cash flow to pay off the lenders; only with this support would they be willing to invest in the project. From a consumer point of view, the proposal was a serious precedent that could leave the public with a double liability. If the pipeline was not completed on time, the customer would pay for the gas he received from an alternate source and for the Arctic Gas charges from which he derived no benefit. As Union and Consumers' Gas in Ontario were both financial partners in the Arctic Gas consortium, their customers also paid through the gas rates for a share of the costs of the consortium and were committed to an equity stake in the final project. When Arctic Gas collapsed in 1977 the Ontario consumers lost their investment. The purpose of the all-events tariff was very clear; the risks involved in the project were too great for the shareholders and bond holders and had to be transferred to the southern customers. In this case, however, the risk-taker had no say in the running of the project.

Quite naturally, the proposed tariff led to regulatory battles between public interest groups and the gas utilities. The Ontario Energy Board held public hearings in September and October, 1975, on the advisability of allowing the Ontario utilities to roll into their rate base the costs of their involvement in the Arctic Gas application, future equity purchases, and any liability flowing from an all-events tariff. Even though they heard testimony from a California state official that there were problems when shareholders were no longer liable for the financial consequences of a project decision, the Board and then the Ontario cabinet approved the proposals.[11] These were announced a year and a half before the federal decision on the rival applications as an indication of the province's clear support for Arctic Gas. The Ontario government viewed Bob Blair and the Foothills project as an extension of Alberta Premier Peter Lougheed's efforts to restrict gas supply to Ontario and force up domestic prices. At this time some industrial expansion in southwestern Ontario had been curbed by the absence of additional gas supply and gas pricing was a factor in deciding if plants were to be located on the Canadian or the American side of the border. While this tariff was unprecedented in Canada, it was argued that the risks faced by potential lenders were too great unless this type of guarantee was in place. In the National Energy Board Report and that of the Federal Power Commission in Washington, the concept of an all-events tariff was approved.

The other fundamental worry of the financial advisers was that cost-overruns would exhaust the capital resources available to the consortium before the system would be operational. The basic financing plan called for the original investors to provide an additional 25 per cent contingency fund to cover cost-overruns. But in the 1970's no major northern project had been confined to a mere 25 per cent overrun. So Arctic Gas proposed a scheme it called government backstopping. Under this proposal, when the 25 per cent contingency fund was drained the government would step in to guarantee further bonds or bank loans required to complete the project. If with this government guarantee the further funding was not forthcoming from private sources, the government would invest the capital required. After supplying capital up to a given figure ($2 or $3 billion was suggested), the government would have the option of terminating the whole project if it was still uncompleted. However, if it exercised that option, the government had to assume the financial liabilities of the pipeline company.[12] The United States government would backstop the American portion of the line and the Canadian government would do the same for the part on its territory. This would result in the bulk of the backstopping being carried by Ottawa while the bulk of the gas would be bound for U.S. customers.[13]

The basic purpose of this scheme was clear, namely, to transfer the risks of cost-overruns and non-completion from the corporate sponsors to the government. Geoffrey Edge of the NEB posed the crucial question that Arctic Gas was never able to answer: "I think the Board is interested in why the Canadian Government should be expected to contribute financially to this problem in the absence of the Alaska producers" who would gross about $2 billion per year thanks to the pipeline.[14] To a lesser extent the same question could have been put to Imperial, Gulf, and Shell, the Delta producers.

The rival Foothills consortium has argued consistently that government backstopping is neither needed nor desirable. Bob Blair, in testimony before the National Energy Board, stated that it was wrong to demand a "government guarantee for the support of a project financed in the private sector." If the lenders demanded such stringent security, Blair argued that he would recommend the formation of a Crown corporation to build part or all of the line as it had been done in the case of Trans-Canada Pipelines: "that would be the Canadian way and the right way."[15] When the Federal Power Commission and National Energy Board reports were released in 1977, both bodies rejected the concept of government backstopping. In 1981, the U.S. partners in the Alaska Highway Pipeline project raised the issue with the Reagan administration and received an emphatic "No." The President argued that such guarantees were contrary to his principles of free enterprise; the pipeline, if it was to proceed, must be financed through the regular private capital markets.

Some financial analysts have argued that without some government support, the $20-billion-plus Alaskan portion cannot be financed. Future Canadian northern pipelines like the Polar Gas Project would appear to be even more dependent on some type of backstopping. The need for backstopping, it would seem, is particularly great during periods when recession has seriously disrupted the capital markets, with inflation virtually eliminating the long-term bond markets and heavy government borrowing to finance deficits cutting seriously into the available capital supply. These market conditions in 1981 and 1982 made the financing of northern mega-projects through the regular capital markets virtually impossible.

There is one further means of attempting to limit the risk to would-be investors through what is called completion insurance. This has been discussed several times in Canada but never formally proposed. Under such a format the applicant would apply to government or some private-sector insurance consortium (such as arranged through Lloyd's of London) for insurance that the project would be completed on schedule. This could be alone or in conjunction with the all-events tariff. In the latter case it would help to ease the burdens on the participating utilities, who could be bankrupted in the event of an extended delay or interruption of service,[16] if they were not allowed to pass on all their added costs to their customers. Once again it was a technique to divert risk from the shoulders of potential investors to ensure that the project would be financed.

Through the 1970's and the early 1980's the availability of capital in Canada has been a serious matter of concern for those planning Arctic mega-projects. To ensure the success of the financing, there would have to be new forms of government intervention to stabilize or regulate the money markets. In 1976 Thomas Dobson, a senior vice-president of the Royal Bank, testified to the NEB that "The ultimate certification by the Canadian Government of an undertaking of this scope would signify that the Government endorses the Project as being in the national interest. It is therefore reasonable to assume that in such circumstances the Bank of Canada would manage the money supply to enable the banking system to accommodate the financing requirements of the Project."

Monetary policy is considered to be a key ingredient in the government's efforts to limit inflation. If Arctic mega-projects require releasing greater flows of money into the economy then it is a very serious macro-economic issue. In addition to this manipulation of the money supply, cabinet would have to ensure that there was no bunching of these large energy projects. Allan B. Hockin, executive vice-president of the Toronto-Dominion Bank, stated: "Cabinet approval, I believe, would also imply a willingness by the Government to use its considerable influence to phase the timing of other major projects thereby avoiding an undesirable bunching of demands, both on the physical and the financial resources of the country." He stressed that this would be necessary to minimize inflationary and balance-of-payments pressures.[17]

This raised yet another fundamental question. On the basis of what criteria would some projects be held up and others allowed to proceed? This could open the way for increased political intervention and interference with normal market forces, thus creating new uncertainty for business. As the government is itself a heavy borrower in these capital markets and its own company, Petro-Canada, is one of the largest players in the northern oil patch, there are areas of potential abuse in this economic scenario. From the testimony of leaders of the Canadian banking community it is clear how extraordinary were the circumstances created by the massive demands of these huge northern projects. To finance such efforts, applicants had to try to ensure that they did not create serious distortions within Canadian capital markets that would cause problems for other sectors of the Canadian economy requiring capital during the same period.

There are other ways as well that the public treasury will have to subsidize Arctic pipelines or drilling in the Beaufort Sea. For pipelines, deferred income tax payments during the years of construction and after would help to supplement available capital from bank loans, bonds, and common stock. Under the plan proposed by Arctic Gas, construction would begin in the first year, cash flow in the fourth year, but corporate income taxes would not begin until year nine. Gas consumers, however, would be charged to cover corporate income taxes from year four. This arrangement would provide interest-free capital totalling $1.4 billion for the intervening years. This was a change from the normal "flow-through" tax accounting where only income tax actually paid is charged through the rate base back to the gas consumer.

Although this was not standard practice for regulated industries, the NEB approved these procedures as a means of limiting the pressure on capital markets and of recognizing the exceptional nature of the problems of financing this type of project.[18] The tax provisions for the Beaufort Sea drilling have been given wide publicity because of their extreme generosity. The super-depletion allowances or the PIP subsidies to companies based on the level of Canadian ownership meant that as much as 90 per cent of the costs of drilling could be covered through the tax system. Yet, in addition to these benefits, the public treasury covers many of the direct costs of northern infrastructure for icebreakers, airports, hospitals, roads, and the like. Hence, the federal treasury has a very important role to play in meeting the costs of northern development in ways that the average taxpayer is not aware of.

The Delta producers at the NEB and the Prudhoe Bay oil companies in Washington have refused to set a selling price for their gas to the pipeline. At the other end, the American gas utilities have been reluctant to sign contracts for gas, the price and the delivery date being uncertain. With such uncertainty at both ends it was difficult to prove the economic viability of the system. The reluctance to set a price or delivery date has caused great annoyance and frustration to the pipeline companies and the regulatory authorities. There were times when the whole project before the NEB appeared to be a house of cards. At one point, Geoff Edge of the Board exploded at Vern Horte, the president of Arctic Gas:

> Well, I guess the problem we are wrestling with is . . . a design which is to a certain extent, hypothetical, because we do not have contracts to look at. We are talking about contracts which do not exist, which someone is expecting in some way to come into existence. We are talking about financing which is hypothetical because there are no contracts to support financing. It seems to me that we are getting close to talking about a hypothetical public interest with a hypothetical certificate with hypothetical conditions in it.

The Board had to have hard details to judge the project.[19] Imperial, Gulf, and Shell assumed that they were in an impregnable position in which they could dictate the gas price to whomever built the pipeline. Even though they were partners in the Arctic Gas consortium, their refusal to disclose fully the vital pricing assumptions or even to give a definite commitment to produce the gas hurt the image of Canadian Arctic Gas before the Board. It was clear from comments outside the hearing room that there were now tensions between the three oil companies and the pipeline staff. Imperial, Gulf, and Shell felt that the longer they held out, the clearer would become the issue of southern prices and the better would be their bargaining position to maximize their own prices and profits.

An essential feature of the Arctic pipeline and the LNG tanker schemes is a gas export component. As the Canadian domestic market can be supplied from Alberta for the next decade, northern natural gas projects have to export to get off the ground. Exploration firms like Panarctic and Dome, which have been drilling for many years, are desperate to get sales and cash flow from production. Thanks to conservation the Canadian market has hardly expanded at all in the last few years. As Canadians have responded to the appeals to conserve, ironically they have contributed to the increasing pressure from industry for exports. But at the same time in the U.S., with gas price deregulation and increasing imports from Mexico, Canadians have had a harder and harder time selling their gas there. Early in the 1980's gas exports were running at only 50 per cent of levels sanctioned by the NEB.[20] Now if inexpensive southern Canadian gas was encountering increasing difficulty in penetrating U.S. markets, Arctic gas with its high delivery costs would experience even greater market resistance. Also, the long lead times for planning and constructing such a system make it hard for utilities because they must commit themselves six or eight years before receiving the gas. Many of the U.S. companies who were anxious to buy Delta or Alaska gas in 1975 are no longer in need of additional supply because the higher American prices have brought on new domestic sources of supply.

Lastly, one aspect of the export question is a serious long-term issue for Canada. To what extent do we as a nation wish to go on exploiting crucial non-renewable energy resources to provide cash flow for Arctic drillers and financing for Arctic pipelines? Critics from outside industry complain that these resources will some day be required for Canadian industrial prosperity. Natural gas is not only the cleanest fuel but also the feedstock for the massive petrochemical and plastics industry. If Canada in the last two decades of the twentieth century turns to a more protectionist approach to conserve its supplies of natural gas for its own future industrial development, this would constitute a further blow to the prospects for projects like the Arctic Pilot Project and the Polar Gas Pipeline. As the United States prices weaken in the eighties Canada may be forced back on LNG exports to Japan or Western Europe.

When the Foothills/Northwest Alaska Project was approved by the American and Canadian governments in the summer of 1977, few observers had any idea of the tortuous road that lay ahead for the victors. Under the controversial and complex Canada-United States Pipeline Agreement signed in 1977 the Alaskan construction was scheduled to begin in January, 1980; work in the Yukon was to commence in January, 1981; and the whole project was to start operating on January 1, 1983. However, by early in 1978 it was clear that the financing problems would preclude any early start on the project. There was no price for the gas to be delivered to the pipeline; there was no sponsor for the gas plants required to extract the impurities before delivery to the pipeline; there were only the roughest estimates of the capital cost of constructing the system; there were no firm figures for the tariff to be charged for transporting the gas to southern markets; and because of the above there were only vague estimates of the cost of the gas to American consumers. Without answers to the above, financing could not be attempted. Yet with each succeeding month the size of the overall package increased as costs escalated.

In 1978 Congress took a few steps that began the preliminary progress toward the above goals. The complex Natural Gas Policy Act was passed, which allowed for a phased deregulation of natural gas prices. More important for the pipeline, the Act allowed U.S. gas utilities purchasing high-cost Alaskan gas to "roll in" such gas with lower-cost southern gas for a blended common price that would be economic for the utility. As Alaskan gas could be two or three times the domestic price for southern gas this averaging of cost was an essential precondition for selling the Alaskan gas. The wellhead price for gas in Alaska was established by the Act at $1.45 per thousand cubic feet (Mcf), which would be adjusted upward yearly for inflation. However, the costs of purifying the gas prior to delivery to the pipeline were still unknown. The overall pricing formula had become so complex because of Congressional compromises required to meet conflicting aspirations of consumer and industry lobbies. The seventeen categories of gas pricing were all proceeding along their separate ways toward deregulation by 1985. How high-cost Alaskan gas would fit into this complex picture was by no means clear to financial institutions or gas utilities, one of which would finance the project and the other of which would buy its gas.

In another preliminary move the U.S. Federal Energy Regulatory Commission, the successor to the Federal Power Commission, attempted to come to grips with the thorny issue of the profit margins for the project sponsors. With all the uncertainties and risks, the rate of return had to be higher than southern projects to attract the necessary equity capital, but not too high to infuriate consumers who could be dependent on a single monopoly pipeline from Alaska. After the Alyeska experience American regulators were determined that tough cost-control measures would be enforced; to achieve their goal they devised an "incentive rate of return" whereby the profit level to the equity owners would be a direct consequence of their ability to complete the project at the estimated price. Shareholders as well as consumers would pay the price of capital cost increases. In the past usually there had been no penalty on the corporate owners, for their costs could be rolled into the rate base.

Yet this was hardly in the public interest. Under the incentive rate of return, if the project was completed within a 30 per cent cost overrun (as allowed in the President's report to Congress), then the backers would qualify for a 17 per cent return on equity. Southern pipelines were getting 12 to 13 per cent. If, however, the company was so zealous in its cost control that the system came on stream with no overrun, the rate increased to 19.7 per cent, and in the unlikely event that some segment of the line was completed at 20 per cent below cost estimates then the rate of return would be 22.6 per cent. On the other side, as the costs rose above the 30 per cent level, the return to shareholders declined on a similar sliding scale – at 40 per cent it was 16.4 per cent. Now these rates of return could mean a great deal to companies who had borrowed at high interest rates to make the investment. They might make virtually nothing or at best net 1 or 2 per cent. Every 1 per cent in the rate of return would add an additional $10 million per year for every $1 billion in equity investment. It was hoped that the investors would now bring much more effective pressure back on the pipeline company to ensure that the pipeline would be built at the lowest possible price consistent with proper engineering standards. However, such a flexible rate of return made investors all the more cautious about committing their money. The National Energy Board in Canada designed a similar incentive rate of return, only for the Canadian portion there was a sliding scale, with higher rates of return for the difficult northern zones and more conventional rates of return further south. In the U.S. Congress there was some criticism that the profit margins in Canada were higher than those for the Alaskan segments, but this was merely a reflection of the higher rates of interest prevalent in Canada.

In Washington, Alaska Northwest complained that this incentive rate of return added a further level of uncertainty to complicate its financing problems. Even more serious were two official government agency reports that cast doubt on the economic viability of the whole project. One of these probed the financial mess Alyeska had spawned; the other focused on the issues confronting the Alaska Highway Project.[21] Both these reports were from the General Accounting Office, and they acted as a catalyst in mobilizing the growing fears that the project would never be built. The GAO drew attention to the growing reserves of low-cost natural gas emerging in the lower forty-eight states, Mexico, and Canada; the estimate by the sponsors that the chances of abandonment had increased from one in eight to one in three; and the assumption that the Alyeska problems of cost control would re-emerge with any further Arctic pipeline. These higher than usual risks were attributable to potential catastrophes like earthquakes, design and construction problems, restrictive regulatory stipulations, government and citizen legal challenges, finite limits to the money available, and even the possibility of "political conflict" within

Canada. This report was leaked to major North American newspapers, causing further loss of confidence in the project.[22]

By the summer of 1979 it was clear that the project was stalled in the United States. Besides the financing questions, there were dozens of regulatory hurdles where progress was agonizingly slow. For instance, it was July, 1979, before the federal inspector, the official coordinator between the government and the pipeline company, was appointed, while within financial circles along Wall Street the serious analytical work on the project had barely begun. Until they had clear answers on the costs involved and filed evidence of signed contracts to sell the gas, the financial institutions would not enter into serious negotiations.

Many analysts and observers were convinced that the Alaska Highway Pipeline would be forced as a last resort to seek government backstopping. In the spring of 1977, as part of its appeal for political support, Northwest had stated that it would not require such guarantees. President Carter in his report to Congress had emphasized that there should be no direct federal involvement in the financing package. Energy officials in Washington believed that the direct beneficiaries of the project, the North Slope producers, the government of Alaska, and the utilities purchasing the gas should provide the needed guarantees. Mobilizing this disparate group of interests was clearly something beyond the powers of the executive wing and the public relations staff of Northwest. The three North Slope producers claimed to be in very different positions in terms of potential support. Exxon, as the largest and wealthiest corporation in the world, was clearly capable of taking a strong financial stake. ARCO (Atlantic Richfield) was less able and Sohio's credit rating had been stretched to the limit in financing its portion of the Alyeska system.[23]

Also, the producers resisted any suggestion that they provide debt guarantees without an equity stake in the company so they would have some say in its management. Yet under American anti-trust regulations oil companies were excluded from equity holdings in natural gas pipelines. The law thus helped to provide a convenient rationalization for something Northwest was wanting to avoid. The producers were also resisting responsibility for building the gas plants required to remove impurities and prepare the gas for the pipeline. These plants would cost $2 to $4 billion and the producers were worried that these added costs would erode their profit margins derived from the wellhead price. The position of the state of Alaska was far from clear; while supporting the pipeline, it was also considering a petrochemical complex to use all or part of the gas needed for supplying the pipeline. Some of the state's consultants' reports that had been made public were quite negative on the Foothills/Northwest project. Because of all this, it appeared that neither the producers, nor the state of Alaska, nor the gas utilities were willing to take a leadership role in supporting the pipeline and contributing to its financing. This left Northwest with no option but to reassess its position on requesting government backstopping.

Both the Carter and Reagan administrations in the United States and the Trudeau government in Canada were united on one point – no government backstopping. This issue, which had been a formal part of the Arctic Gas application, raised a number of fundamental questions about the theory of free-enterprise capitalism. If the risks of a project are transferred from the shareholders to the taxpayer, this is inequitable because most taxpayers will receive no benefit in the form of lower cost or more secure supply. Besides, many believed that the risk-assessment function of the private financial institutions was a healthy means of weeding out uneconomic or impractical projects.

These institutions had to live with their investment decisions in a way that government did not. Any government guarantee would constitute an indirect subsidy to gas companies. In addition, once the government was involved through guarantees it would be subject to the conflict of interest of being both guarantor and regulator of the project. In such a scenario it would be easy for the "public interest" to be confused with the project interest. In the United States, where the theory of free enterprise was enjoying a vigorous revival, these priniciples made it politically impossible for Northwest to press for or for Congress to approve government guarantees, especially after the defeat of the Carter administration in the election of 1980. The only bright spot for the project was the consequences that flowed from the Iranian overthrow of the Shah and the further jump in OPEC oil prices. Americans were certainly sensitive about secure future supplies of oil and gas, but they were by no means convinced that the Alaska Highway Pipeline system was the best available means of securing that supply.

In Canada from late 1978 on there were growing worries that the project was losing momentum and heading for a tailspin. When John McMillian, head of Northwest, appeared before the House of Commons Standing Committee on Northern Pipelines in early 1979 he was closely questioned about some of the negative reports, such as Dr. Arlon Tussing's for the state legislature of Alaska. In answer he lashed out emotionally at his critics in a way that hurt his own cause. "He is a college professor. He is just a solid 14-carat nut running loose. That is one of the nicest things I can say about him. I do not think he has any credibility."[24] Even for those on the committee who shared his view of university professors, the bombastic language cast more doubt on McMillian's credibility than that of his critics. There were worries about the ability of Foothills' partner to complete all the difficult financing and other requirements to get the project off the ground.

Yet it was very clear that something had to be done to revitalize the flagging image of the project. Foothills saw that it was facing two related challenges, either of which could destroy its chances. One was the financing impasse, the other was the growing pressure in Alberta for new gas exports to the United States. Many small and medium-sized Canadian producers were desperate for new markets to sell shut-in gas and generate needed cash flow. However, these new exports could tap markets the Alaska Highway Pipeline had assumed would be theirs. For Foothills the gas exports could turn from a liability to a benefit if they could be channelled to support the start-up of the southern portions of the line. Then this "Pre-Build" would be a functioning revenue-producing operation when the more costly and difficult northern line came to be built. But such a strategy would require Nova to jump in to organize and direct the flow of new exports, which was not likely to be accomplished without a fight.

The National Energy Board Report on Northern Pipelines of 1977 had recognized that some Alberta gas might be available to support the early operation of the overall project. However, there were two very firm requirements for any such action. First, the gas must be replaced at a later date by "swaps" of Alaskan gas when it came on stream; second, no portion of the pipeline could be constructed until the financing for the whole system was in place. In response to strong producer pressure from Alberta, the NEB held gas export hearings in October, 1978, which resulted in the Board declaring an exportable surplus of 2 trillion cubic feet (Tcf). This decision immediately evoked cries of anguish from the industry that these figures were too conservative. To Foothills there was a growing groundswell of pressure for exports, which unless handled carefully could absorb all or part of the market needed for Alaskan gas.

In 1979 Foothills moved aggressively to try to protect its position. Using Nova's gas brokerage affiliate, Pan-Alberta, Foothills organized a slate of new gas export applications that would be committed to using the southern Pre-Build.[25] This campaign was not without its embarrassing angles for Foothills. Early in the debate over the Mackenzie Valley Pipeline, Foothills had attacked Arctic Gas for its plan to export Delta gas to finance the line. In a reversal of his earlier position, Vern Horte, the ex-president of Arctic Gas, was organizing a rival group of export applications called Pro-Gas, who planned to

Figure 25.
Alaska Highway Pipeline Project and Pre-Build. From the Nova Annual
Report, 1981.

operate through existing pipelines, while some eastern Canadians were worried that with all the new exports there would not be sufficient gas to service the expansion of existing markets as well as the new Trans-Quebec and Maritime Pipeline in which Nova, ironically, was a principal shareholder. Some of the western producers were less than enthusiastic about Pre-Build because it would be more expensive than existing pipelines and, as the border price was fixed, it could eat into their profit margins. The heavy emphasis on Canadian nationalism, which spokesmen like Reg Gibbs had used in his opening address to Berger, was moved to the back burner by Foothills as it worked furiously to preserve its project.

In July, 1979, the NEB opened hearings to consider the export applications of Pan-Alberta and twelve other companies. The applications totalled 4.9 trillion cubic feet (Tcf), nearly two and half times the exportable surplus as defined by the Board six months earlier. In spite of efforts from public interest group intervenors, it was clear that there was no longer any effective opposition to massive new exports. In November, 1979, the Board delivered its judgement authorizing 3.75 Tcf in exports, including 1.8 to Pan-Alberta for the Pre-Build. The Board endorsed the concept of the Pre-Build as "in the public interest" while approving 75 per cent of the Pan-Alberta application.[26] However, the volumes approved were not sufficient to finance the Pre-Build on a "stand-alone" basis – i.e., that all the costs could be amortized by Alberta gas flows in the event that the northern portions were never completed. On December 13, Foothills, in a surprising departure from its normal tactics of quiet diplomacy, called a press conference to denounce the NEB Report. The reasons for the desperation were clear; the Clark government, while supporting the project, was not prepared to move on the Pre-Build until the financing for the whole project was in place, as had been stipulated in the Canada-United States Pipeline Agreement. Late in 1979 American resistance to Canadian gas exports increased dramatically when price increases of 30 per cent were announced to take effect at the end of January, 1980. American gas utilities no longer took their full contracted volumes while new gas via the Pre-Build no longer looked so attractive. Then in December, 1979, the Clark government fell from power and policy direction stopped while the ministers jumped into the heated election campaign. Some observers in Washington saw this as further evidence (in addition to Quebec) of the political instability in Canada, which did nothing to strengthen the pipeline prospects. In the United States, 1980 was an election year with all the predictable political posturing that entailed.

While the Canadian winter election campaign plowed along with all its bitterness and emotion, many were at work behind the scenes in the bureaucratic and corporate sectors to press the case for the pipeline. Foothills approached the NEB to demonstrate that the volumes granted were inadequate to provide minimum pressures and economies of scale. The project could not fly. In reply the Board admitted that some unassigned surplus was available and that it would hold special hearings in February to consider the financing problems of Pre-Build, especially as they related to the provisions of the Northern Pipeline Act. Thus the Board was prepared to reconsider the conclusions of its own report only two months after it was issued. These announcements were followed by a number of private meetings between Foothills executives, Mitchell Sharp, the Northern Pipeline Commissioner, and Geoffrey Edge of the NEB; by now Sharp and Edge had become strong supporters of the project, even helping to fine tune its case. In this instance the regulators were no longer operating at arm's length to the corporate applicants as arbiters of the public interest. One of the intervenors in those hearings later wrote: "Edge's involvement raised disturbing questions about the fairness of the upcoming hearings: would he now sit as a judge of a financing plan and an export application he had helped to develop."[27] It was clear from the Board's action that it had already decided to rescue Foothills from the dilemma its previous report had created.

In gaining access to the new markets in the United States, Pre-Build enjoyed one enormous advantage over Pro-Gas or other rival suppliers. The Carter administration made it clear that it was prepared to exclude new Canadian gas imports unless they were part of the Alaska Highway Pipeline system and to hold up approvals of further imports from Mexico. This decision caused some in Pro-Gas to jump to Pan-Alberta in order to ensure their entry into U.S. markets. In addition, Northwest made it plain that any American gas utilities wishing to purchase Pre-Build gas must be prepared to join the consortium supporting the overall project. In Canada the long and sometimes fierce rivalry between Nova and Trans-Canada Pipelines was brought to a close when the Calgary-based Dome Petroleum bought controlling interest in TCP. Thus, by the early months of 1980 the opponents of Pre-Build had been neutralized by government intervention and corporate manoeuvres on both sides of the border.

In February, 1980, the Trudeau government was returned to power with a clear working majority by the Canadian electorate. Obviously one of its first major tasks was to get the stalled pipeline back on the track. However, the new Energy Minister, Marc Lalonde, had attacked only a few months previously the modest export proposals of the earlier NEB report. In the House he had argued that gas exports for the Pre-Build should only be on the basis of an "ironclad commitment" for construction of the whole project. Everything should be "signed, sealed, and delivered" before one cubic foot of gas could be exported for American customers.[28] On the opposition front benches were former cabinet ministers from Ontario like Allan Lawrence, who were determined not to capitulate to Blair,[29] while the NDP, led by Ian Waddell, was committed to all-out war on what it believed to be the sell-out of Canadian resources involved in Pre-Build. Foothills was now pushing full out for increased exports to flow through the Pre-Build and to get amendments to Condition XII of the Northern Pipeline Act, which prohibited the start of construction on any part of the pipeline system until the financing for all parts was in place, and Foothills had allies strategically placed that helped in the critical spring of 1980.

In the same month that Trudeau returned to power Pan-Alberta filed a new export application, which the Board quickly announced it would hear the next month. It seemed clear from the opening minute that the panel would recommend sufficient gas to meet minimum flow rates for the economic operation of the Pre-Build. A further set of hearings chaired by Edge looked at the financing issues that a separate Pre-Build created for government policy of single-unit project financing under the provisions of Condition XII. The government was backed into a corner and chose to swallow its previous statements because it was not prepared to see the whole project collapse. Yet it was a calculated gamble, for if the U.S. felt its gas needs were met by the new Alberta exports, would it bother to press ahead to ensure the completion of the northern portion where financing was obviously so difficult?

In the backroom wheeling and dealing three individuals played key roles: Geoffrey Edge, now acting chairman of the NEB; Mitchell Sharp, the Northern Pipeline Commissioner; and Senator Bud Olson, the Minister Responsible for Northern Pipelines. Edge directed personally the NEB's public hearings on Condition XII and the financing of the pipeline. In the end, Foothills was required to provide financing proof of nothing beyond the Pre-Build while reiterating its commitment to the whole project. But to sell this radical change to the Canadian electorate the Trudeau cabinet had to have hard evidence from Washington that the Americans were determined to press on with the whole project. In March, Trudeau wrote to President Carter to elicit further American action but the President, struggling for his own political life in an election year, was hardly in a position to deliver the kind of guarantee the Canadians sought.[30] When Secretary of State Cyrus Vance visited Ottawa in April he refused to give any commitment that the funds for the overall project could be raised. The NEB had done its job of recommending the necessary changes, but they had to be wrapped in a politically saleable package. The Liberals did not want another pipeline debate like 1956. Canada must not appear to be making all the sacrifices for a project that the Americans were no longer committed to.

In spite of pilgrimages to Washington by Edge, Sharp, and Olson, the Americans were not prepared to make any dramatic move on the project. At this point the pipeline clearly was a far greater political issue in Ottawa than in Washington. When Trudeau met with Carter privately at the Venice economic summit nothing was accomplished because the President had not read his briefing notes on the subject.[31] By June, 1980, many in Canada were beginning to question the wisdom of such a massive commitment to the project when its chances of being completed were slowly eroding. As one official summed up his frustration to the author: "If the Americans won't get off their ass why should we be killing ourselves." The Pre-Build could become a very bad deal for Canada if the northern link to Alaska was never completed.

Realizing that time and events were now working against the project, Senator Olson made one further trip to Washington on June 27 for a working breakfast with key Congressional and regulatory figures. He warned that without further American assurances the project would probably collapse. He outlined the type of commitment Canada needed and why. If Ottawa got such assurances, he promised speedy cabinet approval of the changes to Condition XII and a summer start on the Pre-Build. That morning a joint resolution for the Senate and the House of Representatives was prepared and then was passed that same afternoon. The resolution expressed general support for the completion of the Alaska Highway Pipeline by the end of 1985 but without committing Congress to any specific action to ensure its achievement. However, this symbolic action was sufficient to meet the political needs of the Trudeau cabinet in dealing with its own domestic critics. Cabinet quickly approved the exports and the changes in Condition XII to allow for the separate financing of the Pre-Build. This was done without enthusiasm, for everyone in Ottawa was aware they had been backed into a corner. In the House of Commons, Joe Clark, quoting Marc Lalonde's statements while in opposition, accused the government of an "ironclad flip-flop"; Ian Waddell of the NDP launched a court challenge to the Pre-Build. Everyone recognized that Canada was way out on the limb in its efforts to save the pipeline and that there was no guarantee the efforts would be successful.

As the American election campaign swung into high gear in late summer and early fall, Foothills began construction of the western leg of the Pre-Build through the Rockies and into Washington State. When the Reagan administration entered office in 1981, the overall project was still stalled by the financing barriers. The New York bankers and insurance companies viewed the project as too risky an investment, especially given the size of the capital requirements. The new administration was even more vehemently opposed to financial backstopping, something the President made brutallly clear in his March, 1981, speech to the Canadian Parliament. However, they were prepared to consider a legislative package for Congress that might ease some of the problems in getting private-sector financing. Ottawa pressed the government in Washington to move quickly, but nothing came forward; the administration explained that it wished to allow some of the anti-Canadian feeling aroused by the National Energy Policy to ease before making any attempt. In public statements, however, the U.S. Interior Secretary, James Watt, expressed doubt that the project would ever be built. In the fall of 1981, Mitchell Sharp hurried south again to try to prod the American leaders into action – he feared that once again the project was losing momentum even though the western leg of the Pre-Build was about to begin pumping gas and the eastern leg was about to begin construction. Sharp admitted that any further delays "would be quite dangerous."[32]

Behind the scenes members of Congress sympathetic to Foothills and Northwest were preparing the package. The two main components in it were: a waiver of anti-trust regulations that allowed the North Slope producers to invest in the equity stock of the gas pipeline; a special pipeline tariff that would allow American gas consumers to be liable for pipeline charges for completed sections of the line even if other sections of the system had been delayed. This was a type of all-events tariff. In July, when he was in Alaska, U.S. Energy Secretary James Edwards appeared to reject specifically this option, but obviously by late fall he had changed his mind. Most financial analysts felt this special tariff was essential for the overall project financing and was the only way backstopping could be avoided.[33]

The project, though, was still exceedingly controversial and had many opponents within the American gas industry. Meanwhile, Congressional opposition exploited Canadian-American tensions flowing from the National Energy Policy and other issues in dispute. On the eve of the Trudeau visit in September, 1981, the *New York Times* described relations between Trudeau and Reagan as acrimonious.[34] On the project itself cost-overruns were once again a matter of controversy. With the incentive rate of return, it was now suspected that the company would try to maximize cost estimates as a cushion for later overruns. To curb this potential abuse, the United States government hired private consultants to assess the accuracy of the filed estimates for the Alaskan section, which the company had projected to be $11.3 billion. When the consultants had completed their analysis of this 1,240-kilometre section, they lowered the estimate to $9.7 billion, which seemed to cast doubt on the integrity of the Northwest estimates and hurt its image in Congress. Some in Alaska still believed that all or part of the gas could be used to found a local petrochemical industry if the pipeline fell through.[35]

In September the Reagan administration began to move on the "waiver package" for Congress, although the assassination of President Sadat diverted administration attention for some weeks. Just at this time, the stock market entered its worst period of decline since the depression, while the insurance companies so crucial to the debt package were experiencing a liquidity crisis that restricted their investing capability. On the very day of the announcement of the Reagan initiative, Senator Ted Stevens of Alaska sadly admitted: "The amount to be borrowed is beyond the present capacity of the domestic financial market."[36] Among both supporters and critics there was an assumption that the battle in Congress would be a tough one.

When the package came before Congress in October, it consisted of seven legal waivers to existing regulations to facilitate financing. In addition to the all-events tariff and the stock purchasing by the producers, the legislation allowed the gas plants to be lumped into project financing, regulatory procedures to be abbreviated, prohibition of later changes that could increase the debt charges, and two purely technical changes. The package contained a sixty-day time limit to counter normal Congressional procrastination. The opposition to the legislation was immediate, involving elements from the left and right wings in Congress. The possible billing of gas consumers before gas deliveries triggered most of the controversy, which was centred in the House of Representatives. Illinois Republican Congressman Thomas Corcoran charged that the package was "the greatest consumer ripoff in the history of the United States." The consumer lobby moved into high gear to try to defeat the bill. Ralph Nader called it "the most radical extremist corporate power grab in U.S. history." All the evils of the National Energy Program and the Foreign Investment Review Agency were trotted out to colour opinion against Canada as an untrustworthy ally. Some drew attention to the original cost estimates of $8 billion and the current $40 billion price tag to argue that the finances were out of control.

However, with political instability in the Middle East, a land bridge pipeline to Alaska seemed appealing to those seeking secure energy supplies on American territory. Also, the Canadian Embassy mounted a discreet but effective lobby that the United States had a moral obligation to carry through the deal that both countries had signed in 1977. As one Bronx Democrat put it: "Lord knows we have enough problems with our neighbours to the north without adding to them." After committee approvals the package passed the Senate and came on to the House early in December. In spite of a furious rearguard action by the opponents, the bill passed 233 to 173 only to face a seldom-used procedural device that forced a second vote twenty-four hours later. Here the margin narrowed only slightly to 229 to 188.[37] President Reagan signed the legislation into law before Christmas and the project sponsors breathed a sigh of relief. With this help they might now be able to tackle the private money markets in New York and elsewhere.

Early in 1982, Northwest Alaska and Foothills began what they hoped would be the final round of meetings to complete the financing plans. Following the Congressional action they hoped that the way might now be clear for the project to regain momentum after the long delays. Then five states, twenty-four members of Congress, and some consumer groups combined to file a legal challenge to the waiver bill as a violation of consumer rights. At this latest turn John McMillian, chairman of Northwest Alaska, did not conceal his intense annoyance. "I am extremely concerned that this action, even though unsuccessful, will seriously delay the project and result in major capital cost increases which will have to be borne by the gas consumers." He estimated that each year's delay would add $3 billion to the capital cost of the project. Opponents like Ralph Nader argued that if the pipeline was as necessary and as potentially profitable as Northwest claimed, the banks would finance it like any other commercial venture. If not, then it was unfair to burden the consumer with the heavy financial obligations for a dubious project.[38]

Even more serious than the court challenge were the conditions in financial markets. During the spring of 1982 the recession continued to deepen and the stock market plunged, and as a result new equity offerings were almost impossible to float. There was also market resistance to selling the Alaskan gas through the necessary long-term contracts that the lenders would demand to see as part of financing. Late in the spring of 1982 the project sponsors met with the officials of Northwest Alaska and indicated that there was no way the project could proceed given the above conditions. However, they did agree to assess the situation again early in 1984 to see if conditions had changed sufficiently to make an effort to finance the pipeline at that time. It was a severe blow to the partners on both sides of the border.

During all the trials and tribulations of Foothills from 1977 through 1982, the Trudeau government had always stood firmly behind the project. The reasons for this support were tied up in their belief that mega-projects could provide a great stimulus to the whole Canadian economy and lift it out of recession. In 1977 Ottawa estimated that the Alaska Highway and Dempster Lateral pipelines would contribute nearly 100,000 man years of work to the Canadian economy: 26,800 man years in construction; 40,500 man years in manufacturing (steel pipe, etc.); 31,000 man years in indirect services. During the construction phase there would be 2,200 workers, mainly from the south; during the operations phase following construction there would be only 200 permanent jobs in the North.[39] During the construction phase there would be an induced boom along the route of the pipeline followed by economic slump if other projects did not follow in its path.

This type of capital-intensive mega-project does not create stable economic growth. The pushing up of local wage levels can do serious harm to other local industries, which may go under because they cannot compete for local labour. The high demand for local goods and services can create a steep inflationary spiral of prices. Those who are not working on the pipeline will have trouble maintaining their standard of living because of the increased cost of living they have to face. Some local industries may be seriously hurt by physical impacts caused during the construction phase. Tourism is one of the major employers in the Yukon, but all the extra truck traffic and dust along the highway during the construction phase will certainly cut the flow of tourists.

The impacts on the national economy would be more positive, especially during a period of recession with unused capacity checking inflationary pressures. During the construction phase, with the large capital inflows from New York, there would be upward pressure on the Canadian dollar, which Ottawa might welcome. During the operations phase there would be a small net surplus in the balance of payments involving the pipeline; the tariff paid by the U.S. customers would more than cover the interest and dividends to foreign backers of the project.

Many Canadian industries were anxious to get contracts to supply components in any Arctic pipeline. This was particularly true of steel companies with the capacity to roll large-diameter pipe. Stelco signed a letter of intent with Arctic Gas in 1976 to supply 1.1 million tons of 48″-thick wall pipe at $645 per ton (with an inflation clause). It was the largest order in Stelco's history, which *The Financial Post* estimated would bring an operating profit of $200 per ton or about $1.50 per share per year on the three-year order.[40] It was no wonder Stelco was such an outspoken booster of Arctic Gas! When the agreement was signed between Canada and the United States to build the pipeline it was agreed that each would allow the companies of the other to tender for contracts within its jurisdiction. However, when the NEB opted to change the pipe size from 48″ to 54″ all but one U.S. competitor were eliminated for pipe contracts, causing an uproar in Congress from interests sympathetic to the American steel industry, which had considerable idle capacity.[41]

In assessing the overall economic worth of a massive new energy system like the Alaska Highway Pipeline, it is important to look at the issue of economic rents or super profits, which are often involved with resource development. In this project they could take three forms: profits to the North Slope producers; royalties to the state of Alaska; and price savings to the consumer. In order to get American approval for the Canadian route, Ottawa had abandoned any hope of tapping any of those economic rents through special taxation when it signed the Transit Pipeline Treaty in January, 1977. But while the main economic rents will remain within American territory, many of the environmental and socio-economic costs would be occurring in Canada.

In the negotiations with the Americans in the summer of 1977 Canada insisted on some special form of compensation for these costs, which otherwise would have to be absorbed by the people of the Yukon and the Canadian taxpayer. Under the agreement reached by Carter and Trudeau, Foothills would be liable to pay up to $200 million to cover socio-economic costs related to the project. These funds could be deducted from later taxes to be paid so they were not a special "heritage fund" as the Lysyk Commission had proposed.[42] They were a form of advanced tax payment. During the construction phase Foothills (Yukon) was to pay $35 million in property taxes and a yearly tax of $30 million (indexed to the GNP from the start-up of operations). This should mean that the Yukon would receive tax benefits of at least $1 billion over the twenty-five-year life of the pipeline while the cost savings to the U.S. consumer over the rival El Paso system were estimated to be $6 billion.[43] Thus it was clear that the main post-production economic rents would be flowing to the American consumers. In the delays since 1977 the Canadian economic benefits that Ottawa had to bargain so hard to get have deteriorated significantly because of inflation. The lump-sum payment and the yearly property taxes had lost half their real value by 1985. The indexing begins only after the line is in operation.

When the huge Prudhoe Bay oilfields were discovered in 1968, the industry had expectations of huge profit margins with the high rates of production, and when the OPEC price revolution and further crises in the Middle East pushed up world prices those hopes rose even higher. By early in 1979, with world oil prices at $14 per barrel, the true picture began to emerge. From the wellhead price of $6.16 the producers cleared $1.61 in profits and a further $1.30 from their investment in the pipeline. This produced a 9 per cent rate of return on the $14.3 billion invested in exploration, production, and pipelines. This was significantly below corporate expectations, especially for BP/Sohio, which owned 53 per cent of the 9.4 billion barrels of proven reserves at Prudhoe Bay. These financial returns discouraged their willingness to jump into gas transmission, which had even lower net-backs to the producers.

Alyeska Costs Per Barrel

Operating costs	.57
Depreciation	.85
Removal	.10
Interest	1.57
State property tax	.37
State income tax	.26
Federal income tax	1.19
Pipeline profits	1.30
Total pipeline charge	$6.21

Pipeline charge	6.21	per barrel[44]
Wellhead price	6.16	" "
Tanker charge to Cal.	1.63	" "
California landed price	$14.00	" "

Thus, the combination of much higher costs and higher taxation led the industry to conclude that the Prudhoe Bay field was not the bonanza expected. The companies had made their financial projections on the basis of one series of cash-flow assumptions and were having to live with another set. While the market price was above the estimated level, the net return was about one-half of that projected.

As Prudhoe Bay was seven times the size of any other American oilfield, it provided an enticing target for state politicians anxious to maximize tax revenue. During the 1970's the state taxation of oil and gas was changed thirteen times, increasing by 900 per cent in the process. In 1979, oil and gas revenue of $790 million constituted 74 per cent of the internally generated funds for the state. A number of state politicians, including Senator Gravel, suggested that as the multinationals were now reluctant to pursue development, the state should get into the oil business as it had in most other producer states such as Canada, Norway, and Britain. In rhetoric very similar to that used later against the National Energy Program in Canada, the majors attacked the "predatory" taxing policies of Alaska, which would destroy the financial viability of the industry. Also by 1979, it was evident that all the Prudhoe Bay oil could not be sold in California but had to be shipped in smaller tankers through the Panama Canal at a cost of $3.10 per barrel, cutting away half the profits. Ironically, for Canadians this problem would never have emerged had the route across Canada, offered by the Trudeau government, been accepted.

With the profitability of the Prudhoe Bay oil down so significantly it was hardly surprising that there was growing pessimism about the gas. In 1979 it was estimated that the Chicago city gate price could be as high as $6 per Mcf for Alaskan gas when the current American domestic price was $2.10. Even with the prospect of roll-in provisions for higher-cost sources of supply, it would still be difficult to sell Alaskan gas at a price satisfactory to the producers. Charles E. Spahr, former chairman of Sohio, noted bitterly; "It won't happen in my lifetime and maybe for much, much longer," when asked to comment on the prospects for the Alaska Highway Pipeline.[45]

In the years ahead Dome Petroleum, Gulf Canada, and Imperial Oil will be tapping smaller oil reservoirs in the Beaufort Sea area with even more expensive technology and higher costs of delivery to market. They will face many of the same problems as those experienced in Alaska with escalating costs and taxes. Dome will require more than $10 billion in the next decade for this area and Gulf and Imperial not much less. With world oil prices having stalled in their upward climb, it is difficult to see how the Canadian market price for crude will cover all the expenses involved on the frontier. In 1982 it became clear that the whole Canadian banking system, and especially the Canadian Imperial Bank of Commerce, had over-extended itself in loans to the Canadian oil companies. This lesson will not be forgotten quickly by the normally conservative Canadian banking fraternity, and future loan applications for Arctic exploration, production facilities, or pipelines will be viewed with much greater caution. It will no longer be sufficient to offer oil in the ground as collateral for future borrowing because changes in oil prices may eliminate its value. This has brought a new realism about future oil production from the Beaufort. Even if the reserves for commercial operation are proven, the economics may not justify the capital required and lengthy delays may be in store. Given the Alaskan experience the Beaufort oil does not seem to be viable, unless the government in its drive for new oil supplies is prepared to guarantee or to invest itself in these new and highly expensive facilities.

In the 1980's and 1990's Canada will require heavy new capital investment in energy projects, many of which will be situated in the North. The Royal Bank estimated that the total capital requirements for the energy and non-energy sectors will be about $500 billion (using 1980 prices). Energy investments as a percentage of GNP are higher in Canada than in any other industrialized country, as the following figures indicate:[46]

	1970	1979	1985 (est.)	1989 (est.)
Canada	3.4%	5.2%	7.8%	7.9%
United States	1.9	3.4	4.4	4.4
Japan	1.8	2.0	4.4	4.5
EEC	1.5	1.8	1.6	1.6

The capital requirements for Canada are all the greater because of projects like the Alaska Highway Pipeline, which are designed as delivery systems for American gas to American customers. Now that the Dempster Lateral has fallen through, it will add very little to Canadian energy supply.[47] Traditionally, Canadians have been great savers, either directly or indirectly, such as through insurance companies or pension plans. But the even greater demands in the future for financing energy projects will have to be met either voluntarily or through taxes. In coping with these new mega-projects, the inflationary pressures of price increases must be kept under control. In a special study undertaken by the NEB staff in 1982, they found that pipeline construction costs had been rising much more quickly than the general rate of inflation (50 per cent higher than the rate of inflation in 1981) and that these costs were rising faster in Canada than in the United States. It is useful to use the example of three tarsands plants to show the pattern from 1967 to 1982.

Suncor (1964-67)	cost	$ 4,800 per barrel/day production
Syncrude (1973-78)	cost	$17,600 " " " "
Alsands (1982 est.) would cost	$95,000 " " " "

The above constitutes a twentyfold increase in just over two decades.[48] The problems of capital availability and cost control interact to make the overall financing all the more difficult.

In the spring of 1982 the collapse of the Alsands project and the further delay in any start on the Alaska Highway Pipeline triggered a great deal of soul-searching within government concerning regulatory procedures and financing. Geoffrey Edge, the chairman of the National Energy Board, in speeches and interviews stressed that the regulatory process would have to change if the great energy projects were to get off the ground. While the package offered by the two governments to save Alsands had been generous, the companies involved still viewed the project as too risky. With oil prices in such a weak condition, all the financial assumptions were profoundly uncertain. Long-term debt (the old-style bonds) was almost impossible to float while short-term borrowing was subject to high and fluctuating interest rates. They tried to estimate their future profits by a "discounted rate of return" (discounted for inflation) but this was always an uncertain guessing game when the lead time before production was six years or more. With rare candour the NEB chairman noted that without changes "you just won't get an Alaska Highway Pipeline, it won't be financeable." One of the basic problems was the financial sector's practice of "front-end loading" by which the financing charges are heaviest in the first years of the project and then decline as liabilities are paid off and interest payments decrease. Inflation and high interest rates had caused these front-end charges to double, substantially increasing the tariff and making Alaskan gas uncompetitive in American markets. Edge suggested that regulators and financial institutions had to get together to seek means of levelling out these charges, as had been done with home mortgages. "Obviously you won't get the Alaska Pipeline off the ground without some degree of levelling." The energy mega-projects would not proceed unless Canada could be more "inventive in regulation and financing."[49]

Thus, in the 1980's the North American financing system for major projects is in a period of crisis. Although the above proposals will not solve the problems, they are a recognition of how serious these problems are. They are far more serious than merely the downturn or recession in the economy and are particularly acute for northern projects. A decline in the rate of inflation, a decrease in interest rates, and a firming of world oil prices will all help. But even with these improvements there will still be problems because of the scale of capital requirements and the level of risk perceived by the lending institutions for projects like the Alaska Highway Pipeline.

In the period from 1977 to 1982 Foothills and its American partners received strong endorsement from the Canadian and American governments; yet the free-enterprise money markets could not cope with all the variables involved. Arctic Gas had been right in its firm conviction that government backstopping would be necessary. If the great northern projects currently on the drawing boards are to proceed in the 1980's they will involve new levels of government support, including public ownership in some cases. Rather than massive debt guarantees to private enterprise similar to the era of railroad building at the turn of the century, it would be preferable to see the public utility format or joint ventures between private capital and Crown corporations. In spite of some of the rhetoric from free-enterprise theorists, government must play a central role in the future economic development of the North because, as the markets have demonstrated, it alone has the economic strength to carry the risk.

CHAPTER 11

The Canadian North in the
Circumpolar World

In the preceding chapters, the primary focus has been on domestic policy with only the occasional digression into external matters (such as the comments in the last chapter on Canadian-American economic relations). In this chapter the Canadian Arctic will be seen in a broader international setting, which Canadians have been reluctant to recognize in spite of its growing importance. Included in this analysis are a number of difficult issues that complicate greatly our relations with the United States and are part of the explanation for the growing tensions between Ottawa and Washington in the early 1980's. These tensions involve the intricate interrelationship among the environment, sovereignty, energy policy, and defence.

This bilateral relationship must now be fitted into a wider scenario. The existing alliance system is faced by the logical need for circumpolar co-operation. We are only slowly coming to recognize the ecological interdependency of the nations facing the Arctic Ocean, while our closest military ally is also our greatest challenge in terms of sovereignty and national economic goals in the North. The traditional stereotypes of the "True North Strong and Free" collide with the realities of world politics in the 1980's. Canadians may resent these circumstances but they cannot ignore them. This volume began by viewing the Canadian North as an extension of the northern frontier of Europe; now we must return to that theme to understand properly the current scene.

The first problem we face is our own perception of the Arctic world, which has been conditioned by traditional southern maps that are "open at the top"; yet all the circumpolar nations face each other around the Arctic Ocean. This body of water is nearly landlocked by the territory of the Soviet Union, Alaska, Canada, Greenland, and Norway. The activities of each of these nations interact, the environmental impacts from one area inevitably creating consequences for the surrounding territories. Under these circumstances the only ef-

289

Figure 26.
The Circumpolar North.

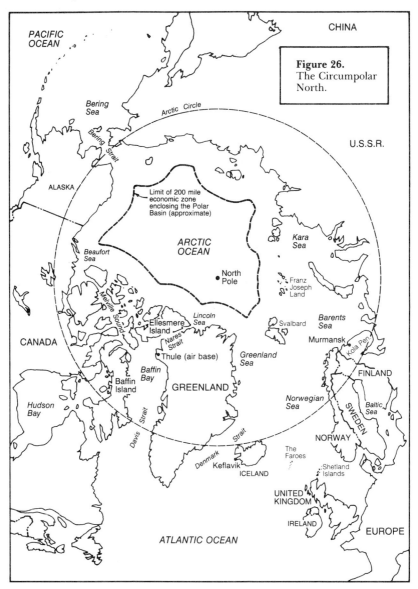

Figure 26.
The Circumpolar
North.

fective means of environmental protection is through international law, diplomacy, and co-operation. Yet the international community was slow to recognize the significance of the scientific research and the overall threat posed for marine ecosystems, including the Arctic. The great powers were reluctant to see coastal states allowed to interfere with the historic principles of the freedom of the seas that their own commercial and military vessels enjoyed.

In the North the need for new regulation became evident in the 1970's when advances in marine technology allowed commercial shipping to penetrate the frozen seas for the first time. In the 1980's and 1990's intense economic development will occur in many areas of the Arctic. Major offshore drilling programs are underway or planned for the Barents Sea (U.S.S.R.), the Svalbard Archipelago and the Norwegian Sea (Norway and the U.S.S.R.), the Davis Strait (Canada and Greenland), the Sverdrup Basin (Canada), and the Beaufort Sea (U.S. and Canada). With all these efforts the urgency for international environmental co-operation is clearly evident, hopefully to avoid but if not at least to contain and to clean up major oil spills in the difficult Arctic conditions.

In the 1960's Canadian fears about its jurisdiction over Arctic waters were limited by the belief that the Northwest Passage would never be used by commercial vessels. These concerns, however, were brought to a focus by the *Manhattan* and *Polar Sea* voyages and the clear refusal of the United States to recognize Canadian claims to these waters. The fears in Canada revolved around two interrelated issues – sovereignty and environmental regulation. The potential damage of an oil spill was brought to public attention in February, 1970, when the tanker *Arrow* sank in Nova Scotia waters, polluting a long stretch of the coastline. There was strong political pressure on Ottawa to take counter-measures to protect Canadian sovereignty as well as the pristine northern wilderness from poorly maintained "flag of convenience" tankers under charter to the Prudhoe Bay producers. Because Canada at this time had never formally claimed the waters through the establishment of baselines around the islands or by proclaiming the sector theory drawn on most Canadian government maps, the American challenge tended to produce bureaucratic confusion and political embarrassment in Ottawa. In the end Canada swallowed its pride and co-operated with the *Manhattan* in 1969 and 1970 while planning future moves to consolidate its position.[1]

The American position on the *Manhattan* was founded on two assumptions basic to the traditional philosophy of maritime powers. The U.S. maintained that the Northwest Passage was an "international strait" where the shipping of all nations enjoyed the rights of "innocent

291

passage," stressing that these principles were enshrined in international law and the historic traditions of the freedom of the seas. As a major world shipping power, the Americans were concerned not only about commercial and military access to Canadian waters but about the effect the Canadian action might have in promoting jurisdictional claims by island nations such as Indonesia and the Philippines. The State Department thus chose to take a hard line with Canada even though the Americans knew that Ottawa had no intention of excluding Arctic-class American vessels like the *Manhattan*. It was the principle of having to apply for permission they wished to eliminate, and they were prepared to accept the necessary damage to Canadian-American relations to establish the point. If the Canadian initiative was allowed to go unchallenged it could become an embarrassing precedent that other nations might seek to follow. With many coastal states around the world seeking to extend their jurisdiction, Washington was highly sensitive about any changes in its own backyard.

Canada chose to respond to the American position by adopting an approach that would achieve its political goals without directly challenging the practices of international law, calling its position a "constructive and functional approach whereby Canada will exercise only the jurisdiction required to achieve this specific and vital purpose of environmental protection."[2] Ottawa justified its action on the basis of the pressing need for environmental protection while avoiding any claim to expanded sovereignty. As international law did not recognize the need for coastal states to intervene to protect the environment, Canada had to act unilaterally at once as a precondition for wider multilateral efforts to mobilize international support. Many nations at the UN recognized the shortcomings of international law as it is related to marine pollution but there was no consensus as to the best means of regulation. With the "Limits to Growth" debate ranging around the world, there was growing concern about the long-term viability of the world's oceans as a food source. Canada used this intellectual climate to wrap its own Arctic plans in a wider idealism that many nations would support. However, some of the principles espoused so eloquently in foreign affairs statements were only faintly evident in federal and provincial efforts at environmental regulation.

At many international gatherings Canadian officials argued that the doctrine of "innocent passage" was not appropriate for Arctic conditions because it failed to allow Ottawa sufficient authority to safeguard the northern environment. Normal tankers could be holed or sunk in the tough multi-year ice of the Northwest Passage. Yet under the traditions of innocent passage Canada had no right to interfere to enforce adequate Arctic standards and to refuse entry when these were not met, even though the food supply and the way of life of the local Inuit could be destroyed by a major oil spill. The Canadians argued that environmental integrity was every bit as valid as territorial integrity and coastal states had a duty to intervene to protect the environment on which so many of their citizens depended. These arguments were challenged continually by representatives of the major marine powers, such as Britain and the United States.

As a first step toward achieving its goal, the Trudeau government in 1970 pushed through Parliament the Arctic Waters Pollution Prevention Act (AWPPA), which established a 100-mile environmental control zone around the Canadian Arctic islands. The regulations included standards of construction and navigation procedures; they applied to through-transit vessels as well as local resource exploitation and development. Sixteen Shipping Safety Control Zones were set up, which reflected the differing levels of ice danger. Vessels failing to meet the required standards could be banned by pollution prevention officers and their cargo seized by cabinet order. Any dispute emerging from the application of the Arctic Waters Pollution Prevention Bill was excluded from reference to the International Court of Justice, which showed the Canadian worries about the status of its legislation under international law. The bill was passed in 1970 but not proclaimed for two years while Ottawa tried without success to negotiate American compliance. The response of the Nixon administration was to cut the Canadian oil import quota and to threaten further retaliation if the act was put into force. Congress approved funds for the "most powerful ice-breaker fleet in the world" so future Arctic voyages by American shipping would not require any contact or assistance from Canadian authorities. These actions aroused indignation in Canada, evoking media comparisons to the American action on the Panama Canal.

The final vote in the House of Commons on the AWPPA was unanimous, with the only criticism being that it might not be enough to protect the national interest and the northern environment.[3] The act was coupled with amendments to the Territorial Seas and Fisheries Acts to extend the limits of Canadian territorial waters from three to twelve miles, which brought the eastern and western "gates" of the Northwest Passage within Canadian territorial waters. Canada's move to a twelve-mile limit followed that of a number of other coastal states. However, it would have little practical significance if the American contention that the Northwest Passage was an international strait was generally accepted and there were no changes in the prevailing assumptions regarding the freedom of the seas within international law. These were serious barriers to acceptance of the Canadian position.

Internationally, the Arctic Waters Pollution Prevention Act was recognized as a significant unilateral attempt to create separate environmental regulations for Arctic waters and as addressing the general issue of expanding the jurisdiction of coastal states to protect the marine environment. Prime Minister Trudeau, a former law professor, attempted to explain some of the thinking behind his government's initiative. He argued that the action would strengthen international law in an important new way. It was "an assertion of the importance of the environment, of the sanctity of life on this planet, of the need for the recognition of the principle of clean seas, which is in all respects as vital a principle for the world of today and tomorrow as the principle of free seas for the world of yesterday." Canada had an international obligation to protect the northern environment.

The Arctic ice-pack has been described as the most significant surface area of the globe, for it controls the temperature of much of the Northern Hemisphere. Its continued existence in unspoiled form is vital to all mankind. The single most imminent threat to the Arctic at this time is that of a large oil spill. Not only are the hazards of Arctic navigation much greater than are found elsewhere, making the risk of breakup or sinking one of constant concern, but any maritime tragedy there would have disastrous and irreversible consequences . . . . Involved here, in short, are issues which even the most conservative of environmental scientists do not hesitate to describe as being of a magnitude which is capable of affecting the quality, and perhaps the continued existence, of human and animal life in vast regions of North America and elsewhere.[4]

This apocalyptic vision helped to entrench the government's position with northern environmentalists and reassure native groups, who rightly assumed that they would be the principal losers in the event of a major Arctic oil spill in their area. American protests achieved little except that the compensation provisions were broadened to allow claims from beyond Canadian territory, which made perfect sense given the pattern of northern winds and currents. The basic policy, however, was non-negotiable for it constituted the central feature of Canada's functional approach to extending its marine jurisdiction. Although it tried to avoid international sensitivities on sovereignty, it was an important initiative in the area of the law of the sea. An article in a Canadian law journal reflected Canadian pride when it claimed that the law was "the most significant unilateral action on the marine environment ever taken."[5] Within Canada it was clearly a political success, which helped to ease the frustrations generated by the *Manhattan* voyages that Ottawa was only an impotent spectator to events in the North.

The AWPPA was a unilateral step, so Canada now began efforts to promote multilateral acceptance of its Arctic legislation. Negotiations continued in Washington, although without success. President Nixon personally phoned the Canadian Prime Minister and when the Canadians refused to back down, the United States State Department released a diplomatic note stressing that "international law provides no basis for these proposed unilateral extensions of jurisdiction on the high seas," which the American government "can neither accept nor acquiesce [to]."[6] At the United Nations, however, Canada got a better response for its efforts. The Canadian government played an influential role in the events leading to and the proceedings of the Stockholm Conference on the Human Environment held in 1972. Here, Canada promoted its concept of "regulation based upon scientific principles," which would give new powers to coastal states. In its proposed "Third Principle," Canada outlined the jurisdictional changes it sought.

> The basis on which a state should exercise rights or powers, in addition to its sovereign rights and powers, pursuant to its special authority in areas adjacent to its territorial waters, is that such rights or powers should be deemed to be delegated to that state by the world community on behalf of humanity as a whole. The rights and powers exercised must be consistent with the coastal state's primary responsibility for marine environmental protection in the areas concerned: they should be subject to international rules and standards and to review before an appropriate international tribunal.[7]

These efforts were strongly opposed by the major shipping powers, but the proposals were passed on for consideration to the Third United Nations Law of the Sea Conference (UNCLOS III), which opened in Caracas in 1973 and continued for nearly a decade.

There is not scope in this chapter for detailed analysis of all the complex negotiations at the Law of the Sea Conference. Canada, however, did achieve partial success in the final version of the Convention through the acceptance of Article 234, the so-called "Arctic clause."

> Coastal states have the right to adopt and enforce non-discriminatory laws and regulations for the prevention, reduction and control of marine pollution from vessels in ice-covered areas within the limits of the exclusive economic zone, where particularly severe

climatic conditions and the presence of ice covering such areas for most of the year create obstructions or exceptional hazards to navigation, and pollution of the marine environment could cause major harm to or irreversible disturbance of the ecological balance. Such laws and regulations shall have due regard to navigation and the preservation of the marine environment based upon the best available scientific evidence.[8]

Enforcement of such national laws would normally be limited to the coastal state seeking redress through the courts of the flag state. "Monetary penalties only may be imposed" on the offending vessels "except in the case of a willful and serious act of pollution in the territorial sea" (Section 230). Thus there is still some legal uncertainty with regard to Canada's jurisdiction to enforce the provisions of the AWPPA outside Canadian territorial seas but within its pollution control zone. Flag states must provide recourse through their courts "for prompt and adequate compensation or other relief" for acts of pollution caused by "natural or juridical persons under their jurisdiction" (Article 235). However, these provisions do not include airplanes, warships, or other vessels owned or operated by a state and involved in "government non-commercial service" (Article 236). Thus, Canada has no jurisdiction over foreign vessels operating for their governments for military or research purposes or for the supplying of these vessels. Canada has hailed the Law of the Sea Treaty as formal international recognition of its jurisdiction over Arctic waters as provided under AWPPA. Unfortunately, the United States' refusal to sign the treaty greatly weakens the importance of the document for Canadian Arctic environmental regulation.

In the 1980's there is still confusion regarding international acceptance of the AWPPA and the United Nations Law of the Sea Convention. Canada maintains that the waters of the Northwest Passage are internal waters subject to complete Canadian sovereignty and regulation. Outside of the waters between the Arctic islands but within the Exclusive Economic Zone, Canada claims the right to enforce the Arctic Waters Pollution Prevention Act equally on all shipping under the terms of the Arctic clause of the Law of the Sea Convention. The rights of innocent passage are qualified by the requirement to meet Canadian environmental standards. The United States rejects Canadian jurisdiction, refuses to sign the Law of the Sea Convention, and declares the Northwest Passage an international strait where nations have the right to unhindered innocent passage. Canada has now drawn baselines around the islands and its claim is founded on the amorphous concept of historic title, that the waters historically have been assumed to be Canadian.

In this scenario, a number of problems are on the horizon. Enforcement of the AWPPA would be difficult in any instance where an American vessel chose to defy Canadian jurisdiction as did the *Manhattan*. The Canadian government presence in the North is so limited that Ottawa might not even be aware of the violation. Also, it is difficult to challenge the American claim that the Northwest Passage is an international strait when there appears to be no internationally recognized definition of what that term means. Canadian arguments have been presented that, as large parts of the passage are locked in landfast ice for so much of the year, the normal meaning of high seas and straits cannot be applied to it. In this case ice assumes a separate legal status from either land or water. Also, as Professor Donat Pharand had argued, "by no stretch of the imagination could the few foreign American crossings constitute sufficient use for commercial navigation to turn the Northwest Passage into an international strait."[9] Yet all these arguments remain an academic exercise given the American position in the world and the determination in Washington to defend vigorously its own interests. The voyage of the *Polar Sea* in the summer of 1985 is one example.

One of the strongest pressure groups for more stringent environmental regulation is the Inuit Circumpolar Conference, linking the Inuit of Greenland, Alaska, and Canada. Their aboriginal claims include the right to continue their traditional hunting on the sea ice in areas like the Northwest Passage where commercial shipping would chew up the ice. This is a unique problem for international law in determining the legitimacy of these competing claims to the sea lanes. To my knowledge there is no basis or precedent in international law for recognition of these traditional rights. Also, even if Canada or Greenland were to recognize their claims, could they enforce compliance by foreign ships when there is no basis for such claims in the wording of the Law of the Sea Convention? In the last decade the Inuit Circumpolar Conference has been steadily raising its political profile, which was clearly evident in the international media attention accorded the third conference at Frobisher Bay in July, 1983. Their strong views on the environment dominate the thinking of the newly autonomous government of Greenland, which achieved "home rule" in 1979. Although foreign and defence policy is reserved to Copenhagen under the new constitution, Greenland has not hesitated to come to Ottawa to lobby directly to stop projects like the Arctic Pilot Project when it opposes them. The Greenland officials stress that current international practices are totally inadequate and the tankers heading for the Northwest Passage will skirt the ice-free coastal waters of Greenland. They are much more radical than the Canadian government in their proposals for protecting the environment. Thus, the Canadian AWPPA is attacked by the United States from one direction and by Greenland from the opposite. The final land claims settlement with the Inuit of Canada will almost certainly have provisions to protect the sea ice and the marine environment, which will be added costs for international resource companies as well as further annoyance to the U.S. State Department.

In regard to the eastern Arctic, Canadian officials have had far fewer contacts with officials from Greenland than is the case in the west with their Alaskan counterparts. Canadian concerns were aroused in 1975 when the Danish government authorized a drilling program off the west coast of Greenland with only a very cursory regulatory structure in place. Danish policy placed full responsibility to plan for and to control a blowout or spill on the drilling company or partnership involved. However, under Danish law, the operator was responsible only as long as he remained on site. When he left his liability ended. Canadian officials were relieved when the drilling program lapsed without incident and then proceeded to approve permits for drilling on the Canadian side of the Davis Strait. In August, 1977, an interim Canada-Denmark Marine Pollution Contingency Plan was signed covering the waters of the Labrador Sea, Davis Strait, Baffin Bay, and Nares Strait. However, without any local coast guard on the Greenland side, the prime responsibility for immediate action would lie with Canadian men and equipment.

Many Inuit in Greenland fear that a major spill from the Canadian side would seriously harm their traditional hunting grounds. Canada has offered a liability regime with a ceiling of $20 million for compensation to Danish nationals for the results of any accidents originating in Canadian waters. In February, 1979, Canada agreed to finance the cleanup of spills within its waters, to recover funds for any direct damages, and to allow access to Canadian courts for the recovery of indirect costs (such as to fishermen).[10] While this agreement met with approval in Copenhagen, there is far less enthusiasm in Greenland, where the issue is not compensation but opposition in principle to the idea of drilling. Greenland is upset with the potential environmental impacts of marine drilling or even tanker traffic through its waters or those of Lancaster Sound. Its suspicion of the Canadian government is all the greater because of Canada's key role in northern oil exploration through the Crown corporation, Petro-Canada.

Another controversial area of the Arctic environment has been the

Beaufort Sea, where in 1976 Canada became the first nation to attempt exploratory offshore oil drilling in the pack ice of the Arctic Ocean. When cabinet approval was given on April 15, 1976, for drilling that summer, a formal U.S. State Department note requested a delay: there had not been formal public Environmental Impact Assessment (EIA) of the exploratory drilling; there was no adequate contingency planning in the event of a spill; and there was no liability regime for potential U.S. claimants. Ironically, after the rhetoric of the *Manhattan* incident, Canada now appeared to be neglecting the environment. Canada proceeded with drilling in 1976 and in each year since. Joint contingency planning was in place by 1977 with Canada establishing a response centre at Inuvik. But if a major oil spill or well blowout occurred during the short summer drilling season, it is impossible to know if containment and cleanup could be achieved *before* the return of the pack ice in October. The oil would pour out under the ice and be carried by the currents and the movement of the ice westward along the Yukon coast and then into Alaskan waters. Government structures are in place on both sides of the border to react to any oil spills and there has been good co-operation between officials in both countries. However, the physical problems of containment and cleanup are great, for existing booms, skimmers, and dispersants require open water free of pack ice.

A further complication for drilling and environmental regulation in the Beaufort Sea remains the disputed offshore boundary. Canada claims that the land boundary between the Yukon and Alaska along the 141st meridian extends due north from the coast, reflecting the sector theory that appears to have influenced so much of Canadian thinking. The line proposed by the United States follows an arc further east, thus cutting into the area claimed by Canada and creating a disputed zone. The American contention is based on the principle of equidistance and therefore reflects the contours of the coast. As the coast angles northward and westward at the border, the American line swings eastward (into territory claimed by Canada) until the influence of Banks Island comes into play and the line then swings westward, crossing the 141st meridian approximately 200 miles offshore. By this point the area is covered by permanent pack ice and is currently of little economic significance.[11]

In proclaiming the Exclusive Economic Zone and the Arctic Waters Pollution Prevention Act, Canada had assumed that its case would be accepted and that its jurisdiction went right to the 141st meridian; Ottawa even issued leases for petroleum drilling in the disputed zone to companies, including its own Petro-Canada.[12] Some Canadians have implied that their case is based on the Anglo-Russian Treaty of 1825, which the United States assumed through its purchase of Alaska in 1867. This point is of dubious historic validity given that there was no concept of jurisdiction over the continental shelf in 1825, let alone any interest in it by either party. The 1977 International Court decision on the North Sea Continental Shelf Cases noted that one of the four possible methods for delimiting the jurisdictional boundaries involved was "the continuation in the seaward direction of the land frontier."[13] Yet the basic fact is that the sector theory has never been recognized in international law. One of the leading Canadian authorities in international law put it bluntly: "the sector theory has no validity as a legal root of title, whether it be in respect of land or water, and Canada would be well advised to abandon any hope of gaining legal support from the theory . . . with respect to jurisidictional claims in the arctic."[14]

At this point in mid-1985 there does not appear to be any resolution of the Beaufort Sea boundary dispute in sight, even though the principle of equidistance has been employed by Canada in negotiations with Greenland and in the Gulf of Maine, where the United States has rejected it.[15] The current Canadian Beaufort drilling may help to show whether or not there is any chance of oil in the disputed zone. Also, if Canada successfully develops the costly technology required for offshore oil production, it will be of immense benefit to the Americans for future marine production off Prudhoe Bay. If, however, there is a massive oil spill in Canadian waters it will trigger environmental controversy in the U.S. that will make it all the more difficult for any American administration to proceed further with its own offshore plans. Initially, the Arctic Waters Pollution Prevention Act did not provide any means for Americans to be compensated in the event of a Canadian blowout, but Ottawa has now made changes to try to meet these concerns.

In the eastern Arctic the marine boundary with Greenland has been almost completely defined on the principles of equidistance. The two exceptions involve the northern extension of the line out into the Lincoln Sea (which has still to be negotiated) and Hans Island, lying at latitude 80° 49' north in the Nares Strait, perfectly on the median line between Ellesmere Island and Greenland. This small uninhabited island about one mile long was claimed by both countries so the decision was made to draw the boundary up to the low water mark at the south end of the island and recommence it at the low water mark at the north end. Hans Island thus remains in dispute, the only example of disputed land sovereignty in the Canadian Arctic.[15]

Inevitably, marine boundary issues have increased greatly in political importance with the recent growing realization of the mineral and petroleum potential. Coupled with these issues has been the rising controversy in Washington about the drive to Canadianize the oil industry that emerged with the announcement of the National Energy Program (NEP) in October, 1980. This was the most radical change in the history of Canadian energy policy. The NEP was designed to divert oil and gas exploration to the northern and offshore frontiers; to increase the level of Canadian ownership and control; and to divert significant economic rents from the producing provinces and the corporations to the federal coffers. It was bitterly attacked by western provinces and the multinational oil companies, the full discussion of which lies outside the scope of this volume. But the NEP northern incentives became a serious irritant in Canadian-American relations, which is central to this chapter. The Reagan administration viewed it as a deliberate attack on American-owned interests in Canada, which, along with the Foreign Investment Review Agency (FIRA), was the focus for American attacks. Washington demanded that Canada revert to its traditional open-door policy that had allowed the foreign-owned majors to capture such a dominant position in the Canadian industry. The Trudeau administration viewed this pressure as an open challenge to Canadian economic sovereignty and its own moderate goal of 50 per cent Canadian ownership of the petroleum industry by 1990.

When the new Republican administration took over in Washington in January, 1981, it injected a new ideological intensity into foreign policy as well as a dogmatic support for American economic interests around the world and a free-enterprise fundamentalism. Within the inner group, no individual showed close knowledge of the Canadian scene such as Vice-President Walter Mondale had shown within the Carter administration. Many of the oil companies who had financed the Reagan victory now expected action to defend their vested interests in Canada. At the same time, several United States oil companies were facing takeovers at home from Canadian interests financed by the Canadian banks operating under regulations not allowed in the United States, which only increased the levels of controversy. At a time when the foreign ownership of the American oil industry stood at about 18 per cent and yet Americans were very sensitive about Canadian takeovers, Ottawa could not understand the American opposition to its own goal of 50 per cent domestic ownership. But the Americans saw the NEP as part of a worldwide pattern of attack on American interests that must be boldly confronted, especially in their own backyard north of the border.[16]

The specific provisions of the NEP were clearly designed to discriminate in favour of Canadian companies and to promote exploration on federal lands north of 60° or the East Coast offshore. Under the PIP grants, a company with 65 per cent or more Canadian ownership would qualify for government support totalling 80 per cent of its exploration costs on federal land while a foreign-owned firm could only recover 25 per cent of its approved costs. These new grants were to replace the depletion allowances, which were a deduction from corporate income taxes. The previous system of fiscal incentives had greater tax advantages for the large, integrated oil companies with extensive downstream profits in refining and marketing as opposed to the smaller Canadian exploration firms. The NEP also included a variety of other regulatory features to achieve the 50 per cent goal. In the event of a major oil discovery the Crown retained the right to a 25 per cent working interest in the field and could exercise this option right up until the field went into production. Although this "back-in" provision was denounced as anti-American and confiscatory in Washington, it applied equally to all companies; in fact, it had the most serious implications for Dome Petroleum with its Beaufort discoveries. The result of the American protests was that Ottawa modified its policy, agreeing to make "ex gratia" payments when exercising its option. In turn, these were denounced as merely token payments unrelated to the asset value of the discovery. Ottawa, however, replied that as the owner of the resource and the provider of the PIP grants, the Canadian public had a right to a share of the production revenue. Also, once in, Petro-Canada would be responsible for its full share of the heavy capital costs of the production facilities, which were normally too great in the Beaufort for any one company to shoulder alone.

When a company wished to convert an exploration lease into a production agreement, the new regulations required that the company or joint venture have a minimum of 50 per cent Canadian ownership. Under the new Canadian Oil and Gas Lands Administration (COGLA) all companies had to renegotiate their existing leases, returning 50 per cent of the land to the Crown. This was designed to open up the huge areas of the North already under lease to the majors but not being actively explored. New regulations were established to require high levels of Canadian content for future Arctic mega-projects while Canadian-owned firms were promised preferential treatment in the awarding of new gas export contracts, an important source for cash flow to finance frontier exploration. Finally, a special tax was placed at the wellhead (the Petroleum and Gas Revenue Tax) to tap production revenues at the source, thus funding the PIP grants and other federal initiatives. A consumer products tax on gasoline and fuel oil helped to finance the takeovers of Petrofina and BP assets by Petro-Canada.

Although none of the large American companies were subject to public-sector takeovers, they objected vigorously to the whole system of increased public ownership and government regulation, claiming that the asset value of their companies decreased under the NEP and that with time they might be forced to sell out at "fire-sale" prices to Canadian buyers. In fact, the takeovers that did take place were all accomplished at a heavy cost to the Canadian purchasers, for the value of the shares was bid up to premium levels by the market forces on the stock exchange. When the world oil prices declined in the following months, the asset value of the properties purchased declined while the revenues declined for both industry and government. The net result of the new fiscal incentives was that foreign-controlled companies like Imperial Oil now sought "farm-outs" or joint ventures with smaller Canadian companies.[17] Many of these Canadian companies did not have the financial resources or the land position (leases) to allow them to participate on their own in the Arctic.

Another factor in the Canadian-American feud on the NEP was the issue of Canadian content in the large northern mega-projects such as the Alaska Highway Pipeline and the Arctic Pilot Project. In the past, most of these huge projects had been constructed by American contracting firms such as Bechtel, which had a built-in bias for American suppliers it was used to dealing with.[18] The government was determined that these industrial spinoffs be captured for Canadians as part of its industrial strategy and its battle against rising unemployment. Thus, a Major Projects Task Force of business and labour leaders was established to propose new policy initiatives. Headed up by Bob Blair, president of Nova, and Shirley Carr, executive vice-president of the Canadian Labour Congress, they tackled directly the supply/procurement problem. Their report stressed that out of the $1 trillion Canada would need for capital investment by the year 2000, $440 billion would be required to finance mega-projects. Procurement policies were needed to ensure that Canadian suppliers would achieve their maximum potential in spite of the traditional patterns of supply from the United States. Their recommendations were translated into a series of guidelines in Bill C-48, the Canadian Oil and Gas Act, and the establishment of the Office of Industrial and Regional Benefits to monitor compliance. The United States protested strongly that this bill was a form of disguised protectionism, for the Canadian bids did not even have to be competitive. Ottawa amended the legislation to include the word competitive and pointed out the frequency of "Buy

America" clauses in American legislation. Washington remained convinced that U.S. companies would lose their traditional position of dominance as suppliers to these large projects and warned the Trudeau government that it would monitor future tendering and procurement practices to ensure that American companies were given equal opportunity in Canada.[19]

In its communications with Canada, the Reagan administration clearly expressed its profound displeasure with Canadian energy policy.

> We cannot, however, continue simply to discuss matters without substantial movement both on the FIRA and on the NEP. . . . We are most concerned about the following discriminatory and inequitable measures associated with the operation of the FIRA and the NEP. . . . It is most important that the first two practices [of FIRA] be eliminated and that the others [of FIRA and NEP] be eliminated or modified as appropriate.

This was exceedingly harsh language to use in a diplomatic note to an ally and trading partner. The specifics of the NEP that Washington demanded to be changed included: exemption from the "back-in" for existing exploration leases; asset value payments for "back-in"; end of the discrimination in the awarding of PIP grants; end of the 50 per cent Canadian ownership requirement for production licences; and Canadian ownership preference for future natural gas export licences. These would have gutted the whole program and Ottawa refused to consider the American position as a legitimate request of one sovereign nation to another. However, Canada did make several small concessions, and in the following months Washington toned down its rhetoric while maintaining the protests. It must have realized that it had badly overplayed its hand.[20]

In June, 1983, Secretary of State Shultz returned to the offensive on the NEP with a strongly worded note of protest delivered by U.S. Ambassador Paul Robinson directly to Allan MacEachen, the Minister of External Affairs. Shultz described the 25 per cent back-in as confiscatory and threatened that unless changed it could lead to a "major issue in Canadian-American relations." The Secretary of State went on to claim that this provision was a breach of international law, which the U.S. might take to the International Court of Justice at the Hague. Shultz included in his communication a thirty-five-page written opinion from a leading Washington lawyer who frequently acted for the majors. Cecil Olmstead's study concluded that the back-in violates international law and unless directly challenged could be followed by similar action by other nations.[21] The Shultz letter worried officials in Ottawa because it appeared that for the first time the American Secretary of State was becoming directly involved in the dispute with Canada, unlike Alexander Haig, his predecessor.[22] Given the importance of Shultz's position with the President, this was viewed as an escalation of the crisis. It appeared also that the Americans had been encouraged by the events at the Progressive Conservative Party convention two weeks earlier, when Brian Mulroney had attacked the NEP and promised to abolish the back-in provisions to improve relations with the United States. All this was happening at a time when the majors were no longer attacking the back-in provision because it could be replaced by higher royalties or other measures, which in the long term could prove more costly. Petro-Canada was now accepted as a legitimate partner in the costly northern joint ventures; in fact, government involvement helped to reassure the investment community that the project would proceed with all dispatch and with a minimum of government regulatory interference. But this growing pragmatism within industry clashed with the ideological purity of the Reagan administration and some politicians on both sides of the border.

By the summer of 1983 the PIP grants were flowing north to promote petroleum exploration. But the costs of the Beaufort wells were rising so rapidly that danger signs for the program were on the horizon. The issue of inflated costs came out into the open when Canterra (controlled by the federal government) refused to pay its share of a joint venture with Gulf Oil, which was charging its partners very high rates for use of its expensive drilling equipment. Canterra claimed that Canmar (Dome's drilling subsidiary) could do the job for half the price charged by Gulf and had the equipment available to do it. Yet Canterra's involvement was critical to Gulf for it to achieve the necessary Canadian Ownership Rating (COR) to qualify for the PIP grants.

Federal officials had been growing increasingly alarmed at the ever-increasing size of the payments while revenues were eroded by weak oil prices and fiscal concessions to industry.[23] To bring some order and control back into the system, the PIP regulations were changed in the summer of 1983 so that all wells over $50 million required individual ministerial approval to ensure their costs were competitive. After the election of the new Conservative government in 1984, the whole system was reassessed in the light of this experience and of the new government's greater concern for its relations with the United States.

In 1985 the Mulroney government moved to respond to the American protests. The Minister of Energy, Pat Carney, announced the phasing out of the PIP grants over several years, to be replaced by a return to a system of depletion allowances (tax deductions for explo- ration work). Also eliminated was the infamous 25 per cent back-in clause and some of the other Canadianization features that had pro- voked the American outrage. The drive for frontier exploration and Canadianization was now put on the back burner; without the huge government PIP grants, exploration plans for the Beaufort were reas- sessed and in some cases abandoned. Gulf put its new equipment up for sale and Dome tried to rent drillships to American companies operating off Alaska. With weak world oil prices and new priorities in Ottawa the downturn in Beaufort activities is assured for the rest of the 1980's.

During the Trudeau years northern energy policies were a major factor in Canadian-American relations. The National Energy Program was designed to Canadianize the oil industry and the Reagan admin- istration was determined to stop it. With southern conventional oil reserves declining since 1972, it was Ottawa's great hope that "ele- phants" would be found in the Beaufort and the eastern offshore to replace the Alberta conventional reserves. The Trudeau government was determined to see the production from these new fields largely in the hands of Canadian companies, and this would have a profound impact on the whole ownership structure of the industry. If Canadians were to pay the bulk of the costs of Arctic offshore production through PIP grants, they should have a majority stake in the profits and control of the patents in the event they could be used under licence by the Americans or the Russians. The NEP was a tough game of power politics where there was clear and deliberate discrimination in favour of the Canadian companies.

With the Conservative government, the balance has now fallen back in favour of the majors. But the Mulroney government can only go so far before it will suffer the same kind of political damage as befell C.D. Howe in 1956. The Canadian public does not share the same perception of continentalism as the majors operating in Canada. As one American oil executive explained to the author: "Part of our great annoyance with the NEP is that we have *never* treated Canada as a foreign country." Like Alaska, it was just another northern territory. After working for years to see the expansion of their Canadian op- erations, they resented the sudden emergence of Dome, Petro-Can- ada, and other Canadian companies through government intervention. With the overall American economic position in the world declining, many Americans felt they must now fight to protect their vested eco- nomic interests, and nowhere more so than in Canada, where they already possess great influence. Many Canadians, however, who see their own policies as much more moderate than such oil producers as Norway, cannot understand or accept the ideological intensity of the American response. Irrespective of the friendly platitudes of Brian Mulroney, sooner or later he will have to come to understand that fundamental Canadian economic interests will have to be sacrificed to continue his present policies. The reality of the Canadian-American relationship is the sharply protectionist forces in Congress who are determined to reverse the American decline. They have no interest in giving anyone "the benefit of the doubt," as Mulroney did as Opposition Leader at the time of the American invasion in Grenada, and they see great opportunities in exploiting the new philosophy in Ottawa.

The military and strategic significance of the Arctic waters has been steadily rising in the last decade. Concern has grown in NATO circles about the increasing naval and military strength of the Soviet forces based in the Kola Peninsula just over 1,000 miles from Ellesmere Island across the Arctic Ocean. In 1981 it was the base for the largest and most powerful Soviet surface fleet, 130 attack submarines (including 70 per cent of ballistic missile capability), as well as aircraft and missile installations. It is only 180 miles by sea to the cover of the Arctic ice pack, which allows submarines to roam across the Arctic into Canadian or American waters.[24] The Soviet Union, with its interests in Arctic offshore oil and fisheries, recognized much earlier than the West the strategic significance of the Arctic areas and became the world leader, with nuclear icebreakers and other northern technology. Its current dispute with Norway over their joint activities in the Svalbard Archipelago is one example of Soviet concerns. Fisheries, in fact, have been an explosive issue in the North Atlantic in the last decade, with incidents such as the Cod War between Britain and Iceland, both members of NATO.

Similarly, the U.S. Air Force base at Keflavik, which monitored Soviet naval activities in the North Atlantic, became the centre of political controversy and anti-American feelings within Icelandic politics. Using the threat of closing the U.S. base and withdrawing from NATO, the Icelandic government won its battle to control its offshore fisheries. Here the linkage between resources and essential security services was one that both Britain and the United States were forced to accept. Former Secretary of State Henry Kissinger later remarked bitterly: "That little tableau in the town hall of Reykjavik – the beseeching superpower, the turbulent tiny country threatening to make war against a nation 250 times its size and to leave NATO . . . said volumes about the contemporary world and of the tyranny that the weak can impose upon it."[25] Now, in the 1980's, the U.S. battle to retain its bases may shift from Iceland to Greenland.

As the world's largest island, Greenland has important resource and strategic significance even though most of the land is covered by the massive ice cap. From 1721 to 1953 the island was a Danish colony; then, from 1953 to 1979, it became an integral part of the Danish kingdom; and finally, since 1979, it has enjoyed home rule with a local assembly. Greenland possesses important mineral deposits that are exploited by such foreign companies as Canadian Pacific. Politically, there is some interest in Greenland in withdrawing from the European community, restricting the American use of the base at Thule, and assuming a neutralist position outside of NATO. Yet Greenland's importance to NORAD and NATO cannot be underestimated given the North Atlantic and circumpolar threats. It is the eastern end of the DEW line radar system currently being refurbished as well as of the Ballistic Missile Early Warning System (BMEWS). If, for political reasons, the American military presence faced future limitations, the adjacent areas of the Canadian High Arctic, such as Ellesmere Island, would take on a totally new strategic significance to military planners in Washington.

In addition, with the United States proceeding with its cruise missile program, there will be increased need for manned bomber bases in the Arctic, low-level specialized radar facilities, and training missions by bomber crews learning to hug the northern landscape.[26] There are also increasing American worries about the Soviet submarine threat to North America. The Soviet Typhoon-class submarines are now operational with the capability of lengthy submerged patrols under the Arctic ice pack and of firing long-range nuclear missiles through several metres of ice.[27] Hence, with the increased submarine and low-level missile threats, Greenland and the Canadian High Arctic islands will play a critical role in overall NATO and NORAD strategy. The American pressure for cruise missile testing in northern Canada may be only the first of a whole series of "requests" for increased American military presence in Canada.

These strategic assumptions can be documented from the writings of American security experts. Lincoln Bloomfield, former member of the U.S. National Security Council, explained the changing American interest in the Canadian Arctic:

> U.S. strategic interests in the Canadian north declined in the 1960's when the ICBM's emerged as the chief strategic threat to the U.S. mainland. Even with a suspected refueling capability for the new Soviet Backfire medium bomber, it seems unlikely that Washington will revive its languishing air defense preparations against potential Soviet bombing attacks. But a new Soviet strategic bomber or Soviet

ALCM (air-launched cruise missile) might generate a whole new air defense program. The enormous Canadian Arctic still provides a precious cushion of time and space to deal with incoming hostile objects well before they could reach American cities, substantially enhancing U.S. defense.[28]

The reality of such a Soviet cruise missile is clear as Moscow scrambles to counter the American cruise program. The Pentagon is also concerned to devise naval defence barriers to thwart Soviet submarines from launching missiles from Canadian Arctic waters. Hudson Bay, for instance, is considered to be dangerously close to the industrial heartland of the United States. This fact is likely to cause even greater American pressure to open up our North for the "common" defence of the continent.

These changes in strategic thinking do not mean that Canadian bargaining power with the U.S. will suddenly increase or that Washington will be more grateful to Canada. To quote Bloomfield again: "The unhappy recent shift in U.S.-Canadian relations to an abrasive and more openly resented dependency relationship is at least somewhat exacerbated by the U.S. strategic perception of Canada as a useful polar barrier against trajectories of weapons targeted on the United States which cross Canadian territory. Put differently, Americans sometimes seem to look straight through Canada as they peer across the arctic at the U.S.S.R."

In fact, security worries may make Washington officials even more determined to get Canada clearly into line through not only the use of territory but financial contributions on a scale as never before. Canada has been taken for granted with its small and ineffective role in NORAD and there is little chance that this attitude will change. Although a few Americans have recognized the problem and are concerned about the future, their writings appear to have evoked no official response: "The fact that only a few Americans are even aware of such sensitivities constitutes the unkindest cut of all for our northern neighbour. Impending developments in the arctic are likely to sharpen rather than dampen Canadian resentment of the perceived American mix of power and indifference."[29] These two factors – American power and indifference – together constitute the essence of the Canadian sense of frustration in dealing with the United States even though they are a natural product of the unequal position of the two nations in much the same fashion as Finland and the Soviet Union.

In the current circumstances there is an acute need for international co-operation in scientific and technological research. Although there have been sporadic efforts for decades, too much of it has been dependent on the "old boy" network of personal friendships, easily disrupted by government financial restraints or Cold War pressures. Even the co-operation between the United States and Canada has been limited by such factors as American security concerns, which stopped the flow of the *Manhattan* ice data. There is considerable potential here for future expansion, especially with the Nordic countries. Sharing of weather data is one critical area of science with clear pragmatic benefits to all countries involved. Also, out of the research links may come important multilateral agreements such as the Polar Bear Treaty of 1973 signed by the United States, the Soviet Union, Canada, Denmark, and Norway. It would seem that a co-ordinated international research program to develop the technology for oil-spill containment and cleanup is essential now that most of the Arctic nations have begun marine drilling in areas of seasonal pack ice. Canada and the United States have developed excellent bilateral relations among officials involved with the Beaufort Sea,[30] but the techniques are still totally inadequate to cope with the nature of the oil-spill problem in pack ice.[31] International co-operation with the Soviet Union was limited even before the Afghanistan invasion; but since then it has become almost non-existent, certainly in terms of North America. Science, like the Olympics, can be highly politicized.

The last decade has seen the North emerge as a fundamental new component for Canadian foreign policy. With the *Manhattan* and *Polar Sea* voyages Canadians were made aware that their traditional complacency constituted a serious menace, for technological change and resource scarcity were ending the isolation of the Arctic. As the first chapter in this book has shown, the North has contributed emotional ingredients to the Canadian identity that are now thrown into doubt. Recently, as Peter Dobell stressed: "The arctic became a kind of test of Canada's resolve to hold onto its birthright."[32] This defensive response must now be channelled into more positive and creative multilateral efforts. We will achieve our goals with the United States only if wider international support can be mobilized, as was done with the Law of the Sea. To our advantage, profound changes are under way right across the Arctic, and these are affecting all nations. We must recognize and seek to mobilize the emerging international concerns that Dosman and others have drawn attention to. "An embryonic international sub-system is in the process of formation in the circumpolar north which requires continuous, rather than sporadic, monitoring. In other words, Canada requires a northern foreign policy and a coherent set of policy instruments for its effective implementation."[33] As a precondition for this initiative, Canada must sort out its own priorities with regard to domestic northern policy. Links to the United States draw us toward a pro-development stance; links to Greenland and the Inuit Circumpolar Conference push us toward a conservationist/environmentalist approach.

In approaching this joint problem of defining a domestic policy to create a foundation for a foreign policy, Canada would be wise to study the efforts of Norway to develop its "Nordpolitik." Norway has jurisdictional disputes with the Soviet Union over the Svalbard Archipelago and the Barents Sea involving fisheries, minerals, and petroleum exploration. Norway is a member of NATO but has no allied troops or nuclear weapons on its soil. In 1981, Johan Holst, the Norwegian State Secretary for the Ministry of Foreign Affairs, defined his country's position in the following manner: "The overall objective . . . is to develop a framework for a stable order in the high North based on a balance of power maintained at the lowest possible level of military activity, and a pattern of cooperation which cuts across and reduces the saliency of the military competition. This is the essence of the Norwegian 'Nordpolitik' which may become an important element in the broader construction of East-West relations in Europe in the 1980's."[34]

A balance of power at the lowest level of military activity, plus economic, scientific, and environmental co-operation, appears to be central to Canadian interests in the Arctic as well. Ottawa obviously has problems ahead with the United States (marine jurisdiction) and the Soviet Union (defence) so we must build new diplomatic bridges to Greenland, Iceland, and the Nordic countries that share many of our concerns. Nordic Europe and Iceland have followed a curious combination of alignment and non-alignment policies. Yet all these nations, including Finland, have demonstrated a commitment to regional stability that makes their area unique in the context of postwar East-West tensions. These are traditions Canada must seek to emulate and mobilize for the wider benefit of all other Arctic nations. Canada should take the initiative in hosting a circumpolar conference of the nations bordering on the Arctic Ocean, to include also Finland and Sweden. This would be a regular regional forum where international Arctic agreements could be discussed without the complications of the other 150 members of the United Nations and allowing the middle powers to exert some pressure collectively on the two superpowers.

The above is not meant to imply that the task will be easy, for there have been few past successes like the Polar Bear Treaty. Norway and the Soviet Union have serious differences in their northern seas, just as Canada and the United States have over the Northwest Passage.

Canada and Greenland have basic differences over tanker traffic in Baffin Bay and Davis Strait, as do Greenland and Norway on fisheries jurisdiction in the Jan Mayen zone. Over all these disputes hangs the bitter Cold War confrontation between the Soviet Union and the United States with its particular Arctic focus. Yet a joint initiative by Canada and one of the Nordic countries would be hard for Washington and Moscow to ignore. The propaganda value to the other would be too high. While the Brezhnev proposal for an Arctic nuclear-free zone was clearly one-sided, yet there are alternatives that countries such as Norway have explored that are far more balanced. If there is to be progress on this issue it must be now, before the full deployment of the rival fleets of cruise missiles and their launching bombers. It is certainly in Canada's interest to keep these bases out of its Arctic islands; unless some progress is made in arms limitations, though, there is little likelihood of the United States allowing Canada any option on this issue, as was the case with the cruise missile testing. A council of Arctic nations might help to put the bilateral talks between Washington and Moscow into a wider framework of debate and improve the chances of success.

As we move through the 1980's human activity in the Arctic will continue to increase and the flow of events will tend to follow one of two roads. Events will be dominated by the competitive economic and military rivalry of the current scene or by a more co-operative approach such as that illustrated by the Nordic countries. Canada, for the sake of its position in the world and for its own selfish interest, must work to see the success of the second option. We cannot become the armed buffer zone for the two feuding superpowers. That would be no future for the Arctic and its peoples.

CHAPTER 12

The Emerging North: Today and Tomorrow

The purpose of this book has been to probe the nature of the debate on northern development that has been raging in Canada since 1968. In this final chapter some of the themes of the last five chapters now need to be brought together to demonstrate the changing roles of the different actors in the last few years and to offer some projections for the future. The principal actors on the northern scene remain: the federal government; the territorial governments; the private-sector resource companies; the native organizations; and the public interest groups. In the period between 1974 and 1977 the policy process was a very public one with the hearings before Berger and the NEB. Environmental and native rights arguments were central to the decision-making. Since 1977 policy formulation has been a much more private in-house operation for government, and economic matters have been the greatest influence. In the mid-1970's northern megaprojects seemed inevitable; now, a decade later, they appear to be financially unsound with one or two relatively small-scale exceptions. Under the Mulroney Conservatives the pendulum has swung back to a more laissez-faire and pro-business philosophy from the strongly interventionist approach exhibited by policies like the National Energy Program. The one check on this process involves specific cabinet ministers in key portfolios. David Crombie as Minister of Indian and Northern Affairs and Tom McMillan as Minister of the Environment ensure that native and environmental concerns will be vigorously defended at the cabinet table.

With so many interests and actors involved, with so many agencies of government, the debate has been a complex and confusing one. This process will continue for many years because it concerns basic questions of economic power and the evolving nature of Canadian federalism. How is power to be shared among the federal ministries and between them and the territorial governments and the native organizations? The new constitution and the Charter of Rights and

Freedoms open the way for new legal avenues for redress. The move toward provincial status and the settling of land claims will entail great debate, and the solutions will involve new political forms that will complicate the policy process and government structures in the North. Given the ongoing debate with Quebec nationalism, Ottawa will be very sensitive about new northern initiatives. Also, discussion of power always involves emotions. Yet over the next decade the territorial assembly of the Northwest Territories will be pressing for greater powers and there will be some movement toward provincial status. But as with the early history of Alberta and Saskatchewan, the federal government will keep land and resources clearly within its own control. This policy will also complicate the negotiations on the land claims, for the Nunavut and Denendeh proposals assume control of resources within their own areas.

This three-way struggle among Ottawa, the territorial assembly, and the native groups will dominate the political affairs for the next few years in the N.W.T. North of the treeline, the Inuit will be working toward the creation of their own province; south and west of it, Dene, Métis, and white elements will be struggling to create new political forms. In the first, the Inuit have a clear majority of the population, while the white population is nearly equal to that of the Dene in the western Arctic. Overlapping with this process will be the land claims where both the Dene and Inuit have made only limited progress, and their political goals have been firmly rejected by Ottawa. There appears to be a growing consensus between the territorial assembly and the native organizations based on a common commitment to settling the land claims and common antagonism to the "colonialism" from Ottawa.

Interfering with any smooth transfer of power in the North is the continuing southern mythology about the region. Since the gold rush of the 1890's, Canadians have had difficulty viewing the North with detachment because their future hopes have always involved the exploitation of its resource riches. Yesterday it was the yellow gold of Bonanza Creek; today it is the black gold of the Beaufort Sea for profits, government revenue, and energy self-sufficiency. But there has always been an element of self-delusion in this northern vision. Our great expectations of northern wealth never seem to materialize, such as in 1920 with Norman Wells or in 1972 with the Delta discoveries. Possibly the same thing will happen with some of our current hopes. The pattern of stalled projects, so clear in the last decade, is a continuation of a long-term problem for northern development.

In retrospect, Canada has been fortunate that so many of these recent projects have been delayed or abandoned. An empty Mackenzie

Valley Pipeline would be an embarrassment to all and a serious financial loss to a great many Canadian companies. Yet in 1972 its construction seemed inevitable. Canada must use wisely this breathing space that economics has forced on us. In the lull before the development resumes we must upgrade our capability to cope with geotechnical problems such as permafrost; to unravel more of the mysteries of northern ecosystems; and to settle native land claims. The chances of a comprehensive and amiable settlement will be much higher if the negotiating environment is not poisoned by mega-projects about to be approved or even under construction. This scenario of impending and ongoing mega-projects is viewed by the native leaders as intimidation, and quite naturally it breeds militancy. Canada has been fortunate, as well, to have traditions of moderation among its native leaders. But this situation may change if the present generation of leaders cannot deliver some results. It is imperative that both sides proceed to serious bargaining before the next round of mega-project applications increases tensions. This is not only a matter of law and morality but of sound business sense, as Bob Blair's testimony to the NEB clearly showed.

The North has created many new stresses and strains, and considerable jockeying for power and jurisdiction, within the federal bureaucracy. As the last chapter showed, External Affairs and Defence are two departments whose northern profile is increasing and will continue to do so through the 1980's. Defence will undoubtedly be stepping up its physical presence as part of a rejuvenated NORAD and for a number of paramilitary functions related to sovereignty. External Affairs will be increasing the number of personnel working on northern foreign policy and diplomacy, especially in terms of rationalizing the conflicting international pressures from Greenland and the United States. Transport Canada and the Coast Guard will have new responsibilities especially when the Class VIII icebreaker is ready in the early 1990's. The current government views activity in the High Arctic as the means of establishing its claims to sovereignty.

This study has tried to show the many confusions and contradictions in federal northern policy. Many of the weaknesses in policy are a reflection of the structural weaknesses in government. Clearly, some changes are needed to meet the difficult challenges that lie ahead in the North. Nowhere is the confusion of priorities more obvious than in the structure of the Department of Indian and Northern Affairs. It is responsible for northern resource development, the trusteeship of native people, and the protection of the northern environment. Traditionally, the development concerns have tended to dominate policy at the expense of the other two. Also, in the never-ending political struggles between departments to control jurisdiction, Indian and Northern Affairs has lost some battles, particularly to Energy, Mines, and Resources. The time has come, I believe, for the abolition of the ministry. The mining, oil, and gas matters could be easily transferred to Energy, Mines, and Resources; environmental protection should be more properly handled by Environment Canada. In turn, there should be a new Ministry of Native Affairs, which could pursue its goals without the complications of economic development priorities. The native land claims negotiations make this portfolio a crucial one in the coming years and the minister should not be burdened with other responsibilities. Also, it may be necessary for the minister to confront directly the northern plans of Petro-Canada and Energy, Mines, and Resources. Major decisions like this should be argued out at the cabinet level, not buried internally within any single department. We need some new thinking within native policy and these structural changes might help to promote it.

Below the ministerial level, the stresses and strains in the regulatory process have been documented in the earlier chapters. At the National Energy Board, a number of internal organizational changes are required to reflect the current requirements of the Board's mandate. A fully staffed environmental and socio-economic section of the NEB is needed, especially for future hearings of northern projects, and one Board member should be appointed with a career background in these areas so that these issues are properly presented in the private deliberations of the Board at its weekly meetings. There have also been external structural problems involving the NEB's relations with the other arms of government. Here the interrelated issues of independence and accountability have taken on new meaning because of the expanding role of government in Canadian society. These issues have harmed the Board's credibility at the very time it is most needed. In the near future Canadians will have to face a number of hard truths about their energy scene, and because of the high level of public cynicism they will not take as seriously as they should any warnings the Board may issue.

The theory of regulatory boards like the NEB is that they provide an independent assessment of complex issues that is technically competent and free of partisan political considerations. They must adjudicate the conflicting claims of the various interest groups seeking to influence policy: corporations versus public interest groups; producers versus consumers; developers versus environmentalists; federal versus provincial; white versus native. They have the difficult job of defining the national interest. Yet the necessary independence and objectivity needed for the job have been strained by our own theory of government and its expanding role in society. Unlike the United States, we do not subscribe to the theory of the separation of the powers of government but to the unity and paramountcy of Parliament. Therefore, regulatory boards as they evolved in Canada entailed an internal contradiction. They were to be independent and yet they were also a part of the internal interdepartmental committee system to define policy. They have been both regulators and advisers. Hence, the NEB is not free of the policy web of the Department of Energy, Mines, and Resources, and its statements are expected to reflect the policy needs of the government in power. Any doubt on this point was exploded in October, 1980, when Marc Lalonde indicated to the House of Commons that he would overrule the NEB if approval was not granted to the Trans-Quebec and Maritime Pipeline. The Board quickly announced its willingness to hold hearings to reconsider its opposition to the project.[1] Parliament is supreme and all the minister is required to do is to suggest the passage of a bill to enforce his wishes. Although the Board is quasi-judicial it does not operate at arm's length, as do the courts.

A second area involving the issue of independence grew out of the steadily increasing government ownership stake in the oil and gas industry. As Petro-Canada and Canterra became larger and larger players on the northern energy scene, the question of the Board's objectivity came out into the open. How could the NEB and EARP deal impartially with competitive applications from these Crown corporations as opposed to those coming from private-sector companies such as Imperial and Shell. As Petro-Canada was the government's instrument for expanding its presence in the industry, it is hard to believe that it would not have hidden advantages when pleading a case before the NEB. The conflict of interest between the corporate and regulatory arms of government appeared to be clear. Each price increase approved by the NEB would bring additional revenue to the federal treasury. Given the levels of the federal deficit, this could be an inducement if and when markets and prices begin to firm.

If the NEB is to be free of these suspicions of conflict, it must be separated off as an independent regulatory tribunal, free of its policy advisory role within the ministry. Second, it should report regularly to Parliament and the relevant Commons committees. The current procedures are too superficial. Here the Board chairman would be subject to detailed questioning on the operations and the energy policy options proposed by the Board. Today, too few MPs have any serious knowledge of the Board's work or of the complex issues involved in energy policy. Currently, parliamentary committees are too restricted in their deliberations on energy policy and need new staff and powers, for the Board has been reluctant to promote discussion even of current policy. By having to answer about matters often not mentioned in its reports, the NEB would be adding to Parliament's assessment of energy options and increasing public accountability. The political climate of Canada in the 1980's would tend to suggest that important interests are pressing for deregulation of energy; they wish to cut back on the power of the NEB, not restructure its operations. Given the complex and conflicting interests involved in northern mega-projects, one can only hope that they fail. The lesson of the northern pipeline hearings is that it took great effort and time by the NEB and Berger to assess properly the technical, economic, and other issues. Deregulation will increase the chances of major mistakes in northern energy policy.

In the northern debate of the 1970's, the Berger Inquiry played a central role in raising fundamental issues and setting new standards for public participation. In his hearings, Berger demonstrated how funds for public intervenors could improve the whole hearing process. Although this lesson has had no impact on the NEB, it has been taken up at a number of provincial and federal regulatory hearings. His report is a remarkable document for the philosophy of decision-making it expounds. For the first time in Canadian history a major project was stopped for environmental and social reasons. Also, his two major conclusions are important precedents. In recommending a prohibition of development across the North Slope of the Yukon and the western fringe of the Delta, he concluded that this was an area where mitigative measures were not enough to preserve environmental standards. This was "critical habitat" where disturbance could not be tolerated. Here he accepted the environmental evidence of the public interest groups and the native people while rejecting that of the consultants of the applicant. In the Mackenzie Valley itself he found that a pipeline could be built, provided proper environmental safeguards were scrupulously observed. But due to the nature of the land claims negotiations and the critical state of Dene and Inuit society, there should be a ten-year moratorium on pipeline construction to allow for a just and proper settlement. These claims were of greater consequence to Canada than was immediate access to Delta gas.

The revolutionary thing about the Berger Report was that it put environmental and social values on an equal plane with the economic considerations. This was profoundly unsettling for many in business and government, for they feared that the arguments Berger had put forward could influence future policy as well as stimulate opposition to other Arctic mega-projects. On the policy side their fears have proved groundless, for the two principal recommendations discussed above have both been breached: the ten-year moratorium by the Norman Wells Pipeline and the prohibition on development on the North Slope by Gulf's need for port facilities along that coast, probably to be located at King Point. Berger and his report diverted the pipeline to the Alaska Highway corridor but he did not create a new environmental regime in the North. In an informal sense he did increase the environmental and social awareness within the federal regime, but it is difficult to find significant policy or process changes as a result of the report.

Many officials in Ottawa found the Berger Inquiry a trying experience they do not wish to see ever repeated. Berger, through his use of the media and his direct access to cabinet, was beyond their control. He promoted expectations among native people, which they believed were unrealistic and harmful to the native land claims negotiations. In their view (as outlined in the Drury Report) they wanted the negotiations confined to a narrow legal definition of the issues under dispute. The Berger Report gave credence to the wider political claims and therefore increased the problems of negotiation. The bureaucrats were also concerned about his efforts to force the public disclosure of internal government research reports. He forced their hand for his own hearings but they succeeded in ensuring that this was a "one-shot" deal not applicable to any other hearing. This was closely in line with their efforts to change the proposed public information act.

In any comparison of the procedures of the Berger Inquiry and the NEB, certain conclusions are evident from the basic statistics regarding the source of evidence heard.[2]

	Berger Inquiry	NEB
Corporate applicants	48%	80%
Native groups	20	1
Berger/NEB counsel	17	0
Public interest groups	12	6
Producers/distributors	0	8
Other	3	4

The Berger Inquiry was far less dominated by the evidence of the corporate applicants and allies; had far more input from native and environmental groups; and allowed commission counsel to sponsor their own witnesses in areas where they considered the record incomplete or contradictory. The strengths of the public inquiry method are evident from the above statistics; when not intimidated by a process, people are more likely to appear. It has often been charged that the National Energy Board has become the prisoner of the industry it is legislated to regulate. This is not true in any direct sense, as the Arctic Gas and other decisions demonstrate. However, it is clearly influenced by the fact that most of the professionally prepared evidence presented in its hearings is from industry spokesmen and this process over time has a conditioning effect on its own thinking irrespective of its own staff research. It must make its decisions on the basis of the evidence presented to it. As a result it tends to reflect industry opinion except in those areas where government policy itself is taking an independent line. The continuous changes in gas export policy in the years between 1978 and 1985 are clear evidence of the success of industry pressures in gradually forcing changes.

Many environmentalists assumed that the EARP process of the federal government would pick up where Berger left off. Over the last decade this office has gradually gained momentum and evolved procedures to allow for public input. The 1982 Beaufort Sea Oil Production Panel was a distinct improvement over earlier efforts, with panel members from outside government and public funding of intervenors. However, the EARP process is not mandatory but subject to departmental and ministerial discretion in terms of when it is applied or whether its recommendations are accepted. EARP needs to be broadened in its scope and made mandatory, as John Fraser suggested when he was Environment Minister. It needs to be given an independent agency status (like the NEB) and its operations entrenched through statute, which would open the way for court challenges if it neglected its powers. Currently, it is subject to discretionary control by ministers and to political influences that inhibit effective environmental assessment and review for policy purposes. At first, everyone was concerned to limit its powers until it had built up its experienced personnel; now, after a decade, it should be granted a clear regulatory role with defined powers and responsibilities. Many in the North are particularly concerned that the military must be subject to environmental regulations irrespective of their special status.

From an environmental point of view the one overriding fear of business, government, and northern native people is a major oil spill from a well blowout or a tanker accident. There are not only the problems in getting equipment quickly on the scene; but in areas of pack ice like the Beaufort Sea the problems are almost insuperable. This is one of a number of cases in Arctic development where the current levels of technology are quite inadequate to cope with the physical reality of the North. Both government and industry have invested heavily in research through programs like AMOP, but we are in no way even close to adequate solutions. Yet the alternative, to close down Arctic offshore drilling in the Beaufort until satisfactory measures are in place, is politically unacceptable to government. So we proceed on the basis of bluff and a gamble that no major oil spill will occur until we have the means to cope. Further, Ottawa is subsidizing this drilling to the tune of billions of dollars because of the private-sector risk involved. These are the type of cruel trade-offs we face in the Arctic, where the costs and the risks are high, and where to a greater extent than in the south the instincts of the gambler are an integral part of the public policy process.

The public interest groups over the last decade have argued that the energy savings from an extensive conservation program would more than equal the additional energy supply from Arctic pipelines. Especially in the early 1980's, during a time of recession, it seemed obvious that labour-intensive conservation schemes would have economic advantages over capital-intensive Arctic mega-projects, especially if it is government policy to restrain inflation. The stresses and strains that mega-projects can place on the capital markets and monetary policy of the country have been discussed in Chapter 10. Dr. David Brooks, in a study for the Economic Council of Canada, tried to assess the importance of the scope of the capital requirements. "This would require that the share of annual capital investment in new energy sources rise some 40% or 50% over what it was on the average in the period since 1950. Similarly, the share of domestic borrowing from Canadian savings that is allocated to energy will have to increase from around 8% to 18%." There is certainly some doubt about our ability to achieve a smooth transfer of these economic resources and still keep in place our current industrial and social policies. An Energy, Mines, and Resources study, which argued that the capital could be found, also assumed that there would be a relative decline in the level of social expenditure in Canada.[3] As the average age of Canadians is increasing, the levels of unemployment are exceedingly high, and social programs are politically difficult to dismantle, this conclusion is open to serious doubt. Northern mega-projects, because of their size, inevitably raise this issue of capital availability and opportunity cost. Yet the NEB has never done a serious study of this critical issue.

In its report on northern pipelines, the Board acknowledged that some intervenors had pressed strongly for an initiative on conservation. It even admitted that "conservation appears to offer the lowest cost option for balancing the energy budget in the near term" while frontier supplies would still be needed over the long term. The Board, however, was not prepared to limit supplies to force conservation, as some individuals had suggested. "Changes normally proceed more slowly than some elements in society wish, and the Board under the

National Energy Board Act clearly has no mandate to force changes."[4] Under the Act, the Board is permitted to recommend to government any proposals it considers to be in the public interest. However, the Board obviously is reluctant to take a controversial stand that may be in advance of public opinion and complicate its relations with the minister.

In the various regulatory formats, Canadian public interest groups have come of age in the last decade. They have been responsible for much of the increased consideration of environmental and social impacts. The National Energy Board noted the "major contribution" they had made in cross-examination of witnesses and in the presentation of evidence. "The decision and the reasons on which it is based would surely have been less comprehensive and might have been different" had not such a thorough discussion of the issues taken place. The public interest groups were also commended for their role in raising the level of public knowledge about northern concerns.[5] These comments were a recognition of the role the public interest groups had played in the hearings even if the Board remained staunchly committed to its position on public funding. By 1982 EARP had bowed to public pressure and had arranged funding for the Beaufort Sea public interest coalition. After an auspicious start, government cutbacks led to an ending of the public funding and the exodus of the public interest groups from the hearings. There was no major public response when this occurred.

In the years since 1977 the public interest groups have declined in number and influence. Many of their leading people fled to government or the universities to earn an adequate salary, and fewer individuals have been moving up to take their place. The universities are no longer the breeding ground for young activists that they were a decade ago. CARC continues its extensive efforts at research and public education but its conference in June, 1983, at Yellowknife was not nearly as great a success as its earlier ones. Industry and government were well represented but only a corporal's guard of *young* activists were present. The public interest groups, such principal actors in the events of the mid-1970's, now appear to be pushed into the wings. The most dedicated activists appear to have swung back to the antinuclear movement and away from northern environmental concerns.

One of the serious corporate criticisms of the Berger-NEB decision-making on northern pipelines was that there was no early warning system to Arctic Gas before it spent over $150 million on its application. A number of individuals in business and the current chairman of the NEB have suggested that the Board Act might be revised to allow approval-in-principle before a company went ahead to invest the large sums on the detailed environmental research. Geoffrey Edge stressed: "More and more companies are refusing to spend many millions of dollars preparing applications for public hearings without getting some indication that it is worthwhile to continue to spend money on delineating the more detailed aspects of the proposals" in case they may be rejected "for non-environmental reasons."[6]

While such procedural changes might speed up the process and limit the costs of unsuccessful applicants, this would seem to suggest that you can separate the environmental issues from the geotechnical and the economic. This present study, however, clearly demonstrates that this compartmentalization is not possible if regulatory boards are to do a proper job. Without the detailed environmental analysis from the Berger Inquiry, the NEB would not have understood the technical weaknesses of the deep burial design and the additional capital costs of several hundred millions. Another problem is the phenomenon of momentum. Once approval-in-principle is given it will be that much more difficult for any regulatory board to reject it later. Compartmentalization of approvals could weaken the whole process.

Earlier in this book I discussed at some length the upsurge of intellectual nationalism in Canada in the early 1970's. The real significance of the pipeline debate was not that the intellectual nationalists stopped the Arctic Gas consortium with its American links but that the new corporate nationalists (of which Bob Blair was a prime example) offered Ottawa a viable Canadian alternative. These new entrepreneurial nationalists were emerging to challenge the traditional hegemony of the majors, such as Imperial, Gulf, Shell, and the other multinational subsidiaries operating in Canada. A recent American corporate report warned of this new class of Canadian businessmen. "The new nationalists provide what the old nationalists could not: a realistic Canadian alternative to foreign ownership and control. The old nationalists talked about the dangers of foreign ownership and control; the new nationalists are able to offer a viable Canadian alternative and they are determined to wrest control of key sectors of the economy out of foreign hands." Because their competitive edge is slight and their capital resources are modest, government action is a critical component in their strategy.[7] Although this approach is far from new in Canadian history, it makes the program antithetical to the Reagan free-enterprise philosophy currently in the ascendent in the United States. This alliance is all the more potent because state capitalism is involved as well as private enterprise. The Canadianization process, which began with the rejection of Arctic Gas in 1977, continued on with the radical expansion of Petro-Canada in acquiring Pacific Petroleum in 1979 and Petrofina in 1981, and reached its full bloom with the fiscal discrimination involved in the National Energy Program of 1980. Even after the election of Brian Mulroney, Petro-Canada expanded further as part of the Canadianization package of Gulf Canada. The old nationalists were significant only in the sense that they helped to prepare the way for the new.

The long-term implications of energy exchanges between Canada and the United States are complex and often difficult to assess. Generally, demand for new energy supply is more pressing in the U.S. than in adjacent areas of Canada. If surplus Canadian supply is exported, the Americans will invest in pipelines, refineries, and the like to utilize the energy flow. If Canadian demand later increases to the point that the supplies are needed domestically, there is a reluctance to cut off the flow. Canadian gas exports help to cover other trade areas where Canada suffers from a chronic balance-of-payments deficit. Yet natural gas is a finite natural resource that is essential as an industrial feedstock for plastics as well as an energy source. Canada may be opting for quick profits to this generation at the expense of the supply needs of those Canadians as yet unborn, and a very generous export policy is an absolute essential for all the major northern gas projects, such as the Arctic Pilot Project or the Polar Gas Pipeline.

Canadian-American relations, so essential for the North, are headed for a difficult period. Both countries are going through an economic crisis with protectionist and nationalist overtones to their respective policies. Americans have become more sensitive about defence and security questions in this hemisphere than at any time since the Korean War. The new generation of weapons now emerging will increase U.S. interest in establishing new air and submarine detection systems in the Canadian Arctic. We own the prime real estate between Russia and the American industrial heartland. These new systems would integrate Canada further into the American defence establishment on a continental basis.

Yet at the same time Canada may feel threatened by American attempts to push supertankers through the Northwest Passage in defiance of Canadian environmental legislation, the provisions of the Law of the Sea, and the Canadian assumptions about marine sovereignty in the Arctic. Ironically, the Americans cannot press their case for an international strait too strongly without opening the way for Russian use of the Canadian waters. Sooner or later the Americans, merely for reasons of their own security, will have to recognize Canadian sovereignty irrespective of their principles of international relations. Elsewhere, tanker traffic and drilling in the Davis Strait may complicate and embitter our relations with the government of Greenland. Here the pressures will be the exact reverse of those from Washington, and the further we go to meet American concerns, the greater will be the tensions with Greenland. Also, the faster we push Arctic energy projects, the more they will be dependent on exporting into the American market and the more American priorities will come to influence our own energy policy and northern policy in general. If Washington can apply American law to the Siberian Pipeline to Western Europe, so can the U.S. seek to regulate a Canadian pipeline exporting to service American customers. Hence the issue of Arctic sovereignty involves mega-projects as well as marine navigation. We must be aware of these trade-offs when we consider the issue of northern development.

As Canadian development moves North the implications are clear for the whole country. From this book I hope it is clear that there is no consensus among Canadians and there has been no clear policy applied to northern development in the past. We have muddled through. Yet for the future that will not be good enough. We are facing a whole series of new and costly challenges in terms of northern technology as well as the social implications of that technology. We are facing a complex series of environmental problems where biological science is still groping for answers. The scale of capital is so great for northern mega-projects that it will probably require a new hybrid of private and public enterprise traditions. The native land claims negotiations will require new legal and constitutional forms. All of these require a will and a flexibility that Canadians have not exhibited in their past. I fear that the future will be dominated by the same *ad hoc* approaches of the past. Yet the people of the North, as they move constitutionally to their three new provinces, deserve something better. But they will not get it. Canadians are still hung up in their dilemma about the North – that ambivalent mixture of greed and idealism.

Notes

Notes to Preface

1. D. Peacock, *People, Peregrines, and Arctic Pipelines* (Vancouver, 1977), p. 195; Earle Gray, *Super Pipe* (Toronto, 1979), p. 174.

Notes to Chapter 1

1. W.L. Morton, *The Canadian Identity* (Toronto, 1961).
2. See, for example, L.J. Burpee, *Henry Hudson* (Toronto, n.d.), in the Ryerson Canadian History Readers Series.
3. S. Leacock, "Introduction," in V. Stefansson, *Unsolved Mysteries of the Arctic* (New York, 1938), p. 7.
4. L.H. Neatby, *The Search for Franklin* (Edmonton, 1970).
5. E.E. Rich, *John Rae's Correspondence, 1844–1855*, Hudson Bay Record Society (London, 1953), pp. 265, 276. At the time, Rae's report was published in a variety of sources, including *Parliamentary Papers*, 1855, vol. XXXV; *Journal of Royal Geographical Society*, XXV, pp. 246ff; and Charles Dickens (ed.), *Household Words*, London, February 5, 1855.
6. David Roberts, "Dickens and the Arctic," *Horizon* (January, 1980), p. 70.
7. M.H. Long, *Sir John Franklin*, Ryerson Canadian History Readers Series (Toronto, n.d.), p. 2.
8. The Weekly *Globe*, April 2, 1869.
9. Carl Berger, "The True North Strong and Free," in Peter Russell, *Nationalism in Canada* (Toronto, 1966), pp. 4–19.
10. Benjamin Kidd, *Social Evolution* (London, 1895), p. 57.
11. House of Commons, *Debates*, 1903, pp. 12816–19, (September 30).
12. V. Stefansson, *The Northward Course of Empire* (New York, 1923), p. 1.
13. *Ibid.*, p. 19.
14. R.J. Diubaldo, *Stefansson and the Canadian Arctic* (Montreal, 1978), p. 3.
15. Leacock, "Introduction," p. 9.
16. Department of Northern Affairs and Natural Resources, *This is the Arctic* (Ottawa, 1958), p. 35.
17. House of Commons, *Debates*, 1978, Vol. V, pp. 2390–91 (May 5).
18. Senate, "Report of the Select Committee Appointed to Inquire into the Resources of the Great Mackenzie Basin," Ottawa, 1888, pp. 10–15.
19. Robert Service, "The Spell of the Yukon," in *The Collected Poems of Robert Service* (New York, 1907).
20. Thomas Berger, *Northern Frontier, Northern Homeland: The Report of the*

Mackenzie Valley Pipeline Inquiry (Ottawa, 1977), Vol. I, p. 52. Hereafter Berger Report.

21. House of Commons, *Debates*, 1902, pp. 3951–61 (May 1); Public Archives of Canada, MG 26, G, Vol. 68, Capt. J.E. Bernier à Wilfrid Laurier, 5 mars 1898. This was the first of a number of attempts by Bernier to get Ottawa to finance his plans for a North Pole expedition.

22. This sector theory is usually dated back to Senator Poirier's motion of February 20, 1907. See Senate, *Debates*, 1906–07, p. 271.

23. See C. Hopkins, *Canadian Annual Review 1903* (Toronto, 1904), p. 389, where he quotes from Quebec *Chronicle*, December 2, 1903, and Halifax *Chronicle*, October 25, 1903.

24. House of Commons, *Debates*, 1902, p. 3978 (May 1).

25. House of Commons, *Debates*, 1903, p. 12819 (September 30).

26. M.W. Morris, "Boundary Problems relating to the Canadian Arctic," in William Wonders, *Canada's Changing North* (Toronto, 1971), p. 317.

27. George Whalley, *The Legend of John Hornby* (Toronto, 1962), p. 130. Whalley, the noted poet and English scholar of Samuel Taylor Coleridge, is a living embodiment of the romantic attraction of the Canadian North.

28. Toronto *Globe*, January 19, February 18, 1932; Dick North; *The Mad Trapper of Rat River* (Toronto, 1972); Alan Phillips, "Who was the Mad Trapper of Rat River?" *Maclean's*, October 1, 1955.

29. Ian K. Kelly, "The Canol Project: Defence, Politics, and Oil" (M.A. thesis, Trent University, 1977), p. 110.

30. PAC, MG 26, King Diaries, Vol. 92, p. 174 (February 17, 1944).

31. Ralph Allen, "Will Dewline Cost Canada Its Northland?" *Maclean's*, May 26, 1956.

32. J.L. Granatstein, "A Fit of Absence of Mind," in E.J. Dosman, *The Arctic in Question* (Toronto, 1976), p. 27

33. Diefenbaker speech, February 12, 1958.

34. Richard Rohmer, *Essays on Mid-Canada* (Toronto, 1970), p. 109.

35. For analysis of the significance of these concepts for international law, see Chapter 11.

36. M.A. Galway, "Arctic Sovereignty," *Canadian Forum* (November, 1969), pp. 179–81; Richard Rohmer, *The Arctic Imperative* (Toronto, 1973), p. 44.

37. E.J. Dosman, "The Northern Sovereignty Crisis," in *The Arctic in Question*, p. 34.

Notes to Chapter 2

1. Helen J. Dawson, "The Consumer Association of Canada," *Canadian Public Administration*, VI, 1 (March, 1963), pp. 92–118.

2. For instance, the author, who headed the CIC effort at the NEB and appeared before Berger as an expert witness for the Native Brotherhood of the N.W.T. (the Dene Nation).

3. W.F. Lothian, *A History of Canada's National Parks* (Ottawa, 1976), I, p. 18.

4. Commission of Conservation, *National Conference on the Conservation of Game* (Ottawa, 1919), pp. 3–6.

5. Janet Foster, *Working for Wildlife* (Toronto, 1978), p. 13; also Foster, "The Federal Government and Migratory Birds," *Canadian Historical Association Report*, 1976, pp. 207–27.

6. S.P. Hays, *Conservation and the Gospel of Efficiency* (Cambridge, 1959), p. 256; Peter Gillis, "The Ottawa Lumber Barons and the Conservation Movement, 1880–1914," *Journal of Canadian Studies*, IX (February, 1974).

7. Commission of Conservation, *Lands, Fisheries and Game, Minerals* (Ottawa, 1911), p. 405.

8. Roderick Nash, "Wilderness and Man in North America," in J.G. Nelson and R.C. Scace, *The Canadian National Parks* (Calgary, 1968), I, p. 75.

9. Roderick Nash, *Wilderness and the American Mind* (New Haven, 1973), p. 104.

10. *Ibid.*; Stewart Udall, *The Quiet Crisis* (New York, 1963); David Lowenthal, *George Perkins Marsh: Versatile Vermonter* (New York, 1958); Arthur Ekirch, *Man and Nature in America* (New York, 1963).

11. W. Drew, "Wilderness and Limitation," *Canadian Forum* (February, 1973), p. 16.

12. *Ibid.*, p. 17.

13. Morton, *The Canadian Identity*, p. 93.

14. B.M. Littlejohn, "Wilderness: Canadian Cultural Heritage," *The Bulletin of the Conservation Council of Ontario* (October, 1978).

15. James K. Woodford, *The Violated Vision* (Toronto, 1972).

16. P.E. Trudeau, speech to annual meeting of the Canadian Press Association, April 12, 1970.

17. Don Chant, "Pollution Probe: Fighting the Polluters with their own Weapons," in A.P. Pross, *Pressure Group Behaviour in Canadian Politics* (Toronto, 1975), p. 73.

18. *Ibid.*, p. 64.

19. Jean Chrétien, speech in Dallas, Texas, March 10, 1971.

20. Doug Pimlott to Members of the Committee, November 12, 1971, reprinted in *Arctic Alternatives* (Ottawa, 1973), p. 23.

21. *Ibid.*

22. D. Pimlott *et al.*, *Arctic Alternatives*; John Livingston in *The Ontario Naturalist*, VIII (December 4, 1970).

23. See, in particular, E. Dosman, *The National Interest* (Toronto, 1975); Pimlott *et al.*, *Arctic Alternatives*, p. 7.

24. Peter Usher, *The Bankslanders*, 3 vols. (Ottawa, 1971).

25. Robert Davis and Mark Zannis, *The Genocide Machine in Canada: The Pacification of the North* (Montreal, 1973).

26. William Ophuls, *Ecology and the Politics of Scarcity* (San Francisco, 1977), p. 152.

27. See recent works by Bruce Hodgins and John Wadland.

28. D. and E. Spring (eds.), *Ecology and Religion in History* (New York, 1974); Ian G. Barbour, *Earth Might Be Fair* (Englewood Cliffs, New Jersey, 1972).

29. Dosman, *The National Interest*.

30. R.L. Heilbroner, *Between Capitalism and Socialism* (New York, 1970), p. xiii.

31. See William Leiss, *Limits to Satisfaction* (Toronto, 1976); Ursula Franklin, *Canada as a Conserver Society* (Ottawa, 1977); K. Valaskakis *et al.*, *The Conserver Society* (Toronto, 1979).

32. George Grant, *Technology and Empire* (Toronto, 1969), pp. 68–70.

33. D. Creighton, quoted in A. Rotstein, "Canada: The New Nationalism," *Foreign Affairs* (October, 1976), p. 113.

34. Daniel Drache, "Harold Innis: A Canadian Nationalist," *Journal of Canadian Studies*, IV, 2 (May, 1969).

35. H.A. Innis, "The Canadian North," *University of Toronto Monthly*, XXX (January, 1930), pp. 163–65.

36. H.A. Innis, "The Teaching of Economic History in Canada," in M.Q. Innis, *Essays in Canadian Economic History* (Toronto, 1956), p. 3.

37. A. Rotstein, "Innis: The Alchemy of Fur and Wheat," *Journal of Canadian Studies*, XII, 5 (Winter, 1977); Karl Polanyi, *The Great Transformation* (Boston, 1957), pp. 163–91.

38. Drache, "Harold Innis: A Canadian Nationalist," p. 12.

39. H.A. Innis, "Great Britain, Canada and the United States," in M.Q. Innis, *Essays in Canadian Economic History*, p. 405.

40. H.A. Innis, *Empire and Communications* (Toronto, 1972), p. 5. For more on the Marxist analysis, see Mel Watkins, "The Staple Theory Revisited," *Journal of Canadian Studies*, XII, 5 (Winter, 1977), pp. 83–95.

41. A. Rotstein, "Nationalism and Technology," *Canadian Forum* (January, 1965), reprinted August, 1973.

42. Ramsay Cook, *The Maple Leaf Forever* (Toronto, 1971), pp. 197–214; George Woodcock, "A Plea for the Anti-Nation," in V. Nelles and A. Rotstein (eds.), *Nationalism or Local Control* (Toronto, 1973), p. 5; Wayland Drew, "Wilderness and Limitation," *Canadian Forum* (February, 1973), p. 18.

43. House of Commons, *Debates*, 1971, p. 10205 (December 7).

44. Bruce Hodgins, "Nationalism, Decentralism, and the Left," in Nelles and Rotstein (eds.), *Nationalism or Local Control*, p. 39.

45. Walter Gordon, *A Political Memoir* (Toronto, 1977), pp. 315–17.

46. The policy papers and resolutions of the conference were published in an edited version: A Rotstein and G. Lax, *Getting it Back* (Toronto, 1974).

47. Elie Kedourie, *Nationalism* (London, 1960), pp. 73–74. For a recent discussion of Canadian nationalism and Canada–U.S. relations, see Richard Gwyn, *The 49th Paradox* (Toronto, 1985).

Notes to Chapter 3

1. P.A. Cumming and N.H. Mickenberg, *Native Rights in Canada* (Toronto, 1972), p. 331.

2. Lewis Hanke, *Aristotle and the American Indians* (Bloomington, 1959); Cumming and Mickenberg, *Native Rights in Canada*, p. 14.

3. Cumming and Mickenberg, *Native Rights in Canada*, p. 14.

4. P.A. Cumming, *Canada: Native Land Rights and Northern Development* (Copenhagen, 1977), p. 23.

5. Cumming and Mickenberg, *Native Rights in Canada*, p. 114.

6. *Ottawa Citizen*, June 30, 1898; *Winnipeg Free Press*, June 20, 1898.

7. Charles Mair, *Through the Mackenzie Basin* (London, 1908), pp. 57–59.

8. Berger Inquiry, Transcripts, April 14, 1976, Vol. 143, p. 21816. Hereafter Berger Transcripts.

9. Mair, *Through the Mackenzie Basin*, p. 58.

10. Treaty 11, Ottawa, July-August, 1921.

11. Bishop Breynat to T.A. Crerar, February 23, 1937, quoted in R. Fumoleau, *As Long As This Land Shall Last* (Toronto, 1975), p. 2.

12. Berger Transcripts, April 14, 1976, Vol. 143, p. 21833; Fumoleau, *As Long As This Land Shall Last*, pp. 255–57. Indians were not allowed to shoot buffalo, although some hunting and trapping of other species was permitted.

13. George Manuel and M. Posluns, *The Fourth World: An Indian Reality* (Toronto, 1974), pp. 84–95.

14. Ministry of Citizenship and Immigration, *Report of the Commission Ap-*

pointed to Investigate unfulfilled provisions of Treaties 8 & 11 as they apply to the Indians of the Mackenzie District, PC 799 (Ottawa, 1959), pp. 8–10.

15. This is a very curious argument as the French-Canadian property rights and civil code were respected in the Quebec Act of 1774.

16. Pierre Trudeau, speech, August 9, 1969, in Vancouver.

17. Berger Report, I, p. 176.

18. Cumming, *Canada: Native Land Rights and Northern Development,* p. 19.

19. P.A. Cumming, "Native Land Rights," *Alberta Law Review,* XII (1974), p. 60.

20. Toronto *Globe and Mail,* February 21, 1973.

21. Yukon Native Brotherhood, *Together Today for our Children Tomorrow* (1973).

22. W.H. McConnell, *Commentary on the British North America Act* (Toronto, 1977), p. 225.

Notes to Chapter 4

1. For those interested in the corporate intrigue between the rival study groups, see Peacock, *People, Peregrines, and Arctic Pipelines;* Gray, *Super Pipe.*

2. Berger Transcripts, August 18, 1975, pp. 7896–900.

3. National Energy Board, Northern Pipelines, *Transcripts,* vol. 218, May 11, 1977, pp. 36940–45; Blair to Strom, May 19, 1970, quoted in Peacock, *People, Peregrines, and Arctic Pipelines,* p. 28.

4. Dosman, *The National Interest,* p. xvii.

5. *Ibid.,* p. 108.

6. The merger agreement was filed in the NEB hearings as Exhibit N–PD–659, "Joint Research and Feasibility Study Agreement," June, 1972.

7. House of Commons, *Debates,* 1973, pp. 8482, 8579 (December 6, December 10).

8. *Ibid.,* pp. 8572–8876 (December 10).

9. Berger Transcripts, August 18, 1975, pp. 7910ff.

Notes to Chapter 5

1. Law Reform Commission, Working Paper #17, "Commission of Inquiry," Ottawa, 1977, p. 10.

2. Berger Report, II, p. 223.

3. Thomas Berger, speech in honour of Frank Scott, Simon Fraser University, February 21, 1981.

4. Thomas Berger, interview with the author, May 19, 1980.

5. Berger Report, II, p. 223.

6. Berger Report, II, p. 224.

7. Thomas Berger, "Commissions of Inquiry and Public Policy," speech at Carleton University, March 1, 1978.

8. Berger, interview with the author, May 19, 1980.

9. Peacock, *People, Peregrines, and Arctic Pipelines,* p. 178.

10. See points raised by Michael Goldie for Arctic Gas: Berger Transcripts, Vols. 1–6.

11. Privy Council, PC 1974–641 (March 21, 1974).

12. Dosman, *The National Interest,* p. 168.

13. Berger Transcripts, Vols. I–VIII, Yellowknife, Inuvik, Whitehorse, and Ottawa.

14. Berger Report, II, p. 227.

15. Berger Transcripts, Vol. 4, pp. 236–50.
16. *Ibid.*, Vol. 8, p. 707.
17. *Ibid.*, Vol. 5, p. 376.
18. *Ibid.*, Vol. 1, pp. 20–21.
19. *Ibid.*, Vol. 7, pp. 611–13.
20. PAC, RG 126, Papers of the Mackenzie Valley Pipeline Inquiry (hereafter, PAC, Berger Inquiry Papers), Vol. 72, CARC file, Berger to A. Thompson, August 23, 1974.
21. *Ibid.*, Vols. 72, 73; Berger Report, II, pp. 225–30.
22. Berger Transcripts, Vol. 4, pp. 280, 306.
23. Dosman, *The National Interest.*
24. PAC, RG 126, Berger Inquiry Papers, Vol. 72, CBC File; Whit Fraser, "The Berger Inquiry," *North* (February, 1977).
25. Arctic Gas spent a great deal of time wining and dining journalists and supplying them with prepared copy, very little of which was ever used except in the financial press.
26. Thomas Berger, *Preliminary Rulings Nos. 1 & 2*, Yellowknife, July 12, October 29, 1974.
27. *Ibid.*
28. See the author's filing, NEB Northern Pipelines Phase 3(c), Socio-Economic, February 10, 1977.
29. Berger Transcripts, Vol. 9, March 3, 1975, p. 766.
30. *Ibid.*, p. 777.
31. *Ibid.*, pp. 784–90. It was ironic that Foothills later came to champion a similar "Panama Canal" across Canadian territory.
32. *Ibid.*, pp. 835–42.
33. *Ibid.*, pp. 804–25.
34. *Ibid.*, pp. 835–42.
35. House of Commons, *Debates*, 1975, pp. 3708–09 (March 3).
36. *News of the North*, March 5, 1975.
37. Berger Transcripts, Vol. 13, March 7, 1975.
38. *Ibid.*, March 6, 1975, p. 1374.
39. *Ibid.*, Vol. 10, March 9, pp. 844–48.
40. Berger Transcripts, Vol. 15, March 11, 1975, pp. 1606–14; PAC, RG 126, Vol. 73, DOE file.
41. Berger Transcripts, Vol. 21, March 19, 1975, p. 2413.
42. Colin Alexander, *Angry Society* (Yellowknife, 1976), pp. 3–7; Dick Turner, *Sunrise on the Mackenzie* (Saanichton, B.C., 1977), p. 43; *News of the North* (Yellowknife), January 29, 1975.
43. Berger Transcripts, Vol. 21, pp. 2202–15.
44. PAC, RG 126, Berger Inquiry Papers, Vol. 72, CBC File, A. Cowan to T. Berger, September 29, 1975.
45. *Ibid.*, Vol. 73, EPB file; and a number of discussions with Carson Templeton by the author.
46. There were three exceptions to this pattern – the white-dominated towns of Hay River, Norman Wells, and Inuvik.
47. Berger Report, II, p. 227.
48. Berger Transcripts, Vol. 52, pp. 5223–31.
49. This is usually referred to as the Staff Report. For press comment, see Toronto *Globe and Mail*, October 30, 1976.
50. Berger Report, II, p. 229.
51. Most of the public interest groups supported the proposal.

52. Toronto *Globe and Mail*, October 30, 1976.

53. Larry Bliss in *Financial Post*, May 21, 1977.

54. Mel Watkins, "The Berger Report," *This Magazine*, II, 4 (August, 1977).

55. Berger Report, I, p. xi.

56. Toronto *Globe and Mail*, May 9, 1977.

57. Berger Report, I, pp. xxii–xxv. Berger's position as a provincial supreme court judge enhanced the importance of his wording on native rights.

58. *Toronto Star*, May 13, 1977.

59. See Toronto *Globe and Mail*, May 11, 13, 25, 1977; *Toronto Star*, May 10, 11, 14, 1977; *Le Devoir*, May 11, 14, 1977; *Financial Post*, May 21, 1977; *Financial Times*, May 16, 1977.

60. Arctic Gas, *Response to the Report of the Mackenzie Valley Pipeline Inquiry* (Toronto, 1977).

61. Toronto *Globe and Mail*, May 7, 11, June 25, 1977; *Financial Times*, June 6, 1977; *Financial Post*, May 21, 1977; and personal discussions with an aide to Gillespie at that time.

62. Toronto *Globe and Mail*, May 13, 1977.

Notes to Chapter 6

1. Law Reform Commission, *The National Energy Board* (Ottawa, 1975), p. 175.

2. Consumers Association of Canada/Pollution Probe challenge on Ontario Hydro exports; Manitoba and six other parties on the Dow-Dome ethylene decision; and Union Gas of Ontario challenged the decision on gas supplies for Trans-Canada Pipelines. See Toronto *Globe and Mail*, August 14, 15, 1974.

3. Morgan had established the Trident Trading and Transport Co. When the CBC presented the evidence to Marshall Crowe, Morgan's resignation was demanded (May 20, 1974).

4. Comments from Bruce Willson, former president of Union Gas, to the author. See also his comments to the NEB, Gas Supply Hearings, 1975.

5. François Bregha *et al.*, *A Case for Delaying the Mackenzie Valley Gas Pipeline*, York University Work Group on Energy, 1974.

6. NEB, *Natural Gas: Supply and Requirements*, 1975, p. 1.

7. Donald Macdonald, statement of July 15, 1975; Toronto *Globe and Mail*, February 18, 1975.

8. NEB, *Natural Gas: Supply and Requirements*, 1975, pp. 85–86.

9. Helliwell's basic arguments can be found in Peter Pearse (ed.), *The Mackenzie Valley Pipeline* (Toronto, 1974).

10. NEB, *Natural Gas: Supply and Requirements*, 1975, p. 49.

11. A.R. Lucas and T. Bell, *The National Energy Board*, Law Reform Commission (Ottawa, 1977).

12. TUA, CIC Papers, Goodman to Macdonald, September 25, 1972, and reply; *Toronto Star*, October 17, 1972.

13. *Toronto Star*, August 30, 1973; and author's meeting with Macdonald, November 21, 1973.

14. TUA, CIC Papers, Political Correspondence, Election of 1974.

15. The groups were: CARC, Canadian Inst. for Guided Ground Transport (Queen's University), CWF, CIC, Committee for Justice and Liberty (CJL), Committee for Original Peoples' Entitlement (COPE), Consumers Association of Canada, Energy Probe, Indian Association of Alberta, Indian Brotherhood of the N.W.T., Canadian Labour Congress, and the Work Group on Energy Policy (York University).

16. At the time of publication it was too early to be sure if the new act would be a serious help for problems as discussed here.

17. TUA, CIC Papers, Ministerial Correspondence and Pre-hearing Memo.

18. NEB, Northern Pipelines, Crowe Panel, Transcripts, Vol. 1, p. 32; Dosman, *The National Interest*, p. 70.

19. El Paso proposed to construct a pipeline across Alaska and then use LNG tankers from Valdez on the south coast to California.

20. François Bregha, *Bob Blair's Pipeline* (Toronto, 1980), p. 72.

21. Comments at the time from Arctic Gas employees to the author.

22. NEB, Northern Pipelines, Crowe Panel, Transcripts, Vol. 3.

23. CBC Broadcast, quoted in Gray, *Super Pipe*, p. 75.

24. James Lorimer article, Toronto *Globe and Mail*, November 4, 1975.

25. Canadian Wildlife Federation and Committee for an Independent Canada.

26. Federal Court, *Reports*, 1976, Vol. 2, Part 1, pp. 20ff.

27. The Supreme Court, *Reports*, 1978, Vol. 1, Part II, pp. 369ff.

28. Stephen Duncan, in *The Financial Post*, November 8, 1975.

29. Jack Stabback, fifty-five, chemical engineer; Geoff Edge, fifty-five, British-born economist; and Ralph Brooks, fifty, electrical engineer.

30. NEB, Northern Pipelines, Transcript, Vol. 1, p. 128. All references from here on are to the Stabback panel and are cited as NEB Transcripts.

31. Northwest Pipeline Company was split off from the El Paso Company through anti-trust action by the courts. John MacMillian, in a lengthy and furious series of court battles, gained control of the company in 1974. For business reasons, he hated El Paso and Exxon.

32. For good analysis of the corporate diplomacy involved, see Bregha, *Bob Blair's Pipeline*, pp. 75–78.

33. NEB Transcripts, Vols. 86, 87.

34. *Ibid.*, Vols. 88, 89.

35. *Ibid.*, Vol. 91, p. 12978; Berger Transcripts, Vol. 174, p. 27137.

36. Toronto *Globe and Mail*, September 29, 30, 1976; *Toronto Star*, September 30, 1976.

37. Ian Blue for the Board had made it very clear that Crowe would not see them.

38. Bregha, *Bob Blair's Pipeline*, p. 208.

39. PC 1973–4065, December 18, 1973, announced in the *Canada Gazette*, January 9, 1974, pp. 212–13.

40. To the author at this time.

41. TUA Archives, CIC Papers, Brian Whittle, acting NEB secretary, to I. McDougall, May 4, 1976; NEB Transcripts, Vols. 8, 10, 17.

42. Toronto *Globe and Mail*, editorial, July 22, 1976.

43. NEB Transcripts, Vols. 70, 72; *Oilweek*, July 26, 1976.

44. NEB Transcripts, Vol. 105, pp. 15421ff.

45. *Ibid*, Vol. 76, p. 10156.

46. NEB, *Reasons for Decision: Northern Pipelines* (Ottawa, 1977), I–153 and I–164. See also the author's "On to the Yukon," *Canadian Forum* (September, 1977).

Notes to Chapter 7

1. Berger Transcripts, Vol. 19a, p. 2294.

2. *Ibid.*, Vol. 20, pp. 2374–81.

3. *Ibid.*, Vols. 16, 17, 18, pp. 1856–2099.

4. R.J.E. Brown, "Permafrost in Canada," Series D, Map No. 1, from *Canadian Geographical Journal.*
5. Berger Transcripts, Vol. 40, pp. 5191ff.; Berger Report, I, p. 17; PAC, RG 126, Vol. 73, Frost Heave File.
6. Berger Report, II, p. 133.
7. PAC, RG 126, Vol. 73, Frost Heave File; NEB Transcripts, Vol. 20, pp. 2378ff; Berger Transcripts, Vols. 69, 73; Peter Williams, *Pipelines and Permafrost* (London, 1979), p. 65.
8. Berger Transcripts, Vol. 195, p. 30584.
9. NEB, *Reasons for Decision: Northern Pipelines*, Vol. II, Chapter III, p. 63.
10. For some NEB sessions Arctic Gas brought in a blackboard to sketch new details not included in printed filings that were a week old.
11. Williams, *Pipelines and Permafrost*, p. 81.
12. Proceedings, Joint United States–Canadian Northern Civil Engineering Research Workshop, Edmonton, March 20–22, 1978, p. 8.
13. NEB Transcripts, Vol. 181, p. 29546.
14. Alyeska, with primarily non-winter construction, never exceeded .44 miles per day in laying pipe and averaged only .14 miles per day for the October, November, April, and May work. See C.A. Champion, Alaska State Pipeline Co-ordinator, NEB, Filed Evidence, N–FH–5–96.
15. Berger Report, I, p. 27; NEB, Public Documents, N–PD–841.
16. NEB, Filed Testimony, N–FH–5–96, C.A. Champion.
17. NEB Transcripts, Vols. 30, 31.
18. *Ibid.*, Vol. 131, pp. 19860–20039.
19. These are Inuktituk words for Arctic jaeger, raven, snowbird, and night hawk.
20. Data supplied by Imperial Oil, Spring, 1982.

Notes to Chapter 8

1. M. Dunbar, *Environment and Good Sense* (Montreal, 1971), p. 53.
2. Dosman, *The National Interest*, pp. 157–76.
3. CARC Conference, May 24–26, 1972, Ottawa.
4. Dunbar, *Environment and Good Sense*, p. 56.
5. George Calef, *Caribou and the Barren-lands* (Ottawa, 1981), p. 15.
6. The section on caribou is based on the testimony of Calef, Jakenichuk, and Banfield to the Berger Inquiry; Nancy LeBlond, *Porcupine Caribou Herd* (Ottawa, 1979); Calef, *Caribou and the Barren-lands*; and the author's own observations in Alaska and the Yukon.
7. *Science*, 179 (1973), pp. 335–40.
8. Berger Report, I, p. 40.
9. U.S. Department of the Interior, *Alaska Natural Gas Transportation System*, Alaska Volume, p. 421.
10. Arctic Gas, *Final Argument to NEB*, Vol. II, p. x–34.
11. Dr. William Gunn, who opted for the interior on the basis of his ornithological research.
12. Berger Report, I, p. 41.
13. Gray, *Super Pipe*, p. 105.
14. *News of the North*, October 9, 1981.
15. Calef, *Caribou and the Barren-lands*, p. 166.
16. *News of the North*, October 9, 1981; *Maclean's*, October, November, 1981.
17. Berger Report, I, p. xxxvi.

18. Calef, *Caribou and the Barren-lands*, p. 162.
19. Berger Report, I, p. 30.
20. DIAND, Communiqué No. 1–7792 (January 23, 1978) and No. 1–7821 (July 6, 1978).
21. George Calef, in *Northern Perspectives*, VII, 2 (1979).
22. A.R.E. Sinclair, *The African Buffalo* (Chicago, 1977), p. 287.
23. Canadian Arctic Gas, Biological Report Series Vol. XIV, edited by William Gunn and John Livingston.
24. NEB Transcripts, Vol. 15, pp. 1869–2083.
25. W.W.H. Gunn, "The Need to Preserve the Integrity of the Mackenzie Delta," LGL Ltd., 1975, pp. 9ff., quoted in Berger Report, I, p. 63.
26. Berger Transcripts, Vol. 93, pp. 14172–74; Vol. 98, pp. 14908–11.
27. U.S. Department of the Interior, Final Environmental Impact Statement, Alaska Natural Gas Transmission System, Alaska Volume, pp. 284, 422.
28. Arctic Gas, NEB Direct Testimony, Phase 3D, Panel 2, Living Environment, p. 26.
29. Berger Community Hearings, Tuktoyaktuk, March 20, 1976, p. 4395; Berger Staff Report, Wildlife Protection, Mammals, pp. 29–30.
30. A.R. Milne and R.H. Herlinveaux, *Crude Oil in Cold Water* (Ottawa, 1977), p. 26.
31. *Ibid.*, pp. 27–30.
32. These reports were published by the Beaufort Sea Project, Department of Fisheries and Oceans, P.O. Box 6000, Sidney, B.C.
33. S.L. Ross, AMOP Technical Seminar, Edmonton, June 30, 1980, quoted in *Arctic Seas Bulletin*, II, 7 (1980).
34. Toronto *Globe and Mail*, December 1, 1981; *Toronto Star*, December 2, 1981; CARC Newsletter.
35. Federal Environmental Assessment and Review Process, *Guide for Environmental Screening* (Ottawa, 1979).
36. National Environmental Policy Act. See Chapter 2.
37. William E. Reeves, "EARP: The Case of McKinley Bay," *Northern Perspectives*, VIII, 2 (1980), pp. 2–12.
38. House of Commons, Special Commons Committee on Northern Gas Pipeline, *Proceedings*, March 2, 1978.
39. D.W. Schindler, "The Impact Statement Boondoggle," *Science*, 192 (May 7, 1976), p. 509.
40. The small post-Keynesian school is an exception to the above comments. They have tried to identify external diseconomies and recover the costs through taxes or pollution control laws. They try to isolate and identify the social benefits that flow from investment in environmental technology.
41. TUA, CIC Papers, copy of H. Inhaber to Dr. John Fyles (Berger staff), August 9, 1976; Berger Report, II, p. 86.
42. Environmental Protection Board, *Environmental Impact Assessment*, Vol. III (Winnipeg, 1974).
43. Don Gamble in *Northern Perspectives*, VIII, 6 (1979).
44. The lemmings are the classic case of this phenomenon. Recent research has indicated that a chemical compound in grasses and sedges that they eat may contain an aphrodisiac promoting their feverish reproductive activity. See *Northline* (newsletter of ACUNS), I, 4 (1981).
45. M.J. Dunbar, *Marine Transportation and High Arctic Development: A Bibliography* (Ottawa, 1980), p. 17.

1. Social Darwinism suggests that there is a basic struggle for survival between races and nations.
2. Berger Community Hearings, Rene Lamothe, Fort Simpson, Vol. 26, p. 2710.
3. *Ibid.*, Chief Frank T'Seleie, Fort Good Hope, Vol. 18, pp. 1777–78.
4. *Ibid.*, Rainer Genelli, Whitehorse, Vol. 23, pp. 2374–75.
5. *Ibid.*, Jim Sittichinla, Aklavik, Vol. 2, p. 87. Sittichinla was in his sixties and had experience as a CBC reporter, clergyman, and interpreter.
6. Bishop Breynat to Hon. T.A. Crerar, February 23, 1937, quoted in Fumoleau, *As Long As This Land Shall Last*, p. 217.
7. Justice W.G. Morrow, Supreme Court of the Northwest Territories, *Reasons for Judgement*, Chief F. Paulette *et al.*, 1973, p. 7.
8. Berger Community Hearings, Philip Blake, Fort McPherson, Vol. 12, p. 1081.
9. *Ibid.*, Chief Paul Andrew, Fort Norman, Vol. 10, p. 874.
10. *Ibid.*, Doulhus Shay, Fort Franklin, Vol. 8, p. 689.
11. *Ibid.*, Charlie Furlong, Aklavik, Vol. 1, p. 17.
12. *Ibid.*, Philip Blake, Fort McPherson, Vol. 12, pp. 1081–82.
13. *Ibid.*, Mrs. Barnabe, Norman Wells, Vol. 21, p. 2126.
14. *Ibid.*, François Paulette, Fort Smith, Vol. 48, p. 4749.
15. Gray, *Super Pipe*, p. 176.
16. Berger Community Hearings, Frank T'Seleie, Fort Good Hope, August 5, 1975.
17. *Ibid.*, Philip Blake, Fort McPherson, Vol. 12, pp. 1085–86.
18. *News of the North*, April 9, 1982.
19. Toronto *Globe and Mail*, March 22, 1982.
20. NEB Transcripts, Vol. 171 (March 14, 1977), p. 27358. The author was present that morning at the NEB and talked with the Dene leaders following the session. Many of the problems for the Board stemmed from its counsel, who did not take seriously intervenors who were outside the corporate group.
21. The private comments of Geoffrey Edge to the author at the press conference, July 4, 1977, when the NEB Report was released. He stressed that the report was a great victory for the environmental and native rights group.
22. NEB Transcripts, Vol. 168, p. 26878; Vol. 187, p. 29000; Berger Community Hearings, Vol. 26, p. 3088; "Alcohol Availability in the N.W.T.," Department of Social Development, Government of the N.W.T., Yellowknife, January, 1976.
23. Berger Report, I, p. 160.
24. *Ibid.*, p. 138.
25. NEB, Filed Testimony of Charles Hobart, Arctic Gas, Socio-Economic, Phase 3c, pp. 8, 30–42; Gray, *Super Pipe*, p. 189; and the oral comments of Hobart to Berger and NEB inquiries.
26. Berger Transcripts, Vol. 158 (July 6, 1976), pp. 24159–64.
27. Directly to the author in the Explorer Hotel (Yellowknife) and the Skyline and Inn of the Provinces (Ottawa). Many corporate officials were frustrated by and deeply hostile to the native and environmental opponents.
28. M. Watkins, *The Dene Nation: The Colony Within* (Toronto, 1977), pp. 84–99; Berger Transcripts, Vols. 154, 155.
29. From personal conversations with members of the Privy Council Office

and cabinet documents the author has seen. Ed Dosman documented the collusion between government and industry in the early stages of the planning for the Mackenzie Valley Pipeline.

30. H. McCullum, K. McCullum, and J. Olthuis, *Moratorium* (Toronto, 1977).

31. Berger Inquiry, Filed Evidence, Project North, "A Call for a Moratorium," June, 1976, p. 7.

32. NEB, Northern Pipelines, 1977, Filed Evidence, Bishop de Roo; NEB Transcripts, Vol. 194 (April 18, 1977).

33. NEB, Northern Pipelines, 1977, Filed Evidence, Archbishop Scott; NEB Transcripts, Vol. 199 (April 21, 1977).

34. NEB, *Reasons for Decision*, Interprovincial Pipeline (NW) Ltd., April, 1981, p. 129, quoting Berger Report, I, p. 163.

35. For a more detailed analysis of these issues, see the author's "Norman Wells: The Past and Future Boom," *Journal of Canadian Studies*, 16, 2 (Summer, 1981), pp. 16–33.

36. NEB, *Reasons for Decision*, Interprovincial Pipeline (NW) Ltd., p. 122.

37. Berger Report, I, p. 122.

38. CJL had challenged the NEB decision on the basis that the Board had not heard sufficient evidence. Mr. Justice Heard of the Federal Court of Canada dismissed the application for leave to appeal. He ruled that in twenty-one days of public hearings the NEB had considered "ample evidence" on which to base a decision. Toronto *Globe and Mail*, July 4, 1981.

39. Page, "Norman Wells: The Past and Future Boom," p. 31; *Toronto Star*, July 31, 1981.

40. *Esso North*, IV, 1 (1985); *News of the North*, May 17, 1985; Toronto *Globe and Mail*, May 15, 1985.

41. *Public Government for the People of the North* (Yellowknife, 1982).

42. George Erasmus, letter to Toronto *Globe and Mail*, May 9, 1982.

43. As the financing plan was not in place at the time of writing, these cost estimates are incomplete, given current interest rates and bond and equity market conditions.

44. Class seven refers to a ship capable of moving through first-year ice seven feet thick with a constant speed of three knots.

45. *Northern Perspectives*, X, 3 (April, 1982).

46. NEB, APP Hearings, ITC Filed Evidence, Environmental Impacts.

47. N.M. Peterson (ed.), *The Question of Sound from Icebreaker Operations*, Proceedings of a Workshop Sponsored by Petro-Canada, Toronto, February, 23–24, 1981.

48. M.J. Dunbar, "The Biological Significance of Arctic Ice," paper delivered to the Sikumiut Workshop, McGill University, April 15, 1982.

49. Marc Denhez, ITC counsel, "Impact of Inuit Rights on Arctic Waters," Sikumiut Workshop, McGill University, April 15, 1982.

50. NEB, APP, Filed Testimony of ITC, February, 1982.

51. *The Northern Miner*, July 13, 1978.

52. Officially, it was the Hamlet of Baker Lake, the Baker Lake Hunters and Trappers Association, and ITC. The Baker Lake RCMP area covers 30,000 square miles. The N.W.T. Council contributed $30,000 to help cover the Inuit legal costs.

53. *Northern Perspectives*, VIII, 3 (1980).

54. *The Northern Miner*, August 16, 1979.

55. *Northern Perspectives*, VIII, 3 (1980).

56. Hamlet of Baker Lake *et al.*, v. Minister of Indian Affairs *et al.* (1980), 1 F.C. 518.

57. *Ibid.*

58. Nunavut means "Our Land" in Inuktituk.

59. *News of the North*, June 11, 1982.

60. *News of the North*, May 14, 21, 1982.

61. Denhez, "Impact of Inuit Rights on Arctic Waters," p. 16.

62. House of Commons, *Debates*, statement by Parliamentary Secretary M.B. Lioselle, July 11, 1980.

63. Don Gamble, research director of CARC, in Toronto *Globe and Mail*, May 27, 1981.

64. Toronto *Globe and Mail*, March 9, 1982.

65. ITC, from some of its NEB testimony, appeared to prefer the Polar Gas Pipeline. See also *News of the North*, February 5, 1982.

66. Toronto *Globe and Mail*, July 2, 1982. On September 1, 1982, the National Energy Board adjourned indefinitely the hearings on the APP.

67. Roy T. Bowles, *Social Impact Assessment in Small Communities* (Toronto, 1981), pp. 87–88.

68. *Ibid.*, p. 85, quoting J.K. Stager.

Notes to Chapter 10

1. LNG rquires large amounts of energy to chill the gas down to the necessary $-162°C$ or $-259°F$.

2. Later, this economic analysis was incomplete, for the oil was surplus in California while it was desperately needed in the Midwest.

3. L.J. Allen, *The Trans-Alaska Pipeline*, Vol. I (Seattle, 1975).

4. NEB Transcripts, Vols. 190, 191, especially pp. 31879–81. This evidence was critical in casting doubt on the winter construction schedule of Arctic Gas.

5. One NEB staff member closely questioned the author in April, 1977, about the possibility of a public interest group challenge to the NEB's report. It appeared that the Board was on the defence on this issue when its legal advice had been wrong on the Crowe case.

6. NEB Transcripts, Vol. 114, p. 17052 (R. Blair); Vol. 107, p. 17757 (J.R. LeMesurier).

7. Bregha, *Bob Blair's Pipeline*, p. 16.

8. Plan as filed in February, 1977, including 25 per cent cost-overrun contingency.

9. NEB Transcripts, Vol. 103, p. 15147.

10. NEB Staff Report, *Pipeline Construction Costs, 1975–1985* (Ottawa, June, 1982).

11. Ontario Energy Board, *Investments by the Ontario Distributors in Natural Gas Projects*, August 26 to October 10, 1975.

12. Arctic Gas, Filed Testimony to the NEB, N–AG–3–140; NEB Transcripts, Vol. 122, pp. 19372ff.

13. The southern laterals to California and Chicago did not require backstopping.

14. NEB Transcripts, Vol. 106, p. 18689; Vol. 125, p. 18919.

15. *Ibid.*, Vol. 114, pp. 17037ff.

16. Arctic Gas, Filed Evidence, Phase 2B, Raymond Gray (Morgan Stanley, New York), N–AG–3–140, p. 8.

17. *Ibid.*, pp. 4ff.

18. *Ibid.*, David Lay, Chart #1; NEB, *Reasons for Decision: Northern Pipelines*, Vol. II, p. 4–72.

19. NEB Transcripts, Vol. 108, p. 15993.

20. *The Financial Post*, November 14, 1981.

21. General Accounting Office, Washington, *Lessons Learned From Constructing the Trans-Alaska Oil Pipeline*, June 15, 1978; GAO, *Issues Relating to the Proposed Alaska Highway Gas Pipeline Project*, October 26, 1979.

22. *Toronto Star*, July 4, 1979.

23. In the *Fortune* 500 listing of May, 1979, Exxon was first in both assets and shareholder equity; ARCO was twelfth in both; Sohio was seventeenth in assets and fortieth in shareholder equity.

24. House of Commons, Standing Committee on Northern Pipelines, *Proceedings*, February 27, 1979, p. 12:45.

25. Pan-Alberta was 50 per cent owned by Nova and Nova in turn held 50 per cent of the Foothills stock.

26. NEB, *Reasons for Decision, Gas Exports*, November, 1979, pp. 9–21 to 9–25.

27. Bregha, *Bob Blair's Pipeline*, p. 212.

28. House of Commons, *Debates*, December 6, 1979, p. 2102.

29. There were strong tensions within the Tory caucus between the Ontario and Alberta members on Pre-Build.

30. NEB, Order No. NPO–2–80, and the NEB Finding in the Matter of Condition 12 (1) of the Northern Pipeline Act, Ottawa, July, 1980.

31. Bregha, *Bob Blair's Pipeline*, p. 223.

32. Toronto *Globe and Mail*, September 11, 1981.

33. Dow Jones wire service report in Toronto *Globe and Mail*, July 14, 1981.

34. Visit to Grand Rapids, Michigan, to join the U.S. and Mexican presidents for the opening of the Gerald Ford Museum. See Toronto *Globe and Mail*, September 17, 1981.

35. Exxon, Shell, and Dow Chemical had all studied this possibility.

36. *Toronto Star*, October 8, 1981.

37. Toronto *Globe and Mail*, October 8, November 20, December 10, 11, 1981; *Toronto Star*, October 8, November 13, 1981.

38. *Toronto Star*, February 3, 1982; "The Perilous Hunt for Corporate Financing," *Business Week*, March 1, 1982.

39. House of Commons, *Debates*, September 9, 1977, statement of Allan MacEachen.

40. *The Financial Post*, May 21, 1977.

41. Foothills preferred a 54″ line at 1120 p.s.i. (pounds per square inch) pressure, which it believed was sounder technically than a 48″ line at 1620 p.s.i. pressure.

42. K.M. Lysyk *et al.*, *Alaska Highway Pipeline Inquiry* (Ottawa, 1977), p. 152.

43. Joint Statement by President Carter and Prime Minister Trudeau on the Pipeline Agreement, September 8, 1977; House of Commons, *Debates*, September 9, 1977, statement of Allan MacEachen.

44. *Business Week*, February 26, 1979.

45. *Ibid.*

46. L. Waverman and A. Donner, "Investments in Energy Supply Industries and the Economy of the OECD," paper given in Toronto, May, 1981.

47. A small quantity of Alaskan gas would be made available to Yukon residents along the right-of-way. Foothills was required to file application for

the Dempster Lateral by July 1, 1979.

48. Geoffrey Edge, speech to the Conference Board of Canada, Toronto, May 11, 1982.

49. *Ibid.*; NEB Staff Report, *Pipeline Construction Costs, 1975–1985*; Toronto *Globe and Mail*, May 14, 1982.

Notes to Chapter 11

1. E.J. Dosman, "The Northern Sovereignty Crisis, 1968–1970," in Dosman (ed.), *The Arctic in Question*, pp. 34–57.

2. J.A. Beesley, Department of External Affairs, speech to U.S. Society of International Law, Syracuse, N.Y., April 8, 1972, p. 9.

3. House of Commons, *Debates*, April, 1970; Dosman, *The National Interest*, pp. 58–59; *Canada Gazette*, Pt. II, V. 106, #16 (23/9/72); D. Pharand, "Canada's Jurisdiction in the Arctic," in M. Zaslow, *A Century of Canada's Arctic Islands, 1880–1980* (Ottawa, 1981), pp. 111–30.

4. Pierre Trudeau, speech to the Canadian Press Association, April 15, 1970.

5. K.M. M'Gonigle, "Unilateralism and International Law," University of Toronto, *Faculty of Law Review*, 34 (1976), p. 189.

6. House of Commons, *Debates*, April 15, 1970, p. 5923,

7. Quoted in W. Rowland, *The Plot to Save the World: The Stockholm Conference on the Human Environment* (Toronto, 1973), p. 107.

8. *United Convention on the Law of the Sea*, A/Conf 62/122.7, October, 1982, New York, p. 103

9. Donat Pharand, "The Northwest Passage in International Law," *Canadian Yearbook of International Law*, 17 (1979), p. 112. On the basis of the Corfu Channel case of 1949, Pharand argues that the International Court has established that "a strait must have been a useful route for maritime traffic" before being called an international strait.

10. E.J. Dosman and F. Abele, "Offshore Diplomacy in the Canadian Arctic," *Journal of Canadian Studies*, 16, 2 (Summer, 1981), p. 11.

11. I.T. Gault, *The International Legal Context of Petroleum Operations in Canadian Arctic Waters* (Calgary, 1983), pp. 66–69.

12. Companies holding exploration leases include Petro-Canada, Canadian Superior, Dome, Amoco, Wainco, and the Alberta/Ontario Group. The Natsek well (dry hole) appears to be just inside the disputed zone. Information from map, *Oilweek*, June 14, 1982.

13. Pharand, "Canada's Jurisdiction in the Arctic," p. 116.

14. *Ibid.*, p. 118.

15. L.H. Legault, "Canadian Practice in International Law," *Canadian Yearbook of International Law*, XIX (1981), p. 321.

16. Stephen Clarkson, *Canada and the Reagan Challenge* (Toronto, 1982), p. 71.

17. Jennifer Lewington, in Toronto *Globe and Mail*, February 17, 1982.

18. Information from interview with Bruce Willson, former president of Canadian Bechtel Ltd.

19. The Blair-Carr report had suggested a 3 per cent preference for Canadian bids, which the cabinet did not adopt. Clarkson, *Canada and the Reagan Challenge*, p. 111.

20. William Brock to Canadian ambassador, December 4, 1981, quoted *ibid.*, pp. 42–44.

21. The letter was leaked to Richard Gwyn of the *Toronto Star*; see Gwyn article of June 25, 1983.

22. The tradition of little interest in Canadian-American relations is a long one for successive U.S. Secretaries of State. For instance, in the Kissinger memoirs there is virtually no analysis of Canadian-American relations and hardly any mention of Canada as a factor in American foreign policy.

23. The scale of PIP grants was: 1981–$608 million; 1982–$1.4 billion; estimate for 1983–$2 billion. In 1982 alone, Dome received $469 million. *Energy Analects*, August 12, 19, 1983.

24. Lincoln P. Bloomfield, "The Arctic: Last Unmanaged Frontier," *Foreign Affairs*, 60, 1 (1981), p. 91. Bloomfield had served on the National Security Council for President Carter.

25. Henry Kissinger, *Years of Upheaval* (New York), II, p. 172.

26. The B-52s have used northern Canada for training purposes for some years, as the author found out when he was buzzed by one while on a canoe trip in northern Ontario.

27. C. Archer and D. Scrivener, "Frozen Frontiers and Resource Wrangles," *International Affairs*, 59, 1 (Winter, 1982–83), p. 65.

28. Bloomfield, "The Arctic: Last Unmanaged Frontier," p. 92.

29. *Ibid.*, p. 94.

30. Dosman and Abele, "Offshore Diplomacy in the Canadian Arctic," p. 5.

31. R. Page, "The High Arctic: Environmental Concerns, Government Control and Economic Development," in Zaslow, *A Century of Canada's Arctic Islands, 1880–1980*, p. 243.

32. P. Dobell, *Canada's Search for New Roles* (Toronto, 1972), p. 24.

33. Dosman and Abele, "Offshore Diplomacy in the Canadian Arctic," p. 3.

34. Johan J. Holst, "Norway's Search for a Nordpolitik," *Foreign Affairs*, 60, 1 (Fall, 1981), p. 66.

Notes to Chapter 12

1. *Toronto Star*, October 30, 1980.

2. Statistical evidence compiled from the transcripts by Mr. Peter Paul (now with Energy, Mines, and Resources), who worked as my research assistant.

3. David Brooks, *Economic Impact of Low Energy Growth in Canada* (Ottawa, 1978), p. 25. See also his *Zero Energy Growth for Canada* (Toronto, 1981); and Energy, Mines, and Resources, *Financing Energy Self-Reliance.*

4. NEB, *Reasons for Decision, Northern Pipelines*, Vol. I, p. 1–68.

5. *Ibid.*, p. 1–60.

6. Toronto *Globe and Mail*, October 16, 1981.

7. *Multinational Forecasts: The Longer Term Environment for Business in Canada, 1981–85* (New York, 1981), quoted in Mel Watkins, "The Innis Memorial Column," *This Magazine*, September, 1981.

Index

Aboriginal rights, 60, 61, 63, 66, 68, 69, 70, 71, 73, 189, 213, 218, 229, 236, 246, 247, 248, 250, 251, 253, 259; claims, 215; title, 213, 248, 250; *see also* Native rights
Access to information, 100
Active layer, 157, 158
Adams, Dr. Ken, 160
Agnew, Vice-President Spiro, 45
Air cushion vehicles, 198
Air-launched cruise missile (ALCM), 309
Alaska, 61, 110, 155, 194; resources, 77
Alaska Boundary Dispute, 12, 13
Alaska Highway Pipeline, 8, 17, 20, 78, 111, 118, 121, 141, 144, 166, 202, 222, 225, 259, 261, 264, 270-72, 273, 274, 276, 278, 283, 285, 286, 287, 303, 319; employment, 282; 48″ express line, 137; original route, 142, 143; *see also* Foothills Pipeline
Alaska native people, claims settlement, 69, 70
Alaskan Arctic Gas, 82, 152, 260
Alaskan Fish and Game Department, 191
Alaskan Gas, 269
Alberta, 86, 113, 126, 127, 140, 159, 161; government involvement in AGTL, 77, 78; mines minister, 78; producers, 125; route for pipeline, 81; Social Credit government, 76
Alberta and Southern Gas, 127
Alberta Court of Appeal, 213
Alberta Gas Trunk Line (Nova), 75, 76, 77, 83, 86, 88, 111, 140, 141, 142, 260, 261; *see also* Foothills Pipeline
Alcohol, 221, 254
Alexander, Colin, 109
Algonquin Wildlands League, 32
"All-events" tariff, 262, 263, 280
Allen, Ralph, 18
Allmand, Warren, 246
Alsands, 286, 287
Alyeska, 44, 133, 164, 169, 257, 258, 271; Alyeska oil pipeline, 142, 157, 179; cost per barrel, 284; experience of and other mega-projects, 258, 259; profit margins, 269; cost control, 270
Amagoalik, John, 243

Amarook, Michael, 190
American Dream, and the North, 223
American Indian Movement, 59, 216
American Pan Ocean Oil, 247
Anderson, Ron, 121
Anglican Book Centre, 228
Anglican General Synod, recommendations on moratorium, 229
Anglo-Russian Treaty (1825), 299
"Annales School," 42
Anthony, Russ, 104-05
Anti-trust regulations, 271
Apache, 61
Archaeology, finds in North, 194; Inuit evidence, 247
Archaeological sites, 60
Arctic char, 206
Arctic ecology, 180
Arctic environment, 179
Arctic exploration, 3, 5, 6; Canadian debate, 7; Norwegian expedition, 13
Arctic Institute of North America, xiv, 39
Arctic International Range (Alaska), 192
Arctic Land Use Research Program, 38
Arctic Marine Oilspills Program (AMOP), 201
Arctic Navigation, 252
Arctic Oil Exploration, 194
Arctic Pilot Project, 152, 196-97, 242, 245, 250, 251, 252, 253, 268, 297, 303, 324; problems of, 243; public hearings, 239, 243
Arctic pipelines, 267; controls for, 282; subsidized by public treasury, 265
Arctic species, 180, 207, 208
Arctic Waters Pollution Prevention Act (AWPPA), 22, 38, 200, 245, 293-97, 299; American response to, 293, 295; and spills and blow-outs, 300; problems of, 297-98
Aristotle, 62
Arrow, 291
Artificial islands, 172, 177, 195, 199
Athabascan language and cultural group, 61
Atkinson Point, 197
Atlantic-Richfield (ARCO), 1, 76, 271
Audubon Society, 38
Atwood, Margaret, 33

Boundary issue, 300-01
Bourassa Government, 71, 72
Bourque, James, 234
Boyle, Harry, 147
BP (British Petroleum), 284, 303
Bradley, R.A., 138
Brant, Joseph, 64
Braudel, Fernand, 42
Bregha, François, 131
Breynat, Bishop, 67
Brezhnev, L., 312
Bridport Inlet, 239
British Columbia, 126
British regime and Indian policy, 64
Broadbent, Ed, 107
Brooks, Dr. David, 321
Brooks, Ralph, 137
Bryce, Robert, 135
Buchanan, Judd, 71, 73
Buffalo, 210; the hunt, 60, 65, 67
Burke, Edmund, 40-41
Bush pilots, 16
Business community, concerns over
    Berger Report, 144

Caisson-retained island, 173, 175, 176;
    Molikpaq mobile Arctic caisson, 174
Calef, George, 182, 189, 190, 193
Campbell Lake, 197
Canada-Denmark Marine Pollution Con-
    tingency Plan, 298
Canada Development Corporation, 56,
    149, 260
Canada First movement, 6, 7
Canada Gazette, 150
Canada-United States Pipeline Agree-
    ment, 268, 275
Canadian-American relations, 324; and
    the *Manhattan*, 292; and the Mulro-
    ney government, 305; and the NEP,
    301-06; and the strategic defence
    of North, 309-10; in the Arctic,
    289-311
Canadian Arctic, 155; military and stra-
    tegic significance, 307
Canadian Arctic Gas, xiv, 37, 54, 57, 75,
    82, 83, 85, 96, 97, 98, 102, 105,
    106, 107, 108, 111, 115, 116, 117,
    118, 119, 120, 121, 126, 127, 133,
    134, 135, 136, 137, 139, 140, 141,
    142, 144, 145, 157, 165, 166, 177,
    180, 187, 188, 189, 192, 196, 197,
    198, 204, 205, 211, 215, 230, 257,
    259, 263, 264, 273, 287, 320, 322,
    323; allies of Ontario government,
    149; and Blair, 86; and media,
    101; and news coverage, 93; and
    permafrost, 157-64; and pro-devel-

opment model, 222-25; and Stelco,
    282-83; application, 130; attack
    by Foothills, 104; backstopping, 272;
    Canadian Arctic Gas system and
    connecting pipelines, 82; consor-
    tium, 260, 267; construction, 164;
    corporate role in society, 227; cor-
    porate sponsors of, 84; end of the
    line, 152; fear of native land claims,
    95; financial plan, 266; financial
    problems, 262; general strategy of,
    138; losing momentum, 151; money
    spent on application, 261; money
    spent on inquiry, 99; opening state-
    ment at Berger, 103-04; proposal,
    29; *raison d'être*, 226; trouble from
    Berger Report, 118-19; view of
    hearings, 95
Canadian Arctic Resources Committee
    (CARC), xiv, 29, 39, 58, 96, 107, 108,
    134, 145, 152, 180, 243, 322; attack
    on government secrecy, 104-05;
    establishment, 37; opening state-
    ments at Berger Inquiry, 104, 105;
    role in preliminary hearing, 97-98
Canadian Bar Association, 130
Canadian constitution, 313; three
    founding nations, 225
Canadian Environmental Law
    Association, 36, 98
Canadian foreign policy, and the North,
    310-12, 315
Canadian Forum, 47, 53, 54
Canadian gas exports, 129; *see also* Gas
    exports
Canadian identity, 2; effect of American
    TV and magazines, 47
Canadian Imperial Bank of Commerce,
    285
Canadian Labour Congress, 99
Canadian National Railways, 79
Canadian Nature Federation, 98
Canadian North, American interest, 18;
    American military need, 17; and
    Berger Inquiry, 102; economic de-
    velopment, 16; economic potential,
    10; impact of exploration on wild-
    life and native way of life, 39; legacy
    of, 16; resource hinterland, 226;
    spiritual escape, 23; strategic line of
    defence, 17
Canadian Oil and Gas Act, 303
Canadian Oil and Gas Lands Adminis-
    tration (COGLA), 302-03
Canadian ownership rate, 305
Canadian Pacific Investments, 260
Canadian Scientific Pollution and Envi-
    ronmental Control Society (SPEC), 98

Canadian Transport Commission, 130
Canadian Wildlife Federation, 131
Canadian Wildlife Service, 192, 217
Canadianization, 323, 324; of American companies, 85
Canmar Drilling (Dome), 172, 173, 305
Canmar *Kigoriak*, 171
Canol Pipeline, 8, 17
Canterra, 305, 317
Capital costs, 262, 268-69
Capital markets, 264, 265, 266
Cargo vessels, 172
Caribou, 118, 164, 180, 198, 244, 245, 250; and native hunters, 186; and offspring, 184-86; biological analysis and Mackenzie Valley Hearings, 180-94; Calef, 182; calving grounds, 185; decline of, 189; disturbances and, 191; environmental factors, 185-87; food, 186-87; herds of the North, 183; hunting, 190; key habitat, 190; migration, 15; Porcupine caribou herd, 151; winter range, 184
Carney, Pat, 305
Carr, Shirley, 303
Carruthers, Jeff, 116, 118, 135
Carter administration, 271, 272, 276, 277, 278, 301
Cash flow, 262
Catholic church, Pope Paul III and thought on natives, 62
Caveat, 67, 71, 213
CBC, 55, 100, 110, 119, 126, 137
CBC Northern Service, 100, 110
C.D. Howe Research Institute, 51
CCF, 26
Chambers, Luther, 247
Champion, Charles, 258
Chant, Donald, 35, 36
Charter of Rights, 313
Chippewas, 64
Chrétien, Jean, 39, 93, 129, 192
Christian theology, role in environmental crisis, 43-44
Churches, 62, 109; and treaties, 213; Anglican and Catholic in northern debate, 228; efforts in pipeline hearings, 230; involvement in pipeline debate, 26; *see also* Missionaries
Circumpolar Conference, 311
Circumpolar co-operation, 289
Circumpolar nations, 289-91; and sharing in scientific and technological research, 309-10
Circumpolar North, 290
Circumpolar threat, 308
Circumpolar world, 289-311

Clark administration, 230, 275
Clark, Joe, 278
Clarkson, Adrienne, 55
Climate, 179; effects on Canadian character, 6, 7, 8; effects on worker productivity, 164-65; challenge of, 8; extremes, 163; protecting North, 22
Climatic forces, 163, 258
Club of Rome, 43, 46
Colonists, 63
Colonialism and dependence of North, xiii, 227
Columbia Gas Ltd., 79
Cominco, 246
Cominco Polaris Mine, 239
Committee for an Independent Canada (CIC), xiii, 47, 54, 56, 97, 99, 129, 130, 131, 132, 140, 145, 149, 157; northern topics, 55; policy issues, 55; role in debate on pipeline, 55; role in preliminary hearings, 96
Committee for Justice and Liberty, 134, 136, 138, 228, 233-34
Committee for Original Peoples Entitlement (COPE), 106, 143, 192, 217, 230, 247, 251
Communal values, 52, 255
Community hearings, 97, 100, 112, 113, 122, 142, 156, 211, 215; and media, 100; and public participation, 216; hearings Vancouver to Halifax, 113; Norman Wells, 110; Old Crow, 111; own language, 94
Company of Young Canadians, 14
Completion insurance, 265
Compressor stations, 170, 196, 197
Computer simulations, 177
Condition XII (Alaska Highway Pipeline), 277, 278
Confederation, 210, 217, 236; and Manitoba, 61; special Indian status, 65
Conference of Catholic Bishops, 229
Conflict-of-interest guidelines, 146
Conservation, 50, 179, 190
Conservation Council of Ontario, 34
Conservation movement, 30, 31; *see also* Environmental movement
Conserver society, 43; and impact on gas markets, 268
Conservative Party, 49, 55, 56, 85, 120
Consolidated Bathurst, 261
Consortiums, 260, 263
Construction, 158, 197, 262, 268-269; costs, 286; toll on machinery, 258; winter, 165; equipment and techniques, 198, 258; problems for, 164

Consumers Association of Canada, 27,
29, 130, 134
Consumers' Gas, 260, 263
Consumer Price Index, 206, 262
Cook, Ramsay, 52
Corcoran, Thomas, 280
Corporate financial planners, 156
Corporate-funded research studies, 204
Corporate social responsibility, xiii, 121,
122, 227; new standards, 209
Corporations, 46, 115
Corrosion, 165, 170
Cost/benefit analysis, 45; and down-
grading social and environmental
costs, 46; traditions, 205
Cost control, 270
Cost estimates, 260, 261, 262, 270, 279
Cost-overruns, 257, 263, 264, 269-70,
279, 280
Council of Yukon Indians, 192, 217,
230
Cowan, Andrew, 110
CPR, 60, 61, 64, 104, 114, 210
Crack arrestors, 165
Cree, 72
Crerar, T.A., 67
Creighton, Donald, 48, 49
Crombie, David, 235, 313
Crosby, Diana, 100
Crowe, Marshall, 44, 133, 135, 136, 146,
150, 228, 259; economic nationalist,
134; trip north, 145
Crowe case, 135, 141, 149, 152; ruling
on, 136-137
CRTC, 137
Crude oil, 199
Cryoanchor, 169-70
Cullaton Lake Gold Mines, 251
Curley, Tagak, 251
Cultural barriers, 220
Cultural erosion, 214, 221
Cultural survival, 210
Cultural traditions, 212
Cumming, Professor Peter, 71

Darwin, Charles, 42
Darwinism, struggle with nature, 15;
racial, 7
Davis Strait, 239, 244, 312
De Roo, Bishop Remi, 229
Decision-making, 204; Berger and NEB
on northern pipelines, 322; govern-
ment, 92, 207
Deep-water wells, 171, 173, 200
Deficiency letters (NEB), 128, 133
Delta gas, 85, 120
Delta producers, 132
Dempster Highway, 118, 189, 191, 192

Dempster Lateral Pipeline, 282, 286
Dene Nation (Native Brotherhood of
Northwest Territories), xiii, 2, 22,
59, 67, 68, 69, 71, 73, 91, 94, 106,
109, 119, 145, 190, 210, 212, 214,
215, 216, 217, 220, 221, 223, 225,
226, 228, 229, 230, 231, 233, 235,
253, 255, 259, 314, 318; and new
political forms, 218; and white advisers, 224; Athabascan, 61; ethnic
group, 60; folk culture, 61; heritage,
194; new pragmatism of, 236; relin-
quishes commitment to ten-year
moratorium, 234; scenario for land
claims negotiations, 240-41; structure of government desired, 236-40;
subgroups, 62; treaties, 66
Dene Declaration, 119; and need for
new political form, 225
Denendeh, 255, 314; difference from
Nunavut, 251; new province description, 236-40; regulation for resource development, 236-38
Department of Consumer and Corporate
Affairs, 130
Department of Energy, Mines, and Resources, 180, 192, 217, 252, 316,
317, 321; establishment, 124
Department of the Environment (Envi-
ronment Canada), 38, 105, 107,
108, 180, 201, 316
Department of External Affairs, 245,
252, 315
Department of Indian Affairs and
Northern Development, 38, 71, 83,
180, 201, 202, 219, 252, 315, 316;
mandate of, 227
Department of the Interior, 44, 45, 141,
188, 198
Department of Justice, 130, 135, 219;
legal presentation against Inuit, 247
Department of National Defence, 217,
315
Department of Northern Affairs, 79
Department of Social Development
(N.W.T.), 221
Department of Transport (Transport
Canada), 201, 217, 315
Deregulation, 153, 318; of natural gas
prices in U.S., 269
Design, 161, 162, 163, 164, 171, 172,
175, 176, 257, 258; analysis, 156;
experimental, 159; new technical
design, 173; original work, 155;
technical, 160
Development Projects, 215
Diamond, Billy, 72
Dickens, Charles, 5, 6

347

Diefenbaker, John, 18, 19, 20, 21, 22,
47, 68; cabinet, 192
Discontinuous permafrost, 159
Distant Early Warning (DEW) line, 18,
19, 20, 308
Disturbances, 196, 197, 198; and snow
geese, 195; impact on caribou, 191
Dobell, Peter, 310
Dobson, Thomas, 265
Doll sheep, 190
Dome, 167, 168, 171, 172, 173, 175,
176, 195, 199, 200, 201, 202, 239,
243, 276, 285, 302, 306; Arctic
tanker, 170
Dome Mobile Arctic Drilling Vessel
(SSDC), 175
Dosman, Edgar, 22, 44, 79, 228, 310
Douglas, Tommy, 106; energy critic,
NDP, 56-57
Drache, Danny, 51
Drake Point, 239
Drew, Wayland, 33, 34, 53
Drill cores, 163
Drilling, 172, 173, 175, 176, 199, 200,
202, 204, 241, 256, 310, 321, 324;
Beaufort, 176; marine and environ-
mental impact, 298; zone in Beau-
fort, 167
Drilling platforms, 175, 176
Drillships, 172, 173, 175, 176, 195, 199
Drury Report, 238
Dumont, Gabriel, 60
Dunbar, Max, 180, 207
Duplessis, Maurice, 56

Earthquake, 166
Eastern Arctic, 240, 241, 253, 298, 300
Ecological activities, 41
Ecological balance, 43
Ecological concerns, 97
Ecological investigation, 76
Ecology, 41; northern, 37; politics of,
29-47
Economic benefits, 283
Economic Council of Canada, 51, 321
Economic development, benefits to U.S.,
226; dilemma of North, 227; evi-
dence, 226; social cost, 102-03
Economic growth, 140; and mega-proj-
ects, 282; most rapid, 42; rate, 229
Economic questions, 108, 323
Economic rent, 283
Economics, analysis of Berger Report,
117; and environmental considera-
tions, 205; as gulf between private
enterprise and environmental movement, 46; benefits of foreign owner-

ship, 54; economic thinking, 46;
environmental movement, 46; exploitation policies and benefits, 233;
free enterprise, 50; integration,
56; Keynesian, 45; laissez-faire, 51;
of deep-water wells, 171; of Norman Wells project, 231; pipelines,
effect on economic life, 75; post-
Keynesian, 45; system, 255; tool for
government and business, 45; tool
for liberal democracies, 50
Economies of scale, 276
Economy, 46, 53, 222, 282-83
Ecosystems, 179, 181, 182, 192, 193,
205, 206, 207, 315
Edgar Jourdain, 201
Edge, Geoff, 137-38, 153, 229, 263, 267,
276, 277, 278, 323
Edmonton Journal, 100
Edwards, James, 279
Eisenhower administration, 192
Ekirch, Arthur, 32
El Paso Project, 81, 93, 95, 96, 101, 134,
138, 140, 142, 259, 283
Eldorado, 16, 17
Ellesmere Island, 300, 307
Emerson, Ralph Waldo, 32
Endangered species, 180
Enders, Thomas, 149
Energy Allocation Board (NEB), 125
Energy investments, 286
Energy policy, 74, 125, 303, 306
Energy reserve, 140
Energy shortage, 132, 222, 238
Engineering, civil, 163; in North, 159;
philosophy of Arctic Gas, 177-78;
data, 157, 171; problems, 155,
170
Engineers, 155, 156, 160, 176, 198;
pipeline, 159, 177
Environment rights, 85, 92
Environmental assessment, 182, 197;
and permafrost, 163
Environmental Assessment and Review
Process (EARP), 132, 176, 201, 202,
203, 230, 231, 239, 317, 320, 322;
public hearings, 204; report, 233
Environmental code, 111
Environmental concerns, 113, 120, 122,
157, 190, 235; of Berger Inquiry,
101; of CARC, 97
Environmental cost, 283
Environmental factors, 205
Environmental impact, 198, 205, 206,
235, 250, 289; of development, 190;
of marine drilling, 298; of tankers
on marine mammals, 244

Environmental Impact Assessment (EIA), 38, 180, 181, 204, 205, 254, 299
Environmental Impact Statement (EIS), 44, 180, 201, 207
Environmental indexes, 206
Environmental integrity, 181; and territorial integrity, 293
Environmental judgements, 205
Environmental movement, 24, 30, 35, 37, 40, 41, 46, 58; early evolution, 29; in U.S., 44
Environmental organizations, 144, 179, 200, 201, 202; against Alyeska, 45; American, 38
Environmental planning, 243
Environmental policy, Canadian, 35
Environmental problems, 244, 325
Environmental protection, 179, 292
Environmental Protection Board, 79, 97, 108, 111, 116, 141, 151, 160, 163, 180, 188, 196, 206
Environmental regulations, 204, 205, 245, 259, 291, 292, 293, 296
Environmental standards, 36, 83
Environmentalism, 24, 39, 59; similarity to nationalism, 58; spiritual ingredients, 43
Environmentalists, 58, 91, 111, 120, 133, 180, 204, 247, 294, 320; concerns about the "commons," 46; funding at NEB, 130; threat of industrialism and growth economics, 48
Equidistance principle, 298-300
Erasmus, George, 220, 224, 234, 236
Erosion, 158, 173, 188
Esso Resources, 234, 235; and Norman Wells, 231
Ethical questions, 227-30
Exclusive economic zone, 299
"Expanded Guidelines for Northern Pipelines," 81, 86, 93, 157, 180
Exploratory wells, 195, 299
Exports, 267-68, 273, 275-77
Exxon, 1, 52, 56, 76, 85, 104, 121, 133, 141, 226, 257, 260, 261, 271

Fairbanks, 142
Falcons, 197
Farmer, Jacques, 134
Faulkner, Hugh, 193, 246
Fault lines, 166
Federal Commission on Conservation, 31
Federal Court of Appeal, 129, 136
Federal government, 60, 95, 99, 115, 122, 180, 195, 200, 213, 228, 235, 252, 313; corporate leadership in

APP, 243; government policy, 100; problems in negotiating land claims, 217; reaction to Denendeh proposal, 238; role in economic development in North, 288; trustee for native people, 72; unhappy with Inuit demands, 245
Federal Power Commission (U.S.), 83, 131, 140, 141, 142, 160, 263, 264, 269
Federalism, 53
Federation of Ontario Naturalists, 32, 98
Flyways (bird migration), 194
Financial advisers, 259
Financial markets, 281
Financial planning, 263; for Pre-Build, 281
Financial Post, 282
Financial problems, 279; Alaska Northwest, 270; and start of project, 268-69; of northern pipelines, 260-70; of Pre-Build, 276
Financial projections, 284
Financing, 256-88; Canadian, 86; of Alaska Highway Project, 271-72
Fisheries, 307, 312
Food chain, 181, 199, 205; effect on of oil spill, 200
Food production, 181
Foothills Pipeline, xi, xiv, 75, 86, 115, 118, 132, 135, 136, 139, 140, 142, 145, 149, 162, 163, 166, 182, 193, 196, 225, 257, 263, 268, 272, 276, 277, 279, 281, 282, 283, 287; against backstopping, 264; corporate role in society, 227; delay help, 137; money spent on application, 261; opening statement at Berger Inquiry, 104; original Alaska Highway route, 143; strategy, 138; system, 87
Ford administration, 149
Foreign direct investment in Canada, 54
Foreign Investment Review Agency, (FIRA), 56, 280, 301
Foreign ownership, 40, 47, 54, 55, 56, 323
Forestry companies, 42
Formal hearings (Berger Inquiry), 94, 122
Fort Good Hope, 166
Fort MacPherson, 120
Fort McMurray, 106
Fort Norman, 233
Fort Simpson, 161, 166, 228, 233, 235
Foster, Janet, 30
Foxe Basin, 201

Fractures, 165
Franklin, Sir John, 3, 5, 6
Fraser, Blair, 34
Fraser, John, 320
Fraser, Whit, 100, 110
Free enterprise, 228; and backstopping,
    272; and capitalism, 215; Inuit
    involvement, 251; philosophy, 211;
    scale required in North, 256; shift
    in Dene attitude toward, 235, 236
Freedom of Information Act, 131
Frobisher Bay, 239
"Front-end loading," 287
Frost heave, 158, 159, 160, 161, 162,
    163, 177
Frost, Leslie, 20
Fumoleau, Father, 66
Fyles, Dr. John, 97, 108, 160

Galbraith, John Kenneth, 25, 45
Galway, Michael, 21
Gas, 157; chill gas, 159, 160, 161, 166;
    supply, 156
Gas Arctic, 81
Gas Arctic Systems Study Group, 79
Gas exports, 273, 275-77, 324
Gas supply hearings, 128
Gas transmission, 284
Gemini North, 224
General Accounting Office (U.S.), 270
Genest, Pierre, 103, 105, 107
"Genocide," 225, 234
Geological formations, 172, 173
Geological Survey of Canada, 11, 97
Geophysical question, 161, 177
Geotechnical, 108, 122, 157, 165, 170,
    199, 315, 323
Gibbs, Reg, 104, 132, 139, 141, 149,
    150, 275
Gibson, Kelly, 86
Gillespie, Alastair, 120, 121, 141
Gillies, Jim, 145
Globe and Mail, 100, 121, 145, 146, 235;
    and Berger Report, 118; coverage
    of Berger appointment, 93
Glomar Beaufort Sea (CIDS), 177
Goldie, Michael, 102, 103, 132, 133,
    139, 149; counsel for Arctic Gas, 95;
    strategy, 96
Goodman, Eddy, 129
Gordon, Walter, 54, 56; as Minister of
    Finance, 55; efforts to counter con-
    tinentalism, 47; key figure in na-
    tionalist forces, 51
Government "backstopping," 262, 263-
    64, 271, 272, 279, 287
Government intervention, 115

Government regulations, 303
Grant, George, 48
Gravel, Senator, 284
Gray, Earl, xii
Gray, Herb, 54
Great Bear Hydro Project, 102
Great Bear Lake, 16
Great Slave Lake, 16, 166, 189
Graham, William, 247
Greenland, 243, 252, 297, 298, 300, 312,
    315, 324; and Canada, 311; Inuit,
    298; strategic significance, 308
Gros Cacouna, 239
Group of Seven, 16
Growth ethic, 36
Gulf Canada, 54, 120, 132, 139, 173,
    175, 195, 197, 199, 226, 264, 267,
    285, 305, 306, 319, 323
Gulf of Mexico, 199
Gunn, Dr. William, 196, 197, 198, 204
Gwyn, Richard, 120

Habitat, 195, 200, 241; and sonar navi-
    gation, 244; critical, 318
Haig, Alexander, 305
Haliburton, R.G., 6
Hall Report, 90, 91; influence on Berger,
    90
Hans Island, 300
Hardy, Rick, 120
Harvard Business School, xiii, 205
Hay River, 144, 210, 215
Head, Governor Bond, 64
Heat probes, 161, 162
Heat-tracing, 161-62
Heilbroner, Robert, 45
Helliwell, John, 127
Helm, June, 107
Hemstock, Alex, 197
High Arctic, 181, 200, 239, 245-46
High Arctic islands, 1, 8, 12, 13, 77, 167,
    171, 172, 194, 243, 256
Historians, 43
History, Berger's reverence for, 91;
    biological factors, 42; Canada, 250;
    Canadian economic, 49; ecological
    interpretation, 43; environmental,
    42; lessons of, 43; social, economic,
    environmental factors, 41-42
Hobart, Charles, 226; and pro-develop-
    ment model, 222-25
Hockin, Allan B., 265
Hodgins, Bruce, 53
Holst, Johan, 311
Honderick, Beland, 54
Hopwood, John, 140
Hornby, John, 15

Horner, Jack, 120
Horte, Vern, 76, 78, 81, 83, 85, 119, 121, 134, 261, 267, 273
House of Commons Standing Committee on Northern Pipelines, 272
Houston, Bill, 150
Howe, C.D., 18, 306
Hudson Bay, 201, 246
Hudson's Bay Company, 5, 14, 16, 60, 68; acquisition of Rupert's Land from, 8
Hudson's Bay Company Charter of 1670, 247
Hudson Bay Railway, 187
Humble Oil, 21, 76
Hurtig, Mel, 55, 130
Husky Oil, 77

Ice, 155, 171, 173, 176; and impact of Arctic Pilot Project, 239; conditions, 172; Inuit claims to, 252; shore fast, 241
Ice-breaking tankers, 256
Ice crystals, 157
Ice islands, 176
Ice jams, 166
Ice lensing, 163, 177
Ice platforms, 172, 241
Ice scour, 155, 166, 176, 172, 199; in Beaufort, 168
Ice sealing, 200
Imperial Oil, xiv, 16, 47, 54, 75, 120, 121, 132, 139, 166, 168, 171, 172, 173, 176, 177, 195, 197, 199, 226, 230, 317, 323, 264, 267, 285; and NEP, 303; and Norman Wells Project, 231; offer to Dome, 232; town, 110
Imperial vision, early exploration of North, 7
"Incentive rate of return," 269
Indians, 62, 65, 71; land policy toward, 63; see also Native peoples
Indian Act, 65, 68, 119, 219
Indian Brotherhood of N.W.T. (Dene), 71, 98; suspicion of inquiry, 94-95
Indian policy, 64
Indian religion, 214
Industrial development, 210
Industrial impact, 179, 180, 221
Industrial psychology, 259
Industrial Revolution, 155
Industrial society, 210; impact on traditional communities, 91
Information Canada, 131-32
Inhaber, Dr. Herbert, 206
In-house assessment, 128, 133, 201
Innis, Harold, 48, 49, 50, 256; analysis

of Canadian-American relations, 49; contribution to nationalism, 50; debate on, 53; influence on Berger Report, 117; school, 51; staples thesis, 48
"Innocent passage," 292
Insects, effect on caribou, 185-86
"Insignificant increments," 207
Institute of Guided Ground Transport (Queen's University), 138
Insulation, 161
International Court of Justice (The Hague), 293, 304
Intellectual ideas, 39-40
International Biological Program (IBP), 197
International law, 292, 293
International Migratory Bird Convention, 66
Interprovincial Pipeline, 168, 171, 230, 231, 233
Inuit, 2, 22, 59, 62, 63, 73, 94, 119, 132, 152, 200, 214, 215, 220, 225, 228, 229, 230, 248, 250, 253, 255, 293, 314, 318; and new political forms, 218; chief concerns about Arctic Pilot Project, 239; claim to ice, 252; concerns over ice, 243; ethnic group, 60; food supply, 198; in Greenland, 298; northern Quebec, 71, 72; protection of marine mammals, 245; rights in North, 64; sense of community, 212; sub-groups, 61
Inuit aboriginal rights, 247, 297
Inuit of Baker Lake, 247-50
Inuit Circumpolar Conference, 252, 297, 311
Inuit Development Corporation, 251
Inuit hunters, 246, 251; and impact of Arctic Pilot Project, 244
Inuit land claims, 247, 298
Inuit Tapirisat of Canada (ITC), 106, 190, 217, 243, 250, 253
Inuvik, 142, 143, 144, 210, 215, 299
Issungnak, 197

Jackson, Michael, 94, 112
James Bay Agreement, 72, 219, 220
James Bay Cree, 214, 219, 220
James Bay Development Corporation, 71-72
James Bay Project, 65, 71, 103, 209, 221, 253
Jamieson, Dr. Stewart, 107
Jan Mayen, 312
Jenness, Diamond, xvii
Johnson, Albert, 15, 16

Johnson, Leo, 40
Judeo-Christian beliefs, 43-44
Jurisdiction, disputes, 311; in North, 292-96; jurisdictional boundaries, 300; of coastal states, 294; offshore boundary, 299-301

Kakfwi, Stephen, 235
Keflavik, 307
Kelly, Brian, 37
Kendall Island Bird Sanctuary, 197, 199
Kidd, Benjamin, 7
King administration, 14
King, Mackenzie, 17, 48
Kissinger, Henry, 307
Klondike, see Yukon
Koakoak, 173
Kopanour, 173
Kulluk, 175

Labatt's, 37
Labine, Gilbert, 16
Lacombe, Father, 66
Lalonde, Marc, 276, 278, 317
Lamar, Fred, 130
Lancaster Sound, 190, 204, 239, 244, 245, 298
Land claims, 59, 62, 69, 71, 73-74, 105, 106, 109, 114, 118, 189, 214, 235, 238, 245, 250, 253, 314; and Berger Report, 119; and lessons of James Bay, 220; and relationship to wider economic system of Canada, 222; legal foundation, 62; native concerns about, 219-20; negotiations, 213; problems of negotiating, 217; see also Native land claims
Land claims benefits, 218-19
Land claims movement, 215
Land claims negotiations, 228, 229, 231, 245, 246, 252, 253, 318; Dene scenario for, 239-40; problems in co-ordinating, 218
Land claims settlement, 215, 218, 221, 222, 223, 225, 230, 231, 234, 236, 251
Land forms, 157, 158
Land rights, 246
Land settlement, 66, 69, 214, 218
Land, the, access to, 215; and land claims, 59; and native people's view, 61, 113, 211-13; Canada's greatest asset, 57-58; ecological viability of, 229; gift of, 230; living off, 215, 255; myth of clearing, 31; future generations, 223; ownership con-

cept, 66; responsibility to, 53; true owners, 62; violence over possession of native lands, 216
Laskin, Chief Justice Bora, 136
Laurier government, 10, 13, 30, 42
Law of the sea, 294, 310, 324
Law of the Sea Conference, 245, 252, 295-96
Law of the Sea Convention, 296, 297
Law of the Sea Treaty, 296
Law Reform Commission, 91
Lawrence, Allan, 277
Laxer, Jim, 40, 54, 55, 56
Leacock, Stephen, 3, 8
League for Social Reconstruction, 26
Leduc, 16
Lemmings, 81
Lewis, David, 85
Liberal Party, 49, 55, 130, 139
Liberal democracy, 25-26
Lichens, 181, 190
Limits to Growth, The, 43, 46-47
Lincoln Sea, 300
Little Cornwallis Island, 239
Littlejohn, Bruce, 34
Livingston, John, 38
LNG, 239, 253, 257; aircraft and tankers, 138; conveyor belt, 138; exports, 268; tankers, 77, 81, 140, 267
Lobbying, 28, 35, 115, 121, 192, 269, 280, 281
Long-term debt, 287
Lougheed government, 126, 263
Lowenthal, David, 32
Lysyk Commission, 283

Macdonald, Donald, 37, 83, 93, 129, 130
MacDonald, Flora, 54, 56
Macdonald government, 61
MacEachen, Allan, 304
Mackenzie Basin, 10
Mackenzie Delta, 1, 60, 76, 126, 127, 140, 159, 164, 168, 172, 188, 190, 194, 196, 198, 226, 247, 256, 314, 318
Mackenzie Delta gas, 127
Mackenzie government, 8, 9
Mackenzie Highway, 180, 197
Mackenzie River, 50, 166, 167
Mackenzie Valley, 61, 91, 92, 107, 117, 118, 120, 122, 152, 160, 166, 210, 212, 230, 239, 318
Mackenzie Valley Pipeline, xi, xiii, 2, 37, 40, 42, 52, 55, 57, 61, 71, 74, 105, 117, 122, 125, 127, 132, 171, 179, 180, 201, 206, 209, 210, 256, 259,

273, 314-15; engineering problems, 155; social and moral chaos, 229
Mackenzie Valley Pipeline Inquiry, *see* Berger Inquiry
Macro-economics, 265
"Mad Trapper of Rat River," *see* Johnson, Albert
Mahoney, Justice Patrick, 246, 247, 248, 250
Major Projects Task Force, 303
Maleuf, Justice, 71
Man-made barriers, 191
Manhattan, 2, 22, 38, 47, 53, 76, 79, 200, 252, 291-92, 295, 297, 299, 310
Manifest Destiny, 63
Manuel, George, 95
Maple Leaf line, 104, 140, 141, 142, 144, 165, 261; map, 87
Marine drilling, 172, 199
Marine environment, 294, 298
Market forces, 51, 178, 205, 266, 303; as self-regulating mechanism, 46
Market price, 285
Marsh, George Perkins, 32
Marshall, Chief Justice John, 63
Marx, Karl, 42, 256
Marxism, 40, 49, 51, 226; economic analysis, 52; Marxist state and native demands, 215; view of multinationals, 51
Matrix method, 206
McClelland, Jack, 55
McCool, Nydia, 131
McCullum, Hugh, 228
McCullum, Karmel, 228
McDermott, Dennis, 56
McDougall, Professor Ian, 131, 146
McKinley Bay, 173, 202
McMillan, Tom, 313
McMillian, John, 272, 273, 281
Media, 110, 116, 121, 128, 132-33, 145, 150, 152, 153, 189, 319; and Berger Report, 120; and NEB opening, 134; at Berger Inquiry, 100-01; environmental commentary, 33; local, 113
Mega-projects, 140, 155, 197, 205, 207, 208, 222, 251, 286, 287, 302, 303, 313, 318, 321, 325; Arctic, 258-59, 260; economically feasible, 256; financing, 265; stimulus for economy, 282
Meighen, Arthur, 30
Melford Point, 239
Melville Island, 239
Melville Shipping, 239

Mental Health Association of the N.W.T., 97
Methane hydrates (frozen natural gas), 173
Métis, 219, 314; ethnic group, 60; folk culture, 61; land claims, 61
Métis Association, 105, 219, 228; desired structures of government, 236-40; political split, 218; relinquish commitment to ten-year moratorium, 234
Metropolitanism, 255
Michigan-Wisconsin Pipeline of Detroit, 76
Mid-Canada Corridor, 20, 21
Mid-Canada Development Foundation, 47
Middle East, 172, 245, 280, 284
Military and strategic significance, 320; and Greenland, 308; of Arctic, 307-09
Mill, John Stuart, 45
Mineral Leasing Act, 45
Mining, 239, 246, 250
Ministry of Northern Affairs and Natural Resources, 192
Missionaries, 228; and treaties, 213; church in North, 16, 22, 66; explaining treaties to natives, 67, 68
Mississaugas, 64
Molikpaq-Mobile Arctic Caisson, 174, 176
Molson, 38
Monetary policy, 265
Money markets, 265, 281, 287
Moose, 190
Morgan, Donald, 126
Morgan Stanley, 85
Morris, Hugh, 130
Morrow, Justice, 71; Caveat case (1973), 67
Morton, W. L., 2, 34
Mosquitoes, 186
Mosses, 181
Mountain Pacific Pipeline, 78, 141
Mowat, Farley, 3
Mulroney, Brian, 307, 324; Canadian-American relations, 305-06
Mulroney government, 153, 175, 235, 305, 306, 313
Multinational oil companies, 125, 134, 226, 235
Multinationals, 48, 51, 52, 54, 56
Munro, John, 231
Muskeg, 170
Muskox, 181, 190

Myth of the North, xii, 1-24

Nader, Ralph, 280, 281
Nares Strait, 300
Nash, Roderick, 31, 32
National and Provincial Parks
    Association, 32
National Energy Board, xii, xiv, 20, 44,
    46, 55, 81, 83, 97, 98, 101, 102,
    103, 105, 108, 111, 115, 116, 121,
    123, 126, 127, 131, 133, 134, 135,
    136, 142, 144, 145, 146, 149, 154,
    159, 161, 162, 163, 188, 198, 204,
    220, 225, 229, 230, 239, 244, 252,
    253, 257, 259, 264, 265, 266, 267,
    268, 270, 273, 276, 277, 278, 286,
    287, 313, 315, 317, 318, 321, 322,
    323; and comparison of procedures
    with Berger, 319-20; appointment
    of members, 153; central features
    of, 230; challenge to CARC, 37; de-
    cline in participation in, 152; differ-
    ences from Berger, 150-51; export
    application of Pan-Alberta, 275;
    final weeks, 151; funding groups,
    137; hearings, 92, 96; informal
    advisory function of, 147; internal
    organizational changes, 316; origins,
    124; procedural matters, 152; pro-
    ceeding steps, 128; representation
    on interdepartmental committees
    and task forces, 147-49; regulatory
    function, 125; staff members, 150;
    technical jargon, 129
National Energy Board Act, 322
National Energy Board Guidelines for
    Regional Socio-Economic Impact
    Assessments for Pipeline Projects,
    209
National Energy Board Report, 128,
    129, 151, 234, 263, 275, 276; and
    Norman Wells project, 233; condi-
    tional approval to Foothills, 151-
    52; on northern pipeline require-
    ments, 273
National Energy Program, 279, 280,
    285, 301-06; and Canadian-Ameri-
    can relations, 301-06; and Imperial
    Oil, 303; "back-in" clause, 304-
    05, 306
National Environmental Policy Act
    (U.S.), 44, 45, 202, 259
National Film Board, 16, 100
National Geographic, 16
National Indian Brotherhood, 95, 105,
    109

National Museum of Man, 60
National Oil Policy, 124
National Research Council, 161
Nationalism, 51, 59, 133, 323; American,
    53; and environmentalism, 58; and
    patriotism, 57; contribution of Innis,
    50; description, 52; emerging in
    late 1960's, 47; in Canada, 57; intel-
    lectual debate, 53, 323; Pearson's
    view, 56; physical independence, 48;
    responsibility to, 53; rise of eco-
    nomic nationalism, 54; roots of in-
    tellectual nationalism, 48, 49;
    spiritual identity, 48; Stanfield's
    view, 56; suspicious of, 56; philoso-
    phy of Bob Blair, 77; theme of
    Foothills Pipeline, 104
Nationalist movement, 47, 56, 57
Nationalist response, 47-58; between
    Trudeau and Nixon governments,
    53; challenge to northern lands, 47
Native communities, 59, 214, 228, 254;
    and problems with development,
    233
Native culture, 213
Native economies, 254
Native educational system, 213-14, 222;
    and development of expectations,
    223; proposals for, 236
Native entrepreneurs, 234, 235
Native organizations, 110, 133, 144, 213,
    224, 225, 234, 235, 250, 294, 313,
    314; and Arctic Gas, 215; caution to
    land claims negotiations, 217-18;
    present evidence on traditions, 102
Native hunters, 189, 199; and caribou,
    186-87
Native land claims, 209, 259-60, 315;
    negotiations, 316, 319, 325; settle-
    ment, 55, 81, 90, 91, 102, 117, 144,
    190, 193, 226, 230, 236
Native land rights, 73; cases, 70-71
Native language, 213, 236
Native leaders, 59, 65, 73, 94, 113, 119,
    120, 189, 190, 211, 220, 222, 233,
    315; and James Bay Agreement, 72;
    and "Red scare" tactics, 215
Native peoples, 58, 63, 65, 67, 71, 72,
    105, 109, 113, 122, 209-56, 259,
    318; and gold rush, 66; and movies,
    214; and oil development, 233;
    basic problems, 254; crisis, 210; how
    came to North America, 60; jobs
    in construction, 235; lost their lands,
    61; maximize economic benefits
    to, 236; renaissance of Canada's, 59;

354

right to land, 62; sense of history, 60; Watkins' analysis, 226; way of life, 181
Native rights, 59, 60, 83, 85, 92, 113, 139, 215, 217, 250, 313; and Berger Inquiry, 101; federal authorities, 65; to homeland, 62; *see also* Aboriginal rights
NATO, 18, 307, 308, 311
Natural Gas Pipeline of America, 76
Natural Gas Policy Act (U.S.), 269
Natural resources, 49
Naturalist clubs, 30
Naylor, Tom, 40, 51
Navaho, 61
Navisivik mine, 239
Nelson Commission, 68
New Democratic Party (NDP), 40, 56, 85, 106, 107; and pipeline inquiry, 92
New York Stock Exchange, 261
New York Times, 279
Nerysoo, Richard, 253
Newman, Peter, 54
News of the North, 107, 109
Nishgas, 70-71, 90, 92, 259
Nixon administration, 45, 53, 56; and AWPPA, 293, 295
No-strike clauses, 259
Non-renewable resources, 235, 268
Non-status Indians, 219
NORAD, 308, 315
Noranda, 246
"Nordpolitik," 311
Norman Wells, 16, 17, 66, 79, 110, 166, 168-69, 212, 215, 230, 231, 233, 314
Norman Wells Pipeline Report, 129
Norman Wells Oil Pipeline, 152, 168, 232, 234, 235, 239, 319
North American Air Defence Command, 18
North Sea, 199
North Sea Continental Shelf Cases, 300
North Slope of Yukon, 122, 141, 186, 187, 188, 190-91, 193, 194, 196, 271, 279, 318, 319
Northern Assessment Group, 98
Northern boundaries, 8, 9
Northern development, 93, 120, 122, 176, 178, 217, 226, 253; and financing, 266-67; and mines and oil potential, 300-01; and social change, 220; social costs, 103
Northern development policy, 71, 91, 104-05; ethics of, 227
Northern development projects, 79, 224

Northern Engineering Services, 162
Northern Land Use Regulations, 38
Northern Miner, 246-47
Northern Natural Gas (U.S.), 79
Northern pipelines, 126, 225, 227, 321; economic viability of, 256-88
Northern Pipeline Act, 276, 277
Northern Pipeline Agency, 204
Northern pipeline applications, 126, 134
Northern pipeline hearings, 124, 125, 128, 131, 147, 153, 154, 318; controversial procedural matters, 149; most difficult problems, 142-43; *see also* Berger Inquiry; National Energy Board
Northern policy formation, 208
Northern projects, 287
Northern whites, 108-10
Northern Yukon Wilderness Park, 193
Northwest Alaska Project, 141, 142, 268, 270, 271, 272, 276, 279, 280, 281
Northwest Passage, 2, 3, 5, 21, 168, 252, 291, 292, 296, 297, 298, 311, 324
Northwest Project Study Group, 76, 77, 78-79, 86
Northwest Staging Route, 17
Northwest Territories, 30, 59, 62, 67, 68, 71, 76, 78, 92, 210, 214, 219, 227, 230, 238, 247, 256
Northwest Territories Assembly, 120, 233, 234, 314
Northwest Territories Association of Municipalities, 97, 144; problems of major development, 106
Northwest Territories Chamber of Commerce, 100, 144
Northwest Territories Métis Association, 120
Nortran, native apprentice program, 222
Nova, 239, 243, 261, 273, 275, 276; *see also* Foothills Pipeline
Norway, 291, 307, 312; and Nordpolitik, 311
Nuclear waste, 179
Nunavut proposals, 250-51, 255, 314; difference from Denendeh, 251

Office of Industrial and Regional Benefits, 303
Offshore boundary, 299-301
Offshore drilling, 199, 200, 201, 202, 299, 320; exploration, 172-79, 199, 241; fields, 197
Offshore oil production, 300

Ogilvie Mountains, 186
Oil and Gas Land Regulations, 20
Oil blobs, 200
Oil industry, 54, 101, 113, 214, 215,
    257; failure to appreciate concept of
    public ownership, 49
Oil production system, 173, 231
Oil spill, 167, 195, 200, 201, 293, 294,
    298, 299, 300, 320, 321; and *Arrow*,
    291; technology for, 310
Oil tankers, 176, 243, 244, 245, 253,
    257, 292, 324; accidents, 320; de-
    sign, 175; Dome tanker, 170;
    through Arctic waters, 169
Old Crow, 111, 191, 192, 194, 245, 255
Olmstead, Cecil, 304
Olson, Senator Bud, 277, 278
Olthuis, John, 131, 228
Onshore fields, 197
Ontario Energy Board, 263
Ontario, government of, 149
Ontario Hydro, 49
Ontario Naturalist, 38
OPEC, 83, 125, 272, 284
Ophuls, William, 41
Orders-in-Council, 89
Ornithologists, 197
Osler, Sandford, 37
Ottawas, 64

Pacific Gas and Electric of California,
    79, 127
Pack ice, 172, 173, 176, 199, 299, 310,
    320
Page, Robert, 131
Pan-Alberta, 275, 276, 277
Pan-Arctic, 172; consortium, 239, 243,
    273; oil, 145
Parks, Algonquin Park, 29, 30, 33;
    armed occupation by native peoples,
    216-17; Banff, 29; national and
    provincial, 29, 30; Quetico, 33;
    Wood Buffalo, 68; *see also* Wilder-
    ness parks
Parks Canada, 93, 217
Parry, Sir William, 5
Parti Québécois, 72
Paschen, Jerry, 140
Passmore, Dick, 37
Peacock, D., xii, 93
Pearl Harbor, 17
Pearson, Art, 144
Pearson, Lester, 18, 20, 21, 27, 47, 55,
    56
Peel River, 186
Pemmican, 191
Peregrine falcon, 180

Permafrost, 75, 155-64, 165, 166, 169,
    170, 173, 176, 177, 205, 258, 315
Penner, Edward, 161
Petro-Canada, 49, 56, 108, 239, 243,
    252-53, 266, 298, 299, 302, 303,
    305, 306, 316, 317, 323, 324
Petrochemicals, 75, 271
Petrofina, 303
Petroleum and Gas Revenue Tax, 302
Petroleum Club, 115
Pharand, Professor Donat, 297
Philips, Edward, 141
Pickering nuclear power plant, 118
Pimlott, Doug, 37
PIP grants, 175, 266, 302, 304, 305, 306
Pipeline Application Assessment Group,
    97, 98, 128
Pipeline construction problems, 157-78
Pipeline route, 156-57, 164
Pipeline technology, 155-79
Pipelines, 39, 55, 57, 58, 59, 60, 75, 77,
    79, 81, 85, 92, 93, 95, 96, 97, 99,
    103, 105, 108, 109, 111, 113, 118,
    127, 129, 132, 137, 145, 146, 167,
    169, 170, 176, 195, 198, 206, 211,
    257; and Mel Watkins, 226; and UN,
    122; applicants for northern pipe-
    line, 82-83; applications, 102; as
    a catalyst for environmental groups,
    24; boom-bust cycles, 50; chill, 166;
    companies, 215; critics, 40; debate,
    22; environmental forces on, 162;
    elevate, 159; equilibrium, 187; final
    compromise, 83; guidelines, 94;
    impact on native society, 102; Lib-
    eral policy, 85; moratorium, 118;
    project, 156; proposals, 214; right of
    way, 143; Trans-Canada natural
    gas, 124; U.S. multinationals, 47;
    wintering, 165; *see also* Mackenzie
    Valley Pipeline; Northern pipelines
Polanyi, Karl, 46
Polar bears, 190, 200, 244
Polar Bear Treaty, 310, 311
Polar Gas Pipeline, 145, 162, 196, 224,
    239, 264, 268, 324
Polar Sea, 2, 22, 291-92, 297, 310
Political parties, 25
Pollution, 182, 195, 197, 200; biochemi-
    cal impact, 43; control, 79; control
    in Arctic, 245; economic growth
    and industrial expansion as cause,
    42; in North, 35; marine, 292
Pollution Probe, 35, 36, 37, 96, 97, 98,
    99
Polynyas, 244
Ponding, 158, 159

Sector theory, 14, 291, 300
Seismic experts, 166
Seismic survey lines, 195
Senate Select Committee, 10
Sense of community, 212
Separatism, 72
Service, Robert, 11
Shallow Bay, 197, 198
Sharp, Mitchell, 106, 276, 277, 278, 279, 287
Shehtah Drilling Limited, 235
Shell Oil, 54, 120, 132, 139, 197, 226, 260, 264, 267, 317, 323
Shore-fast ice, 199
Shultz, G., 304-05
"Shut-off" theory (permafrost), 160-61, 178
Siberia, 155, 166, 194
Siberian Pipeline, 325
Sierra Club, 32, 38, 58, 192
Sifton, Clifford, 31
Sigler, Murray, 106
Simcoe, Lord, 64
Simpsons-Sears, 38
Sinclair, A. R. E., 193-94
Six Nations Confederacy, 64
Smith, Adam, 45, 256
Smith, Jack, 140
Snow geese, 151, 181, 195-98
Social alienation, 214, 254
Social analysis, 224, 255
Social barriers, 222; and alcohol, 221
Social casualties, 210-11
Social change, 210, 255; and northern development, 220
Social costs, 210, 223, 233, 253, 254; of booze and drugs, 221; of economic development, 102-03
Social Darwinism, 211
Social environment, 233
Social Gospel, 26
Social impacts, 209, 210, 225, 233, 253
Social Impact Assessment (SIA), 209, 253, 254
Social planning, 243
Social questions, 108, 113, 115, 117, 122, 139
Social roots, 215
Social science, 209, 211, 253, 254
Social stability, 210, 222
Social structures, 212
Social tensions, 225
Socio-economic, 91, 180; concerns of native people, 105; costs, 283; data, 224, 226; impacts, 209
Soloway, Hyman, 134, 135, 139, 150
Sonar navigation, 244

Sovereignty, 9, 10, 12, 14, 79, 289-311; and law of sea, 294-296; and *Manhattan* and *Polar Sea*, 291-92; Arctic, 252, 325; Canadian economic, 301; election issue, 19; erodes, 54; erosion of Canadian, 226; *Manhattan*, 22, 38; marine, 324; press reports, 18, 19
Soviet cruise missile, 309
Soviet Union, 200, 252, 291, 307; experience in North, 159; jurisdictional disputes, 311; strategic problems within the North, 307-09
Spahr, Charles, 285
St. Laurent government, 18, 19
Stabback, Jack, 137, 138, 151, 153, 220, 229
Staff Report (Berger), 116, 122
Standard of living, 46
Stanfield, Robert, 56, 85
Staples theory, 49-50, 51, 117, 226, 256
Steel Workers Union, 56
Stefansson, Vilhajalmur, 7, 8, 9, 10, 14
Stelco, 282-83
Stevens, Senator Ted, 280
Steward, Willard, 261
Stock market, 280, 281, 303
Stockholm Conference on the Human Environment, 295
Strait of Canso, 239
Strategic Air Command, 18
"Super agency," 111, 116
Super-depletion allowance, 266-67
"Super-ditcher," 164
Super profits, 283
Supertankers, 171
Supreme Court of Canada, 70, 72, 90, 136, 137, 145, 149, 246, 259
Svalbard Archipelago, 307, 311
Sverdrup Islands, 14
Sykes, Mayor R., 113, 114-15
Syncrude, 118

Taglu gas, 197
Tar sands, 286
Tarsiut N-44 well, 173
Task Force on Churches and Social Responsibility, 228
Task Force on Northern Oil Development, 79, 80, 180
Task Force on Structure of Canadian Industry, 54
Technical viability, 171, 176
Technology, 162, 163, 165, 169, 171, 172, 173, 176, 177, 196, 255, 325; adequacy of, 156; and computers, 52; and physical forces, 155, 163;

White, Lynn, 43
White man's burden, 7
White Paper of 1969 (on Indian policy),
    70, 73, 92
White Sea, 252
Whitehorse, 142, 144, 145
Wilder, William, 83, 85, 120, 133, 261
Wilderness, 32, 193-94; advantages for
    modern society, 32; art, 34; Wayland
    Drew, 53; myth of clearing the
    land, 31; preservation, 33; rhetoric
    of dissent, 33; Trudeau, 35; value
    of, 31
Wilderness experience, 194
Wilderness parks, 193; at Polar Bear
    Pass, 239
Wilderness Society, 38, 58, 192
Wildlife management, 218, 250
Wildlife population, 181
Wildlife preservation movement, 30
Wildlife questions, 181, 208; survival,
    205
Williams, Dr. Peter, 160-61, 162, 163
Willson, Bruce, 131, 140

Wolves, 182, 186, 187, 189, 191
Wood Gundy, 259, 261
Woodcock, George, 52-53
Woodford, James, 34
Worker productivity, 188, 258, 259; ef-
    fects of climate, 164-65
World oil prices, 178, 303
Wounded Knee, 216
Wrigley, 166, 233

Yellowknife, 108, 112, 131, 142, 144,
    210, 233
Yellowknife Bay, 17
Yellowknife hearings, 102
Yukon, 22, 59, 60, 117; boom-bust, 50;
    gold discovery, 11, 12, 17; gold
    rush, 66
Yukon Conservation Society, 144
Yukon Minerals Bill, 38
Yukon Native Brotherhood, 72

Zama Lake, 233, 235
Zooplankton, 200

Canada in Transition: Crisis in Political Development
General Editors: David V.J. Bell and Edgar J.E. Dosman